In the Name of Liberalism

Illiberal Social Policy in the USA and Britain

DESMOND KING

OXFORD

UNIVERSITY PRESS

OXFORD

UNIVERSITY PRESS

Great Clarendon Street, Oxford OX2 6DP

Oxford University Press is a department of the University of Oxford.
It furthers the University's objective of excellence in research, scholarship,
and education by publishing worldwide in

Oxford New York

Athens Auckland Bangkok Bogotá Buenos Aires Calcutta
Cape Town Chennai Dar es Salaam Delhi Florence Hong Kong Istanbul
Karachi Kuala Lumpur Madrid Melbourne Mexico City Mumbai
Nairobi Paris Sào Paulo Singapore Taipei Tokyo Toronto Warsaw

with associated companies in Berlin Ibadan

Oxford is a registered trade mark of Oxford University Press
in the UK and in certain other countries

Published in the United States
by Oxford University Press Inc., New York

© Desmond King 1999

The moral rights of the author have been asserted
Database right Oxford University Press (maker)

First published 1999

British Library Cataloguing in Publication Data

Data available

Library of Congress Cataloging in Publication Data

King, Desmond S.
In the name of liberalism: illiberal social policy in the USA and Britain / Desmond King.
Includes bibliographical references.
1. United States—Social policy. 2. Great Britain—Social policy.
3. Public welfare—United States. 4. Public welfare—Great Britain.
5. Liberalism—United States. 6. Liberalism—Great Britain.
7. United States—Politics and government—20th century.
8. Great Britain—Politics and government—20th century. I. Title.
HN57.K54 1999 361.6'1'0941—dc21 99-19785

ISBN 0-19-829609-6
ISBN 0-19-829629-0(Pbk.)

1 3 5 7 9 10 8 6 4 2

Typeset in Times
by Best-set Typesetter Ltd., Hong Kong
Printed in Great Britain
on acid-free paper by
Biddles Ltd. Guildford and King's Lynn

For
Carolyn

ACKNOWLEDGEMENTS

During the 1997–8 academic year I was fortunate to hold a Nuffield Foundation Social Science Research Fellowship, which provided release from my normal responsibilities and enabled me to complete this manuscript. I am extremely grateful to the Trustees of the Foundation for their support. I should also like to thank the British Academy for the valuable support provided by its Research Leave Scheme. My archival research in the USA was facilitated in significant part with assistance from Oxford University's Mellon Fund and I should like to thank the Fund's Trustees and its chairman, Byron Shafer, for responding generously to requests for travel grants. My college in Oxford, St John's, has provided some financial support toward the cost of the research required for this book, for which I am grateful. I have received assistance from archivists at the National Archives and the Manuscript Division of the Library of Congress in Washington, the Public Record Office at Kew, and from Judith May-Sapko at the Truman State University's Pickler Memorial Library.

At Oxford University Press, this project has benefited greatly from the encouragement and support of the Senior Editor for Political Science, Dominic Byatt, to whom I extend my genuine thanks. Dominic has not simply ensured an efficient and professional production of the book but offered his unwavering support throughout this process, as has his assistant Amanda Watkins, to whom I also extend my thanks. For careful and constructive readings of early drafts of this manuscript I should like to thank Alan Deacon, Nigel Bowles, Roger Crisp, Michael Freeden, Ross McKibbin, David Miller, Serena Olsaretti, Daniel Tichenor, and OUP's four readers. Randall Hansen undertook some research for one section of this study, for which I am grateful. Part of this research material, used in Chapter 3, comes from a paper which Dr Hansen, now a Research Fellow at Christ Church, Oxford, and I co-authored, entitled 'Experts at Work' and published in the *British Journal of Political Science*, 29 (1999), 77–107. The list of colleagues who have generously contributed to this volume through conversations, suggestions about readings or sources, or comments on drafts is long and includes Edward Berkowitz, Michael Burleigh, Carolyn Cowey, Harvey Feigenbaum, David Goldey, Robert Goodin, Randall Hansen, John Holmwood, Ira Katznelson, Jane Lewis, Rodney Lowe, Chris Pickvance, Nancy Leys Stepan, Byron Shafer, Julie Suk, Robert Taylor, Sarah Vickerstaff, Alan Ware, Albert Weale, Margaret Weir, Mark Wickham-Jones, Gavin Williams, Stewart Wood, and the organizers and participants in seminars at the Universities of Essex, Kent, and Oxford. I am grateful to each of them for their contribution which has undoubtedly saved me from many errors; those which remain are my responsibility.

D.K.

Oxford
October 1998

CONTENTS

LIST OF FIGURES

LIST OF TABLES

ABBREVIATIONS

AFDC	Aid to Families with Dependent Children
AFL	American Federation of Labor
AMC	Association of Municipal Corporations
CCA	County Councils' Association
CCC	Civilian Conservation Corps
COS	Charity Organization Society
CP	Cabinet Papers
CWES	Community Work Experience Program
D	Democrat
FBI	Federal Bureau of Investigation
FRS	Fellow of the Royal Society
FSA	Family Support Act
GI	Government Issue
GPO	Government Printing Office
GTC	Government Training Centre
HO	Home Office
HR	House of Representatives
IC	Instructional Centre
IEA	Institute for Economic Affairs
ILO	International Labour Organization
INS	Immigration and Naturalization Service
JOBS	Job Opportunities and Basic Skills
LC	Library of Congress
LSE	London School of Economics
MH	Ministry of Health
MHA	Mental Hospitals' Association
MRC	Modern Records Centre
NAACP	National Association for the Advancement of Colored People
NA/NARA	National Archives and Record Administration
NSF	National Science Foundation
NUWM	National Unemployed Workers' Movement
NYA	National Youth Administration
PP	*Parliamentary Papers*
PRO	Public Record Office
PRWORA	Personal Responsibility and Work Opportunities Reconciliation Act

PWA	Public Works Administration
RG	Record Group
TANF	Temporary Assistance for Needy Families
TIC	Transfer Instructional Centre
TUC	Trades Union Congress
UAB	Unemployment Assistance Board
USES	United States Employment Service
WPA	Works Progress Administration

Introduction

In August 1996, President Bill Clinton signed a welfare reform act mandating workfare for welfare recipients and imposing a lifetime limit of five years for the receipt of benefits. Workfare (under which programmes recipients of income support must undertake a work activity) was introduced in Britain in April 1998 by Tony Blair's New Labour government. In the 1920s and 1930s, eugenic arguments, which defined some individuals as inferior to others and therefore objects for special policies, were widely propagated amongst policy-makers in both the USA and Britain, and in the former country they were legitimated by the Supreme Court. In this study, I investigate examples of such social policies which conflict with liberal democratic precepts by treating some individuals differently from others. My central thesis is that existing accounts of American and British political development neglect how and why illiberal elements are intertwined in the creation of modern liberal democratic institutions and the significance of their being so. Such elements are explicable in terms of the liberal democratic framework itself and thus illustrate paradoxical features of these polities: measures promoted 'in the name of liberalism' permit a surprising variety of social policies. It is an important topic because of the recurrence of such policies throughout the twentieth century.

Government use of social policy to alter society perhaps marks out the twentieth century more distinctively than previous centuries. From the horrific metamorphoses of totalitarian regimes to the terrors of fascism and diluted forms of socialism, the landscape of state intervention is extensive and, in some countries, baneful; as James Scott remarks, 'the idea of a root-and-branch, rational engineering of entire social orders in creating realizable utopias is a largely twentieth-century phenomenon.'[1] The implementation of ambitious social policies which succeed in respecting basic rights of political democracy is not to be taken for granted, especially since even liberal democracies such as the USA and Britain 'became, in the context of war mobilization, directly administered societies'.[2] This rarity makes the experience of successful market democracies especially compelling since they have not been immune to initiatives designed to modify

---

[1] Scott (1998: 97).   [2] Ibid.

the social order in a way potentially conflicting with liberal democratic values. Undertaken in political systems premissed on a liberal equality of treatment and rights, social policy is implemented within the institutional and political opportunities presented, and boundaries imposed, by the democratic system: government freedom to act occurs within significant limits, formal and informal. Such measures themselves influence these democratic boundaries by redefining what is acceptable and unacceptable government policy. This book investigates three examples of such social policies in the United States and Britain: eugenic policies in the 1920s and 1930s; work camps as part of the response to unemployment in the Great Depression years; and modern workfare schemes.

The case for such a study is pressing. If the claim that liberal democracy represents the most attractive set of political institutions is valid,[3] there is a need to know more about the internal workings of successful and entrenched democracies. Panegyrics about the success of liberal democracies overlook the way in which the political boundaries of such polities are shaped dynamically, and how new policies often echo earlier ones, prompting familiar questions about the rights of citizenship and membership in new contexts. Second, the political cultural limits of government policy in a strong civil society has been the subject of scholarly interest.[4] Social policy is illustrative in this context since it tests the democratic limits of public policy: for those targeted, the policies may reveal an illiberal and inegalitarian face of liberal democracy. Third, the inexorable requirement for strong government in purportedly market democracies—whether to maintain these markets or to facilitate liberty—has been a key issue in the USA and Britain since the 1970s. How such interventions, in social policy, are promoted, implemented, and dismantled points to a paradox of American and British democracy: each polity's political culture celebrates individualism and liberty,[5] yet governments find themselves regularly compelled to formulate social policy with which to direct some members' behaviour. Defending that liberal individualism has required government policy, a practice manifest in a range of government initiatives during the last century including New Liberalism, Progressivism, the New Deal, the Great Society, the New Right, New Labour, Gingrich's Contract with

[3] In Francis Fukuyama's popular thesis, it is the ' "end point of mankind's ideological evolution" and the "final form of human government," and as such constitute[s] the "end of history" ' (Fukuyama 1992: xi).

[4] This takes two forms: the debate about trust and attention to the design of political institutions. On the former see *inter alia*, Putnam (1993), Fukuyama (1995), Gambetta (1988), Seligman (1992), and Misztal (1996). On the latter, see, for instance, Goodin (1996*a*), Copp, Hampton, and Roemer (1993), and Elster and Slagstad (1988).

[5] The idea of community has, however, played a not insignificant role in British political culture: see Miller (1989), ch. 9.

America, and New Democrats. Michael Freeden comments: 'liberals ... have as a rule, endorsed a strong state precisely because they have entertained a passionate respect for the integrity of the individual and the need to protect that integrity from harmful intrusion.'[6]

To examine these issues, I present a study of selected examples of illiberal social policies, whose sources are identified and whose development is traced. The cases demonstrate the range of motives for such intervention (though the aim of affecting behaviour is a constant) and the consequences for democracy. I argue that each of these policies is defended as compatible with liberal democracy, but for different reasons, thereby demonstrating the political and intellectual breadth of liberalism. Historically, the defence and expansion of liberal democratic ends appears to necessitate, on occasion, the use of illiberal measures. Crucially, I am not advancing a proposition about the theoretical inconsistency or coherence of liberalism as a normative framework but rather presenting conclusions about two major liberal democratic polities on the basis of historical studies.

Social policies are purposeful programmes, associated with political ideologies and programmatic ambitions to modify individuals' behaviour and society. They recur in American and British politics. The impetus for such initiatives lies in the democratic political system. Democracy permits freedom of expression of ideas, in populist and rationalist versions, and party political competition ensures both that some of them will be implemented and that there is the potential to rescind them. The two-party system in Britain and the USA undergirds these processes while the expansion of publicly funded social research, often in universities, and the proliferation of think tanks has facilitated the making of purportedly well-informed choices.

Central to social policy is the employment of ideas and expertise in public policy programmes. Politicians, acting within the constraints of democratic institutions, willingly use ideas to serve their ends, whether short-term electoral ones or grander ideological ambitions. Although ideas, or expertise, are the instrument of political ends they must be intellectually plausible; they are manifest in several forms, ranging from detailed policy specifications to a guiding ideological orientation. As justifications of public policy, expert knowledge or ideational claims are indispensable since both citizens and policy-makers in liberal democracies value rationality highly and expect coherent explanations for policy choices. Explaining how these claims have been reconciled historically and politically with liberal democracy is, however, a neglected topic.

[6] Freeden (1996: 268)

STRUCTURE OF THE BOOK

Chapter 1 introduces liberalism and a threefold typology of 'illiberal' social policy. Both are located in the substantial literature on liberal democracy. Chapter 2 explicates the book's argument about the role of knowledge or expertise (terms used interchangeably) in social policy, and explains how the study relates to existing theoretical concerns in comparative politics. The subsequent chapters illustrate the theoretical points introduced in Chapters 1 and 2 through a series of empirical case studies. The cases address the questions of why and how knowledge operates in policy-making; how the illiberal dangers of some defensible and rational policy options are avoided; and how policy-makers validate knowledge in the context of competing arguments about the apposite course of action. They are organized in terms of the types of social policy introduced in Chapter 1. Chapters 3 and 4 examine the influence of eugenic arguments in respect of sterilization policy in Britain and immigration regulations in the United States respectively. Chapters 5 and 6 compare the way in which work camps were used in Britain and the United States in the 1930s as part of strategies to counter unemployment. Chapters 7 and 8 extend this focus upon labour market participation through an examination of workfare programmes. The discussions are based on primary and archival sources. Chapter 9 discusses the broader implications of the case studies.

PART I

Politics, Policy-Making, and Ideas

1

Liberalism and Illiberal Social Policy

THE intellectual and political dominance of liberal ideas in the United States and Britain is incontestable. The political theorist Michael Freeden describes liberalism as 'a pre-eminent ideology in Western political thought, extensively articulated and amplified, and a familiar component within the ideological spectrum of the past century and a half'.[1] Although scholars adopt different emphases, at its core liberalism accords primacy to individual freedom in political arrangements:[2] that is, there is a commitment to enabling all citizens to engage in freedom of choice to as great an extent as possible without harming others. It is also a fundamental principle of democracy that members of the political community receive equality of treatment.[3] As Brian Barry summarizes: 'the basic idea of liberalism is to create a set of rights under which people are treated equally in certain respects, and then to leave them to deploy these rights (alone or in association with others) in pursuit of their own ends. In the past two hundred years, western societies have been transformed in accordance with *the precept of equal treatment*';[4] or as Winston Churchill pithily declared, opposing immigration restriction, in 1904, 'all should be free and equal before the law of the land'.[5] Liberal democracy imputes a set of rights to citizens as the basis for autonomous action;[6] unreasonable or

---

[1] Freeden (1996: 141).

[2] See *inter alia*, Kymlicka (1990), Bellamy (1992), Freeden (1996), Waldron (1993), Raz (1986), Powell (1992), and Holmes (1995). In Michael Freeden's most recent book (1996: 142–3) he distinguishes four variants of the liberal tradition: Millian classical liberalism; reformist or new liberalism; American (Rawlsian) philosophical liberalism; and libertarianism.

[3] Alan Brinkley (1998: xi) correctly warns that 'liberalism has never been a uniform or stable creed', an observation especially germane to the United States; nonetheless as defined here the core values of liberalism find expression in the political institutions of both countries.

[4] Barry (1996: 538), emphasis added; and see Gray (1989, 1995).

[5] Quoted in the *Jewish Chronicle*'s report on the Aliens Bill 1904, 15 July 1904, p. 721.

[6] These rights are not static but have been expanded to cover previously excluded groups and new spheres. See Smith (1989). For an historical analysis of the development of the idea in the United States see Howe (1997), and for the theoretical context see Taylor (1989).

unconstitutional delimitation of these rights results in what the political theorist Stephen Holmes terms an 'illiberal' society.[7]

A liberal political system provides equality of treatment of individuals and access to the due process of law for the redress of violation of individual rights. It is premissed on the impartial treatment of its members and places a high value on individual autonomy. This latter assumption implies that members of the polity possess the necessary reasoning powers or ability to lead fulfilling lives and prudentially to plan for their future. Importantly, the state is portrayed as neutral in respect of the validity of competing ways of life and is expected to enforce that neutrality through the rule of law.[8] Twentieth-century accounts of liberalism have given an especial prominence to equality. Thus, Thomas Nagel remarks that 'modern political theories agree that a society must treat its members equally';[9] this equality principle has become far more salient since 1945.[10] Over and beyond the principle of equal treatment, many modern liberals argue that the conception of equality must be made a richer one which systematically addresses some of the inequalities resulting from market processes. This shift reflects an emphasis upon the rights considered inherent to the individual citizen in a liberal society: the definition of the equality of these rights has become central to Rawlsian liberal theory and its exponents.[11] Finally, a liberal democratic society is one which places a premium on ideas and their expression: it is a feature of reasoning individuals that there be freedom of expression and multiplicity of opinions.[12]

Within these general principles, however, some policies in the United States and Britain treat some citizens differently from others and, historically at least, other policies have differentiated amongst citizens in terms

[7] Holmes (1993: xv). In his book, *The Anatomy of Antiliberalism*, Stephen Holmes proposes the following succinct definition: 'liberalism's four core norms or values are *personal security* (the monopolization of legitimate violence by agents of the state who are themselves monitored and regulated by law), *impartiality* (a single system of law applied equally to all), *individual liberty* (a broad sphere of freedom from collective or governmental supervision, including freedom of conscience, the right to be different, the right to pursue ideals one's neighbor thinks wrong, the freedom to travel and emigrate, and so forth), and *democracy* or the right to participate in lawmaking by means of elections and public discussions through a free press.' Holmes (1993: 4).

[8] As recently expounded in Rawls (1993). It should be noted, however, that there is a significant debate about state neutrality amongst political theorists.

[9] Nagel (1991: 63).

[10] Indeed Freeden (1996: 159) remarks that 'the profile of liberalism in the nineteenth and twentieth centuries has not depended on the salience of equality. Rather, the intension of equality has been shaped mostly by features of the core concepts of rationality and individuality.'

[11] Rawls (1993); see also Arneson (1990*a*).

[12] See J. S. Mill's *On Liberty* (1972 edn.) for a classic statement.

of their suitability to lead autonomous, self-sufficient lives. Such cases contribute to the practices and institutions of liberal democracy; these political institutions change over time in ways consequential for the relationship of citizens and the state. Identifying such 'illiberal' social policies is not always straightforward. It is plain that certain issues fit this category (such as the unequal treatment of children or prisoners) and I propose not to deal with such comparatively uncontroversial restrictions.[13] Furthermore, what seems a reasonable justification at one point in time— for instance, the use of 'scientific racism' to rationalize racial segregation —loses its legitimacy over time: thus the US Supreme Court's own constitutional acceptance of segregated race relations was rescinded in 1954. Although it is hard not to see such instances as manifestations of simple prejudice rather than reasoned argument, the latter was invoked by defenders of segregation who attempted to reconcile their racialism with liberal values,[14] and the legacies of this illiberality for American political development are elemental. Defenders of workfare, for example, present it as consistent with liberal values, but I argue that this apparent compatibility does not mask its illiberality because of the way in which it differentially treats those affected from other citizens. It aims to direct individuals' behaviour in specified ways.

Liberal democracy implies that the political system, to retain legitimacy, rests in some notion of consent amongst its citizens, or as political scientist Bo Rothstein remarks: 'it is scarcely possible to carry out a program successfully if it does not enjoy the confidence of the group towards which it is directed, or of the citizens at large.'[15] In fact, Rothstein's assertion neglects cases in which illiberal social policies, such as workfare or eugenic-inspired programmes, are targeted on the relevant population irrespective of their willingness to accept the programme (a practice with implications for the importance of trust in government for a strong civil society). Analytically, it is important to ascertain how such measures are justified, a point Rothstein neglects, rather than to assume their consensual establishment. Indeed, as Schneider and Ingram have argued, the 'cultural characteristics or popular images of the persons or groups whose behavior and well-being are affected by public policy' does not assume a homogeneous population but is calibrated by the type of target population for a particular policy. In respect of policy-makers, they conclude that there are 'strong pressures ... to provide beneficial policy to powerful, positively constructed target populations and to devise punitive, punishment-oriented

---

[13] The example of children has become more controversial recently, however, with a nascent children's rights movement identifiable.

[14] Fredrickson (1987) and Barkan (1992).

[15] Rothstein (1998: 72).

policy for negatively constructed groups'.[16] It is, I argue, the case that there is sufficient scope within the core values of liberal democracy to justify them, as the next section explains.

ILLIBERALISM AND SOCIAL POLICY

Illiberal social policies violate the liberal principles identified above in one of three ways:[17] first, by making judgements about the mental competence and reasoning powers necessary for citizenship; second, in using collectivist solutions to social problems; and third, by requiring activities of recipients of welfare benefits. Each of these measures entails differential treatment (sometimes involuntarily or quasi-voluntarily) for the citizens concerned, on grounds which provide justififcation of the policies within a liberal framework. Below I set out three sources of justification employed in such cases.

Type I: liberal unreason

Social policy arises from the competing pressures created by the tradition of rationality and science, bequeathed by the Enlightenment, combined with the electoral pressures articulated through democratic institutions and the expansion of the state's capacity to implement policy. Democratic institutions are themselves an expression of commitment to the potential for rationality in human affairs. The idea of a perfectible social order paralleled that of the success of market forces in regulating economic affairs, a coincidence urbanely surveyed by Albert Hirschman.[18] The Enlightenment inheritance gives a particular force to proposals proffered on the basis of their intellectual plausibility and rationality, a point Daniel Kevles makes in respect of the United States: 'we Americans still operate under the Enlightenment propensity, fostered by science, for an empirical adventurousness.'[19] James Scott adds that an Enlightenment-inspired conception of government responsibility effected 'a fundamental transformation' in the state's role. Prior to this new expectation, 'the state's activities had been largely confined to those that contributed to the wealth and power of the sovereign . . . The idea that one of the central purposes of the state was the improvement of all the members of society—their health,

[16] Schneider and Ingram (1993: 334).
[17] For a valuable threefold categorization of the liberal tradition into nineteenth-century classical liberals; interventionist social liberals; and modern neo-liberals see Brittan (1996).
[18] Hirschman (1977, 1982).
[19] Kevles (1988: 107).

skills and education, longevity, productivity, morals and family life—was quite novel.'[20]

This Enlightenment influence is apparent in policy-making. Thus, Donald Winch explains how nineteenth-century legislators recognized social research as an instrument for improved law-making. He writes that the 'underlying aim of many philosophers who adopted naturalistic approaches to man in society during the Enlightenment was to construct a science of the legislator capable of doing for their own generation what Aristotle and Machiavelli had done earlier, but to do so on a fresh foundation that incorporated an improved Newtonian methodology of observation and experiment; access to more cosmopolitan historical and anthropological evidence; and a more profound understanding, as they saw it, of the psychological "springs" of human action.' In the nineteenth century, the British parliament was transformed into a law-making body which enacted legislation on the basis of 'extensive social investigation' (of which the 1834 Poor Law is illustrative), implemented 'through bureaucratic modes of intervention'.[21] In a similar vein, Hugh Heclo marvels at the growth of British parliamentary reports during the nineteenth century, reporting that by 1850 the '*annual* product of parliamentary papers in terms of number, size, and circulation was greater than the product of all of the centuries before 1800 put together'. This explosion in government investigation of problems arose, he reasonably concludes, from 'the increasing problems being thrust upon the state by a rapidly changing society'.[22]

Liberal democracy and its theorists value rationality and reason. The common emphasis upon autonomy and self-sufficiency implies a particular conception of who should be included and excluded in the polity: that is, a Lockian assumption about citizens' capacity meaningfully to enter a contract. This value is forcefully articulated, for example, in John Stuart Mill's 1859 text, *On Liberty*, in which he stresses the importance of individuality (and the prior reasoning powers) as aspects of liberty. Mill writes that

he who lets the world, or his own portion of it, choose his plan of life for him, has no need of any other faculty than the ape-like one of imitation. *He who chooses his plan for himself, employs all his faculties.* He must use observation to see, reasoning and judgment to forsee, activity to gather material for decision, discrimination to decide, and when he has decided, firmness and self-control to hold to his deliberate decision.[23]

---

[20] Scott (1998: 91).   [21] Winch (1993: 66).   [22] Heclo (1974: 44).

[23] Mill (1972: 117, emphasis added). In his valuable discussion of American liberalism, the historian Gary Gerstle (1994: 1046) singles out three values, those of emancipation, rationality, and progress, as the core of this perspective, and concludes that 'liberalism's evolution can be understood as a series of efforts to reinterpret these principles in light of unexpected historical developments'.

The ability to plan and to select among alternatives are key Millite qualities of the free citizen in a liberal polity: 'the human faculties of perception, judgment, discriminative feeling, mental activity, and even moral preference, are exercised only in making a choice.'[24] Mill criticized those who assent 'undoubtingly to what they think true', demanding instead that a person be able to defend a belief: 'whatever people believe, on subjects on which it is of the first importance to believe rightly, they ought to be able to defend against at least the common objections.'[25] The development of intellectual skills not only improved the individual concerned but added value to society as a whole: 'in proportion to the development of his individuality, each person becomes more valuable to himself, and is therefore capable of being more valuable to others.'[26]

  This Millite assumption of a thinking and planning individual implies an important boundary between citizens possessing the requisite reasoning powers to be full members and those depleted in this respect. Despite a liberal democratic assumption that all members of society deserve equal inclusion, some policies pursued in the United States and Britain have been premissed explicitly upon judgements about suitability for membership of the polity. Such policies point to the challenge posed by the assumption of competent reasoning power principle of liberal democracy to the equality of treatment precept.

  I treat the example of eugenic arguments whose advocates self-consciously presented claims about the need to exclude some individuals from citizenship (though one could equally examine the fate of women citizens prior to enfranchisement). The language and argument for these assessments rested in 'scientific' doctrines derived from eugenic research. As Mathew Thomson concludes from his study of eugenic social policy, 'mental deficiency provided a new biological boundary-line for good citizenship, with social, moral and intellectual incompetence all deemed to be manifestations of an underlying mental defect.' Eugenic arguments exposed the 'deep-rooted belief that there was a fundamental difference between the mentally defective and the normal'.[27] The success of these doctrines and their influence with policy-makers in liberal democracies arises in part from the emphasis upon reason foundational to the USA and Britain. Liberal democrats' high valuing of reason implies the exclusion of those people considered ill-equipped in this attribute. Such arguments were not only held by both the left and right but were not viewed as incompatible with liberal precepts. Eugenic-based arguments are a historical phenomenon, whose legitimacy was unequivocally eliminated by Nazi

---

[24] Mill (1972: 116).   [25] Ibid. 95, 96.   [26] Ibid. 121.
[27] Thomson (1998: 297, 298).

policies, but the intellectual appeal of which illuminates the character of liberal democracy.

Eugenic proposals are not the only example of such policies, since the definition of who is a member of society has been limited in several respects. Although liberalism is defended as an inclusive doctrine (for example, in Brian Barry's definition quoted above), bestowing equality of citizenship and rights on all members of the political community, historically membership has in fact been restrictive; the breaking of such restrictions is a feature of American and British political development. In both the USA and Britain, women were treated unequally until the twentieth century and in the former state many African Americans endured inferior citizenship rights only.[28] Segregated race relations probably constitute the most powerful example of the qualified membership historically associated with liberalism as an ideology and political institution.[29] However, whereas simple prejudice and racism galvanized the exclusion of African Americans, apart from claims about mental inferiority, it was the latter which alone was at the core of eugenic arguments.

Type II: liberal amelioration and collectivism

Liberal principles imply a limited generosity toward the needy and vulnerable, constituting a strong ameliorative streak (whether of a minimal or generous form). Thus politicians, in both the United States and Britain, partly influenced by liberal claims about responsibilities toward the less fortunate, played key roles in instituting modern welfare state programmes.[30] Philosophically, Robert Goodin constructs a complementary argument for social reform in terms of a society's obligation to protect the vulnerable: 'the social assistance programs of the welfare state are best seen as devices to protect vulnerable and dependent beneficiaries. That is at one and the same time their intention, their effect, and their justification.' Sociologically, Goodin continues, 'protecting the vulnerable is the primary (though not the sole) function of such programs. Historically, that was their advocates' principal (though not sole) argument for them, and it continues to be one of the most prominent arguments offered for their expansion.'[31] There is now an established tradition of social obligation by the state to the needy, though the content of this commitment is not fixed.

---

[28] See Smith (1997).
[29] Smith (1995, 1997).
[30] The respective roles of Lloyd George, William Beveridge and Franklin Roosevelt illustrate this point.
[31] Goodin (1985: 145–6); and see Goodin (1988).

Such liberal amelioration has often been undertaken because the force of compelling circumstances, for example mass unemployment, demands government action even in the absence of an obvious solution. The example examined in this study is the use of work camps in the 1930s to alleviate unemployment (though clearly other social policies would have some of this type's characteristics). The collectivism necessitated by a work camp strategy conflicts with the liberal principles of self-sufficiency and individualism; it had therefore to be rendered acceptable politically, as a pragmatic measure which would not undercut market activity. State-fostered improvement within the constraints of individualism was formulated as a response.

Intellectually, liberal ameliorative policies have an identifiable locus in Britain's New Liberalism and the United States' Progressive movement. In the closing decades of the nineteenth century and opening ones of the twentieth, both societies saw the development of social policies undertaken by the state but often based on ideas and research generated by social reformers or researchers. In Britain this period culminated in the social policies of the 1906–11 Liberal administration, and the articulation of New Liberalism. In the United States this period is the heyday of social Progressivism. These frameworks, part of an international movement,[32] formed the intellectual background to liberal ameliorative or re-educative policies.

British reform movements, beginning with revision of the New Poor Law and the work of the Charity Organization Society (founded in 1869), and culminating in New Liberalism and Fabianism assumed that state policy could be mobilized for social amelioration without compromising unduly the individual freedoms of the democratic polity.[33] The Fabians were explicit about their aim of restructuring society, within a democratic framework, to create a new social order. At its foundation, the Fabian Society strove for the 'cultivation of a perfect character in each and all'.[34] Avowedly socialist, the Fabians pursued this ambition by reform rather than revolution. Other (ultimately more influential) New Liberals rejected the socialist agenda and the assumption that the state could effectively reform society but embraced social reform in terms of morally improving members of society partly with government policy. Beatrice Webb is an articulate voice of this position. Even as late as the early 1930s, she warned

[32] The intellectual convergence of American Progressivism and European social democracy (which includes English Fabianism) is the subject of James Kloppenberg's study in which he argues that key thinkers created a '*via media* in philosophy' consisting of a 'genuinely new approach to the problems of knowledge and responsibility'. Kloppenberg (1986:11).
[33] The outstanding account of the ideological context remains Freeden (1978) and for the political context see Bentley (1987).
[34] Edward Pease, *The History of the Fabian Society* (New York: E. P. Dutton, 1916), 43.

the Royal Commission on Unemployment Insurance that benefits without sanctions induces idleness:

yet to be able to escape fatigue, the uncomfortable conditions, and the discipline of continuous work is so tempting to a large proportion of men at all times, and probably to all men at some times, that the universal offer of Subsistence Allowance whenever unemployed without some unpleasant conditions, must undoubtedly lead to a certain amount of slackness in seeking employment, and of indifference to being dismissed from employment.[35]

Michael Freeden argues, convincingly, that 'the new liberals constituted an explicit social and cultural reaction to the glaring evils of the industrial revolution, evils exposed in increasing detail by surveys and research into the condition of the poor.'[36] In terms of policy achievements, the years 1906–11 saw the foundation of the British welfare state (by a Liberal government) with programmes for pensions and unemployment, sickness and accident insurance first enacted in, for example, the Old Age Pensions Act 1908 and the National Insurance Act 1911.[37] Intellectually, Beveridge and Keynes were products of the New Liberal tradition.[38]

In the USA, the movement stemming from scientific charitable work, absorbed into the general tendency toward Progressivism and culminating in Roosevelt's New Deal, a period covered in Hofstadter's grandiloquent sobriquet 'the age of reform', was also one entrenched faithfully in the assumptions of a market economic system and a democratic polity.[39] There was 'a frequent demand', in the Progressive era, in Veysey's words, 'to replace partisan politicians with experts, so that decisions might be made fairly and impartially—"scientifically", as it was said—from then on into the future'.[40] It was the background to Roosevelt's New Deal programmes, the collectivism of which constituted, in terms of the USA's history, a precarious balance of democratic individualism, market forces, and government intervention.[41] Yet both in the Progressive and New Deal periods, American liberalism was formulated as an interventionist doctrine. The historian, Hugh Brogan, conveys the ambition and significance of Progressivism as an exercise in social reform: 'epochs which generate

[35] Royal Commission on Unemployment Insurance, (London: HMSO, 1931), Minutes of Evidence, from Mrs Sidney Webb, p. 1326, 12 Nov. 1931.
[36] Freeden (1996: 194).
[37] Thane (1982, 1984).
[38] On Keynes and New Liberalism see Clarke (1988: 78–83); and for Beveridge see Harris (1977).
[39] Hofstadter (1955a). He deals with the years between 1890 and 1940. See also H. Croly, *Progressive Democracy* (New York: Macmillan, 1915), Dewey (1935), Hamby (1985), and Gerstle (1994).
[40] Veysey (1988: 24).   [41] Brinkley (1998) and Gerstle (1994).

reform over a wide span of life and years ... occur when a society is confident and efficient enough to contemplate large-scale innovation unafraid, and when there is a consensus among its rulers and shapers that such innovation is desirable. A consensus of this sort emerged rapidly in the first years of the twentieth century, until by the beginning of the second decade it seemed that all Americans were now reformers.'[42] The conservative critic, Michael Tanner, makes a similar point though admonishingly, observing that Progressivism 'caused many Americans to believe that "experts" were required to solve most problems, and that only government could provide the needed expertise'. Before the Progressive era, 'the purpose of government had been seen as protecting individual rights. Now, government was seen as a problem solver.'[43]

Brogan correctly singles out the role of the 'new middle class' as reformers during Progressivism; they constituted the 'age of the expert', to whom was accorded a remarkable freedom and deference. In graceful prose, he elaborates further on the scale of the Progressivist social experiment: 'the new middle class ... was anxious to get hold of American society and remake it according to plan. All round were problems that needed solving—crime, disease, bad housing, drunkenness, political corruption—and the new class thought it knew what to do about them.' This ambition had to be reconciled with American values: 'it was still very American in its outlook, very traditional: just as the experts themselves had taken advantage of a society open to the talents to rise, so they wanted their disadvantaged fellow-citizens to rise also; and the democratic individualistic ideology made it seem perfectly legitimate to bid for political power, that is, for votes; to go down into that arena was simply to carry out one's civic duty.'[44] His analysis captures precisely the way in which this quintessential market democracy, the United States, found its individualist political ideology subject to social policy necessitated by the need to ensure that the most vulnerable members of the polity could (and in some cases, would) in fact become full and active participants in both market and politics.

Intellectual support for such progressivist reform came from the American thinker, John Dewey, who advocated a 'positive state': 'the majority who call themselves liberals today are committed to the principle that organized society must use its powers to establish the conditions under which the mass of individuals can possess actual as distinct from merely legal liberty. They define their liberalism in the concrete in the terms of a program of measures moving toward this end.' Dewey dismissed the opponents of such intervention as anachronistic, unwilling to recognize

---

[42] Brogan (1985: 455).   [43] Tanner (1996: 37).   [44] Brogan (1985: 460).

that the state should not act 'simply [as] a justification of the brutalities and inequities of the existing order'.[45]

Dewey's argument for a more active government was manifest in Franklin Roosevelt's New Deal. He provided an intellectual framework for public policy which appeared successfully to combine an invigorated federal authority with appropriate respect for individualism. From his analysis of Roosevelt's 1932 Commonwealth Club Address (a speech which Alan Brinkley judges the 'most important of the campaign'[46]), Sidney Milkis remarks that the 'need to establish a broader security, and thereby revitalize democratic individualism, provided the text for Roosevelt's' address.[47] In the context of economic depression, Roosevelt argued, the federal government had new obligations—themselves arising from a desire to protect the very basis of individualism—which required historically innovative programmes, declaring that 'the day of enlightened administration has come'.[48] Milkis concludes that Roosevelt's address to the Commonwealth Club—a speech which benefited from the expert advice of Roosevelt's so-called 'brains trust' group of academics—set out a new philosophy for the state:

the final version delivered by Roosevelt made clearer the extent to which the New Deal presupposed a fundamental reconsideration of the state's obligations—the traditional emphasis in American politics on individual self-reliance should give way, Roosevelt suggested, to an expansive understanding of rights, characterized by a continuous identification of new problems and the search for methods by which those problems might be solved.[49]

Building directly upon the Progressivist tradition, conjoined with an appreciation of the USA's unique constitutional tradition, Roosevelt legitimated Deweyite progressive principles 'by imbedding them in the language of constitutionalism and interpreting them as an *expansion* rather than a *subversion* of the natural rights tradition'.[50] No interpretation of the US Constitution and the powers and responsibilities it bequeathed to federal government and the executive was ever likely to be definitive but the Progressives and New Dealers formulated one which justified public policy of a sort consistent with liberal amelioration.

The charitable impulse to address problems of poverty and unemployment in the 1880s and 1890s, the rationalist concern to 'improve' the national stocks, and debates about who should be admitted to membership of the polity and who segregated became pressing political and social issues. Manifestations of both political pressures (agitation about

---

[45] Dewey (1935: 27).   [46] Brinkley (1998: 13).   [47] Milkis (1993: 40).
[48] President Franklin D. Roosevelt quoted in Milkis (1993: 41).
[49] Milkis (1993: 42).   [50] Ibid. 43.

unemployment or undesirables, for example) and economic development (the severe logic of the market), social policy was advanced mostly by 'progressive' reformers driven by the need to foster an efficient social order. I take the example of work camps whose collectivism was a direct challenge to the individualism of liberal democracy.

The New Liberal and Progressive eras marked the complete acceptance of systematically produced research and data as the basis for policy-making married with mild social engineering ambitions: policy, based on apposite expertise, could be used to reform society. Such ambitions have not dissipated. Although articulated in eras whose faith in rationality and progress was less critical than the present one, their historical significance in legitimating such an approach has long outlived them.

Type III: the liberal coercive contract

Rights of citizenship are constitutive of liberalism. Often expressed as part of a contract, rights beget obligations. It is this claim which informed the nineteenth-century New Poor Law in both the United States and Britain, and has underpinned the formulation and dissemination of workfare since the late 1970s. Intellectually, a contractual view of the liberal polity has been a core idea in political theory since Hobbes and Locke, revived in Rawlsian and post-Rawlsian analysis since the 1970s.[51] The stimulus to an enormous literature in political theory, this contractarian debate is overwhelmingly normative in content. As Freeden observes, this framework's theorists value abstraction and precise conceptualization over application or empirical groundedness: 'it is almost entirely ahistorical despite superficial allusions to the historical liberal tradition; it adopts the conceptual purism of some philosophers in its attempts to isolate the synchronic constitutive principles of liberalism "as such"; it is formalistic and rule bound.'[52] Rogers Smith has similarly laid bare the empirical inadequacy of leading liberal political theorists regarding the consequences of illiberal elements in the US political culture.[53] In respect of Rawls's theory, George Klosko concludes, from a review of social science surveys, that the results are 'troubling' because the 'pervasive intolerance of liberal citizens is one of the best attested facts of modern social science'. He adds that 'a series of empirical studies conducted over the past half-century has established that Americans are surprisingly willing to abridge the rights of dif-

---

[51] That is, the ideas introduced by John Rawls in his 1971 book *A Theory of Justice* and developed both in a huge commentary literature and in Rawls's own work. For informed reviews see Frazer and Lacey (1993), Mulhall and Swift (1992), and Kymlicka (1990).
[52] Freeden (1996: 227), and see Klosko (1993).   [53] Smith (1997).

ferent groups. Among the rights they are willing to cast aside are many that fall under Rawls's basic liberties.'[54]

Nonetheless, the contractarian approach is well established as a model for justifying a liberal democracy. The liberal polity is conceived of as the product of an implicit contract between citizens and the state:[55] the former grant certain powers to the state, principally the implementation of the rule of law, in exchange for social stability and the enforcement of rights of citizenship. Contractarian political theorists aim to infer moral principles for the organization of society from an analysis of rational individuals reaching decisions under conditions of uncertainty and ignorance about their likely place in the agreed-upon polity (an exercise expected to produce preference for a rights-based rule of law and a welfare function for the state since market processes will generate inequalities). Its proponents assume a society with the panoply of liberal rights enunciated above, and in classic liberal fashion, place the individual (rather than classes or other abstract economic or social forces) at the centre of the analysis (an assumption which has provoked the communitarian critique of liberalism and the liberal-communitarian 'debate' among political theorists[56]). For our purposes, the important trait to take from the contractarian tradition is its juxtaposition of rights and obligations in a liberal democracy.

Amongst scholars of social policy the articulation of claims about the social rights of citizenship has been immensely influential in both Britain and the USA.[57] In Britain, it was associated with one of the two dominant post-war figures in the discipline of social policy and administration—T. H. Marshall, the other being Richard Titmuss[58]—who advocated universal social policy and subscribed to a social democratic conception of welfare programmes.

T. H. Marshall argued that social rights formed the third element of a triumvirate of citizenship, the others being civil and political rights. Citizenship was conceived, by Marshall, very much in terms of the equality of treatment identified above in respect of liberal democracy:

Citizenship is a status bestowed on those who are full members of a community. All who possess the status are equal with respect to the rights and duties with

---

[54] Klosko (1993: 352).

[55] For attempts to make the contract explicit see the useful discussion in Hardin (1982).

[56] There is a vocal communitarian critique of liberal arguments, whose proponents argue that an individual's sense of self is not forged prior to membership of a political community but is an intrinsic part of that process. For accounts see, *inter alia*, Sandel (1982), Goodin (1996*a*), Etzioni (1995*b*) and Mulhall and Swift (1992).

[57] See Marshall (1964) for the seminal claim. See also King and Waldron (1988), Lister (1997), Plant and Barry (1990), Barry (1990), Andrews (1991), Faulks (1998), Roche (1992), Oliver and Heater (1994), Stewart (1995), van Steenbergen (1994), and Twine (1994).

[58] Deacon (1996).

which the status is endowed. There is no universal principle that determines what those rights and duties shall be, but societies in which citizenship is a developing institution create an image of an ideal citizenship against which achievement can be measured and towards which aspirations can be directed. The urge forward along the path thus plotted is an urge towards a fuller measure of equality, an enrichment of the stuff of which the status is made and an increase in the number of those on whom the status is bestowed . . . Citizenship requires a direct sense of community membership based on loyalty to a civilization which is a common possession. It is loyalty of free men endowed with rights and protected by a common law. Its growth is stimulated both by the struggle to win those rights and by their enjoyment when won.[59]

The rights about which Marshall is writing are first, civil rights, rights associated with individual freedom: 'liberty of the person, freedom of speech, thought and faith, the right to own property and to conclude valid contracts, and the right to justice';[60] second, political rights, those associated with democratic political participation: 'the right to participate in the exercise of political power, as a member of a body invested with political authority or as an elector of the member of such a body';[61] and finally, social rights, the entitlements acquired by citizens under welfare state programmes: 'the whole range from the right to a modicum of economic welfare and security to the right to share to the full in the social heritage and to live the life of a civilised being according to the standards prevailing in the society'.[62] The latter were presented as a means through which some citizens could modify the effects of market processes on their lives, as Raymond Plant observes: 'rights of citizenship can be an important counterpart to the power which the consumer has in the market'.[63] These rights are associated, quite explicitly by Marshall, with obligations or duties: 'we have here a personal right combined with a public duty to exercise the right'.[64] In one interpretation, an argument in favour of social rights of citizenship can be derived from recent Rawlsian contractarian theory.[65]

The Marshallian version of the development of the social rights of citizenship was enormously influential with both policy-makers and social policy advocates in the decades before 1980, despite its obvious flaws in respect of gender in what Jane Lewis terms strong 'male-breadwinner' states of which Britain is a classic example.[66] Social citizenship rights were less entrenched in the USA but nonetheless detectable, and would not be incompatible with President Franklin Roosevelt's comments cited above.[67]

---

[59] Marshall (1964: 84, 92).   [60] Ibid. 71.   [61] Ibid. 72.
[62] Ibid. 72.   [63] Plant and Barry (1990: 29).   [64] Marshall (1964: 82).
[65] King and Waldron (1988).   [66] Lewis (1992), and see Lister (1997).
[67] See Schorr (1986), Wilensky (1975), Janoski (1998), and the discussion in Mead (1997c).

An important institutional distinction between the United States and Britain, with consequences for knowledge creation, was the establishment of social policy and administration as a university discipline in Britain and its absence in the United States where professional schools of social policy developed but without a distinctive intellectual base.

Discussion of social rights overshadowed that of duties until the 1980s. Since then, however, it is the idea of obligations which has been marshalled in social policy debates in both the United States and Britain. Intellectually, this political mobilization of arguments about the social obligations of welfare recipients constitutes a break with the post-war social democratic welfare state consensus; the new rhetoric is consistent with liberal contractualism, however.[68] It has also been promoted by communitarians, such as Amitai Etzioni, who have called for a moratorium on rights in an effort to re-establish the obligations and duties accruing to citizens as the basis of a vibrant civil society.[69]

Workfare (the requirement of a work activity in exchange for state benefits) is a classic expression of the contractual obligation entailed by liberalism and is the example examined in this book. Workfare now enjoys political support from the political left and right, and is defended as consistent with liberal democracy. This justification rests upon claims both about 'improving' or removing aspects of individuals' behaviour judged morally unacceptable and about the duties incumbent upon citizens. Designing welfare institutions which avoid moral hazards and disincentives are commonly allied with claims about the obligations of citizens in a liberal polity.[70] For conservative critics of welfare programmes, the emphasis upon obligations or duties in workfare is welcomed for both its directive paternalism and its punitive effects. In Lawrence Mead's widely cited version of this argument, the US welfare state is excoriated as an institution which established over-generous welfare entitlements and rights while neglecting the need to require obligations of welfare recipients.[71]

Even political theorists advance the obligations associated with workfare as an acceptable—and indeed necessary—element of citizenship in a liberal democracy. Thus, Gutmann and Thompson formulate the notion of 'fair workfare' (a concept which succinctly conveys the presence of

---

[68] Glennerster and Midgley (1991).

[69] Etzioni (1995a). White (1998: 26) contends that in a liberal democracy there are 'important civic responsibilities' and that the state 'may and often should act to enforce the obligations which derive from these responsibilities'.

[70] Goodin (1988). Stuart White (1998) argues that there is a British tradition of civic liberalism, manifest in the works of writers such as Tawney, Marshall, and Beveridge, which accords a strong role to the state in the enforcement of obligations and responsible individual behaviour.   [71] Mead (1985).

illiberal elements in liberal democracy) to render this coercive obligation compatible with liberal democratic precepts. They write,

fair workfare takes individual responsibility seriously as a requirement in welfare reform. But it is grounded on a value of mutual dependence, which is implied by reciprocity, rather than the value of independence or self-sufficiency, which libertarians stress. The obligations of welfare should be mutual: citizens who need income support are obligated to work, but only if fellow citizens fulfill their obligations to enact public policies that provide adequate employment and child support.[72]

The final sentence of this formulation is unfortunately rarely matched in political practice.

'Fair workfare' is rendered consistent with what these two theorists call the 'basic opportunity principle', according to which all citizens are entitled to 'an adequate level of basic opportunity goods' such as education, health, income support, and work.[73] Aiming both to support workfare and to defuse conservative proponents of tough work requirements policies, Gutmann and Thompson assert that while the opportunity principle is 'consistent with imposing an obligation to work on able-bodied citizens', this obligation must arise from citizens' mutual dependence instead of a libertarian regard for self-sufficiency or autonomy: 'a more appropriate foundation adopts a concept of individual responsibility that regards citizens as mutually dependent, each obligated to contribute his or her share in a fair scheme of social cooperation. The obligation to work is matched by an obligation to provide for others when they cannot provide for themselves.'[74] Why mutual responsibilities result in an obligation to work as well as one to assist one's fellow citizens is unclear in this framework.[75] Suffice it to note that two distinguished theorists, evidently unattracted to conservative or libertarian rationales for workfare, are nonetheless prepared to formulate an obligation to work in a way compatible with liberal democracy. An alternative view is contained in Phillipe Van Parijs's work in which he argues for an unconditional basic income awarded to all individuals without consideration of their income. Crucially, this unconditional basic income includes no stipulations about willingness to work or about demonstrating that one is 'actively seeking work'.[76] The political prospects for such a scheme are unpromising in either the USA or Britain, nonetheless Van Parijs's approach would clearly be violated by a workfare requirement of the sort Gutmann and Thompson, amongst others, are advancing.

---

[72] Gutmann and Thompson (1996: 276).   [73] Ibid. 273.   [74] Ibid. 292.
[75] For a valuable complementary discussion focused on basic income see White (1997).
[76] Van Parijs (1995) and see White's important commentary (1997).

The salience of the rights or obligations of citizenship has varied historically in both the United States and Britain.[77] This dynamic character illustrates how the ideological and political boundaries of liberal citizenship change. A striking aspect of the recent welfare initiatives from the Clinton and Blair administrations, which have weakened the state's granting of rights and underscored the obligations of welfare recipients, is their resonance with earlier ones such as the nineteenth-century Poor Law reform (as explained in later chapters): this is not to imply a simplistic return to the poor law but to underline how liberal democratic policies often have historical overtones. This historical resonance is manifest in three traits of the new programmes: first, to ensure that potential malingerers are discouraged from depending on public assistance; second, to inculcate the work ethic amongst the unemployed or welfare dependent since labour market participation is central to the definition of membership and citizenship in these two political systems; and third, the policies are justified in terms of the obligations members of a liberal polity incur. It is assumed that such measures will improve the circumstances of the participants and modify their behaviour by changing the regime of benefits and sanctions: the increasingly elaborate training measures associated with modern workfare also distinguishes the more recent versions. Excoriating the 'malingerer' or 'scrounger' is a historically popular theme,[78] and one fairly easily justified by politicians with reference to electoral pressures from taxpaying voters.

Ideological appeal and expertise

Social policies justified by the three sources of legitimation identified above commonly manifest two characteristics. First, they appeal across the conventional left–right ideological spectrum. Such initiatives are conceived of by their architects as compatible with liberal democratic values and almost invariably gain support from political parties on the right and left, as the case studies will make clear. The political scientist David Mayhew's analysis of divided party control in US national government is instructive here. Mayhew argues that even during periods of partisan division between the executive and legislature, nonetheless there is 'enactment of a standard

[77] Some writers dispute the entire contractarian claim in respect of welfare policy. Norman Barry argues (1990: 84) that the principle of social rights of citizenship is inconsistent with the liberal contractarian approach: 'despite the use of liberal language in citizenship theory, there is something illiberal at the heart of it. The attempt to establish the ethical identity of persons by reference to "ways of life" is potentially an *exclusive* doctrine: the criterion of identity, because it is specifically not a universal feature of men but is a local and particular one, can be used as a barrier to outsiders, most obviously in the enforcement of strict immigration rules.'   [78] Deacon (1976).

kind of important legislation: From the Taft–Hartley Act and Marshall Plan of 1947–48 through the Clean Air Act and $490 billion deficit-reduction package of 1990, important laws have materialized at a rate largely unrelated to conditions of party control.'[79] Mayhew's conclusion concerns a far broader range of policies and varying circumstances but his central point that certain sorts of policy-making transcend ideological cleavages is pertinent.[80]

Second, the policies are advanced on intellectual or scientific grounds (their advocates claiming a germane expertise). The way in which expertise—and the associated policy experts—are employed in these policy types contributes significantly to their political appeal. New welfare interventions are invariably distinguished by reference to novel expertise or knowledge, including negative evaluations of existing programmes. The welfare debate preceding the USA's 1996 workfare reform was dominated by competing claims about the effects of existing federal welfare programmes,[81] particularly parts of Lyndon Johnson's Great Society initiative. Critics argued that the programmes fostered welfare dependency and exacerbated social problems by enabling traditional social institutions (such as marriage) and support structures (such as community obligations to the needy) to collapse.[82] Defenders of the status quo rejected the claim about welfare dependency, doubted the capacities of the so-called traditional support system and argued that government programmes improved a significant number of people's lives.[83] Each side marshalled supporting statistical data and evidence. The final decision reflected the dominance of the critics' view in political discourse and electoral calculations. In these examples, knowledge is cited in the political arguments but its influence comes both as part of the pressure for policy and continues once the decision to act has been established. (The salience of such expertise is the subject of the next chapter.)

CONCLUSION

Some policies in liberal democracy—pursued by governments for political reasons—assume illiberal characteristics insofar as they violate the two core principles of liberalism, that is equality of treatment and respect of individual freedom. Analytically, such policies, although apparently illiberal, have found justification within a liberal framework in the three ways explained in this chapter. These three sources of legitimation are not

---

[79] Mayhew (1991: 4).   [80] And see Weir (1998), ch. 1. for similar points.
[81] Weaver (1998), Teles (1998).   [82] Murray (1984), Mead (1985).
[83] Edelman (1997), Mink (1998), Quadagno (1994).

rigidly self-contained: indeed, in many empirical examples, aspects of each type are manifest, though one dominant characteristic, the basis for a policy's categorization, can normally be delineated. Arguments about dependency for instance overlap across these types of liberal policy: the obverse of independence and self-sufficiency, its loss is a continuing concern of liberal reformers whether it arises from misfortune or idleness.[84]

My categorization of illiberalism is intended to be neither comprehensive nor exhaustive. It may not be applicable beyond social policy; but that such policies are identifiable is not in doubt. The policies all entail the state directing some citizens' behaviour or choices (whether quasi-voluntarily or compulsorily), interventions which may affect levels of trust in the government. The case studies are designed to illuminate these issues.

Analytically, the accommodation of illiberal policies in liberal democracies can be considered in three ways. First, it can be conceived of in terms of a perennial struggle between liberal and illiberal ideas and programmes. Hence, Rogers Smith's argument that the US political tradition contains conflicting, ascriptive values—such as racism—in addition to the liberal egalitarian one, commonly celebrated in a Tocquevillian reading of US history.[85] Specifically, in the USA its republican tradition, whose proponents prioritize community and virtue, has provided a consistent source of ideological counterpoise to liberal individualism in American political thought.[86] Republicanism is one of the multiple ideological traditions which has informed US political development; others include especially notions of racial, ethnic, and gender hierarchy that long have warred with liberal egalitarian values in the American political culture. Smith's 'multiple-traditions thesis holds that the definitive feature of American political culture has been not its liberal, republican or "ascriptive Americanist" elements but, rather, [a] complex pattern of apparently inconsistent combinations of the traditions, accompanied by recurring conflicts'.[87] Because liberalism and ascriptive inequalities are equally powerful American civic ideals, Smith maintains, we would expect government policy to alternate between these competing traditions. Thus, Smith writes that the overall pattern of US political development, will be 'one of fluctuations between more consensual and egalitarian and more ascriptive and inegalitarian arrangements with the long-term trends being products of contingent politics more than inexorable cultural necessities'.[88]

[84] See the valuable discussion in Goodin (1988), ch. 6 and Fraser and Gordon (1997).
[85] Smith (1993, 1997) and see also Shklar (1998).
[86] Bailyn (1971), Burtt (1993), Macedo (1990), and Morone (1990).
[87] Smith (1993: 558).   [88] Smith (1997: 9).

Second, some scholars propose a direct link between liberal and illiberal policies in these political systems. Thus, rather than identifying liberal republicanism and ascriptive hierarchies as distinctive and contentious ideological traditions, Ira Katznelson argues that the philosophical shallowness or breadth of liberalism itself renders its adherents susceptible to 'illiberal temptations'.[89] In place of the continuous struggle between alternative traditions, this second view points to the intricate entanglement of liberal and illiberal values. For instance, it is impossible to give an account of US political development without an analysis of the illiberal segregation of African Americans, and that illiberal legacy is germane to issues in contemporary US politics. Such a perspective implies not so much warring philosophical traditions as it does an extraordinary entanglement—or uneasy symbiosis—of liberal and illiberal values.

Third, a final view builds and expands upon the Katznelson position by viewing illiberal policies as intrinsic to liberal democratic politics for three reasons. First, in the search for solutions to urgent problems prompted by crises such as mass unemployment, politicians may come to employ illiberal policies as a means of achieving sought-after reform (as I argue later in respect of workfare). Second, illiberal policies may help politicians reach that part of the electorate they consider to be their principal constituency, for example, taxpayers or public sector workers. By manipulating the balance of rights and obligations available to citizens, the dynamic relationship between liberal and illiberal values is retained. Third, since liberal principles accord such importance to rationality, individual autonomy and choice, and to knowledge, these constitute the grounds for illiberal policies (for example, attaching a high value to autonomy and reasoning has implications for those deficient in these qualities) in ways which can be justified with liberal principles.

It is this third perspective which the ensuing empirical studies best explain. Illiberal policies are intrinsic to liberal democracy itself and their adoption reflects an internal contradiction in these polities: policies adopted democratically conflict with expectations about the role of the state in such a policy but governments use them, from time to time, to promote liberal democratic ends under the stimulus of electoral pressures.

In sum, the presence of these illiberal measures in the American and British polities reflects two sets of issues: first, that allegedly liberal democratic governments undertake, from time to time, illiberal policies and assume or proclaim their compatibility with liberal values, exercises which are relatively unsurprising politically; and second, that these illiberal measures are undertaken, paradoxically, to advance liberal ends. Addressing

---

[89] Katznelson (1996a) and see Gerstle (1994: 1045), who observes that 'the protean character of American liberalism . . . is in part traceable to its role as a surrogate socialism'.

the accommodation of illiberal elements in liberal democracy is both a historical and a theoretical question: what liberal theory requires of a liberal polity, that is, that the principles of equality of treatment and individual freedom be respected; and second, what governments in liberal democracies do that constitutes illiberal policy. I focus on the historical dimension. The book's analysis is not concerned with the universe of logical inconsistencies scrutinized by political theorists but instead upon what has happened historically in the field of social policy. What the historical analysis illuminates in respect of the theoretical arguments is that illiberal elements appear to be part of liberalism itself. It is a defining but neglected feature of liberal democracy.

2

Liberal Democracy and Policy-Making:
Knowledge and the Formation of Social Policy

PUBLIC policy reflects multiple sources, including electoral pressures, regulation of and accommodation with market forces, elite and popular pressures, incrementalism, and bureaucratic innovations. Democratic systems which coexist with a market economy require government interventions to facilitate the operation or maintenance of the market, an institution deemed a guarantor of choice and efficiency. Karl Polanyi observed that 'the road to the free market was opened and kept open by an enormous increase in continuous, centrally organized and controlled interventionism,'[1] a judgement which may overstate the level of government intervention but not its significance. Commenting on the implementation of the New Poor Law in 1834 in Britain, Hugh Heclo concludes that 'during this period of supposedly laissez faire government, a shift becomes perceptible from the medieval policy of largely negative state prohibitions to new attempts at deliberate social engineering... The nineteenth century British poor law was a manifestation of the period's most enlightened principles of Malthusian social science and political economy, a heroic attempt at social planning in the broadest sense.'[2] The commitment to the sovereignty of individual democratic rights has to be balanced with an apparently ineluctable need for government intervention in social and economic policy;[3] such intervention must, however, be rendered compatible with democratic rights. In this century it is also presented and partly justified in terms of expertise. A consequence of this characteristic is the particular role assumed by 'knowledge' in the making of social policy.

Social policy clearly serves political purposes and, I argue, expertise is fundamental to fulfilling those purposes.[4] To devise social policies, policymakers require an 'evidential' or 'knowledge' base. How this knowledge is identified and employed in policy choices is a key issue in comparative politics. Its influence is twofold: first, as part of the intellectual and political

---

[1] Polanyi (1944: 140).　　[2] Heclo (1974: 60–1).

[3] A view shared by Marxist and liberal analysts, though for different reasons.

[4] For a related point see Breslau (1997) and for a study of the influence of expertise in municipal reform see Finegold's important (1995) volume.

discourse within which politicians operate (the content of which of course varies over time[5]); and second, as the basis for detailed policy initiatives,[6] this second being the more germane. The way in which knowledge is established and used varies between policies: in some cases, it is presented by civil servants, in others it is drawn from think tanks or university researchers, and in yet further cases expertise is based on the emulation of policies in other countries. Many policies are amalgams of several sources. The role of expertise as a source of justification for policy choices is constant, however. The empirical case studies have been selected to provide some purchase on these patterns.

In this chapter, I offer an explanation for how ideas which result in illiberal social policy are adopted, on some occasions, politically. Two sets of factors are germane: first, general features of liberal democracy, manifest in the policy-making process,[7] and second, the way in which policy ideas are promoted and become institutionalized administratively.

One dominant approach in political science to policy-making is to focus upon the influence of publicly expressed preferences and priorities, as articulated in electoral outcomes, a framework formalized in Downsian spatial voting models.[8] Political parties and politicians design their electoral campaigns to win elections, and attempt to formulate commitments consistent with voters' preferences. One significant source of public policy issues therefore is that of public opinion expressed through elections. This takes several forms including the traditional expression of support or opposition to party political and presidential electoral manifestos. Politicians keenly register such statements of electoral interests. Better to monitor voters' views, there has been a marked increased use of public opinion polling and focus group meetings.[9] Public opinion is not the only source of input to policy-making. Three other general features of liberal democracy contribute to the formation of social policy. These are: the importance of ideas and debate, which politicians seek to influence; the privileged position accorded expertise or specialist knowledge; and the contraints imposed by political institutions and policy legacies.

---

[5] Schwarzmantel (1998).

[6] Amongst scholars of international relations, there is a considerable and interesting literature about the role of ideas in policy-making: see Goldstein (1988, 1989), Jacobsen (1995), McNamara (1998), and Yee (1996).

[7] For engaging and erudite accounts of the vast literature on theories of policy-making, see Stone (1997), Hood (1983, 1998), Lindblom (1980).

[8] Downs (1957); for an overview of subsequent developments see Goodin and Klingemann (1996), part III.

[9] A point Weir (1998: 5) also makes.

THE MARKET FOR IDEAS AND KNOWLEDGE

Democracy permits debate and the diffusion of ideas—within the limits of free speech and respect for the rights of others—in a way which few political systems can emulate or contemplate. Consequently, ideas and ideological ambitions become the stuff of politics and of party political competition in a conventional Downsian form.[10] The expansion of the public sector in the USA and Britain enabled advocates of ideas to promote these systematically with senior policy-makers and to expect some of them to be adopted. The diffusion of think tanks and expectation that these will provide practicable proposals for public policy choices is now a commonplace in both Britain and the United States.[11]

In stressing ideas and policy-making, I concur with political scientist Deborah Stone's view that 'the essence of policy making in political communities [is] the struggle over ideas.' She adds that 'ideas are a medium of exchange and a mode of influence even more powerful than money and votes and guns. Shared meanings motivate people to action and meld individual striving into collective action. Ideas are at the center of all political conflict.' The pivotal place of ideas and expertise renders the policy-making process 'a constant struggle over the criteria for classification, the boundaries of categories, and the definition of ideals that guide the way people behave'.[12] In a similar vein, John Kingdon argues that 'ideas' are an 'important pressure in . . . the [policy] processes'.[13] In respect of academic research, he identifies a process of 'gradual accumulation of knowledge and perspectives among the specialists in a given policy area, and the generation of policy proposals by such specialists'.[14] More recently, in his valuable study of American welfare, Steven Teles underlines the importance of ideas to policy formation:

ideas are not a side story in understanding political events and are not simply the reflection of more 'fundamental' things. For many actors in the political process, ideas are the reason why they engage in political activity in the first place rather than a mere cloak for economic or power interests . . . The essence of politics is the interaction of ideas, interests, conditions and institutions.[15]

The openness of the USA and Britain to such influences differs, however: the United States' separation of powers and bureaucratic agencies offers multiple points of access but not necessarily of influence since,

---

[10] Downs (1957).

[11] For one account of their role in the Thatcher period see Desai (1994); see also Cockett (1994) and Stone (1996).

[12] Stone (1997: 11).   [13] Kingdon (1995: 206).   [14] Ibid 17.

[15] Teles (1998: 182).

aside from the White House, there is an absence of centralized authority and decision-making; nonetheless close contacts between individual government departments, congressional committee staff and policy experts is common.[16] As both the Great Society and the recent (1996) American welfare reform reveal, ambitious initiatives in social policy are not impossible in the USA. To be enacted they require, at the least, either presidential leadership based on a strong electoral mandate (such as Johnson had in 1965 and Reagan in 1981) or a coalition of congressional members and the President (manifest in 1988 when the Family Support Act was passed), the latter a more precarious basis from which to reach agreement.[17] Policy advocates can influence this process at numerous points notably with expertise presented to congressional committees and their staff or by winning influence with policy-makers in the executive.

The British polity is highly centralized, concentrates decision-making power in the political executive and, for the most part, makes civil servants instruments of party political ends. If ideas reach and are accepted by politicians, they can be acted upon when those politicians are in office; equally, if disregarded by the principal policy-makers a proposal is unlikely to be adopted. Hugh Heclo's judgement, formed in 1974, retains a broad validity: 'the inclusion of groups outside the civil service has remained an occasional, usually haphazard, event in Britain rather than a routinized political procedure; non-civil service groups have typically been treated as parties to be consulted rather that as participants integrated into the formulative policy deliberations.'[18] The resistance to Keynesian economics in the 1930s is a good example of this phenomenon. However, Heclo's characterization needs some updating. Since the 1980s the presence of influential advisers in Nos. 10 and 11 Downing Street has unquestionably strengthened the diversity of policy advice provided to these two offices' incumbents. Civil servants' knowledge of policy debates amongst academics and think tanks has also increased greatly in the last decade, and briefings by outsiders of such ministers is not uncommon. (For instance, the Secretary of State for Social Security was regularly exposed to academic and other opinions in Britain during the 1980s and 1990s.) Civil servants responsible for social policy are also normally cognizant with policy developments in other countries: for example, government departments of social policy in European Union member states often hold a conference of civil servants and academics during the period that their country holds the EU presidency.[19] In respect of workfare in Britain, for instance, its advocacy and evaluation was neglected by the academic social policy

---

[16] On the historical tenacity of this pattern see Weir and Skocpol (1985).
[17] Though not impossible as Mayhew (1991) amongst others attests.
[18] Heclo (1974: 45).   [19] As for instance Ireland did in November 1996.

establishment, as think tanks (both Conservative and New Labour ones) propagated its merits and defended its practicality.

Whether inspired by populist prejudices and pressures or purportedly scientific theories and evidence, social policy in market democracies implies a privileging of 'knowledge' or 'expertise': policies are legitimated and rationalized by reference to a claim about their intrinsic validity.[20] It is a crucial source of a policy's legitimacy. Liberal democracy necessarily creates the need for expertise as a basis for social policy since it, first, permits freedom of ideas and competition amongst ideas, and, second, politically requires government intervention to establish equality of opportunity (though not necessarily of outcomes) amongst citizens by rectifying sources of inequality or by expanding choice. 'Expertise' is a commodity provided by a range of specialists including civil servants, policy analysts and academics, and used by politicians. The latter's motives for selecting expertise includes its compatibility with their ideological aims (for example, a government determined to reduce public spending will most likely be keen on 'expertise' which identifies wastage or mistargeting in current expenditures) or with their desire to satisfy populist pressures ('expert' claims about the effect of immigrants on labour market trends will be attractive to a government under political pressure to restrict immigration) or their aim of modifying the social order (for example, selecting universal over means-tested welfare benefits). Alternatively, on rare occasions, the evidence may be sufficiently robust to require acceptance by policy-makers of whatever ideological hue.

None of these features abrogate the profoundly political nature of policy choices. This point is worth emphasizing and qualifying. According to a dominant view in political science, there is little need to look beyond politicians' or parties' self-interest to understand policy choices. In this perspective, ideas or arguments are merely the material exploited by politicians for electoral gain. To view ideas or arguments as autonomous is therefore inappropriate and empirically inaccurate. Such a purely interest-driven account of policy-making is not without appeal but has limitations. While interests are unquestionably of importance they do not provide a complete account of the process. Many ideas or proposals lack the scientific or evidential basis to be independently compelling (that is, independent of political debate); rather, they are used by politicians to advance their ends (and commonly, competing explanations for a particular issue are available). That ideas are used as instruments of political ambition does not, however, dispel their significance as legitimators and,

---

[20] In non-democratic systems, such measures are justified by ideological goals or appeals to national needs.

on occasions, stimulants of policy decisions. Furthermore, on some issues —often 'social policy' ones—identifying the political centre is not straightforward (and concern about budgetary limits may constrain any initiative[21]) while politicians will logically seek to structure perceptions of issues, as political scientist Margaret Weir comments: 'politicians may seek to frame issues in distinctive ways so that a center is easier to locate, or they may take advantage of complexity to press for some policies and not for others.'[22]

Social policy-making is an activity of government in market democracies peculiarly susceptible to the deployment of the commodity 'expertise'. Whether intentionally or indirectly, social policy is a mechanism designed to induce significant social change—for example, the efforts of the New Poor Law (1834) to modify the behaviour and incentive structures of paupers or the modern debate about workfare—and the issue of expertise as a commodity is thus central to its analysis. Initiatives designed to improve people's circumstances need plausible measures or expertise to address this task: government policies, whether new or revisions of existing policy, are invariably defended as measures consistent with expertise. This propensity is complemented by the politics of liberal democracy which place a premium on ideas (or ideologies) as a source of differentiating between parties and politicians (though, in practice, the differences are rarely as real as sometimes claimed).[23]

The relationship between expertise and experts is a dynamic one. The fortunes of individual experts fluctuate (compare the fate of Keynesian economists with monetarists in the 1980s[24]), but expertise *remains* a valued and sought-after commodity amongst policy-makers and politicians. This is a crucial distinction. Living in liberal democracies committed to the Enlightenment values of progress and rationality, it is inconceivable for a politician to propose a new social policy simply on grounds of hunch or intuition about its likely value. This point is well illustrated by the observation of the Clapham Committee (enquiring into social research in Britain), in 1947, that 'in simpler societies it may have been safe to base social policies on hunch and traditional wisdom. But in more complex conditions such a basis is not enough';[25] planning, based on systematic research, was required, and by 1965, in a widely cited work, Andrew Shonfield assessed advanced industrial democracies by their commitment to planning.[26] The justification for a policy must be rooted in scientific

---

[21] See Pierson (1994).   [22] Weir (1998: 5); and see Dunleavy (1991).
[23] See Brittan (1975).   [24] Wickham-Jones (1992).
[25] *Report of the Committee on the Provision for Social and Economic Research*, chaired by Sir John Clapham (London: HMSO, 1946, Cmd. 6868), 3.
[26] Shonfield (1965).

evidence (for example, eugenists' claim that evidence about the inherited source of mental illness meant that sterilization would reduce pauperization) or empirical research (for example, the widely articulated claim that welfare programmes have engendered dependency instead of its defeat[27]). Although notions of both rationality and progress are contentious, nonetheless their place in the public presentation of new policies is firm.

The influence of experts and expertise has grown.[28] In both countries since the Second World War, the professionalization of social research and the proliferation of a 'problem-oriented knowledge elite' (based in universities, research institutes and foundations, and think tanks) has facilitated a greater role for expertise or knowledge in social policy, resting on the implicit (or sometimes explicit) assumption that the quality of such research is sufficient to justify its application in policy choices. Governments have institutionalized public funding regimes for social research.[29] Recent scholarly discussion of this phenomenon has established the inherent (and largely unresolvable) tension in such public organizations between funding research focused on identified policy needs and projects justified in terms of a general contribution to knowledge. Schematically, the British public funding regime was rationalized and justified in terms of the former strategy—the likely contribution of social research to resolving identifiable societal problems—while the equivalent body in the United States (and independent foundations) placed their primary emphasis on expanding knowledge in a more universal sense. Thus, the Clapham Committee, whose report urged an expansion in Britain of public funding of social science, revealed a problem-oriented understanding of these disciplines: 'it is a platitude that modern industrial communities rest on knowledge of the subject matter of the natural sciences. It should be also a platitude that their smooth running and balance rest upon a knowledge of social needs and social responses.'[30] At the US National Science Foundation's social science division, officials found themselves politically lauding the value of publicly funded social research for addressing pressing social problems: funding basic research would enable the social sciences to 'demonstrate concretely their ability to assist in a practical way in the solution of operating and policy questions'.[31] The establishment of these two public funding regimes constituted a commit-

---

[27] Dean and Taylor-Gooby (1992). [28] Crane (1972), Polanyi (1967).

[29] See Bulmer, Bales, and Sklar (1991), Bulmer (1987), Katznelson (1996b), King (1997, 1998b), Kleinman (1995), and Larsen (1992).

[30] *Report of the Committee on the Provision for Social and Economic Research*, 3. For the general context see Shonfield (1965).

[31] NARA RG 307 Records of the NSF, Office of the Director, General Records 1949–63, Dr Waterman's Subject Files Box 20, Memorandum from Harry Alpert to Dr Waterman 1 July 1955, p. 18.

ment to expanding 'knowledge' and 'expertise' through systematic support and organization, which in turn contributed to the general assumption that social research can benefit society. This latter claim has often been advanced by the respective institution's defenders. The unparalleled expansion of university level education is further testimony to the principle that 'knowledge' is pivotal in modern industrial societies.

Governments claim to improve either individuals or society (or both) through social policy, and need expertise legitimately to do so; the latter constitutes a signal as to the appropriateness of a policy choice. As already noted I am not suggesting that politicians' choices of ideas and evidence is independent of their basic interests: indeed, rational choice theorists would view ideas as mere epiphenomenon upon politicians' electoral interests (which may themselves be rooted in deeper convictions). That is the crux of the rational choice framework.[32] But this view marginalizes ideas and the results of scientific debate excessively from political decisions. For instance, have New Labour politicians embraced workfare because (*a*) it is electorally appealing or (*b*) because it fits their political beliefs, which then become their interests, or (*c*) for a combination of these factors? At the least, some credence to the third option is necessary and that permits us to recognize that while ideas are instruments of political ambition they are far from irrelevant analytically.

Experts acquire influence, and sometimes fame, in exchange; furthermore, their reputations (both among colleagues and the public) are often enhanced by the successful marketing of their knowledge. These aspects of the process have increased vastly in the last few decades, though eminent reformers were far from unknown in the early twentieth or nineteenth centuries. In social policy, expertise is validated by one signalling mechanism: the fact that politicians decide to pursue a particular policy (and will do so even when confidence in the precise causal relations assumed is low[33]). This does not imply the absence of disagreement about the policy or consensus about the status of the relevant research (experts notoriously disagree about the apposite course of action or about the inferences to be drawn from research); for example, the recent debate in Britain amongst welfare policy experts as to the relative importance of increasing or reducing benefit payments reveals significant divisions of opinion (divisions which have not prevented the government following the advice of

---

[32] Downs (1957), especially ch. 7.

[33] Rothstein writes: 'the idea that an indubitable causal theory must first be available lacks an empirical basis, and theoretically it assumes an excessively rationalistic conception of politics (and indeed of human action generally). Successful policy implementation is often a question of so organizing the implementation process as to accommodate the need for flexibility and the uncertainty in the policy theory,' (1998: 113).

the cutters). Rather, those disagreements about knowledge are resolved in favour of one version through political endorsement: the selection of that view by policy-makers privileges and confirms its validity *at that point in time*. Or as John Kingdon writes, from his research about agenda setting in politics, 'if any one set of participants in the policy process is important in the shaping of the agenda, it is elected officials and their appointees, rather than career bureaucrats or nongovernmental actors.'[34]

This signalling process is fundamentally different to that in other areas where competitive claims to expertise can more easily flourish. For instance, opinions about a new film or novel will diverge between reviewers, and no one reviewer can dominate the choice of consumers (though which is most profitable commercially may be taken as a measure of success). In social policy, political endorsement does validate one set of expertise, by excluding others (at least in the short term) from the decision; political choice constitutes a signal about confidence in the selected knowledge. Politicians have their own signals about the expertise (including the quality of the research, the reputation and standing of the researchers producing it) which presumably gives them confidence in it and a political motive for its adoption. What is fascinating about this process is, arguably, that the central place of expertise (though not its content) remains relatively constant over time. I stressed the phrase, 'at that point in time', above to underscore the fact that the content of knowledge or expertise employed in social policy-making changes; its role as a source of policy formation does not, however. Despite criticism of the optimism of post-1945 assumptions about the ability of governments rationally to formulate and implement public policy and frequently voiced criticisms of experts themselves for lacking neutrality or real knowledge,[35] the expectation that governments will adhere to such practices endures. That part of the need for new policies stems from the failure of earlier institutions has not diminished belief in the general principle of intervention and its utility (for example, the Blair Labour government, elected in 1997, quickly made the Bank of England independently responsible for monetary policy through the setting of interest rates). Even to 'end' intervention requires social policy, though too many 'new' initiatives may erode electoral trust in the ability of a government to make effective policy.[36]

---

[34] Kingdon (1995: 19).   [35] See e.g. Bledstein (1976).

[36] The privileging of knowledge or expertise by politicians depends on trust in the government's judgement and authority. For instance, the US government has major responsibilities in the regulation of drugs and food production. Americans rely on the government to assess the relevant knowledge or expertise regarding new drugs or production standards, and are overwhelmingly less interested in the details of these expertises. For a discussion about declining levels of trust in the US government see the essays in Nye, Zelikow, and King (1997).

Crucially, trust does not have to be shared by all the population: those targeted by workfare, for instance, are less relevant politically than the remainder of the population.

The rise of expertise

The influence of expertise in social policy is not a new phenomenon.[37] Even before 1945, the influence of professional associations and university research students was exercised through experts in the United States, as Finegold observes in his study of reform politics in New York, Cleveland, and Chicago: 'the municipal experts of the Progressive Era were the first products of the new doctoral programs in American universities.'[38] In a recent volume, Rueschemeyer and Skocpol bring together a set of papers examining how what they term 'social knowledge' was utilized by governments at the end of the nineteenth and early twentieth centuries in the design and implementation of social policies. Correctly observing that an emphasis upon the class bases of such schemes inadequately takes account of the influence of the 'new knowledge-bearing elites', and that modern social policy reflects multiple sources (including civil servants' labours and the initiatives of political parties not directly associated with employers or organised workers), these two scholars argue that 'amidst the variation, there is one constant: intellectual expertise and authority invariably left their imprint on the formation of early modern social policies.' They argue that 'we need to understand more deeply both the ideas and the socio-institutional locations of the bearers of new knowledge about society who figured so importantly in the origins of early modern social policies.'[39] Obviously, the way in which ideas and social knowledge were injected into the making of modern social policy varies significantly with the nature of party competition, relative openness of government agencies, and socio-economic context,[40] but the claim that knowledge is itself an important factor and something employed by politicians, often in innovative ways, is compelling.[41]

Two examples illustrate how knowledge can become central to the policy-making process. First, the British Poor Law Act of 1834 was based on the extensive researches of the Poor Law Commission established in 1832. Composed of nine commissioners and twenty-six assistant

---

[37] See also Goldman (1987, 1998).
[38] Finegold (1995: 24). Rodgers (1998: 62) explains how may American Progressives benefited from university study in Germany.
[39] Skocpol and Rueschemeyer (1996: 6–7).
[40] Issues explored in Weir and Skocpol (1985).
[41] See also the 'Introduction' in Hall (1989) and see Rodgers (1998).

commissioners, the Commission distributed questionnaires to rural districts and towns, and the assistant commissioners undertook 3,000 field trips, to approximately a fifth of existing Poor Law authorities. The data compiled from these investigations were appended to the final report and used as the basis for the analysis and recommendations prepared by the commissioners. Heclo appreciates the innovation in the use of systematic research that the New Poor law represented. He writes: 'what marked 1834 policy as novel was the tighter and more deliberate intellectual and administrative framework for the workhouse idea . . . [T]he 1834 act followed a "scientific" royal commission investigation. The commission investigation was an unprecedentedly detailed study of existing poor relief conditions.'[42] Second, the advocacy of eugenic-based sterilization of the so-called mentally ill was recommended in Britain by the Brock Report in 1934. This study was based on two years' investigation of the scientific research on the causes of mental illness (in particular, scientific confidence in claims about its hereditary form), appropriate remedies and international practices, acquired through meetings and questionnaire responses from local health authorities. It met for two years, compiling a substantial amount of data. In these examples, specialist knowledge was central to the process of policy-making. Although the Brock Committee's recommendation was not implemented its intellectual framework defined the problem and its solution. The policy-makers enjoyed some autonomy from short-term political pressures, and provided what they believed to be strong evidential bases for their proposals. However, members of the elites in each case had clear views (which other experts would have challenged or rejected) about the solution to the problems addressed. The Poor Law Commission secretaries, Edwin Chadwick and Nassau Senior, possessed firm convictions about social improvement, the importance of market forces, and the role of government, all of which assumptions structured the report, as Heclo underlines: 'instructions to the roving commissioners had been written personally by Nassau Senior, Britain's leading political economist, and it was the tight theoretical structure of political economy that provided the systematic, intellectual underpinnings to the investigation.'[43] In 1932 the members of the Brock Committee, including the chairman Brock, had multiple connections and beliefs with eugenists, which again influenced their conclusions. The degree of autonomy and political confidence enjoyed by such expert committees will vary historically and ultimately whether their advice is acted upon remains a political judgement.

These observations suggest a pattern to social policy formation (not dissimilar from that enumerated in John Kingdon's agenda-setting model[44]).

[42] Heclo (1974: 56).   [43] Ibid.

[44] Kingdon (1995). See also Baumgartner and Jones (1993), Cobb and Elder (1972), and Walker (1969).

First a political problem either becomes too great to be neglected (such as unemployment) or a lobby group pushes an issue onto the political agenda (as in the case of eugenic arguments for sterilization policy); problems also arise as a result of earlier measures, such as the size of the welfare budget.[45] John Kingdon argues that 'problem recognition is critical to agenda setting', adding that 'some problems are seen as so pressing that they set agendas all by themselves'.[46] This description is apt in respect of the problems associated with eugenics, unemployment and workfare examined in this study. Second, this initial interest compels a systematic study or collection of relevant data to determine the scope of the problem and the best way to alleviate it (or a proposal, dormant but supported by some policymakers, may be mobilized). Both of these stages may well be structured to favour a particular interpretation (especially since policy advocates usually have a firm view about the problem and how to address it), and hence resolution of the issue. Kingdon writes about the selection of policy alternatives as analogous to a biological process of selection: 'through the imposition of criteria by which some ideas are selected for survival while others are discarded, order is developed from chaos . . . These criteria include technical feasibility, congruence with the values of community members, and the anticipation of future constraints, including a budget constraint, public acceptability, and politicians' receptivity.'[47] Such criteria will be in evidence in the ensuing chapters, though Kingdon's description does not give sufficient attention to the conflicting views evident amongst think tanks. Baumgartner and Jones add an emphasis upon the non-incremental way in which issues become dominant and policy options feasible.[48] Finally, bipartisan agreement on the issue is common: the major parties concur about the problem and its solution, as the case of workfare in both the USA and Britain richly illustrates.

In sum, in both the United States and Britain a general market in ideas and research findings, funded partly through public resources (including research grants to universities) and partly from private sources has developed. It is hardly controversial to make this proposition in the closing decades of the twentieth century: since the 1950s, think tanks, interest groups, and other forms of idea 'generators' and enterpreneurial efforts have arisen in political capitals. To some extent, the new visibility of think tanks and independent research institutes since the 1960s arises from both a frustation among their members with the lack of policy relevance of much professional university-based social science (whose practitioners'

---

[45] Pierson (1994).   [46] Kingdon (1995: 198).
[47] Ibid. 200. Rodgers (1998: 415) argues, from his consideration of the New Deal, that at this stage in the policy-marking process, proposals which have been around for some while often suddenly receive attention in response to the political urgency of the problems facing policy-markers.   [48] Baumgartner and Jones (1993).

career-need to emulate 'scientific' standards has accelerated and become a principal source of professional status), in addition to a greater openness to ideas and schemes for problem-solving amongst policy-makers. The influence of such organizations upon policy was decisively demonstrated by the Reagan and Thatcher administrations;[49] and the openness of politicians to such influences has hardly diminished in the Blair and Clinton eras, (although it is plain that ideas continue fundamentally to serve political ends).[50] Such 'idea generators' have been in existence, in one form or another, since the nineteenth century (though, before the 1950s, they were principally of a voluntary nature) and there are now substantial policy communities linking experts from government, academy, business, and independent institutes. The knowledge or expertise resulting from these intellectual and political activities has become part of policy-making.

POLICY IDEAS AND LEGACIES

The factors examined in the previous section provide a context within which illiberal social policies may be adopted. These latter were defined in Chapter 1 as policies possessing an ideological appeal across the left–right spectrum, some intellectual or scientific plausibility (even if controversial), and promulgated as compatible with liberal democracy but which actually violate the equality of treatment principle in some way such as by making participation in government programmes for selected citizens involuntary. How such ideas become part of the political agenda must now be examined, a process dependent on the activities of lobbyists, think tanks, and interest groups, activities which build upon or reverse the legacies of earlier policy choices.

The articulation of ideas

There is a substantial literature on 'policy networks', or 'policy communities' or 'issue networks' to use the varying labels. Each term attempts to depict the groups to which experts belong and through which expertise is communicated to decision-makers.[51] The different terms embrace several

---

[49] Stone (1996), Cockett (1994). And see Godfrey Hodgson, 'Now is the time for all Right-thinking men' *Sunday Times Magazine*, 4 Mar. 1984, for profiles of influential figures.

[50] In Britain the roles of the think tank Demos and network Nexus are illustrative in this context: see 'Top Blair adviser steps down as director of Demos think tank', *Observer*, 18 Oct. 1998, and 'Ex-Labour aides selling the inside track on how to block party policy', *Independent*, 7 Sept. 1998. For an analysis of academic sociologists' failure to provide proposals of relevance to policy-makers see Christie (1999).

[51] See Marsh and Rhodes (1992a), Dowding (1995).

common features: the existence of a network or community of experts, civil servants, academics and others, working in their different institutions on the same policy and aware of each other's research. Interest groups feature in these issue networks too; indeed, what distinguishes these new networks from earlier 'iron triangles' or 'subgovernents' is that the latter featured one dominant interest group while the former are more permeable to a host of advocacy groups. What makes interest group representatives influential is their ability to understand and contribute to policy expertise, a characteristic germane to my thesis about the importance of expert knowledge in social policy formation. Policy communities are not, of course, immune to faddish ideas, even when the evidence for them is thin at best. Political scientists writing about policy networks focus mostly upon how these networks function.

This circle overlaps conventional distinctions between the public and private sectors, and directs scholars toward the study of decision-making within this group. In her valuable study, Diane Stone identifies 'epistemic communities' centred on think tanks, whose research feeds directly into policy-making: 'epistemic communities are knowledge based networks who articulate the cause-and-effect relationships of complex problems.' She places think tanks at the locus of this process: 'think-tanks are a strategic location for epistemic communities. In particular, they play a role in the development of an epistemic community's consensual knowledge and the diffusion of this knowledge to influence government agendas.'[52] Stone's proposition about the centrality of think tanks in intellectual communities or networks through which ideas are generated or rediscovered and promoted is sound.[53]

However, the idea of networks underestimates the dominance of politicians and civil servants in the determination of policy choices, especially in Britain, and the extent to which political choices and calculations can easily dissipate apparent 'concern' about policy options. I concur with John Kingdon's observation, writing about the USA, that 'in the shaping of the agenda' the most important participants are 'elected officials and their appointees'.[54] Furthermore, political scientists' descriptions of networks gives no indication about the content of their discussions and how the agenda for them is set. Most descriptions of policy networks tend to exaggerate the degree of consensus shared by experts. In respect of welfare reform in the USA, Teles demonstrates how think tanks and research foundations lined up with the various sides of the debate rather than offered a shared view about desirable legislation. Furthermore, think tanks—despite their members' claim to expertise—often express more deeply held

[52] Stone (1996: 37).　　[53] See also Solomon (1998).　　[54] Kingdon (1995: 19).

ideological or political convictions. Teles writes that 'it is at the think-tank level that the cultural division of the American elite starts to become clear.'[55]

In respect specifically of social policy, Hugh Heclo advanced the term 'issue networks', defined as a 'shared-knowledge group having to do with some aspect (or, as defined by the network, some problem) of public policy'. Networks comprise a large number of participants with variable 'degrees of mutual commitment or of dependence on others in their environment'. He adds: 'participants move in and out of the networks constantly. Instead of power commensurate with responsibility, issue networks seek influence commensurate with their understanding of the various, complex social choices being made.'[56] The precise delineation and operation of policy or issue networks is less important than that they can be said to exist, and contribute to the processes by which ideas and expertise are communicated with decision-makers. Some of the empirical case studies in this study have rested on precisely these sorts of intellectual issue communities.

Second, as in other creative activities, such as art (think of Picasso's reworking of Ingres's painting *The Source*), imitation or adaptation of policy elsewhere is common. Here, the specialist literature on policy transfer across nations[57] is a source for students of how knowledge shapes policy choices. If policy networks do not stretch automatically to cross-national linkages, experts certainly draw on experience and research from other countries. For example, the shift to workfare in British social policy since the 1980s has been informed by ministerial and civil servant visits to Sweden, Australia, New Zealand, and above all the United States.[58] Leading American 'experts' and exponents of particular views have found their approaches reproduced in Britain and their expertise sought in think-tank-organized seminars.[59] This emulation of another country's policy is historical. Eugenics was an international movement, with advocates—familiar with each other's work—in several countries. Workfare shows these features too: British policy has been fundamentally influenced by the arguments of American experts and has emulated American practice. In both countries political parties have played a key role in communicating these ideas—borrowed from think tanks and experts—into government

[55] Teles (1998: 67).   [56] Heclo (1978: 102–3).
[57] See Dolowitz and Marsh (1996), Bennett (1991), Deeg (1995), Oliver (1996) and Rose (1993). For an excellent discussion of the transfer of European ideas to the United States in the first four decades of the twentieth century see Rodgers (1998). Of this period, Rodgers remarks 'that American progressives should have found themselves drawing so much more heavily on the experience and ideas of their European counterparts than Europeans did on theirs has no historical given' (1998: 70).
[58] Dolowitz (1996, 1997) and King (1995).
[59] Mead (1997*b*), Murray (1990), and Dolowitz (1997).

policy, particularly in Britain. However, a deficiency in this literature is the failure to recognize—in the US–British context—the dominance of US policies: British policy has imitated the US model but the reverse pattern is unusual (for example, little American emulation of British privatization policy occurred in the 1980s, though many American progressives aimed to emulate European social and economic legislation).

Policy legacies: the solidification of ideas

Consideration of the role of ideas or expertise in public policy is strikingly at variance with one influential framework in comparative politics: the emphasis, shared by a range of scholars, upon the importance of institutional arrangements in policy choices and the relative inflexibility of policy-making processes to new ideas once a course of action has been established.[60] I think this perspective marginalizes the importance of ideas and exaggerates the rigidity of institutional arrangements for policy-making and implementation.

The principal scholarly claim is that government policy and intervention in the social realm can assume a self-sustaining character. Once an area is identified as a task for public policy—immigration or labour market participation, for example—then institutional arrangements created to oversee and manage policy are put in place which significantly constrain the options of subsequent policies.[61] The recommendation of the Poor Law Commissioners to revise the poor law in 1834 was accompanied by a new administrative institution for its implementation; this institution evolved into the Ministry of Health a hundred years later. Comparable administrative arrangements appeared in the United States from the 1880s, necessitated by the Progressive-inspired social and political reforms commencing at the end of the nineteenth century.[62] Several scholars emphasize how 'policy legacies', the effects of earlier decisions, constrain subsequent policy choices about what innovation is permissible.[63] This is not a new claim, and indeed Heclo singled it out in his comparative study of British and Swedish social policy: 'the context of modern social policy begins to flesh out one major theme: the considerable impact of policy inheritances upon the substance of policy making.'[64] The same sort of

[60] Hall (1986), Immergut (1998), and March and Olsen (1989). For assessments see Katznelson (1997, 1998).
[61] For debates about historical institutionalism and policy legacies see Steinmo, Thelen, and Longstreth (1992) and Weir and Skocpol (1985).
[62] Skocpol (1992) and Polsky (1991).
[63] As Margaret Weir argues in respect of US employment policy, in which New Deal initiatives constrained policy choices in the 1960s: Weir (1992), and see Mucciaroni (1990).
[64] Heclo (1974: 63).

argument is expounded by path dependency theorists, who seek to argue more than 'history matters' (a self-evident truth).[65] Rather, their claim is that apparently small choices in institutional arrangements can have remarkable consequences at a later date (regardless of whether they were adopted purposefully or unthinkingly), and that some policy choices may prove almost irreversible (for example, the image of employment services in Britain and the United States as purveyors of benefits rather than placement agencies despite innumerable reforms[66]). From his study of New Deal relief, Edwin Amenta emphasizes how existing bureaucratic resources and priorities structure policy options: 'the puzzling of domestic bureaucrats is highly structured. The perceptions of administrators are typically limited by the programs and the configuration of bureaucratic capabilities in existence.'[67] This point underscores that made by Heclo.

Undoubtedly, the emphasis upon institutional or bureaucratic solidity has merit. For instance, the influence of New Liberalism in Britain and Progressivism in the United States is indisputable both in making the government an appropriate agent of social reform and in influencing the content of such initiatives. The institutionalization of liberal democratic values in British and American social policy is a manifestation of this legacy and, as explained in Chapters 7 and 8, this inheritance made the establishment of workfare programmes easier. The racialist bias of the US welfare policy adopted in the 1930s resonates in modern income assistance programmes.[68] It does not, of course, preclude some, often significant, policy breaks, a difficulty with too rigid a path dependency view: twenty years ago, a prediction that both Britain and the United States would have implemented robust workfare programmes would have seemed improbable.

The analytical focus upon institutional stability complements the view of those policy experts critical of this very durability. For critics of liberal social policy, it is precisely administrative tenacity which is lamented. They argue that bureaucracies become self-sustaining and inefficient at their job, contributing to, instead of alleviating, the problems which they were designed to address. Such a view informs ideological agendas critical of the post-1945 expansion of government. Whether a budget-maximizing or programmatic view of civil servants is adopted,[69] that civil servants are committed to retaining administrative structures is an assumption common to most theories of bureaucratic behaviour,[70] a commitment a frequent object

---

[65] David (1985). For applications see Berman (1998) and Pierson (1996).
[66] King (1995) and Weir (1992).   [67] Amenta (1998: 35).   [68] Lieberman (1998).
[69] Dunleavy (1991).
[70] Most recently, Amenta claims that 'the greater the number of people in such bureaucracies, the more people working from within the government to promote social spending and to provide aid and information to reformers outside the government' (1998: 28).

of conservative critics. These claims have been voiced forcefully in respect of welfare policy.[71] In Lawrence Mead's judgement, 'traditional approaches to social reform have been exhausted. Government has failed to overcome poverty simply by expanding opportunity, the traditional American solution to social problems.'[72] Reflecting on the declining support for social citizenship in the United States, Hugh Heclo reports that, 'there is now a deeply embedded cynicism about the ability of government programs to produce desired social changes. This is the result, not only of conservative rhetoric, but of hard experience as well-meaning efforts have collided with the unforgiving complexity of social reality.'[73] The embeddedness of a bureaucracy does not preclude deploying public resources to address problems—Mead in fact perceives a new paternalism in policy[74] —but suggests that part of the problem stems from earlier solutions. 'Knowledge' thus retains its special place.

Two general points about administrative legacies are worth making. First, institutional arrangements clearly do embody certain principles and assumptions which may constrain later options but, second, the political pressure to undertake social reform combined with the market in ideas has given expertise a greater potential influence than this assumption of institutional durability appreciates: if there is no change, analysis of public policy would be rather trivial. The solidity of administrative arrangements can be overstated and the role ideas in policy changes underestimated (even if those ideas simply recycle ones influential in earlier periods). The major workfare measures implemented in both Britain and the United States in the last two years rest upon an explicit rejection of existing institutional structures in respect of the poor. The fact that these initiatives resonate with nineteenth-century measures does not diminish the need to explain their adoption and how they are justified as liberal democratic.

CONCLUSION

This discussion suggests that the following factors are germane to the formulation and, in some cases, adoption of social policies which conflict with liberal democracy. First, the policy proposals enjoy close to bipartisan political party support, despite the electoral incentive for party political competition. The policies serve identifiable political ends and the fact that there is bipartisan support implies both that the policies are acceptably liberal democratic and concerned with general problems. For instance, the argument that 'welfare dependency' is a major (detrimental) consequence

---

[71] See e.g. Murray (1984).   [72] Mead (1992: ix).   [73] Heclo (1995: 684).
[74] Mead (1997a).

of welfare programmes is a view shared by the political left and right in Britain and the United States, as manifest in recent reforms. Second, ideas form an important part of the three types of policies identified in the last chapter. Both eugenic arguments and workfare schemes have been promoted in terms of strong ideational claims. Even the collectivism of inter-war labour camps, while less rigorously formulated as a public policy initiative, nonetheless rested on claims about the benefits of such schemes for participants. Third, the policies examined empirically need to be considered in relation to existing institutions and policies. These latter formed the background from which new initiatives were either conceived to be significant breaks or laudable developments. Finally, the people for whom illiberal policies are designed do not constitute the mainstream of the electorate: they are often politically marginal and apparently bereft of the qualities necessary for citizenship in a liberal democracy, suggesting that their consent to the schemes has played a smaller part in their adoption than the intellectual or political motive (crucially, shared across political parties) apparent amongst the relevant policy-makers.

This overview should not conceal the extent to which all social policy initiatives have distinct features. The role of politicians, the way in which evidence is collected and employed, the presence or absence of electoral pressures (and their intensity) for reform, the interaction between government officials and interest groups, and the reliability of predictions about the changes likely to occur as a result of proposed measures, will vary over time and between polities. In terms of the core questions addressed in this study, the investigation of these policies throws light upon the dynamic nature of liberal social policy (and its influence upon American and British political institutions), the role of expertise and experts in policy formation and how ideas interact with politicians' calculations and decisions. Although the analysis of such policies is germane to a range of current debates about topics such as social citizenship, liberalism and the preconditions for democratic institutions, and the role of the state in a democratic polity, there is a dearth of empirical studies of them. One partial example is Tony Kushner's discussion of the reaction to the Holocaust in the United States and Britain. Kushner's book is an 'attempt to explore the reactions of liberal societies when confronted with an *illiberal* phenomenon—the isolation of a minority and the eventual murder of six million of its members'.[75] In this book I examine public policies embarked upon internally within the USA and Britain during more routinized political eras and the reasons given for supporting them. From the reconstruction of selected policies a picture of the political culture and

[75] Kushner (1994: 18).

tenets of a polity can be distilled, richer for its treatment of illiberal elements.

With these issues in mind the criteria for selection of the case studies include: examples which are historical as well as contemporary; policies in which scientific knowledge or expertise was salient; and policies which posed challenges to citizenship or contributed to its redefinition. A number of contrasts and comparisons are built into the selected cases. First, the United States and Britain constitute a useful comparative coupling. Democratic institutions are entrenched in both the USA and Britain, and liberal assumptions about the importance of equality of treatment pervade their political cultures. The successful matching of individualism and market forces has made the USA and Britain influential, indeed crucial, examples of twentieth-century democracy.[76] This shared inheritance masks significant differences which influence the making and implementation of policy. Institutionally, the USA's separation of powers renders decision-making complex and cumbersome in contrast with Britain's centralized parliamentary system in which political decisions can be achieved with relative ease. This distinction is reinforced by the role of the USA's written constitution in structuring politics and facilitating rights-based arguments[77] compared with the UK's unwritten constitution and lack of judicial review.[78] These differences result in distinct forms of market democracy (both culturally and institutionally) which influence public policy choices. Thus, on several apparently similar policy questions the response has differed between the two countries in that policy-makers in one have been more enthusiastic about the scheme than in the other. The empirical discussion is mindful of this contrast, as for example in the success of the Civilian Conservation Corps experiments compared with the British interwar reconditioning camps: indeed, any illiberal tendency in the CCC was completely sidestepped at its establishment.

A further difference concerns the democratic and historical constraints upon policy in the two countries. For instance, eugenic arguments found favour amongst policy-makers in the United States (and won Supreme Court endorsement) whereas in Britain political scepticism about their compatibility with the individualism of liberal democracy ultimately precluded their adoption. An obvious contrast is provided by work camps. The USA's experience of work camps, as illustrated by the New Deal Civilian Conservation Corps, was one which emphasized that institution's transparent and democratic features (as documented in Chapter 6) whereas the

---

[76] This claim is problematic in respect of the USA, of course, because of its denial of civil and voting rights to many African Americans until the 1960s.   [77] Sandel (1996).
[78] For a recent demonstration of the comparative consequences of this difference see Hart (1994).

British policy was circumspect and according to some critics violated the affected citizens' equality of treatment by making attendance involuntary. This comparison—reported in Part III—permits conclusions to be drawn about how the illiberal potential of a major policy initiative can be curtailed. In the case of workfare another pattern is manifest: adopted earlier and more comprehensively in the USA than in Britain (where the influence of American practitioners and advocates was clear) it is nonetheless a mandatory programme in both countries, specifically limiting the choices of those required to participate in it.

PART II

Liberal Unreason

PART II

Liberal Interests

Introduction

RACIAL categories and eugenic arguments were commonplace assumptions amongst intellectual and political elites in the late nineteenth and early twentieth centuries. Writing in 1912, Leonard Darwin, an activist in the Eugenics Education Society (and later the Society's President), described the eugenic project as one which replaced the 'slow and cruel methods of nature' with 'some more rational, humane and rapid system of selection by which to ensure the continued progress of the race'. He envisaged an 'all-wise government' identifying whom to 'prohibit from figuring amongst the parents of the rising generations' and whom 'to encourage to marry'.[1] Such a vision illustrates how expectations about the requisite intellectual ability to be full members of a democratic polity have featured in liberal democracy.

Coined by Francis Galton, in 1883, the term 'eugenics' received its first institutional recognition in 1904 when Galton endowed a Research Fellowship in National Eugenics at University College, London. Karl Pearson, whose work in statistics facilitated the quantitative development of eugenic studies, was already well established there.[2] Galton's gift enabled the Eugenics Record Office to be opened, which in 1906, was renamed the Galton Laboratory for National Eugenics with Pearson appointed as its director.[3] The Laboratory was later incorporated into a new Department of Applied Statistics, of which Pearson was professorial head. The Department's research—undertaken by a growing band of students and scholars—included a concentration upon eugenic studies of heredity and medical questions. Daniel Kevles, in a leading scholarly account of the eugenics movement, describes the research supervised by Pearson: 'studies emanating from the laboratories typically explored the relationship of physique to intelligence; the resemblance of first cousins; the effect of parental occupation upon children's welfare or the birthrate;

---

[1] Leonard Darwin 'First Steps toward Eugenic Reform', *Eugenics Review*, 4/1 (Apr. 1912), 26. See his later statement also: 'Programme of Eugenic Reform', *Eugenics Review*, 15/3 (Oct. 1923), 595–6.

[2] See MacKenzie (1981).

[3] Edgar Schuster, 'Methods and Results of the Galton Laboratory for National Eugenics', *Eugenics Review*, 3/1 (Apr. 1911), 10–24. Schuster was a Research Fellow in Eugenics in London.

and the role of heredity in alcoholism, tuberculosis, and defective sight. It was tedious labor, but between 1903 and 1918 Pearson and his staff published some three hundred papers.[4] Such work was overwhelmingly aimed toward the broad question of how to ensure mental and physical strength and improvement in the national race. Pauline Mazumdar emphasizes eugenists' initial focus upon the 'pauper class', the post-New Poor Law marginal group in society, whom eugenists 'saw in biological or hereditarian terms as a breeding isolate at the margins of the human race'. The pauper class was the special interest of British eugenists: 'in each country, the eugenists' *Wunschbild*, their ideal type, and its negative image, were determined by national background and historical context. In Britain, it was the casual labourers or pauper class whose low intelligence and high fertility were dangerous to society, as it had been throughout the nineteenth century.'[5] Alfred Tredgold, later a member of the Brock Committee, certainly envisaged eugenic policies as a solution to degeneracy and pauperism.[6]

The American equivalent of the Galton Laboratory was the Eugenics Record Office established at the Cold Spring Harbor Laboratory, funded by the Carnegie Institution in Washington, and directed by the biologist Charles Davenport. Davenport secured funding from the philanthropist, Mrs E. Harriman, in 1910.[7] It was well endowed, from several sources, enabling Davenport to award scholarships to an army of research students and to run summer schools imparting skills in human heredity and statistical techniques of field research. Trained researchers began compiling a copious supply of records on the life histories and inherited traits of diverse groups and families throughout the USA. Dr Harry Laughlin, later employed as a eugenics expert by the US Congress, was Davenport's assistant.

Initially, the American researchers applied Mendelian laws of inheritance, experimenting on animals but always with an eye on the implications for heredity in humans. This latter interest encouraged the sort of data compilation of life histories associated with eugenic research. The fruits of this endeavour were included in Davenport's 1911 book, *Heredity in Relation to Eugenics*.[8] Dissecting the hundreds of life histories he had acquired through questionnaires, Davenport went in search of inherited sources of 'feeble-mindedness', pauperism, and other disagreeable traits.

---

[4] Kevles (1986: 39).   [5] Mazumdar (1992: 2,3).

[6] A. F. Tredgold, 'Eugenics and the Future Progress of Man' *Eugenics Review*, 3/2 (July 1911), 94–117.

[7] Allen (1986). For a contemporary account see Charles B. Davenport, 'The Work of the Eugenics Record Office', *Eugenics Review*, 15/1 (Apr. 1923).

[8] See H. H. Laughlin, 'Eugenics in America', *Eugenics Review*, 17/1 (Apr. 1925), 28–35.

He reproduced the prevailing views about racial differences (views influential to US immigration policy-makers) and energetically proselytized the need to engage in the building of a strong national stock. This 'positive' form of eugenics—fostering good marital choices for instance or as Ronald Fisher of the Eugenics Society put it, 'to increase the birth-rate in the professional classes and among the highly skilled artisans would be to solve the great eugenic problem of the present generation and to lay a broad foundation for every kind of social advance'[9]—was combined with an equally strong 'negative' eugenics, the need to control the reproduction of the least desirable members of society.[10]

This negative eugenics fed directly into a restrictionist US immigration policy, with selection based on individuals and families—tested appropriately for eugenic worthiness—rather than the identification of nationalities to exclude. Negative eugenics implied, as Kevles observes, 'preventing the reproduction of the genetically defective, possibly by state-enforced sterilization. If the state could take a person's life, Davenport judged, surely it could deny the lesser right of reproduction.'[11] Although marriages of so-called 'defectives' and a 'normal' person could result in 'normal' offspring, the risk of the opposite outcome fuelled advocacy of institutional segregation of the 'feeble-minded' and, ultimately, of their sterilization. Long-term reduction in the number of such citizens would have obvious fiscal dividends for society, it was argued.

The illiberal implications of this burgeoning eugenic approach to racial mixing and treatment of the mentally ill are roundly condemned by Kevles:

Davenport was prepared to curtail other people's rights in order to promote the race—to ensure the common protoplasmic good. He remarked to a prospective patron that 'the most progressive revolution in history' could be achieved if somehow 'human matings could be placed upon the same high plane as that of horse breeding.' His protoplasmic vision was on the whole offensive, in part cruel. Equally indefensible, although it was advanced with the authority and prestige attendant on one of America's most powerful biology directorships, it proceeded from science that, even by the standards of his own day, was usually dubious and often plain wrong.[12]

The limitations of this scientific base, and its implications for drawing inferences, were insufficiently attended to by Davenport and his colleagues. As a scientist, Davenport's approach suffered from 'shallow carelessness'.[13] In fact, Kevles concludes, Davenport's 'negative eugenics simply expressed in

---

[9] R. A. Fisher, 'Positive Eugenics', *Eugenics Review*, 9/3 (Oct. 1917), 206–12, p. 206.
[10] See also Darwin, 'First Steps toward Eugenic Reform', 38, who uses the terms 'constructive eugenics' and 'restrictive eugenics' to describe the same dichotomy.
[11] Kevles (1986: 47).   [12] Ibid. 48.   [13] Ibid. 52.

biological language the native white Protestant's hostility to immigrants and the conservative's bile over taxes and welfare'.[14]

As Daniel Kevles has meticulously documented, from the labours of Pearson in Britain and Davenport in the United States, national eugenics movements unfolded, popularizing the need for vigilance in racial breeding. Inspired by the aims of Francis Galton, these new proselytizers found receptive audiences in both countries (and of course formed part of a movement with organizations and advocates in many other countries). Ardent eugenists, such as Raymond Pearl, were confident that inherited behaviour could be such as to warrant sterilization, as he wrote in 1919: 'the investigations of Pearson and his co-workers in England, and of Davenport and the staff of the Eugenics Record Office in the United States, leave no room for doubt that a very considerable number of criminals, paupers, feeble-minded, epileptic and insane persons who come under institutional care owe their defective condition in greater or less degree to heredity.' The equating of pauperism or criminality with severe learning disability is notable. Pearl continued:

The pedigrees of such persons usually show plainly that they are defective in innate, hereditary constitution. They are the bearers of a germ-plasm which carries definite determiners for abnormal or defective somatic characters. If such persons produce offspring, even though in so doing they are mated to persons of normal, sound hereditary constitutions, it is to be expected from our present knowledge of the principles of inheritance (and experience bears out expectation) that a certain definite proportion of the offspring will not only be defective somatically, as were their parents, but will in turn pass on to their progeny, in some proportion, the defective germ-plasm.[15]

Eugenics organizations were formed to promote the new science and its policy proposals.[16] The data had a broad appeal, winning adherents from both ends of the left–right political spectrum, an important source of its popularity. Eugenists offered advice eagerly sought in intensely urbanized and industrialized societies. In the USA, this was the 'age of the expert' celebrated in Progressive social reforms. Eugenists basked in the new reputation gained by members of the knowledge-bearing elite in the opening decades of the twentieth century. This role interacted favourably with the claim that not just physical traits were reproduced generationally but that behaviour had biological sources. Social Darwinism pandered to this tenet, as claims about the extent to which the offspring of the poor, or the

[14] Kevles (1986: 51).
[15] Raymond Pearl, 'Sterilization of Degenerates and Criminals Considered from the Standpoint of Genetics', *Eugenics Review*, 9/1 (Apr. 1919), 1–6, pp. 1–2.
[16] See e.g. Leonard Darwin, 'How should our society now strive to advance?', *Eugenics Review*, 13/3 (Oct. 1921), 439–55. See also Adams (1990).

criminal, or the feeble-minded were themselves likely to reproduce these parental failings were made by eugenists.

This approach leads directly into the family histories undertaken and popularized in the United States from the 1890s. It resonated amongst progressive reformers in the United States and the middle-class social reformers in Britain, stirred by the threat of physical deterioration and national degeneration in the opening decades of the twentieth century.[17] Again, such views found improbable supporters across ideological divisions and sat comfortably with prevailing racial assumptions since, 'Anglo-American eugenicists embraced the standard views of the day concerning the hereditarily biological inferiority of blacks.'[18] The eugenists' alarm about racial degeneration consolidated, in both Britain and the United States, around the popular term 'the menace of the feeble-minded'. This priority privileged arguments about sexually segregating, sterilizing, or excluding (in the case of immigrants) the 'feeble-minded'. The slaughter of young British men in the First World War exercised some eugenists who feared that the 'best stock' had been disproportionately weakened. However, racist hostility toward some immigrants in Britain was not dependent upon this war.[19]

For familiar historical reasons racism was probably more evident in the United States, though social imperialism in Britain was hardly compatible with racial mixing.[20] In a characterization which is probably too strong, Peter Fryer unequivocally places racism at the core of British imperial thought: 'from the 1770s onwards the empire and the pseudo-scientific racism that served it developed side by side ... From the 1840s to the 1940s, Britain's "native policy" was dominated by racism. The golden age of the British Empire was the golden age of British racism too.'[21] Furthermore, as Nancy Stepan argues, the notion of 'race' was pivotal to the intellectual framework of scientists, including British ones, at the opening of the twentieth century: 'the nineteenth century closed with racism firmly established in popular opinion and in science.' Scientific support was fundamental: 'belief in the racial superiority of whites, and the practice of racial discrimination at home and abroad, if often deplored on moral grounds, had nevertheless acquired some sanction in the seemingly objective findings of modern science.'[22]

What was shared by eugenists in the two countries was an illiberalism, a willingness systematically to judge some members of the community as

---

[17] Searle (1971) and Pick (1989), ch. 7.   [18] Kevles (1986: 75).
[19] For example see G. P. Mudge, 'The Menace to the English race and to its Traditions of Present-Day Immigration and Emigration', *Eugenics Review*, 11/4 (Jan. 1920), 202–12.
[20] On the general context see Barkan (1992).   [21] Fryer (1984: 165).
[22] Stepan (1982: 111); see also Barkan (1992).

less worthy of equality of treatment than others. The argument was pre-sented as a 'scientific' one because of the assumption that eugenic research provided such a compelling case for violating the equality of treatment precept, both compulsorily and quasi-voluntarily. What the scientific research explained, it was claimed, was the cerebral limits to membership of the liberal democratic society. There was, for different reasons in the two countries, a disdain of the lower orders. Such views were arguably logical consequences of the eugenics framework. Kevles makes the same point more harshly: 'an unabashed distrust, even contempt, for democracy characterized a part of eugenic thinking in both Britain and America.' He continues, reflecting on eugenists' equal disdain for industrialists: 'the eugenics movement enabled middle- and upper-middle-class British and Americans to carve out a locus of power for themselves between the cap-tains of industry on one side and lower-income groups—both native and foreign-born—on the other.' This professional role was more powerful than ideological loyalties: 'socialist, progressive, liberal, and conservative eugenicists may have disagreed about the kind of society they wished to achieve, but they were united in a belief that the biological expertise they commanded should determine the essential human issues of the new urban, industrial order.'[23] The democratic limits on these tendencies, com-pared with dysgenic political regimes, is of elemental importance.

The two chapters in this section examine a case study each from Britain and the United States in which eugenic arguments and evidence were employed to advance policy proposals. In both instances, experts and researchers associated with eugenic views gained access to crucial policy-makers: in Britain through membership and close collaboration with rele-vant officials in the Ministry of Health and Board of Control; and in the United States through an official appointment with the House of Representatives Immigration Committee. In this instance, the different institutional structures of the two polities were less significant in impeding access for this expertise than in some other policy areas: eugenists found themselves at the heart of decision-making and their arguments were widely disseminated (and accepted) amongst the political elites of each state. However, the political success of eugenic arguments in the two coun-tries differed significantly. Although the Brock Committee recommended the introduction of a programme of voluntary sterilization in Britain, politicians failed to act upon this suggestion. In the United States, eugenists' arguments about the need to define who were appropriate immigrants to the country had a decisive influence upon immigration leg-

[23] Kevles (1986: 76).

islation enacted in the 1920s, thereby building on the position eugenic arguments had already achieved politically in this polity and program-matically in such state laws as sterilization. Fears of the illiberal implica-tions and consequences of eugenic-influenced public policy plainly weighed on politicians in Britain (despite the acceptability of such views) but received wide endorsement in the United States, a difference discussed in the chapters. That eugenics implied social policy which violated the equality of treatment principle is, however, documented amply.

THE AMERICAN MODEL

When the Brock Committee evaluated the appropriateness of sterilization for Britain in 1932 and 1933, it was able to observe considerable interna-tional practice of this policy. It was the most common eugenic measure in liberal democracies. The subsequent British discussion and call for legislation was informed of the purportedly scientific American research demonstrating that 'feeble-mindedness', or 'mental deficiency', or 'mental disorder' had a hereditary basis.[24] Since this US research was so influential internationally and in Britain, it is worth documenting its main findings for sterilization.

By the 1930s, laws permitting sterilization—voluntary or compulsory—existed in over half the states of the United States, two Canadian provinces (Alberta and British Columbia), Denmark, the Swiss canton of Vaud, and Germany.[25] Its introduction was under consideration in Tasmania, New Zealand (where it was rejected), Finland, Norway, and Sweden. Of New Zealand, the Prime Minister's Office informed British colleagues that 'the progressively increasing public burden imposed on the community by mental deficiency, degeneracy, and sexual delinquency, has given rise to much public concern during recent years and special enquiries have been made in an endeavour to deal with the situation.'[26] The US example was

---

[24] American practice and legislation also had a powerful influence in Germany; indeed it was the primary source for German laws according to Kuhl (1994).

[25] For the international context see, *inter alia*, Adams (1990), Broberg and Roll-Hansen (1996), Dikotter (1998), Graham (1977), MacKenzie (1981), Nye (1993), Proctor (1988), Reilly (1991), Schneider (1990), Searle (1979), and Weiss (1987).

[26] PRO MH58/104A 31974. Memorandum from Prime Minister's Office Wellington to His Excellency the Governor-General, 26 Sept. 1932, p. 1. A New Zealand committee, appointed by the Minister of Health in 1924, had recommended the creation of a Eugenics Board with the power 'in suitable cases to make sterilisation a condition of release from any of the insti-tutions under the charge of the Department of Mental Hospitals or removal of their names from the register on probation, but that in no case should the operation be performed without the consent of parents or guardians of the persons concerned'; cited in memoran-dum, pp. 2–3.

paramount for other countries, however, as Philip Reilly maintains: 'the triumph of eugenic sterilization programs in the United States during the 1930s influenced other nations. Canada, Germany, Sweden, Norway, Finland, France, and Japan enacted sterilization laws. In England, sterilization was ultimately rejected, but in Germany the Nazis sterilized more than 50,000 "unfit" persons within one year after enacting a eugenics law.'[27]

Eugenic policies, such as sterilization of the mentally ill or so-called 'degenerates', became popular at the end of the nineteenth century in the United States.[28] Rapid industrialization, urbanization, and the arrival of immigrants proved a potent coagulation within which class and social divisions became pronounced, and arguments about racial calibrations propagated. These latter operated both against new immigrants and black Americans.[29] New immigrants were frequently associated with the problem of a growth in the number of feeble-minded (see Chapter 4). The assimilability of new immigrants was a subject of intense debate in national politics. Trent observes that 'census data about the propensity of feeble-mindedness among immigrants seemed to confirm what superintendents, philanthropists, and some politicians had been claiming for several decades: immigration was responsible for much of the increase in feeble-mindedness.'[30] As Larson concludes, 'applying recent developments in genetics and evolutionary biology, eugenicists offered a means to breed better people just when rising middle-class progressives were seeking to cope with an apparent increase in the number of urban paupers, criminals, and mentally ill or retarded persons.'[31]

The principal US evidence in favour of sterilization (and other eugenic strategies) consisted of a limited number of family cases whose genealogy was traced by advocates of sterilization and presented as grounds for the new policy.[32] The most famous cases were the 'Jukes' family, investigated by Richard Dugdale, a social reformer,[33] and the 'Kallikaks', studied by Henry Goddard.[34] For the Jukes study, Dugdale retraced a family tree, over five generations, of 709 persons, a strikingly high proportion of whom ended up in institutions for the feeble-minded, almshouses, or

[27] Reilly (1987: 162).
[28] Bowler (1993), Haller (1963), Hofstadter (1955*b*), and Ludmerer (1972).
[29] One American observer, Professor A. L. Beeley, informed the Brock Committee that the reason for high rates of castration and sterilization in the state of Kansas was its large black American population: Proceedings of the 15th meeting of the Brock Committee, 13 Mar. 1933, pp. 4–5, in PRO Folder: MH51/226 31100.
[30] Trent (1994: 167).   [31] Larson (1995: 31).
[32] This section benefits from the important work of Philip Reilly (1983, 1987); and see Gould (1981), ch. 5.
[33] R. L. Dugdale, *The Jukes: A Study in Crime, Pauperism, Disease and Heredity* (New York: G. P. Putnam's Sons, 1877), cited in Reilly 1983.
[34] H. H. Goddard, *The Kallikak Family* (New York: Macmillan, 1912).

prisons. Dugdale's research 'created a sensation', in Larson's words,[35] and Reilly observes that 'the public seized his study as proof that crime, pauperism and mental illness were somehow transmitted from generation to generation. It would be difficult indeed to overestimate the impact of *The Jukes* and the studies spawned by Dugdale's work on the American imagination and on social policy from 1877 until about 1920.'[36] The fertility of the Jukes clan—confirmed in other studies—alarmed the burgeoning profession of eugenists, who argued the need to control such a trend, and received support from administrators at mental institutions. Both the cost of maintaining these individuals in institutions and the harmful effects for the American 'race' attracted pro-sterilization advocates.

The Kallikak family had two lineages, one benign, the other degenerate, a combination complicating the eugenic remedy. Goddard traced the family's tree, working backwards from an 8-year-old girl, Deborah. According to Goddard, her great-great-great grandfather, Martin, spawned two familes, one with an allegedly feeble-minded girl, which produced hundreds of feeble-minded descendants and other 'degenerates' such as criminals, epileptics, alcoholics, and prostitutes. The other family, descending from Martin's marriage with a pious Quaker, a scion of virtue, consisted of respectable and mentally fit citizens. Goddard's study had a dramatic impact. It appeared to confirm the 'causal link between vice and retardation'; according to Goddard, 'urban filth, poverty and disease were not the causes of the blight of Deborah Kallikak. Rather, her great-great-great grandfather's one-time peccadillo had ruined her and many other generations of Kallikaks . . . Added to the effects of heredity was the fecundity of the feebleminded.'[37] These family studies were increasingly aligned with a heredity view of genetic formation which negated the importance of environment. 'Feebleminded' thus became an inherited attribute.[38] To the disappointment of eugenic supporters of sterilization in Britain the Brock Committee rather dismissed this research. Thus Leonard Darwin wrote that 'the Committee seem to me to be unjustly severe in the tone of their comments on the work of Dr H. H. Goddard . . . at the date of its publication no English work at all comparable to Goddard's *Feeblemindedness*, and to indicate what was at all events possible in the way of systematic research was in itself an achievement of considerable value.'[39]

---

[35] Larson (1995: 19).   [36] Reilly (1983: 640).   [37] Trent (1994: 164).
[38] H. H. Goddard, 'Heredity of Feeble-Mindedness', *Eugenics Review*, 3/1 (Apr. 1911), 46–60.
[39] See Leonard Darwin, 'Analysis of the Brock Report', *Eugenics Review*, 26 (1934), 9–13, p. 11.

The feeble-minded research implied that policy should be designed to regulate the fertility and reproduction of generations of such feeble-minded citizens, likely to be a social burden and fiscal cost on the community. Measures including sterilization, segregation (placing so-called feeble-minded persons in institutions where they could be monitored and kept from sexual reproduction, a strategy pursued in the USA) and tough marriage laws were the logical remedies of the eugenic goal, measures which the eugenics movement in the USA pursued energetically at the state level between 1895 and 1945.[40] Beginning with Connecticut in 1896, marital restrictions were enacted in more than half the US states by 1914, all identifying various mental 'defects' precluding marriage. Larson notes that 'only South Dakota and Nebraska went as far as establishing central registries for all their members' defective residents and precluding any listed individual from obtaining a marriage license unless one of the wedding partners was sterile.'[41]

The importance of Goddard's work to US legislators was underlined by an American sociologist, A. L. Beeley, in his evidence to the Brock Committee in Britain. Beeley considered it elemental to the success of eugenic legislation in the USA: 'the eugenic movement in USA was in a great measure due to Goddard who in 1911 published the details of the Kallikak family.'[42] Beeley believed this movement was far more significant than claims about the economic burden of the feeble-minded in stimulating sterilization measures. Intellectually, the Goddard research was, in Barker's words, 'both long-lived and influential ... [E]minent geneticists continued to endorse it into the late 1920s and early 1930s and at times their respect for Goddard bordered on the reverential.'[43]

Laws premissed on the need to control inferior citizens began in the states,[44] in many of which 'young retarded women were institutionalized during their reproductive years. State laws were passed to forbid marriage by alcoholics, epileptics, the retarded and persons with chronic diseases. A few superintendents of asylums actually engaged in mass castration.'[45] As Reilly explains, a young Chicago surgeon, Albert Ochsner, developed, in 1899, a method for sterilization which felicitously accommodated the

---

[40] Not without success: see W. G. H. Cook, 'English and Foreign Marriage Laws in Relation to Mental Disorder', *Eugenics Review*, 13/1 (Apr. 1921), esp. pp. 357–8. And see Larson (1995).

[41] Larson (1995: 22).

[42] A note of the proceedings of the 15th meeting of the Brock Committee, 13 Mar. 1933, p. 1, in PRO Folder: MH51/226 31100.

[43] Barker (1989: 353).

[44] For an early inventory see R. Newton Crane, 'Recent Eugenic and Social Legislation in America', *Eugenics Review*, 10/1 (Apr. 1918), 24–9. And see Trent (1994).

[45] Reilly (1987: 154).

eugenic arguments prevalent at this time.[46] By 1917, seventeen state legislatures, led by Indiana (which passed a law in 1907 establishing compulsory sterilization), had enacted laws permitting the sterilization of
'defective' persons;[47] these laws consolidated state statutes already in place
to limit marriages of so-called mental defectives. This rapid pace of legislative enactment suggests political support for such measures and the
influence of eugenists, as Kevles comments: 'eugenicists did not single-
handedly cause the passage of the large variety of restrictive marriage laws
enacted in the first quarter of the century; they were part of a coalition
that put the laws on the books, and they provided prior (or, at times, post
hoc) biological rationalizations for what other interest groups wanted. But
American eugenicists played a dominant role in bringing about the
passage of state sterilization laws.'[48] The Indiana statute identified selected
'confirmed criminals, idiots, rapists, and imbeciles'[49] for compulsory sterilization, if their condition was diagnosed as incurable by a committee of
three physicians. The state conducting the most sterilization operations was
California, whose law focused upon the insane.

In 1927, the US Supreme Court found sterilization constitutionally
lawful, with the distinguished Justice, Oliver Wendell Holmes, imprecating
gloomily that 'three generations of imbeciles are enough'.[50] Sterilization
appeared to provide a solution to this problem *une fois pour toutes*.

This landmark judgement was over two decades in the making as earlier
state sterilization laws persistently encountered legal challenges. Almost
half of the first sixteen state laws were invalidated on various grounds
including (unsurprisingly) violations of due process, freedom from cruel
and unusual punishment, or the equal protection clause. Indiana's law was
closed under court order in 1920. Holmes's Supreme Court 1927 judgement reversed these setbacks, facilitating an upsurge in state sterilization
laws. Writing in a way which implicitly endorsed eugenic assumptions and
the appositeness of disregarding equal treatment for the so-called inferior,
he declared: 'we have seen more than once that the public welfare may call
upon the best citizens for their lives. It would be strange if it could not call
upon those who already sap the strength of the State for these lesser
sacrifices, often not felt to be such by those concerned, in order to prevent
our being swamped with incompetence.' Thus 'reason' or 'competence'
were singled out as a necessary quality for full membership of the liberal
democracy. The Supreme Court's (8:1) judgement imparted constitutional

---

[46] Reilly (1983).
[47] For an early inventory of the 'sterilization of the unfit', see Leonard Darwin,
'Sterilization in America', *Eugenics Review*, 15/1 (Apr. 1923), 335–44.
[48] Kevles (1986: 100).   [49] Quoted in Larson (1995: 27).
[50] *Buck* v. *Bell* 274 US 200 (1927); see Lombardo (1985) and Dudziak (1986).

authority to the sterilization of over 60,000 Americans by the 1960s,[51] including 8,300 inmates in Virginian state mental institutions between 1927 and 1972.[52] There was a distinct class and racial bias to these sterilizations: 'state sterilization laws applied only to the inmates of public mental institutions, whose residents were disproportionately from lower-income and minority groups. In Virginia, the overwhelming majority of those sterilized were poor; perhaps as many as half of them were black. In California, more than half the insane males sterilized were unskilled or semi-skilled laborers.' Immigrants were vulnerable: 'the foreign-born were more likely to be admitted to state mental institutions and to be sterilized once there. While they accounted for about a fifth of the California population in 1930, they represented at least a third of the group compelled to undergo the sterilization procedure.'[53]

Although the American research was influential, few of the advocates or practitioners of sterilization had systematically analysed the effects of this programme, as the minutes of a meeting of the Brock Committee record:

One would have thought that California would have kept very careful records of the 8,000 persons they had sterilised, but no such records were available. The persons who have proposed sterilisation have done so with a definite bias and it is strange they have so far produced no analysis of their work. Sterilisation might be described as a religion with these people—but even eugenics has become a religion in the USA.[54]

The influence of Goddard waned in the USA after the publication, from the late 1920s, of highly critical studies by Abraham Myerson, a neurologist.[55]

Eugenists in the United States were part of the new knowledge-bearing elite associated with the Progressive movement. The scientists amongst them imagined a new and improved social order attainable through the application of scientific solutions to social problems. The broad appeal of eugenics helped propel it into a national movement. The appeal of eugenics across the ideological spectrum is effectively illustrated by Edward Larson when he notes that three presidents of different beliefs— the progressive Republican Theodore Roosevelt, the liberal Democrat Woodrow Wilson, and the conservative Republican Calvin Coolidge— each expressed support for eugenic type arguments at various stages. In

[51] Larson (1995: 28) and Reilly (1987: 161).   [52] Lombardo (1985: 31).
[53] Kevles (1986: 168).
[54] A note of the proceedings of the 15th meeting of the Brock Committee, 13 Mar. 1933, p. 3.
[55] See A. Myerson, 'Some Objections to Sterilisation', *Birth Control Review*, 12 (1928), 81–4; and his later work *Eugenic Sterilization* (New York: Macmillan, 1936).

Larson's view, the 'eugenics movement was characteristically progressive because it involved middle-class professionals applying scientific expertise to solve pressing social problems through governmental intervention'.[56] This view is supported by Trent's study of administrators at institutions for the feeble-minded;[57] and by Lombardo's careful reconstruction of the circumstances preceding the *Buck* v. *Bell* decision. Lombardo argues, from an impressive range of primary sources, that '*Buck* does not merely represent the popular triumph of eugenical theory, but also the success of a small group of professionals who were able to use the specious "scientific" tenets of eugenics to legitimate their private prejudices.'[58] As a eugenically supported practice, sterilization was applied until the 1960s despite growing criticisms of the policy from the mid-1930s influenced by critics of Nazi Germany,[59] though the negative impact of the latter's policies is doubted by Reilly: 'no revulsion against Nazi sterilization policy seems to have curtailed American sterilization programs. Indeed, more than one-half of all eugenic sterilizations occurred after the Nazi program was fully operational.'[60] South Carolina repealed its 1937 sterilization statute only in 1985.[61] As in Britain, the Catholic Church was a consistent opponent of sterilization in the United States, active after the First World War and confirmed in their hostility by Pope Pius XI's 1930 *Casti Connubi* encyclical, which included a formal condemnation of eugenical sterilization. Combined with Abraham Myerson's work for the American Neurological Association in the mid-1930s, the tide began to turn against sterilization.

[56] Larson (1995: 30).　　[57] Trent (1994).　　[58] Lombardo (1985: 33).
[59] In 1936 the American Neurological Association's special committee on sterilization issued a critical report. It was chaired by Abraham Myerson and concluded that 'there is at present no sound scientific basis for sterilization on account of immorality or character defect' and that no 'definite conclusions' could be drawn about the 'part which heredity plays in their genes'. Quoted in Kevles (1986: 166).
[60] Reilly (1987: 161).
[61] Larson (1995: 163–4).

3

'Cutting off the Worst' Voluntary Sterilization in Britain in the 1930s

EUGENICS, a commitment to modifying the national gene pool for the benefit of society, enjoyed significant support among influential British politicians in the late nineteenth and early twentieth centuries, and a number of Mental Deficiency Acts incorporated some eugenist aims.[1] The lobbying of eugenists resulted, in 1932, in the appointment of a special committee by the Minister of Health to report and make recommendations on the sterilization of the 'feeble-minded' in England and Wales. The Committee was designed to generate support for a Royal Commission on the question, an inquiry which would in turn provide the basis for legislation. It was potentially the most substantial policy achievement of the eugenics movement in Britain.

This chapter undertakes three tasks. First, it reviews, briefly, the historical and intellectual context in which eugenics developed. Second, it analyses the context of the Brock Committee's appointment, the content of its deliberations, and subsequent efforts to create sufficient momentum in favour of eugenist legislation.[2] This discussion demonstrates how knowledge or expertise was deployed to justify this social policy initiative. Third, it examines why the initiative to establish voluntary sterilization failed in Britain when it succeeded in the United States.

The chapter presents three claims on the basis of this case study. First, it shows how the campaign for voluntary sterilization was conducted within the policy-making elite, insulated from societal forces (and in the absence of strong electoral support) until efforts to implement the recommendation commenced. Second, the arguments for and against the proposal turned fundamentally on the quality of the scientific evidence or expertise presented by advocates of voluntary sterilization: however, although the Committee reached a firm view about the evidence, it failed to convince sceptics. Finally, the importance of political considerations in resisting this illiberal measure is demonstrated. The evidence establishes that policy can

---

[1] For a history of the Eugenics Society and its aims, see Mazumdar (1992). For the movement generally see Kevles (1986), Stepan (1991) and Jones (1980).

[2] For the best existing studies see Macnicol (1989, 1992) and Thomson (1998), ch. 5.

be driven by experts and advocates acting autonomously from societal and political pressure, but any decision about implementation is firmly a political one. As the archival material illustrates, the committee members were doubtful about the political feasibility of a eugenist programme in Britain, chiefly because of public opposition and the hostility of the Catholic Church. Nevertheless, convinced of the desirability of sterilizing those whom they felt to be mentally incompetent, despite the doubtful scientific case in its favour, the committee members saw their deliberations as an instrument for marshalling support for a controversial policy, support for which they then hoped to use to sway a sceptical British public in favour of legislation. The committee was thus principally a mechanism for furthering the self-defined aims of certain members of the scientific and political elite, principally the protection of the British genetic pool from the dangers of uncontrolled reproduction.

Eugenic proposals have had a continuing allure for policy-makers and intellectuals. Thus, from its development at the end of the nineteenth century in Chicago, sterilization had become a widely cited medical remedy to the problems of mental illness and alleged fecundity of the mentally ill. In Reilly's concise phrase it constituted the 'surgical solution'.[3] Intellectually, eugenic proposals found wide support. Writing the majority decision in the US Supreme Court's 1927 *Buck* v. *Bell* case, which upheld a Virginia state law permitting sterilization of a 'feeble-minded' and 'moral delinquent', Carrie Buck, the US liberal jurist Oliver Wendell Holmes declared that 'three generations of imbeciles are enough', and that it was legitimate for the state to prevent the reproduction of so-called 'degenerates'.[4] Buck was duly sterilized as were many citizens in other American states which enacted comparable laws.[5]

The desire to improve the lower orders, invariably well intentioned but commonly revealing notions of social superiority, recurs in politics. In October 1974, the then shadow Home Secretary, Sir Keith Joseph, made a speech advocating the selective use of mandatory birth control to address the 'cycle of deprivation' and problem families.[6] Joseph took one example of the problems eroding 'civilized values' in British society. This was that 'the balance of our population, our human stock is threatened'. He continued thus:

a high and rising proportion of children are being born to mothers least fitted to bring children into the world and bring them up. They are born to mothers who were first pregnant in adolescence in social classes four and five. Many of these

---

[3] Reilly (1983).   [4] *Buck* v. *Bell* 274 US 200 (1927), 207; see Lombardo (1985).
[5] As meticulously recounted in Larson (1995); see also Kevles (1998).
[6] As reported in *The Times* 21 Oct. 1974.

girls are unmarried, many are deserted or divorced or soon will be. Some are of low intelligence, most of low educational attainment.

This trend augured badly for the future: 'they are producing problem children, the future unmarried mothers, delinquents, denizens of our borstals, subnormal educational establishments, prisons, hostels for drifters.' Without remedial action, society 'moves towards degeneration, however much resources we pour into preventative work and the overburdened educational system'. He proposed birth control to control these trends, judiciously weighing up the pros and cons:

Yet proposals to extend birth control facilities to these classes of people, particularly the young unmarried girls, the potential young unmarried mothers, evokes entirely understandable moral opposition. Is it not condoning immorality? I suppose it is. But which is the lesser evil, until we are able to remoralize whole groups and classes of people, undoing the harm done when already weak restraints on strong instincts are further weakened by permissiveness in television, in films, on bookstalls?[7]

His proposals provoked widespread condemnation.

Joseph's concerns resonate in twentieth-century Britain and the United States across the left–right political spectrum. Thus, in August 1997, the New Labour government announced plans to target adolescent girls most likely to become pregnant and to educate them about the folly of this. In the USA almost half the states enacted sterilization with constitutional authority. The Fabian Sidney Webb criticized the Poor Law for its 'anti-eugenic influence', noting despairingly that 'as things stand at present the Poor Law Authorities cannot even try to check the continued procreation of uncertified mentally defective persons. Indeed, such influence as they exercise in the granting of relief to such persons is all the other way.'[8] By providing medical help to unsuitable mothers, the Poor Law system was 'actually selecting, in practice, the inferior stocks for its subsidies', in Webb's view.[9] Seven years after the US Supreme Court's ruling in *Buck* v. *Bell*, the Brock Committee on sterilization, in 1934, advanced similar arguments in Britain about the dangers of so-called mental defectives reproducing themselves generationally:

Facts must be faced. It is idle to expect that the section of the community least capable of self control will succeed in restraining one of the strongest impulses of mankind. The mere suggestion is so fantastic that it carries its own refutation. Without some measure of sterilisation these unhappy people will continue to bring into the world unwanted children, many of whom will be doomed from birth to

---

[7] Speech reproduced ibid.
[8] Sidney Webb, 'Eugenics and the Poor Law', *Eugenics Review*, 2/2 (Nov. 1910), 233–41, p. 233. [9] Ibid. 234.

misery and defect. We can see neither logic nor justice in denying these people what is in effect a therapeutic measure.[10]

In raising the spectre of a national population policy, Keith Joseph's proposals unavoidably echoed pre-1940 debates about eugenics and sterilization policy, of which the Brock Report was a core element. At that period, Britain, in contrast to most of her major peers (such as the United States, Germany, Denmark, or Canada though not most Catholic countries), failed to implement such schemes despite an official recommendation to do so. Sterilization was advanced, in Britain as elsewhere, as a modern and scientific way of dealing with social problems. One observer noted that the advanced nature of eugenic measures explained why a state such as California—located in the West, the 'most progressive part of the Union'—was in the vanguard of operations.[11] The American Western states' progressivism contrasted with the dominance of Catholicism in the eastern states. This 'progressive' model was one to which many European states turned after 1918. The model assumed that the sources of mental illness were hereditary, and that this inherited gene was necessarily stronger than environmental factors.

THE CAMPAIGN FOR VOLUNTARY STERILIZATION

The context of the Brock Committee's appointment was one in which eugenist arguments commanded considerable sympathy among the political and intellectual elite. At the turn of the century, British intellectuals and policy-makers were exercised by fears of a deterioration in the nation's physical health,[12] and they sought a model of 'national efficiency'.[13] The commitment to improving efficiency was linked with arguments about the 'national racial stock': race improvement could be achieved through wise marriage choices and selective breeding, the information for which could be assembled by eugenists.[14] The Charity Organization Society expressed alarm in the 1890s about degenerate children and the Elementary Education (Defective and Epileptic Children) Act was passed in 1899. The Eugenics (Education) Society was founded in 1907.[15]

---

[10] *Report of the Departmental Committee on Sterilisation* (Brock Report) (London: HMSO 1934, Cmd. 4485), 55.

[11] Mrs C. B. S. Hodson, 'General Obervations on the Position in the United States', 27 Mar. 1933, prepared for the Brock Committee, in PRO Folder: MH51/228 31100.

[12] See *Report of the Interdepartmental Committee on Physical Deterioration* (London: HMSO, 1904, Cd. 2175).

[13] Searle (1971: 54).

[14] See Freeden (1978: 185–94) and Searle (1976).

[15] The Society's foundation was part of an international trend: the German Society for Racial Hygiene was founded (in Berlin) in 1905, the Eugenics Record Office in the USA in 1910, and the French Eugenics Society (in Paris) in 1912.

Eugenics attracted support from an eclectic group of scientists, Fabians,[16] upper-class conservatives, and civil servants,[17] and enjoyed support from across the ideological range of views held by politicians. Its aims achieved limited success in the Mental Deficiency Act, 1913[18] and the later Mental Deficiency Act, 1927. Its organizational focus was the Eugenics Education Society, which, from the late 1920s until the late 1930s, led a campaign for voluntary sterilization.[19] Sterilization was one of four strategies embraced by eugenists, the others being marital regulation, birth control, and segregation of the unfit. A long-running argument amongst eugenists over whether defectives should be segregated or sterilized was won by the proponents of the latter view;[20] (the 1913 legislation signalled a rejection of segregation[21]). The eugenics movement united in its campaign for sterilization. The Eugenics Society executed a three-phase plan: first, the compilation of data to establish the hereditary basis to mental deficiency and the use of this evidence to create scientific, political, and popular support for eugenics; second, the organization of a lobbying effort directed at parliament to secure the passage of a bill legalizing voluntary sterilization in an (appropriately regulated) manner which would satisfy a suspicious public; and third, securing the passage of legislation providing for the compulsory sterilization of all people defined by eugenists to be socially 'inefficient'.[22] The campaign for sterilization peaked in its unsuccessful efforts to complete the second phase.

The impact of eugenics on public debate is suggested by Winston Churchill's decision, in 1909, to circulate, as a Cabinet paper, an address

[16] Fabians, rather than liberals, found the eugenic views about improving the race through systematic and putatively scientific measures most attractive. See Freeden (1979).

[17] The composition of what can broadly be called the 'eugenics movement' is a matter of some scholarly debate. See in particular, Freeden (1979), Jones (1982, 1986), Paul (1984, 1992), and Searle (1976). On the social bases of the British eugenics movement see MacKenzie (1976, 1979), Ray (1983). For an authoritative and cogent critique which locates support for eugenics in a narrow occupational group see Searle (1981). For the best recent discussion see Thomson (1998).

[18] The Act was a watered-down version of legislation recommended by the *Royal Commission for the Care and Control of the Feeble-Minded* (1908). The powers realized in the Act diluted those initially proposed, as legislators worried about the implications for individual liberty of the eugenic project. The final Bill included no direct use of the term 'eugenics', and the definition of the persons 'defective' was circumspect. It did however retain the right to impose mandatory institutionalization of certified mental defectives. On the 1913 Act, see Barker (1989) and Larson (1991). The debate, Larson concludes, revealed a clear distrust of eugenics and eugenists.

[19] For the eugenists' own version see C. P. Blacker, 'The Sterilization Proposals: A History of their Development', *Eugenics Review*, 22 (1930), 239–47.

[20] On this division over strategies see Barker (1983) and Larson (1991).

[21] The Mental Deficiency Act of 1913 did give a role to involuntary institutionalization, which constituted *de facto* segregation.

[22] Macnicol (1992: 428).

by the eugenist Alfred Tredgold,[23] (who was to be a member of both the Wood (1929) and Brock (1934) committees). In common with other reformers, Churchill supported eugenic principles to address the problem of poverty.[24] The historian, Harvey Simmons, maintains that 'one cannot overestimate the influence of the eugenics movement [in the decade before 1914], for the work of Sir Francis Galton on the inheritance of ability, the growing fear of physical and moral deterioration of the English race and the work of the Royal Commission [on the Care and Control of the Feeble-minded] all combined to spread eugenic ideas among the English political elite.'[25] Nancy Stepan makes a similar claim, contending that 'the appeal of eugenics as a science and as a political programme is indicated less by the size of the membership of the Eugenics Society, which was never great, than by its quality. At one time or another many of the leading thinkers in Britain were counted among its number.'[26] Pauline Mazumdar points to the overlap between members of the Eugenics Society and other middle-class social reform organizations, cohering around a set of agreed themes: 'their common appeal was to the "educated class", and their common goal the control of pauperism and the management of the class they called the residuum.'[27] Eugenists were exercised by the high birth rate of the lower classes compared with the middle and upper classes: most advocates of eugenics believed the working class innately inferior and in need of control.[28] E. J. Lidbetter, another eugenist and witness before the Brock Committee, wrote in 1932 that the group suffering from mental illness together with paupers, sufferers of hereditary blindness, and lunatics formed 'a race of sub-normal people, closely related by marriage or parenthood, not to any extent recruited from the normal population, nor sensibly diminished by agencies for social or individual improvement'.[29] These characteristics implied, logically, that 'Britain was breeding a race of degenerates'. As Searle notes, 'in this mood of hysteria, the Eugenics Movement made considerable headway and catch-phrases, like "the sterilization of

---

[23] Cited in Freeden (1978: 188–9).

[24] 'I am convinced that the multiplication of the Feeble-Minded, which is proceeding now at an artificial rate, unchecked by any of the old constraints of nature, and actually fostered by civilised conditions, is a very terrible danger to the race. The number of children in feeble-minded families is calculated at 7.4; whereas in normal families it is but 4.2. . . . [There are] 12,000 feeble-minded and defective children in the Special Schools; many others are in residential homes. . . . The girls come out by the thousand at 16, are the mothers of imbeciles at 17, and thereafter with surprising regularity frequent our workhouse lying-in wards year by year. The males contribute an ever broadening streak to the insane or half insane crime which darkens the life of our towns and fills the convict prisons.' In *The Asquith Papers* MSS Asquith 12, letter from Churchill to Asquith Dec. 1910. See also PRO HO144/1098/197900, and Addison (1992).

[25] Simmons (1978: 395).   [26] Stepan (1982: 119).   [27] Mazumdar (1992: 10).
[28] Barker (1983: 207).   [29] *Eugenics Review*, 24/1 (Apr. 1932), 9.

the unfit", found their way into general political controversy.'[30] Soloway argues that the influence of eugenic ideas was manifest well beyond the limited purview of the Eugenics Society: 'rooted deeply in a tradition of hereditarian determinism and qualitative ideas of class, eugenics permeated the thinking of generations of English men and women worried about the biological capacity of their countrymen to cope with the myriad changes they saw confronting their old nation in a new century.'[31]

The first (and principal) success of this eugenic lobbying occurred with the passage of the Mental Deficiency Act in 1913 (based on the Royal Commission on the Care and Control of the Feeble-Minded[32]). It set out procedures for the compulsory detention of the 'feeble-minded'. The Act specified four categories of persons (idiots, imbeciles, the feeble-minded, and moral imbeciles) liable to detention in mental institutions. Feeble-minded was defined as: 'persons in whose case there exists from birth or from early age mental defectiveness not amounting to imbecility, yet so pronounced that they require care, supervision and control for their own protection or for the protection of others, or, in the case of children, that they by reason of such defectiveness appear to be permanently incapable of receiving proper benefit from the instruction in ordinary schools'.[33] The draft legislation was very broad and, as Michael Freeden points out, its breadth stirred some opposition: 'the liberal press was quick to take up the issue. *The Nation* conjured up visions of a ruthless machine with a totalitarian aura, hounding out the unfit. Amazing indeed was the clause that defined the feeble-minded as incapable of "competing on equal terms with their normal fellows" or "of managing themselves and their affairs with ordinary prudence." '[34] But it was exactly this assumption of inadequate reasoning ability which gave eugenic proposals their significance in a liberal democratic context. Only one Liberal MP, Josiah Wedgwood, presented substantial objections to the bill on the grounds of its diminution of individual liberty. The term 'feeble-minded' remained imprecisely defined and conceptually confused until the passage of the 1913 law. The powers realized in the Act diluted those initially proposed, as legislators worried about the implications for individual liberty—raised forcefully by Wedgwood—of the eugenic project: it is certainly difficult to reconcile with a view of liberal democracy as an inclusive framework. The final Bill included no direct use of the term 'eugenics', and the definition of the

---

[30] Searle (1971: 61).   [31] Soloway (1995: xxviii–xxiv).

[32] *Royal Commission for the Care and Control of the Feeble-Minded*, which met between 1904 and 1908, issuing its report in 1908. *Minutes of Evidence and Reports*, Cmd. 4215–21; 4202 (London: HMSO, 1908).

[33] Mental Deficiency Act 1913, Part 1, Section 1 (C).

[34] Freeden (1978: 191–2).

persons 'defective' was circumspect. 'Defect' had to be proved from birth or an early age and had to be certified by doctors.

Aside from 'defectives', the Act dealt with persons who were: (i) neglected, abandoned, without visible means of support, or cruelly treated; or (ii) brought before a court of law and were liable to be sent to an industrial or reformatory school or prison; or (iii) undergoing detention in an industrial or reformatory school or prison; or (iv) a child between 7 and 16 notified by the local education authority as being unable to benefit by education; or (v) a woman in receipt of Poor Law Relief when giving birth to or pregnant of an illegitimate child. The last category was used in some areas to institutionalize young pregnant women. The Act established the right to impose institutionalization of certified mental defectives when judged apposite, its most significant element.

The Mental Deficiency Act counted as a success for eugenists although its final content was hardly a faithful reproduction of eugenic concepts or ambitions. It was administered by the Board of Control,[35] which established thirty-five 'certified institutions', eight workhouses, ten certified houses, eighteen homes (approved by the Board), and other homes in which to place the feeble-minded.[36] The First World War curtailed the implementation of the Act, some local authorities administering it more diligently than others. An early survey of the law's operation unearthed 'marked diversity in the standards of certifying officers' across local authorities, revealing considerable ambiguity about the definition of the key terms 'defective' and 'mental deficiency'.[37] Eugenists regretted the narrowness of categories of persons deemed to fall within the legislation's parameters, and its casual implementation, with one observer complaining, in 1923, that the Act had 'never, as a whole been fully brought into operation or zealously administered'.[38]

The Wood Committee, appointed in 1924, was charged with ascertaining the number of mental defectives.[39] Its membership included prominent eugenists: Sir Cyril Burt, Evelyn Fox, Dr A. F. Tredgold, and Dr Douglas Turner. The Committee soon associated itself with the then widespread

[35] The Board of Control was established, in 1913, as the successor to the Lunacy Commission (in existence from 1845), with responsibility for pauper lunatics; all other responsibility for public health was assumed by the Ministry of Health when, in 1919, it replaced the Local Government Board. For an account see Thomson (1998) ch. 2.

[36] Anna H. P. Kirby, 'Notes on the Present Working of the Mental Deficiency Act, 1913', *Eugenics Review*, 7/2 (July 1915), 133–5.

[37] Evelyn Fox, 'The Mental Deficiency Act and its Administration', *Eugenics Review*, 10/1 (Apr. 1918), 1–17, p. 5.

[38] H. B. Brackenbury, 'The Mental Deficiency Acts and their Administration', *Eugenics Review*, 15/2 (July 1923), 393–401.

[39] *Report of the Interdepartmental Committee on Mental Deficiency* (Wood Report) (London: HSMO, 1929).

fear that mental deficiency was accelerating.[40] It reported in 1929, and it specified three descending types of deficiency: idiocy, imbecility, and feeble-mindedness, the last defined as persons capable of living in the community if carefully monitored and performing low-grade jobs to pay for their keep; they were unable to make plans for their future however or to 'maintain an existence independently of external supervision'.[41] The language of the Wood Report revealed a eugenic influence:

if, as there is reason to think, mental deficiency, much physical inefficiency, chronic pauperism, recidivism are all parts of a single problem, can it be that poor mental endowment manifesting itself in an incapacity for social adjustment and inability to manage one's own affairs, may not be merely a symptom but rather the chief contributory cause of these kindred social evils? If so, then the problem of mental inefficiency of which mental deficiency is an important part assumes a yet wider and deeper significance and must indeed be one of the major problems which a civilised community may be called to solve.[42]

The Wood Committee's report galvanized the Eugenics Society to intensify its lobbying efforts in favour of sterilization:[43] the Committee for Legalizing Eugenic Sterilization was formed to draft a sterilization bill and to build a coalition of support, drawn from the social work, public health, and mental care communities.[44] The relevant professional associations were exercising a new influence.

Eugenic ideas were, therefore, influential in the early 1930s, and the 1929 Wood Report contributed to an atmosphere which Greta Jones characterizes as one of 'moral panic': the hereditarily inferior, although a minority, threatened to overrun society.[45] The Brock Committee was a response to these fears.

The Eugenics Society's parliamentary campaign for voluntary sterilization began, and largely ended, with the request by Major A. G. Church, a Labour MP (and a member of the Society's Committee for Legalizing Eugenic Sterilization) in 1931, for leave to introduce a Private Member's

[40] Macnicol (1992: 429).   [41] Wood Report, Part I, pp. 11–12.   [42] Ibid. 83.

[43] See for instance the letter from the Eugenics Society's President, Sir Bernard Mallet to the Minister of Health, 18 Feb. 1929, which ended thus: 'if this most shocking of human afflictions is not to increase indefinitely, gravely imperilling the nation's racial health, the present faulty and utterly inadequate system of segregation must either be enormously improved and enlarged, or else be supplemented by some other policy. It is to be regretted that cost seems to preclude the first; and sexual sterilization, which has everywhere been successful, is therefore worthy of the very fullest investigation and consideration, as a supplementary, but not alternative policy.' Reprinted in *Eugenics Review*, 21/1 (Apr. 1929), 41.

[44] Macnicol (1992: 429).

[45] Jones (1982: 726). There were critics of the Wood Report (notably the Distributist League which characterized the study as a 'gratuitous advertisement of the eugenic theory'). See PRO, MH58/103, Letter from the League to the Minister of Health, Arthur Greenwood, Sept. 1929. These were, however, a minority of elite opinion.

Bill legalizing the operation.[46] The request, which was portrayed by its opponents as anti-working class, was defeated by 167 votes to 89.[47] Attempts by the Eugenics Society's secretary, C. P. Blacker, to recruit Labour Party supporters to the cause in order to undermine this charge were mostly unsuccessful.[48] The failure of this direct parliamentary pressure led the Society to focus instead on civil servants in the Ministry of Health and its Board of Control. Through lobbying, and through deputations by ostensibly less partisan bodies such as the Central Association for Mental Welfare,[49] the Association of Municipal Corporations, and the County Councils' Association,[50] the eugenists' movement succeeded in securing the appointment of a Departmental Committee on Sterilization under the chairmanship of Sir Laurence Brock.[51]

The movement was aided by the presence of sympathetic listeners within the Ministry of Health. The Permanent Secretary, Arthur Robinson, wrote to the Minister in April 1929 that 'I am myself of the opinion that the time is coming when this question of sterilisation of the mentally deficient will have to be very seriously considered and the appropriate machinery will be a Royal Commission, with strong expert representation to advise on the heredity factors and strong lay representation on the moral and social factors.' He expatiated further that, 'it has seemed to me for some time repugnant to common sense that, if a mentally deficient parent or parents on the average produce or reproduce similar children, the state should allow them to continue to do so and thereby throw on the

---

[46] A copy of the Bill is reprinted in the *Eugenics Review*, 23 (1931), 153–4.

[47] *House of Commons Debates* (Hansard) 5th ser, vol. 255, 21 July 1931, cols. 1245–58; the supporters included Sir Donal MacLean, Lieutenant-Colonel Walter Guinness, and Lieutenant-Colonel Freemantle. Macnicol (1989) argues that Church was an untypical Labour Party member, holding his seat briefly (in 1923–4 and 1929–31) and representing a white-collar union. He cites the Roman Catholic Labour MP, Dr Hyacinth Morgan—who led the opposition in the Commons to the Bill—as more representative of the Labour Party's stance on sterilization, particularly of the party view that such measures would be concentrated on a single class of citizens.

[48] Soloway (1995: 198–9).

[49] The Association passed a resolution in July 1929 calling for an inquiry into sterilization. See PRO, MH58/103, Resolution passed at meeting of the Executive Council of Central Association for Mental Welfare, 8 July 1929. The Association had links with the Eugenics Society—see reference to work by Brackenbury above—and it was an active promoter of sterilization.

[50] The County Councils' Association, the Association of Municipal Corporations, and the Mental Hospitals' Association had lobbied for well over a year to be seen by the Minister; see for example PRO, MH58/103, letter from the Mental Hospitals' Association to the Secretary, Ministry of Health, 27 Nov. 1931. For the eventual deputation in Feb. 1932, see PRO, MH58/103, Deputation from CCA, AMC, and MHA, Brief for the Minister's reply.

[51] Macnicol (1992: 430). The influence of the Eugenics Society in the appointment of the Committee is beyond doubt. The Society wanted to create the impression that the demand for an inquiry originated with these groups, when in fact it led the campaign.

next generation problems of segregation or supervision which this generation has conspicuously failed to solve.'[52] Robinson thought it too important to be 'tackled in the last months of a government'.[53] Writing two years later, the same official stressed to the Minister the complexity of a sterilization policy and the need for systematic study before enactment: 'it is emphatically the sort of problem which needs full enquiry by the strongest Royal Commission which can be got together—medical experts, sociologists, ethical and religious persons and ample ballast in the way of common sense view. A very detailed expert enquiry into the facts will anyhow be needed.'[54]

Securing the appointment of the Brock Committee was a measure of success of the influence of the Eugenics Society amongst the policy-making elite. From this point forward the campaign was led by a partnership between eugenists in Whitehall and in parliament, and eugenists in British society. The ambition of both groups, by the Committee's own admission, was to create sufficient support for sterilization to secure the appointment of a Royal Commission and, ultimately, the enactment of legislation.[55]

THE BROCK COMMITTEE

In 1934, the Brock Committee recommended in favour of voluntary sterilization. A Royal Commission was, however, never appointed, and Brock's recommendation, as well as the Committee itself, was discreetly forgotten as the cruelty of compulsory sterilization in Nazi Germany was exposed from the mid-1930s. Of scholarly interest is the content of the Committee's recommendations and the role of these proposals in the extra-parliamentary campaign for a sterilization bill.

The Departmental Committee on Sterilization was assigned the task of assessing the extent to which mental illnesses were hereditary and to evaluate the utility of sterilization as a means to limit the dissemination of such illness. Eschewing departmental neutrality, civil servants at the Ministry of Health expressed the hope that the Brock inquiry, by its specialist nature, would be buffeted from the fears of public opinion which a Royal Commission would face.[56] Its embrace of eugenic arguments led the Committee members to recommend an illiberal programme which would

[52] PRO, MH58/103, Minute from Arthur Robinson to Minister for Health, 18 Apr. 1929, p. 2.
[53] Ibid.
[54] PRO, MH58/103, Minute to Minister by Arthur Robinson, 14 Jan. 1932.
[55] PRO, MH58/103, Minute at the Ministry of Health, 8 Dec. 1931.
[56] PRO, MH58/104A, Minute, Ministry of Health, 21 Mar. 1932.

treat some individuals differently from others. The Brock Committee held thirty-six meetings, took evidence from sixty witnesses and received a plethora of statistical data,[57] and reported in 1934.[58]

Sir Laurence Brock was a senior civil servant who had spent much of his career dealing with health matters (serving as assistant secretary at the Ministry 1919–25) and was chairman of the Board of Control from 1925 to 1945; he had close contacts with eugenics activists. The other committee members were: Dr Alfred F. Tredgold, chairman of the Medical Committee of the Central Association for Mental Welfare, Consulting Physician in Psychological Medicine, University College Hospital, and a member of the Consultative Council of the Eugenics Society; Dr (Sir) Ronald A. Fisher, vice-chairman of the Eugenics Society, a member of the statistical department, Rothamsted Experimental Station, and an internationally honoured scientist; Mr Wilfred Trotter, Consulting Surgeon, University College Hospital, and a member of the Medical Research Council; Dr Ralph Crowley, who rose to be Senior Medical Officer at the Board of Education; Dr E. O. Lewis, an inspector at the Board of Control; and Miss Ruth Darwin, a Senior Commissioner at the Board of Control from 1932 to 1949. Two members of the Committee—Crowley and Tredgold—had served on the 1929 Wood Inquiry into mental deficiency and committee member Dr E. O. Lewis had undertaken that study's empirical research.

The evidence considered and commented upon by the Brock Committee is massive. It is bound together with one leitmotiv: the predisposition of the Committee's members to favour eugenic sterilization. Key members of the Committee—Fisher, Tredgold, and Brock himself—were not impartial, and consequently inadequately evaluated the contradictory and inconclusive evidence emerging from British scientific inquiry. In common with other members of the political and intellectual elite at this time, they were enthusiasts of eugenics; Brock regularly supported the Eugenics Society, while Fisher belonged to the Committee for Legalizing Eugenic Sterilization.[59] Reflecting on the Committee's work after the enquiry was complete, Brock remarked: 'no one can approach a controversial question with an entirely open mind, and I confess that I began with a slight prejudice in favour of sterilization in theory, and a doubt of its efficiency in practice, combined with a strong dislike of the controversial methods of certain eugenists of the

---

[57] A letter was sent to each health and local authority (that is, the Clerk to the County Council, the Town Clerk, and the Clerk to the Mental Deficiency Committee) requesting it to fill in a form about defectives' children in its area. See PRO, MH51/209, draft letter and questionnaire 28 Oct. 1932.

[58] *Report of the Departmental Committee on Sterilisation* (Brock Report) (London: HMSO 1934, Cmd. 4485) in *Parliamentary Papers*, xv (1934), 611.

[59] Macnicol (1989: 157, 165).

baser sort.'[60] For one who doubted the practicality of sterilization—in a letter to Robinson, Brock stated that 'while there is a great deal which is repellent in what one might call positive genetics, I believe there is a strong case for what one might call negative genetics, or, in other words, cutting off the worst'[61]—Brock felt notably able to aid the campaign for a sterilization bill. He gave the Eugenics Society advice on drafting its bill for voluntary sterilization. Brock was instrumental in having the Committee appointed under his own leadership as a means to serve the sterilization cause, and he dominated the proceedings.[62] Brock was in personal correspondence with C. P. Blacker, General Secretary of the Eugenics Society, and aware of its efforts to end the 'formidable and well-organised' opposition to a sterilization bill. This opposition was fuelled by Labour Party concerns that 'sterilization was . . . anti-working class.'[63]

The autonomy enjoyed by Brock in the appointment of the Committee was in all likelihood responsible for the partiality of its investigation, since it limited the potential for a critical evaluation of the evidence. Brock's commanding role in the Committee left little room for serious challenge, and it increased the potential for the Committee to act as little more than a validation of the pre-existing views of its key members. A more widely drawn committee membership, or the establishment of an advisory body, might have avoided this problem. As Collingridge and Reeve argue in respect of scientific evidence: 'the only way to ensure a genuine, healthy debate between rival groups of experts is to motivate them to scrutinize their opponents' views critically.'[64] This is particularly important when a committee's recommendations would constitute the main source of expertise for the government.

The Committee members' support of eugenics had three consequences: a toleration of imprecision in the terms defining those who would be encouraged to submit themselves to 'voluntary' sterilization; an inadequate understanding of consent; and a need to discount all evidence, which became stronger in the 1930s, that 'mental deficiency' was the effect of environmental, as well as hereditary causes, and that the relative significance of each could be established only equivocally.

[60] PRO, MH51/210, Chairman's Memorandum, n.d.

[61] PRO, MH79/292, Brock to Robinson, 16 Mar. 1932.

[62] PRO MH79/292, letter of 22 Apr. 1932 from Brock to Robinson about the Committee's membership; and Macnicol (1989: 167).

[63] See EUG./D 50., Brock to Blacker, 31 July 1934, EUG./D 214, Blacker to Lord Moynihan, 7 Aug. 1931 and EUG./D 50, Blacker to Brock, 25 May 1936, all cited in Macnicol (1989: 163). The claim that sterilization was class-biased dogged the committee throughout and led it to the debatable claim that 'sterilisation ought to be regarded as a right and not as a punishment'. Brock Report, 40.

[64] Collingridge and Reeve (1986: 17).

The Committee's proceedings

Speaking at the first meeting of the Committee, chairman Brock noted that pressure for legislation on sterilization had come principally from local authorities and public assistance committees, who urgently wanted an inquiry into 'the sterilisation of the mentally unfit'. However, as he explained, sterilization was 'very controversial', and therefore 'it would be difficult to secure legislation unless public opinion had first been prepared by the recommendations of a Royal Commission.'[65]

In an important memorandum prepared after the Committee had held its first four meetings, Brock distilled its purpose and working method. The former reduced to two key questions: 'the causation of mental disorder and deficiency, which is a medical and scientific question'; and secondly, 'the value of sterilisation as a preventive measure, which is partly a scientific question and also partly sociological'.[66] Brock acknowledged the difficulty facing the Committee in sifting through the scientific and medical evidence, especially since many experts were divided over fundamental questions such as the relative balance of heredity and environmental factors in determining mental illness.[67] He was, however, confident that, with a 'restricted view of our objective', the Committee could sidestep these complexities and still deliver a persuasive report:

I submit that we are not prevented from discharging our real task by the fact that the purely scientific problem is still unsolved. *The primary purpose of our enquiry is to advise the Government what sort of case may be made out for sterilisation*, not to attempt to reconcile the geneticists with the behaviourists, still less to attempt to decide which is right. We ought to take account of any scientific work which has been done; but we shall have met the first part of the Government's demand if we can show that there is evidence which would satisfy a reasonable body of men that the offspring of defectives is likely to include a substantial proportion who will either be defective in the legal sense or so backward as to be, if not socially unadaptable, at least socially useless.[68]

This assessment suggests that the committee members saw their purpose as primarily about convincing others of the suitability and importance of sterilization.

To realize the Committee's brief, Brock proposed a focus upon the

---

[65] PRO, MH51/212, Minutes of the first meeting of the Brock Committee, 23 June 1932, p. 2.

[66] PRO, MH51/216, Chairman's Memorandum, 19 Oct. 1932, p. 1.

[67] A point of context is important here. At this time, it was acceptable and not uncommon to acknowledge that the exact genetic cause of a condition was unknown, but to cite genealogical tables demonstrating that it was transmitted over generations within a family, suggesting that it was inherited.

[68] PRO, MH51/216, Chairman's Memorandum, 19 Oct. 1932, p. 2, emphasis added.

family history method, that is, unravelling the family histories of so-called 'defectives' and determining whether their offspring reproduced feeble-mindedness, the approach popularized in the USA. Methodologically, this approach reduced to extensive consultation with medical superintendents and specialists around the country about their observations and analyses. Despite the poor condition of much mental hospital records and incompleteness or circumspection of this method, Brock argued that such an exercise had instrumental value: 'we have to satisfy public opinion that we have been at pains to hear all the witnesses who had a reasonable claim to be heard.'[69] The greater the 'scientific' gloss the Report ultimately had, however doubtful this would have seemed on closer inspection, the greater the probability of allaying the suspicious and persuading the sceptical.

Who should be sterilized?

The Committee concluded that there was a population of a quarter of a million who were potentially candidates for sterilization. It believed this group both personally unhappy and a source of malaise for the rest of society. In a memorable phrase, the Committee was excited by the 'dead weight of social inefficiency and individual misery' implied by the 'existence in our midst of over a quarter of a million mental defectives and of a far larger number of persons who without being certifiably defective is mentally subnormal'; this language is hardly neutral, though it is not inconsistent with extant eugenic assumptions. Furthermore, 'this mass of defectives and subnormals is being steadily recruited and is probably growing.'[70] This latter view was regularly communicated by expert witnesses such as R. Ruggles Gates, professor of botany in London who proclaimed: 'the proportion of feeble-mindedness is much higher than it is supposed to be.'[71] This argument was a favourite theme of eugenists.[72]

The importance of distinguishing between mental defect and mental disorder was stressed by Committee member Wilfred Trotter, a doctor and fellow of both the Royal Society and the Royal College of Surgeons. Carriers of the first were the primary focus for eugenists as the Committee's Report explained:

[69] PRO, MH51/216, Chairman's Memorandum, 19 Oct. 1932, p. 3.

[70] Brock Report, 55.

[71] PRO, MH51/228 31100, Note of the proceedings of the 16th meeting of the Committee, 20 Mar. 1933, pp. 1–2.

[72] For instance, see H. B. Brackenbury, 'The Mental Deficiency Acts and their Administration', *Eugenics Review*, 15/2 (July 1923), 393–401, who asserted (p. 393): 'feeble-minded persons are more fecund that the normal; they have a tendency to mate together, and so to produce offspring markedly partaking of the parental characteristics. [The Royal Commission's estimates] are almost certainly an under-estimate.' Brackenbury was vice-president of the Education Committee of the Central Association for Mental Welfare.

mental defect may be described as arrested development of mind, whether con-genital or induced by injury or disease before development is complete. It is in almost all cases a permanent condition and in the present state of knowledge is beyond real cure. . . . Mental disorder is the generic term which includes all the various disorders affecting the mind which prior to their onset has been function-ing normally. . . . [T]hough both conditions may occur in the same individual they are clinically distinct from one another.[73]

There was considerable variation in the precision and accuracy of most characterizations of mental defects. The Brock Committee identified a single element beneath the conceptual fog: 'the point we wish to empha-sise is that general terms such as "mental defect" and "feeble-mindedness" represent classes or groups of conditions, all of which exhibit one common feature, arrested development of mind.'[74]

In attempting to define the target of sterilization, the Committee turned to the notion of a 'Social problem group', a term adopted by the Wood Report[75] and praised by the Eugenics Society.[76] The term originated with the 1908 Royal Commission for the Care and Control of the Feeble-minded.[77] It was then refined by the Wood Report's investigator, Dr E. O. Lewis (also a member of the Brock Committee), into three categories: idiocy, whose sufferers have a mental age of 1 to 3; imbecility, adults with a mental age of between 3 and 5; and finally, the feeble-minded with mental ages of between 5 and 8. Crucially, the last group were supposed to have been born principally to parents with similar characteristics (thus imply-ing a hereditary component) and numerically to constitute by far the largest group. The Wood Report believed it comprised a tenth of the popu-lation of the social problem group. Lewis found the same families pro-ducing the feeble-minded: 'these families who in various ways were useless and burdensome to the community, presented "social problems". From these families, it was found, were recruited the bulk of unemployables, incorrigible slum makers, prostitutes, inebriates, habitual criminals, chronic paupers and *high grade defectives* that exists in the community. This group

[73] Brock Report, 7.   [74] Ibid. 8.

[75] Its genesis lies in late nineteenth-century characterizations of the urban poor: see Jones (1971: 285–90), and Macnicol (1987).

[76] Sir Bernard Mallet 'The Social Problem Group: The President's Account of the Society's next Task', *Eugenics Review*, 23 (Oct. 1931), 203–6. Referring to the Wood Report's estimate that the group numbered 4 million, Mallet expatiated on the implications (p. 205): 'four million persons in England and Wales who are the great purveyors of social inefficiency, prostitution, feeble-mindedness and petty crime, the chief architects of slumdom, the most fertile strain in the community! Four million persons in a socially well-defined group forming the dregs of the community and thriving upon it as a parasite thrives upon a healthy and vigorous host. It is difficult to conceive of a more sweeping or socially significant generalization.'

[77] PRO, MH51/228 31100, Memorandum 'The Social Problem Group', n.d.

was christened the "social problem group." '[78] Unlike the lower two types of mentally feeble-minded, the third category of feeble-minded could, if suitably dealt with, be expected to live in the community, an option unimaginable for the others.[79] The Eugenics Society considered voluntary sterilization an instrument with which significantly to address the problems posed by the presence of such a group in society:

viewed as a preventive measure, we regard the legalising of sterilization for mental defectives as but a preliminary move towards this wider application of the principle. Members of the Social Problem Group frequently have many children, of whom the later-born are often unwanted. None of the methods of preventing parenthood which have been suggested as feasible for certifiable mental defectives—such as segregation and legal prohibition of marriage—is applicable to members of the Social Problem Group; and by them existing contraceptive methods are largely impracticable.[80]

Eugenists argued that the 'feeble-minded' required sterilization both because they were unfit to care for these children and because they were said to have had an increased fertility. The assumption of greater fecundity had long punctuated the pages of the *Eugenics Review*, though the Committee's own evidence alleging the excessive fertility of the feeble-minded was inconclusive.[81]

The Committee's scientific problems were compounded by difficulties in isolating the 'carrier', who passed on the hereditary vices manifest in the Social Problem Group. At its first meeting, Dr Alfred Tredgold gave his account of the complexity in identifying the appropriate people to sterilize. Tregold

thought that sterilisation would have to be looked upon as a preventive measure. Mentally defective children were not necessarily children of mental defectives or insane persons. They were the children of carriers and it was these carriers who it might be necessary to look upon as the persons to be sterilised. Many mental defectives are the offspring of parents who are normal but these normal persons may be the carriers of mental deficiency and this thereby makes them possible parents of mentally defective children. If sterilisation is to diminish the number of mental defectives then sterilisation must be applied to these people, i.e., apparently normal people.[82]

[78] PRO, MH51/228 31100, Memorandum 'The Social Problem Group', n.d. Emphasis in original.
[79] This interpretation was reproduced in the Eugenics Society's submission to the Brock Committee. See PRO, MH51/228 31100, Evidence submitted by the Eugenics Society to Mr L. G. Brock's Sterilization Committee, 1 Mar. 1933, 31 pp., p. 22.
[80] Ibid. 25–6.
[81] PRO, MH51/217, Minutes of the 6th meeting of the Brock Committee, 14 Nov. 1932, p. 3.
[82] PRO, MH51/212, Minutes of the 1st meeting of the Brock Committee, 23 June 1932, pp. 6–7.

The target for sterilization included not only 'the recognisably defective, but also the *apparently* normal but actually defective'; indeed, the obviously 'defective'—helpless 'idiots' or schizophrenics—were viewed as less of a threat to the human race than the numerically larger, socially more threatening *Lumpenproletariat* which constituted the social problem group.[83]

The problem of consent

The Brock Committee rejected compulsory sterilization, but argued that, for those 'mental defectives' likely to return to the community, there was a strong argument for establishing the opportunity to voluntary sterilization. The rejection of compulsory sterilization is significant. The decision reflected evidence about patterns in Britain and policies implemented in other countries.[84] As early as 1910, Havelock Ellis had argued, in the pages of the *Eugenics Review*, that sterilization of the 'unfit' should be by choice: 'the sterilisation of the unfit, if it is be a practical and humane measure commanding general approval, must be voluntary on the part of the person undergoing it, and never compulsory . . . It is essential that the refusal of the procreative part in life, as well as its acceptance, should be the outcome of a deliberate and responsible act of will.'[85] The Committee's ruling was prompted powerfully by political calculation, as Brock explained at an early meeting of the Committee: 'the Parliamentary case for sterilisation is really going to turn on the mental defective rather than on the Mental Hospital case. It would be impossible to get Parliament to sanction sterilisation solely for Mental Hospital cases.' He continued: 'it was doubtless the case that there were many persons discharged from Mental Hospitals as not recovered but improved whose relatives would be much more willing to take them back if they were sterilised first. But this would not provide a sufficient case to place before Parliament.'[86] The Committee looked askance upon the US practice of sterilizing those confined to a mental hospital.

As the Committee recommended in favour of voluntary consent for strategic reasons, it needed to claim that such consent could be meaningfully given by a 'defective'. This proved troublesome. Brock firmly believed that the consent of mental defectives indeed could be reliably obtained:

---

[83] Mazumdar (1992: 208).

[84] For the USA see Dowbiggin (1997), Reilly (1987), and Trent (1994).

[85] Havelock Ellis, 'The Sterilization of the Unfit', *Eugenics Review*, 1/3 (Oct. 1909), 203–6, p. 205.

[86] PRO, MH51/216, Minutes of the 5th meeting of the Brock Committee, 31 Oct. 1932, p. 9.

'the fact that many people are easily persuaded by those in whom they have confidence does not mean that they are really incapable of understanding the issues involved. I believe that high grade defectives are perfectly capable of understanding what sterilisation means, and I am confirmed in this view by letters I have seen from patients.'[87] Yet if the individuals could truly understand the gravity of such an irreversible decision, then it is doubtful that they were so mentally incapacitated as to require the operation, even by the Committee's standards.[88] If they could not, the sterilization lost its voluntary character. One witness from Devon, a medical professional, argued that any consent given by a 'defective' would be worthless: 'defectives are so open to suggestion that they would readily adopt the views of someone else and could be persuaded to submit to sterilisation or refuse consent to the operation by any Officer of the Institution whom they respected and trusted.' He added that, 'if defectives saw any possibility of securing freedom through sterilisation they would give consent without any thought for the nature and effect of the operation.'[89]

Inheritance versus environment

The Committee's desire to justify its case for sterilization led it to emphasize any evidence of hereditary causes of defects and, conversely, to discount (and almost disregard) evidence suggesting environmental elements. Even where an environment was so deprived as to be an obvious factor in creating defectives, 'enquiries into the family history of such cases show that in the majority there is evidence of morbid inheritance'.[90] The Committee was nonetheless forced to admit that such a pattern could at least be made worse by poverty: 'there is evidence that in the poorest districts neighbour marries neighbour, and like marries like.'[91]

The Committee's reluctance to stress environmental factors was chal-

---

[87] PRO, MH51/210, Confidential, Chairman's Memorandum, pp. 8–9.

[88] Eugenists' arguments tended to belie their claim that the operation would be purely voluntary. Dr C. P. Blacker reported that the Eugenics Society was 'convinced that there are large numbers of people who do not want large families, especially those in the lower grades of society who cannot afford to bring up a number of children. The motives which will lead these people to undergo sterilisation is the desire to limit their families.' Subsequently questioned by the Committee about applying sterilization to recipients of outdoor relief, Blacker thought that 'if a man was naturally disinclined to work, *pressure in such a case [to sterilize] would be justified*' (emphasis added). PRO, MH51/228 31100, Proceedings of the 17th meeting of the Brock Committee, 3 Apr. 1933, pp. 6, 10.

[89] PRO, MH51/226 31100, Evidence to the Committee on Sterilization by Charles William Mayer, Superintendent of the Royal Western Counties Institution for the Mentally Defective, Starcross, Devon, p. 4.

[90] Brock Report, 20.   [91] Ibid. 21.

lenged by some of the evidence it received.[92] The Portsmouth Branch Inspector of the National Society for the Prevention of Cruelty to Children, for example, reported that 'many who, in their former squalid surroundings, were extremely dull and backward, have shown great improvement [in improved council houses]. . . . [T]he closely confined slum family [was] a prime factor in the product of mental and moral degeneracy.'[93] Even witnesses who claimed a hereditary basis betrayed an implicit assumption of environmental conditioning: thus the expert on Leeds mental health observed that 'mental deficiency was mainly hereditary. The poor and degenerate class of parent naturally lived in poor and unsuitable areas, e.g., slum districts, and the feeble-minded person was usually found to come from parents of these types.'[94]

The Committee itself repeated this argument when it claimed that the concentration of sufferers in an identifiable social problem group was an argument in favour of voluntary sterilization. The danger of two carriers of recessive genes interacting in poor neighbourhoods alarmed the Committee. It asserted that 'defectives drift to the slums'. Within the slums, marriage produced defectives, as the Report commented in its baldest sociological section:

like marries like, and not only is the incidence of defect greater in this group, but the proportion of carriers is correspondingly greater. This means that the chances of two carriers mating is many times greater than it is in any other section of the population. It would be idle to expect of this group, most of whom are of subnormal mentality, a proper sense of social responsibility. But we believe that many of them would be glad to be relieved of the dread of repeated pregnancies and to escape the recurring burden of parenthood, for which they are so manifestly unfitted.[95]

This characterization of the 'social problem group'—about whom there was 'abundant evidence' that it 'contributes much more than its numerical proportion of the total volume of defect, and an equal or even larger proportion of children of low intelligence'[96]—reveals some of the working assumptions of the Brock Committee.

---

[92] To be sure, the Committee succeeded in locating many witnesses who argued that mental defect was caused by hereditary factors. Unsurprisingly, this view was endorsed by the Eugenics Society, whose submissions were, of course, taken very seriously. See PRO, MH51/228 31100, Evidence submitted by the Eugenics Society to Mr L. G. Brock's Sterilization Committee, 1 Mar. 1933, pp. 22, 25.

[93] PRO, MH58/102, Statement of Evidence by William J. Elliott, Director of the National Society for the Prevention of Cruelty to Children, 35 pp., pp. 33–4.

[94] PRO, MH51/217, Minutes of the 6th meeting of the Brock Committee, 14 Nov. 1932, p. 5.

[95] Brock Report, 41–2.   [96] Ibid. 41.

The Committee undervalued the views of experts doubtful of the hereditary argument, of whom the distinguished geneticist J. B. S. Haldane was a leading representative. Haldane told the Committee that 'mental deficiency is not due to a single gene defect'. He added: 'we have insufficient knowledge as to the genes in human beings.'[97] Haldane stressed also the ambiguity surrounding the categorization of severity of mental illness: 'different people drew different lines in different places: one would regard a person as normal and one would regard him as mentally defective; yet another would consider him only dull or backward.'[98] He was supported by Lancelot Hogben, professor of social biology at London. A keen anti-eugenist, Hogben believed some mental 'deficiency' to be hereditary but was unwilling to support sterilization, stating firmly that 'the scientific evidence available is not sufficient to indicate any policy as regards sterilisation at present'.[99] Hogben and Haldane were significant opponents of the sterilization approach.[100]

Scepticism about the primary importance of heredity factors received substantial support from a subsequent massive seven-year survey of cases of mental deficiency in Colchester, undertaken by Dr Lionel Penrose for the Medical Research Council, published in 1938. In *A Clinical and Genetic Study of 1280 Cases of Mental Defect*, Penrose firmly stressed the relevance of environmental, genetic, and pathological factors in the formation of many sorts of mental illness.[101] In her study of the Eugenics Society, Pauline Mazumdar argues that in the decade prior to 1933, increasing doubts about the relative importance of inherited compared with environmental factors in determining ability were unearthed, particularly in Ronald Fisher's statistical agricultural research. This difficulty explains eugenists' dependence on, and preference for, the genealogical, pedigree-type study especially in its lobbying for legislation: 'the best answer the [Eugenics Society's Research] Committee could find to the environmental problem was a completely non-quantitative one: a pair of contrasting pedigrees, showing two families who lived next door to each other in Bethnal Green. One of them

[97] PRO, MH51/234 31100. Haldane, an FRS, was Professor of Genetics at University College, London. Minutes of the proceedings of the 23rd meeting of the Brock Committee, 27 June 1933, p. 1.

[98] Ibid. See also J. B. S. Haldane, *Heredity and Politics* (London: George Allen & Unwin, 1938).

[99] PRO, MH51/225 31100 Proceedings of the 14th meeting of the Committee, 6 Mar. 1933, p. 6, and 'Summary of the Evidence Given by Professor Lancelot Hogben'.

[100] Richard Soloway (1995: 196) judges Hogben the 'most devastating' and 'worrisome' critic faced by the eugenists; on Hogben see Dahrendorf (1995: 254–66), Kevles (1986, ch. 9), and Stepan (1982: 146–53).

[101] *A Clinical and Genetic Study of 1280 Cases of Mental Defect* (The Colchester Survey), by Lionel S. Penrose, Medical Research Council Special Report Series 229 (London: HMSO, 1938).

was studded with paupers, the other had not a single one. It was the traditional *ad oculos* demonstration of the pedigree study, and the Society used it over and over again throughout the thirties, as part of their sterilisation campaign.'[102]

The Committee was aided by the fact that the majority of those making submissions, who were approached by Brock and the others, supported at least in part the hereditarian case. Some of these, reflecting the divisions in the scientific community, came from experts. Professor Ruggles Gates argued that since many physical defects and abnormalities were inherited—anticipated in Mendelian laws of inheritance and demonstrated on plants and animals—the same pattern could logically be imputed to mental defects. He maintained that the 'evidence indicates that feeblemindedness is usually recessive in inheritance'. He approvingly cited the Kallikaks and Jukes families:

I have made no reference to the well-known studies of the Kallikaks, Jukes, Nams, Wins, Hill Folk, Zeros, Tribe of Ishmael and other groups of similar character, whose members through many generations have produced large numbers of paupers, prostitutes, feebleminded and criminals. While convincing as showing the inheritance of mental defect on a large scale through many generations, they have not usually been analysed in such a way as to throw light on the manner or law of the inheritance. In each the descendants, numbering thousands, have been traced back to one or a few individuals, whose sterilization would have prevented an enormous amount of crime, vice and unhappiness and would at the same time have enabled better stocks less burdened with taxation to multiply and fill their places in a happier and more efficient way.[103]

This is a fulsome statement of the validty of imputing a hereditary source of feeble-mindedness and the attainable *beau monde* of preventive procreation. C. J. Bond, a physician at the Royal College of Surgeons and a member of the Eugenics Society, confirmed this pattern: 'although mental deficiency may be due to the influence of a dominant gene or genes in some cases, and may represent a multifactorial recessive character in others, the fact that the manner of inheritance resembles that of Deaf Mutism, Myoclonic Epilepsy (Rudin), Juvenile Amaurotic Idiocy, Von Sjogren and some form of eye defect suggests that mental defect is, like these, transmitted on Mendelian lines.'[104] Bond was a keen advocate of voluntary sterilization:

[102] Mazumdar (1992: 140). For a representative study see E. J. Lidbetter's *Heredity and the Social Problem Group* (London: Arnold, 1933).

[103] PRO, MH51/228 31100, 'Inheritance of Mental Defect', Professor R. Ruggles Gates FRS, 21 pp., submission to the Brock Committee, p. 20. See also his earlier discussion 'Heredity and Eugenics', *Eugenics Review*, 11/4 (Jan. 1920), 193–201.

[104] PRO, MH51/232 31100, Evidence given before Mr Brock's Committee on Behalf of the Eugenics Society, 3 Apr. 1933, by C. J. Bond CMG, FRCS, p. 4.

I am convinced that as genetic knowledge spreads, and a 'racial' conscience is aroused in the minds of our citizens, an increasing number of persons, who, from a study of their family histories, have reason to believe that they are the carriers of serious mental or other forms of defect, will, in the future, regard voluntary sterilisation as a privilege rather than as a privation, and as a means of harmonising conflicting individual, communal, and racial interests.[105]

The advocacy of 'voluntary' sterilization is important here in reconciling this policy with liberal democracy, though as we saw above, serious caveats attached to the reliability of any such 'voluntary' consent.

The difficulty in establishing the hereditarian thesis dogged the Committee. Dr Crowley observed of the penultimate draft that 'the discussion of the inheritance of mental disorder seems very inadequate. *If necessary we may have to insert some padding taken from the evidence of the numerous psychiatrists who came before us as witnesses* [emphasis added].' He added: 'in view of the fact that we had on the Committee— rather unfortunately as it turned out perhaps—no representative of psychiatrists practising in Mental Hospitals, it is specially important that we should subject ourselves to no unfavourable criticism from such a body as, for example, the Royal Medico-Psychological Association.'[106] Mindful of the inconclusive evidence, the Royal Medico-Psychological Association had in fact found itself lacking a 'sufficient measure of agreement among their members to enable them to formulate any collective view'.[107] In the Brock Committee's case, by contrast, where the evidence was strongly against heredity, it could be ignored; where the evidence was weakly in its favour, it could be 'padded'. As another committee member put it, 'I have too a good deal of sympathy with Dr Crowley's remark that in our discussion of the inheritance of mental disorder "we ought to say more, even if there is no more to say"!'[108]

Other endorsements of sterilization rested on administrators' personal experience. From Somerset, the Brock Committee received a submission indicating a 'definite family history of mental deficiency' amongst the county's records (though since not all defectives were recorded accurately this incidence may have been exaggerated).[109] The Nottingham Education Committee provided similar conclusions from a study of those treated for

    [105] PRO, MH51/232 31100, Evidence given before Mr Brock's Committee on Behalf of the Eugenics Society, 3 Apr. 1933, by C. J. Bond CMG, FRCS, p. 14.
    [106] PRO, MH51/210 31100, Notes by Dr Crowley on Draft Report, p. 3.
    [107] PRO, MH51/221, Brock in a letter to Mr E. H. Curtis, London Mental Hospitals Department, 2 Dec. 1932. Mathew Thomson (1998: 194) puts this position down to the Association's 'professional self-interest, as much as support or opposition to eugenics'.
    [108] PRO, MH51/210, Letter from Adams to Brock, 29 Sept. 1933.
    [109] PRO, MH51/231 31100, Norah L. C. Hurle, Chairman Mental Deficiency Acts Committee, G. W. J. MacKay, Medical Superintendent and C. E. Newman Secretary, 'Mental Deficiency Act 1913–1927, County of Somerset', 27 Apr. 1933, p. 4.

mental deficiency between 1913 and 1927. From this analysis, its Senior Medical Officer addressed the hereditary factor: 'fairly intimate acquaintance with many of the parents has convinced me that many of them would have been diagnosed as mentally defective or dull and backward if ascertainment had been more adequate in former years. A large number of the parents of defectives are thriftless and lacking in wisdom and forethought.'[110] Such anecdotal evidence is unreliable.

Professor E. W. MacBride, a zoologist at Imperial College, 'thought sterilisation might be justified as a punishment for bringing too many children into the world who would subsequently have to be supported by the State'. He criticized immigrants from 'South Ireland' who were 'large breeders', adding, 'they have swamped Glasgow, Liverpool and even the coal-fields of Durham.' Articulating an appealing but dubious conflation, he added: 'they may not be mentally defective but they are a very poor type.'[111] In MacBride's view, 'broadly speaking stupid people will produce stupid children.'[112] In light of such rebarbative evidence, Dr Crowley's conclusion is hardly surprising: 'we probably ought to discuss rather more fully, including reference to witnesses and literature, the question of the mental condition of the parents of defectives. *On the face of it*, some of the statistics included in the Report certainly do not justify the conclusion to which we arrive.'[113]

The Committee recognized that a defensible programme for sterilization required demonstrating that hereditary rather than environmental factors be paramount in the reproduction and diffusion of mental defect. The contradiction propelled Brock into the odd claim that while the Committee could not be expected 'to arrive at any definite scientific conclusion' about the hereditary form of mental deficiency, nonetheless the government 'wanted to know whether there was a risk of certain definite classes of persons having mentally defective offspring'.[114] How the second objective could be achieved without resolving the first is not addressed (a problem of policy-making probably experienced by other 'expert' committees).

The Committee's motivation for its robust defence of a hereditarian explanation of mental defect arose from politics and propaganda. At its

[110] PRO, MH51/225 31100, Evidence of Dr A. A. E. Newth, Senior Medical Officer, Nottingham Education Committee, pp. 22, 23.
[111] PRO, MH51/224, Minutes of the 13th meeting of the Brock Committee, 20 Feb. 1933, pp. 4–5.
[112] Ibid. 7.
[113] PRO, MH51/210 31100, Notes by Dr Crowley on Draft Report, p. 1; emphasis in original.
[114] PRO, MH51/212, Minutes of the first meeting of the Brock Committee, 23 June 1932, p. 9.

fifth meeting, Brock argued that 'from the Parliamentary point of view it *did* matter if the Committee could show that there was substantial evidence in favour of the view that mental deficiency was hereditary. If the Committee came to the conclusion that there were no hereditary element, then the Parliamentary agitation would drop.'[115] Such opposition, as Brock recognized, was most likely to come from Labour MPs wary of a class bias in eugenic arguments: 'it was already being urged in some quarters that, if sterilisation were made legal, it would operate against the poor and would not affect the rich.' He continued: 'it was however the case that some of the Labour members were in favour of it. It would be necessary for the Committee to satisfy Parliament that there was a grave risk of mental defectives having mentally defective children, e.g., an appreciably greater risk than with normal persons.'[116]

Opposition would not only be parliamentary. The British public was suspicious of sterilization, and an appreciation of the need to assuage public concern is present throughout the Committee's deliberations. In one of the more blatant instances, Trotter observed that, 'it would be necessary to visualise considerable opposition if sterilisation were to be permitted. This would come from very ignorant persons who would allege that patients were being "cut up" in Institutions.'[117]

Trammelled by ambiguous evidence, the Brock Committee underlined the validity of its conclusions: 'though there may be no certain prognosis in any particular case, we know enough to be sure that inheritance plays an important part in the causation of mental defects and disorders.'[118] It argued that, 'in spite of the paucity of statistics, it would appear to be the general opinion of psychiatrists of experience that, whilst an attack of mental disorder is often the resultant of many factors, the chief and most important single factor is an inherited predisposition.'[119] The evidence was not so decisive, however. On this tenuous foundation, the Committee constructed its final conclusion:

we know also that mentally defective and mentally disordered patients are, as a class, unable to discharge their social and economic liabilities or create an environment favourable to the upbringing of children, and there is reason to believe that sterilisation would in some cases be welcomed by the patients themselves. This knowledge is in our view sufficient, and more than sufficient, to justify allowing and even encouraging mentally defective and mentally disordered patients to adopt the only certain method of preventing procreation. In this view we are unanimous and we record it with a full sense of our responsibility.

[115] PRO, MH51/216, Minutes of the 5th meeting of the Brock Committee, 31 Oct. 1932, p. 6.
[116] Ibid. 10.   [117] Ibid.   [118] Brock Report, 25.   [119] Ibid.

There was, the Committee declared, an 'overwhelming preponderance of evidence in favour of some measure of sterilisation'.[120]

In his confidential 'Chairman's Memorandum', Brock conceded that his aim was ultimately to secure legislation for voluntary sterilization and, implicitly conceded that the sort of hereditarian case necessary to such legislation was lacking.[121] There was, he recognized, no reliable evidence about the proportion of mental defect transmitted from one generation to another. '[H]eredity and environment are not mutually exclusive,' a realization which implied that 'there are few cases in which it is possible to forecast with any reasonable degree of probability the chances of the offspring of any particular union exhibiting defect.'[122] Despite this, somehow the 'overwhelming preponderance of evidence' was in favour of sterilization: 'for myself, I should be prepared to press strongly the desirability of legalising the voluntary sterilisation of defectives.'[123] This is persuasive evidence of the partiality under which this committee of experts laboured.

THE FAILURE TO IMPLEMENT STERILIZATION

The Eugenics Society welcomed the Committee's work, its recommendations, and its unanimity.[124] It judged voluntary sterilization as politically feasible: 'if the general public could be educated to distinguish between sterilization and castration, many members of the Social Problem Group would avail themselves' of the option the Society believed. Such education required the creation of a 'eugenic conscience and a racially conscious public opinion'.[125] Those who would most benefit from sterilization had to be educated into recognizing the appropriateness of such a choice, in the Society's view.[126] The Report, the Society hoped, would promote such a eugenic consciousness.

---

[120] Ibid. 39.

[121] PRO, MH51/210. Confidential. Chairman's Memorandum, pp. 2–3.

[122] Ibid. 4. This imprecision led Brock to reject compulsory sterilization; it would require 'a degree of certainty as to the results of the union of defectives which at present does not exist'. Yet if the scientific case for compulsory sterilization was weak, then surely it was equally so for voluntary, for sterilization of any sort gained its eugenist justification from the fact of heredity.

[123] Ibid. 5. In fact, Brock's enthusiasm for sterilization led him to propose, to his colleagues, its application in areas outside the Committee's remit—'notably certain forms of blindness'—on the grounds that restricting it to sufferers of mental illness gave the policy 'a quasi-penal character'. Ibid. 5–6.

[124] See Leonard Darwin, 'Analysis of the Brock Report', *Eugenics Review*, 26/1 (Apr. 1934), 9–13. Darwin observed that 'one of the most remarkable features of this report is that it is signed without dissent by every member of the committee', p. 9.

[125] PRO, MH51/228 31100, Evidence submitted by the Eugenics Society to Mr L. G. Brock's Sterilization Committee, 1 Mar. 1933, p. 26.   [126] Ibid.

The publication of the Brock Committee's report was followed by petitions in favour of legislation on sterilization. At the Ministry of Health, Arthur Robinson suggested to the Minister, Sir E. Hilton Young, that he should try to get a debate on the report through a private member's motion.[127] Young wrote to Wing Commander A. W. H. James MP, asking him to convince as many MPs as possible to ballot in favour of a motion on voluntary sterilization.[128] A deputation to Sir Hilton,[129] composed of representatives from the Joint Committee on Voluntary Sterilization, the County Councils' Association, the Association of Municipal Corporations, and the Mental Hospitals' Association presented him with a draft bill for voluntary sterilization. It cited the support of an impressive litany of professional bodies.[130] Unable to marshal explicit support from the Church of England, the Joint Committee nonetheless reported that 'many of the clergy, at present distressed at having to marry couples highly unsuitable for parenthood, would welcome such legislation.'[131]

The government, however, was extremely reluctant to legislate: 'as regards legislation, the attitude of the Government has been that they must give ample opportunity for all shades of public opinion to find expression on this grave issue'; it sought clarity about the 'dictates of the public conscience'.[132] The same civil servant expanded on the problem of public opinion in this area: 'Can it be said that public opinion has so clearly declared itself that the Government can fairly be invited to decide whether they should introduce a Bill such as the deputation suggests?'[133] It was recommended that the Minister assure the deputation that the proposal to

[127] PRO, MH58/104B, Minute, Ministry of Health, 25 Jan. 1934.

[128] PRO, MH58/104B, Letter from Young to James, 26 Jan. 1934. To advance health professionals' support of sterilization, the Joint Committee on Voluntary Sterilization (composed of representatives from the Central Association for Mental Welfare, the Eugenics Society, and the National Council for Mental Hygiene) was created to apply pressure for legislation. It drafted a bill for voluntary sterilization. PRO, MH58/100, Letter to the Secretary Ministry of Health from the County Councils' Association, the Association of Municipal Corporations, the Mental Hospitals' Association, and the Joint Committee on Voluntary Sterilization, 3 Apr. 1935, enclosing draft bill.

[129] Succeeded, as Minister of Health, in June 1935 by Sir Kingsley Wood.

[130] These were: the Magistrates' Association, the Royal College of Physicians, the Royal Medico-Psychological Association, the Society of Medical Officers of Health, the Association of County Medical Officers of Health, the National Association for the Feebleminded, the Mental Hospital Matrons' Association, the National Association of Blind Workers, the National Council for Equal Citizenship, the National Council for Women, the Women Public Health Officers' Association, the Conservative Women's Reform Association, the Women's Co-operative Guild, the Women's National Liberal Federation, and other local organizations.

[131] See PRO, MH58/100, Opening Statement of the Deputation to the Minister of Health, 23 May 1935, p. 6.

[132] PRO, MH58/100, Notes for the Minister, 'Deputation on Voluntary Sterilization', 17 May 1935, p. 4.   [133] Ibid. 4–5.

legislate on sterilization was 'receiving the active attention of responsible Ministers'.[134] 'Active attention' in fact meant inaction.

Sir E. Hilton Young listened to the deputation but remained sceptical about legislation. He told the group that while 'much public opinion had undoubtedly been massed in favour of the report', conversely, 'the effect of the report had also been to intensify the activity of those who opposed, generally on religious grounds, the principle of sterilisation'. As a consequence, Brock's report had 'formed fresh opinion in favour of sterilisation but had left the old opposition unshaken'.[135] Young admitted to being persuaded of the 'desirability' of the Brock proposals but was extremely anxious about their opponents: 'it was necessary to build up a case and choose the right moment for action. It would be a mistake to strike too soon, and in his judgement the time had not yet come for the introduction of legislation.' Before a bill could be introduced, Young believed, 'the public would require further reassurance that nothing was to be done which would offend the conscience of the nation.'[136] This line was adopted from the time of the publication of Brock's report. The Minister told Dr Blacker in July of the same year that public opinion remained unprepared for sterilization.[137] The Report was taken up further in the House in July 1934 by Wing Commander James when his Order Paper motion was heard. He complained about the lack of legislation given 'a unanimous report on this very important subject by so weighty a committee'.[138] James maintained that a 'very large number of people' had been stirred by the Brock Report; and argued that 'if the Government are holding back by reason of imagining that there is not sufficient volume of support in the country for the implementation of the recommendations of the Brock Report, I can assure them that they are mistaken.'[139] This discussion, however, was the extent of parliamentary debate and it did little to facilitate passage of a sterilization bill.

The Deputation's visit to Young marked the high point in the post-publication campaign for sterilization.[140] No proposals were enacted and the imminent election precluded the pursuit of controversial policy by the government. Over the longer term, four reasons account for the failure of the campaign in favour of voluntary sterilization. First, the Minister of

---

[134] Ibid. 5.
[135] PRO, MH58/100, Report of the meeting between the Minister of Health and deputation of associations, 23 May 1935, p. 2.
[136] Ibid.
[137] PRO, MH58/100, Minute to Miss Sharp, 15 Mar. 1935.
[138] *Hansard* (Commons), 3 July 1934, col. 1825.
[139] *Hansard* (Commons), 3 July 1934, cols. 1825, 1826.
[140] The National Health Service (Family Planning) Amendment Act 1972 legalized voluntary vasectomies; this measure was unassociated with any eugenic ambitions, making the efforts of the eugenists in the 1930s all the more explicit.

Health, Young, was uncooperative. Although Young himself had reservations about sterilization—'the authority is a doubtful question. To leave it
to the assent of the mental defective is absurd. He is disqualified *ex hypoth-
esi*. I would not trust the parent or guardian, in the interest either of the
mental defective or the community. Unfortunately the democracy will not
allow such a question to be decided on its merits'[141]—it is unquestionably
true that politicians worried about a lack of public support for the Brock
Report (and the generally favourable response amongst newspapers suggests that this political reluctance was decisive in halting the initiative[142]),
even though the 1913 Mental Deficiency Act had passed by 358 to 15 votes.
The limits of public acceptability were recognized by the eugenics movement as early as the 1908 Royal Commission on the Feeble-Minded,[143] and
the public remained hostile to sterilization.[144] This opposition reflected a
confusion (much bemoaned by eugenists) between sterilization and castration, a belief that sterilization was part of a callous effort to reduce
spending on institutions for those with severe learning disabilities and a
rejection of sterilization by the labour movement, which believed the very
idea to be anti-working class.[145] Although the advocates of sterilization
were sufficiently well placed to get a government report issued in its favour
and enjoyed close relations with senior civil servants, this intellectual and
professional community evidently lacked a decisive political component.

Second, the labour movement was joined in its opposition by the
Catholic Church. The Church opposed further enquiries about the treat-
ment of the mentally ill with sterilization at the time of the Wood Report.[146]
Its opposition to the Brock recommendations was consolidated with the

[141] Quoted in Thomson (1998: 75).
[142] Newspaper responses to the Brock Committee were mostly favourable or neutral, suggesting that Young's reservations were considerable. See report in PRO, MH79 292.
[143] *Royal Commission on the Care and Control of the Feeble-Minded* (London: HMSO,
1908, Cmnd. 4215), vol. ii.
[144] Though in fact illegal sterilizations were not uncommon, as evidence to the Committee
indicated.
[145] Macnicol (1992: 431–2). Certain witnesses revealed such a bias. Professor Ruggles
Gates expressed the view that 'when feeble-mindedness appears amongst the higher type
of family, it is unusual for that child to reproduce. His parents will look after him and protect
him for the rest of his life, but in the poorer classes of society the same type of person will
marry and will have children who will carry on the taint.' PRO, MH51/228 31100,
Proceedings of the 16th meeting of the Brock Committee, 20 Mar. 1933, p. 3. See also
Soloway (1995: 200–2).
[146] See e.g. PRO, MH58/103, letter from the Catholic Federationist, in Salford to the
Minister of Health, 26 Feb. 1929, which concluded that 'sterilisation is immoral, unnatural and
inhuman'. The Catholic Church's concern was echoed by the Birmingham-based Distributist
League (whose president was G. K. Chesterton), which argued that eugenist calls for an
enquiry were confined to a 'comparatively small number of people' and did not emanate from
popular demand. See PRO, MH58/103, letter from the Distributist League to the Minister
of Health, 5 Mar. 1929, and PRO, MH58/103, letter from the Distributist League to
Chamberlain's successor, Arthur Greenwood in the ensuing Labour government, Sept. 1929.

1930 papal encyclical *Casti Connubi*, which argued that too little was known about the mechanisms of inheritance for eugenics to have predictive power and that sterilization itself violated a God-given right to reproduce. Catholics, as Macnicol argues, were only 6 per cent of the population but constituted a group whom ministers did not wish to offend.[147] This concern about the public opinion limits to legislation had long exercised the senior civil servants involved at the Ministry of Health.[148] Indeed, that public opinion might limit legislation was acknowledged by eugenists themselves. Thus Leonard Darwin, conceded in 1912, that 'no existing democratic government would go as far as we Eugenists think right in the direction of limiting the liberty of the subject for the sake of the racial qualities of future generations.' Ironically this 'practical limitation' was recognized as a real one and Darwin warned against laws which failed to 'pay attention to the prejudices of the electorate'.[149] Eugenists, at least, were conscious of the democratic limits to illiberal measures introduced by a too powerful state.

Third, although the Brock Report cited a strong scientific case for sterilization, an absence of sufficient confidence in this evidence further weakened the eugenist case. The British Medical Association refused to endorse voluntary sterilization, and eugenists themselves were unable to agree on the number of defectives whose condition resulted from hereditary factors.[150] The scepticism and attacks by distinguished scientists, such as Haldane, undoubtedly diminished the appeal of sterilization proposals. Expertise was modified in practice.

Finally, the Nazi sterilization programme irreparably discredited its proposed British counterpart. The German law, operative from 1 January 1934, quickly became interlocked with pernicious medical practices, including compulsory sterilization and 'euthanasia'.[151] Nazi practices were, of course,

[147] Macnicol (1992: 432).

[148] See e.g. PRO, MH58/103, Minute to Minister by Arthur Robinson, 14 Jan. 1932. The public opinion problem did not dilute the deputation's enthusiasm, however, who maintained that in the seventeen months after Brock's report was promulgated, it had 'received a volume of public support sufficient to justify the Government in accepting the responsibility of introducing a Bill into Parliament'. See PRO, MH58/100, Opening Statement of the Deputation to the Minister of Health, 23 May 1935, p. 6.

[149] Leonard Darwin, 'First Steps toward Eugenic Reform', *Eugenics Review*, 4/1 (Apr. 1912), 35.

[150] Tredgold put it down to 17%, Fisher to 5%, and Mallet (President of the Eugenics Society) to 80%. Macnicol (1989: 159). At the same time, environmentalist arguments gained support: Mazumdar (1992, ch. 5), and M. P. Thomson, 'The Problem of Mental Deficiency in England and Wales' (University of Oxford: Unpublished D. Phil. thesis, 1992), 165.

[151] As meticulously explained by Michael Burleigh (1994). Soloway (1995: 302) reports that the Eugenics Society's secretary feared that 'Nazi policies might turn the British public against the modest, voluntary sterilisation proposals being evaluated by Laurence Brock's interdepartmental committee,' a concern reproduced in the pages of the *Eugenics Review*. And see Webster (1981: 9).

not uniformly condemned: Edward Larson quotes Alabama's health officer telling his state's legislature, in 1935, that 'with baited breath, the entire civilized world is watching the bold experiment in mass sterilization recently launched in Germany'.[152] Nonetheless, revelations of the Nazi practice were particularly damaging for the Brock Committee, as it had praised the German arrangements.[153] By as early as the mid-1930s, and certainly by the end of the decade, it was clear that the bill for which the eugenists lobbied would not be placed before parliament.

CONCLUSION

The Departmental Committee on Sterilization represented the most coherent case formulated by members of the British political elite in favour of eugenic sterilization. That the proposals failed to achieve their supporters' goals is a matter of considerable historical and political interest. The content of the Brock Committee's deliberations themselves prompt a revision of any overly laudatory view of policy experts' autonomy. The members of the Brock Committee, in cooperation with sympathetic listeners in the Ministry of Health and with systematic support from eugenists, reacted to the perceived failings of previous policy, and their intellectual efforts to construct a case in favour of voluntary sterilization were central to the policy process. The Committee acted independently of societal pressure in that it attempted to secure the implementation of a programme which did not correspond to the demands of the public; indeed, the electorate was suspicious of sterilization for eugenist purposes and the Committee conceived of its role as partly one of educating the uninformed British public into an appreciation of the virtues of this policy. Yet although the intellectual case for voluntary sterilization was presented in as powerful terms as the Brock Committee could muster, the next step—policy implementation or quiet abandonment—was a political one which in this case proved a counterweight to the zealousness with which eugenic experts advanced their cause.

As a consideration of eugenics in Britain, the deliberations of one com-

[152] Larson (1995: 146). See also M. E. Kopp, 'Legal and Medical Aspects of Eugenic Sterilization in Germany', *American Sociological Review*, 1 (1936).

[153] 'We propose that recommendations in a prescribed form should be required from two doctors, one of whom should, if possible be the patient's family doctor and the other a doctor on a list to be approved by the Minister of Health.' Brock Report, 43. Ultimately, it was the Minister of Health who would have to approve each individual sterilization of a mental patient. On the problems of involving GPs in the decision see PRO, MH51/210 31100, letter from Brock to E. J. Maude, Solicitor's Department, Ministry of Health, 16 Oct. 1933 and Maude's reply 30 Oct. 1933.

mittee might be said to be insufficiently representative, particularly given that its efforts failed. The Committee was not, however, simply one committee among many: it represented the most substantial policy advance, before or since, in the efforts of eugenists to implement a policy of sterilization of 'mental defectives'; its members represented precisely that cross-section of civil servants and experts who feature in social policy debates. Its recommendations were the closest Britain came to adopting such a policy. Given the extent to which eugenic policies were implemented in other western democracies and the influence this movement achieved in the first four decades of the twentieth century,[154] the content of the Brock Committee Report is of significance since it represented the most substantial advance in the effort of eugenists in Britain to implement a policy based on these principles.

The analysis points to the dangers of an exaggerated view of the power of a policy community getting its ideas implemented. While parts of the policy-making elite pursued their self-defined eugenic interests, they did so partly as a consequence of a campaign waged by the Eugenics Society. A tacit partnership existed between the Society and supporters in the Ministry of Health, and it was with the aid of the latter that eugenists penetrated the policy-making process and used it as the basis for pursuing their programme. The appointment of the Brock Committee, which constituted the pinnacle of the British campaign for sterilization, resulted from a subtle interaction of state and societal interests.[155] The Brock Committee was appointed at a period when eugenist arguments commanded considerable elite sympathy, and though it cannot be proved, it is likely that this context shaped the aims and blurred the judgement of its members. Its members' commitment to building an argument for voluntary sterilization biased its assessment of this aim. The influence of eugenics on the Brock Committee is revealed, most obviously, in the close personal and institutional links between Brock and committee members Fisher and Tredgold on the one hand, and the Eugenics Society on the other. These men were not insulated, in their civil association or in their research, from the

---

[154] For the international context see, *inter alia*, Adams (1990), Broberg and Roll-Hansen (1996), Graham (1977), MacKenzie (1981), Reilly (1991), Schneider (1990), Searle (1979), and Weiss (1987). Nils Roll-Hansen observes, of Scandinavian experience, that the 'introduction of sterilization lawswx in the Nordic countries in the 1930s was carried by the ideology of reform eugenics. In public debates more mainline and partly racist views were still influential.' 'Conclusion: Scandinavian Eugenics in the International Context', in Broberg and Roll-Hansen (1996: 270).

[155] Peter Hall (1993) suggests that state autonomy approaches draw an excessively sharp dichotomy between the state and society and ignores the importance of intermediate interests—political parties, committees, certain interest groups—that stand at the interaction of state and society, a view with which I concur.

dominant intellectual and ideological trends of the day. They personified some of the main tenets of contemporary expertise.

Analysis of the Brock Committee's work suggests that the possession, by relatively insulated experts, of considerable policy autonomy may result in the adoption of an illiberal social policy. Had civil servants and policy experts succeeded, they would have created in Britain a programme which, though practised in North America and Western Europe, is widely viewed today as an infringement of personal liberty (and we have seen the doubts raised about how voluntary a sterilization programme would be, concerns fully vindicated by other countries' experiences). Such a possibility gives rise to suspicions about expert autonomy in this policy-making instance; and it demonstrates the analytical value of detailed study of the workings of any committee purporting to impartiality and expertise.

This assessment raises, finally, questions about retrospective judgements. Political beliefs and policy choices should be judged by the values of their time and not condemned by the retrospective application of current beliefs.[156] Nonetheless, the legacies and effects of eugenic-based sterilization programmes are powerful reminders of the undesirability of these schemes.[157] While it is not within the scope of this chapter to engage in a discussion of the morality of eugenics, other countries' experience suggest that Britain was fortunate to resolve against the implementation of a sterilization programme. It is also worth underlining that the values of many in the 1930s, including the Catholic Church and parts of the British electorate, viewed sterilization and eugenics with genuine concern.

British eugenists, marshalling what they deemed to be compelling scientific expertise, and enjoying close relations with leading politicians and senior civil servants nonetheless failed to effect policy. Politicians, despite sharing some of the beliefs of eugenists, were wary of implementing policy. In the United States, eugenic experts also attained political influence and, as the next chapter demonstrates, found their expertise incorporated into legislation.

---

[156] Clearly, though, there are limits to such revisionism. The values of the 1930s justified many practices which we would wish to condemn absolutely, and sterilization is, equally arguably, one of these.

[157] See the recent revelations in Alberta, Canada ('Sterilised in Alberta', *The Economist*, 9 Nov. 1996), or Gould's discussion of Carrie Buck—the subject of the US Supreme Court's 1927 case, *Buck* v. *Bell* which permitted sterilization—(Gould 1981: 336), or Edward Larson's investigation of sterilization legislation and practices in southern American states in the 1930s and 1940s (Larson 1995). For recent revelations about Sweden, where Social Democratic governments coerced over 60,000 women into being sterilized between 1935 and 1976, see 'Sweden sterilized thousands of "useless" citizens for decades', *Washington Post*, 29 Aug. 1997.

4

'The Gravest Menace?' American Immigration Policy

The time will come when this country will have to face, more courageously than it has at the present time, the matter not only of race and
of individual quality, but also of pedigree or family stock, and we will
have to face boldly and courageously the matter of race. It is a matter
of conservation of nationality. After the Chinese exclusion act, the
greatest step that the American people took in relation to the nationality of race was, of course, the quota laws of 1921 and 1924. It is now
clear that the country has in its recent legislation entered definitely
upon the biological basis, a farsighted policy, of immigration control.—
Dr Harry Laughlin.[1]

I HAVE identified the criterion of 'liberal reason' as one of the sources of
illiberal social policy. To be a full member of a liberal democracy, there is
an expectation about citizens' possession of the requisite mental and reasoning powers. In the United States, concern about the 'mental fitness' of
potential members arose powerfully as a political issue in the opening
decades of the twentieth century when the question was raised in respect
of prospective immigrants some of whom, it was alleged, failed on this criterion. Immigration was salient politically and eugenists found themselves
(willingly) articulating the basis of a restrictionist policy in terms of immigrants' mental (and physical) suitability. The restrictions eventually
enacted in the national origins system (in 1924) remained in place until the
mid-1960s, despite criticisms from a string of presidents including Harry
Truman, Dwight Eisenhower, and John Kennedy. Social policy thus contributed decisively to limiting citizenship in the USA rather than expanding its terms of inclusion.

From broadly accepting all comers in the nineteenth century, in the
twentieth century American immigration policy became restrictive and
selective. The change began in 1882, 100 years after the Republic's founding. In this chapter[2] I use archival research to examine the policy's

[1] 'The Eugenical Aspects of Deportation', Hearings before the Committee on
Immigration and Naturalization, HR 70th Congress, 1st Session, 21 Feb. 1928, pp. 20–1.
[2] The leading scholarly study remains Higham (1988, first published in 1955), to which I
am indebted. While Higham discusses the influence of eugenics on US immigration policy

formulation between 1900 and 1930 and principally to illustrate how racial quotas and eugenic categories shaped these restrictions. Immigration policy proved to be a forum in which eugenists' arguments, partly as a consequence of propitious political and social circumstances, flourished. Eugenic priorities are the thread coalescing the debates and arguments advanced by restrictionists in the years before 1930.[3]

A number of tasks are undertaken here. First, the political and social context at the turn of the century which placed immigration on the public policy agenda is explained. Second, in the bulk of the chapter, the influence of eugenic arguments upon the legislation of the 1920s is explicated. By that decade, eugenic propositions were already well established in the United States, and sterilization was widely practised; eugenists enjoyed a respect which translated into policy influence. In the case of immigration policy this influence was powerfully assisted by the close connections developed between leading eugenists and key congressional figures in immigration policy. Finally, the illiberal implications and effects of eugenic arguments in immigration policy-making are examined: these arguments, setting out criteria about who were suitable immigrants and who were not, were fundamentally illiberal and compromised the USA's traditional commitment to equality of treatment.

THE UNDESIRABLE IMMIGRANTS

The restrictionist turn in American immigration policy necessarily rested upon assumptions about classes of, and suitability for, citizenship: it parallels the debate in Britain about the mental qualities deemed requisite to membership of the polity. The formulation of immigration policy in the early twentieth century rapidly focused upon the assimilability of potential immigrants. The debate was almost exclusively about European immigrants. There was a fear of southern and eastern European immigrants, considered less desirable (because of their Catholicism and alleged inferior intelligence) than those migrants emanating from north-western Europe, the major source of nineteenth-century immigration. The shift, between the 1880s and 1900s, in the sources of European immigration to the United States from north-western countries to south-eastern ones

after 1914, he spends less time in examining in detail this framework than I have done in the remainder of this chapter. For other important studies see Divine (1957) and Archdeacon (1983). For a valuable documentary guide see, Hutchinson (1981).

[3] For an earlier discussion see Kevles (1986) and Allen (1987). For consideration of eugenics and immigration policy see Ludmerer (1972), Dowbiggin (1997), and see also Hofstader (1955*b*).

excited public debate and comment. In 1882, the principal sources of European immigrants were Belgium, Britain and Ireland, France, Germany, the Netherlands, Scandinavia, and Switzerland. In the same year, 648,186 European immigrants arrived in the USA, of whom 13.1 per cent came from southern and eastern European countries, comprising Austria-Hungary, Greece, Italy, Montenegro, Poland, Portugal, Romania, Russia, Serbia, Spain, and Turkey. In 1907, these countries suppled 81 per cent of a total of 1,207,619 European immigrants.[4]

Hostility to economic migrants became subsumed into a more general fear of alien groups and racially 'undesirable' immigrants. It was this latter worry which became the leitmotiv of American immigration policy, effected in legislation in two stages: first, the allocation of quotas to European countries within an aggregate annual immigrant figure, a policy which distinguished north-western from south-eastern Europeans; and, second, the refinement of this quota system into one based on the principle of 'national origins', which separated Americans of direct settler descent from all other European groups. Late nineteenth-century legislation anticipated part of this new racial-based policy in its exclusion of epileptics and so-called 'idiots' and lunatics from the right to immigrate and its exclusion of Chinese immigrants. These categories of exclusion were supplemented and expanded in the new century.

Rationalization of hostility to the new immigrants was married with the research of eugenic scientists. It proved a felicitious match. The application of biological principles of evolution to social development, so-called Social Darwinism, was hugely popular. It not only reified the assumptions of racial calibrations within American society (including in respect of the largely 'invisible' African American population), but provided explanations for social differences and for the USA's relative economic success compared with other countries.[5] The scientific aim of eugenists was to determine genetic sources of 'feeble-mindedness' (associated with 'racial degeneracy'), principles for its eradication and the bases of selective breeding. Such concerns were widespread amongst academics, reformers, and politicians in the two decades before the First World War.[6] They were strengthened by perceptions of immigrants.

Political and social pressure to limit immigration were powerfully

---

[4] *Report of the Immigration Commission* (Washington: GPO, 1910), i. 13.

[5] Social Darwinism 'could be used to defend cutthroat competition as natural, to condemn governmental interference in the economy as contrary to the more efficient action of natural laws, and to dismiss radical efforts to ameliorate social conditions as inconsistent with the inevitably slow improvement inherent in an evolutionary scheme' (Archdeacon 1983: 160).

[6] See Trent (1994), ch. 5, Ludmerer (1972), Dowbiggin (1997) ch. 4, and Kevles (1986). On Britain see Mazumder (1992).

manifest by the 1890s; they did not abate until 1930. Immigration was a hotly disputed issue, with the congressional committees on immigration subject to intense lobbying by both restrictionists and opponents of limits. The proposal, advanced in the Lodge Bill in 1897, substantially to introduce restrictions of immigrants and a literacy test had plenty of supporters but also provoked petitions of opposition. The German-American Society protested that demarcations between immigrants would deter the 'better' migrants and produce false economies: 'perhaps the half-educated foreigner who has nothing to lose in his own land will readily submit to such humiliating conditions. The conservative farmer, the sturdy laborer, will shrink from the same, however, and thus the country will be deprived of the most desirable class of immigrants.'[7] Another organization opposing the educational test wondered how many of the 'founders' of the USA, themselves immigrants, would have been able to satisfy the new 'illiberal' criterion.[8]

The American Protection Association, founded in 1887, and boasting a membership of over 2 million by the mid-1890s, was an energetic exponent of the need to limit the number and type of immigrants to the United States; it was joined, in May 1894, by the Immigration Restriction League founded by a group of Harvard graduates, led by Robert De C. Ward, a professor at his alma mater.[9] The League's self-proclaimed aims were the 'limitation of immigration and a more careful selection, to the end that we shall receive no more aliens than can be properly assimilated'.[10] The League was active until the 1920s.[11] Its national committee included the liberal economist John Commons, the eugenist Madison Grant (author of the widely read *The Passing of the Great Race*), Lawrence Lowell, president of Harvard, Robert De C. Ward, and Franklin MacVeagh, who served as Secretary of the Treasury under President Taft between 1909 and 1913. It was enthusiastically restrictionist, warning against the 'dangerous flood of immigrants', and advocating legislation for the 'selection of those only who will make the most valuable citizens.'[12] Lightly veiled intellectual disdain for the new immigrants was obvious in many petitions favouring the legislation, such as one organization's lament that 'one of the gravest

---

[7] NA RG 233 Records of the US House of Representatives, 55th Congress, Committee on Immigration and Naturalization, Box 174, Folder: HR55A-H7.2, 13 Dec. 1897–5 Jan. 1898, 'Protest against any further Restriction of Immigration' petition.

[8] Ibid., petition from the North-American Turner Bund (Gymnastic Union).

[9] Solomon (1956).

[10] LC MD Papers of Franklin MacVeagh, Box 31, Folder: Immigration Restriction League 1905–28, Immigration Restriction League flyer, c.1923.

[11] Ibid., letter from John Dorr Bradley to MacVeagh 11 Jan. 1902. See also Solomon (1956).

[12] Ibid., letter from John Moors, president, to MacVeagh, 18 Sept. 1922.

menaces to our country's welfare is the free and unrestricted admission of illiterate, incapable, and pauper immigrants within our borders'.[13]

The Dillingham Commission

The debates at the turn of the century set the terms for those of the twentieth century: immigration was a source of intense controversy and often vituperative opinion in the new century's first three decades. The arguments marshalled during passage of the Lodge Act (1917 and see Table 4.1), continued to be rehearsed but were increasingly conjoined with racist and 'scientific' claims; and indeed Senator Henry Cabot Lodge himself anticipated this propensity in his attempt statistically to determine the distribution of ability amongst the American population according to national origins (a study which emphasized the English racial heritage).[14] The Anglo-Saxon milieu cultivated the initially jaundiced and then increasingly bilious eye turned upon immigrants to the United States from the 1890s. The connection between scientific arguments about race and patrician alarm about the new 'hordes' received its first explicit formulation in the Dillingham Commmission, its massive report setting the terms for the restrictionist measures incorporated in the 1924 law and favoured by eugenists, such as Charles Davenport, who had propagated eugenic arguments in the USA from 1910.

In analysing the pattern of immigrants, the Dillingham Commission (established by Congress in 1907 and reporting in 1910), established a conceptual dichotomy which structured ensuing debate. It characterized northern and western European immigrants as 'old immigration', reserving the term 'new immigration' for migrants from southern and eastern Europe, categories based on the significant change in the source of immigrants. It ascribed a set of significant differences between the two types. The former group 'was largely a movement of settlers who came from the most progressive sections of Europe for the purpose of making themselves homes in the New World'. They entered a range of occupations, settled throughout the United States, and integrated with the existing population: 'they mingled freely with the native Americans and were quickly assimilated.' Although many of them belonged to 'non-English-speaking races, this natural bar to assimilation was soon overcome by them, while the racial identity of their children was almost entirely lost

---

[13] NA RG 233 Records of the US HR, 55th Congress, Committee on Immigration and Naturalization, Box 183, Folder: HR55A-H7.2, 21 Feb. 1898, letter from President of the Washington-based Waugh Chautaugua Literary and Scientific Circle to Congressman Daniel Ermentrout, 14 Feb. 1898.
[14] See the discussion in Higham (1988: 141).

TABLE 4.1 Major Immigration Laws in the United States 1882–1929

Year	Act	Content
1882		Law excluding idiots, lunatics, paupers, and convicts.
1882	Chinese Exclusion Act	Excluded Chinese immigrants from the USA for a decade; renewed in 1892, 1902, and made permanent in 1904.
1885	Contract Labour Act	Prohibited employers recruiting labour in Europe and paying their passage to the USA.
1891	Immigration Act	Key piece of legislation, assigning responsibility for assessment of new immigrants to the federal government. Congress established Superintendent of Immigration in the Treasury Department to oversee this work in Ellis and Angel Islands. Main element was a medical evaluation.
1897	Literacy test	Literacy test for new immigrants passed by Congress but vetoed by President Grover Cleveland.
1903		Added anarchists, epileptics, and beggars to list of proscribed immigrants.
1907	Immigration Act	Established Dillingham Commission which reported in December 1910.
1917	Literacy test	Literacy test introduced (over President Woodrow Wilson's veto; also vetoed in 1913 and 1915), applicable to all immigrants over 16.
		Doubled the head tax on immigrants. Significant achievement for the restrictionists.
1921	Immigration Act	Law restricting European immigration, through new quota system: limited immigration to 3% per annum of each European nationality already resident in the USA, taking the 1910 census as a baseline. Limited total number of immigrants to 355,000 a year, 55% from north-western Europe, 45% from south-eastern Europe. Renewed in 1922 to terminate on 30 June 1924.
1924	Johnson–Reed Act	From 1927 immigration limited to a total of 150,000 annually, of whom nationalities resident in the USA according to 1890 census could claim 2% each.
		Set out a commission to determine quota for a system based on national origins to be introduced in 1927.
1927		Implementation of the national origins plan of 1924 Act postponed.
1929		National origins quota formula came into effect after successive postponements in 1927 and 1928. It apportioned quotas on the basis of the estimated national origins distribution of the white population in the USA in the 1920 census.

Source: derived from E. P. Hutchinson, *Legislative History of American Immigration Policy 1798–1965* (Philadelphia: University of Pennsylvania Press, 1981).

and forgotten'.[15] For these immigrants America was the promised New World.

The 'new immigration' movement was depicted unfavourably. It was composed of unskilled labourers 'from the less progressive and advanced countries of Europe in response to the call for industrial workers in the eastern and middle western States'. They lived in ethnically concentrated communities in large cities, thereby avoiding assimilation. From a meticulous study of seven cities (New York, Chicago, Philadelphia, Boston, Cleveland, Buffalo, and Milwaukee) in which the Commission's investigators visited 10,206 households, the report generalized that the new 'immigrant races live largely in colonies, many of whose characteristics are determined by the predominance of a foreign population';[16] the ability to speak English was often confined to school-age immigrants. This assessment, of course, overlooked the bars, enacted by state legislatures, excluding immigrants from certain occupations in the USA.[17] The new arrivals were 'as a class far less intelligent than the old'. A third were illiterate. And 'racially they are for the most part essentially unlike the British, German and other peoples who came during the period prior to 1880, and generally speaking they are actuated in coming for different ideals'.[18] This characterization of new immigrants' low intelligence illustrates how inadequate mental ability was employed as an attribute for potential citizens.

The unassimilability of the new immigrants alarmed the Dillingham Commission.[19] Its evidence suggested a failure to assimilate, arising from the absence of families and the predominance of single men. The Commission paid particular attention to the immigration of criminals and the 'mentally defective', and to the incidence of immigrants in receipt of charity or engaged in crime. These concerns resonated through immigration debates. Stories about the criminality and penury of southern and eastern European immigrants had fuelled the debate in the 1880s and 1890s, and indeed had contributed to the founding of the Commission. Detailed studies were undertaken. Relatively few immigrants became charity seekers, despite widespread assumptions to the contrary, a reflection, in the Commission's view, of existing stringent immigration tests.[20] Of those with learning difficulties, the Commission accepted that

[15] *Report of the Immigration Commission*, i. 13. 'Native Americans' refers to descendants of colonists, not to American Indians.
[16] *Report of the Immigration Commission*, vol. xxvi, *Immigrants in Cities* (Washington DC: GPO, 1910), 143.
[17] For details see Higham (1988: 161–2).
[18] *Report of the Immigration Commission*, i. 14.
[19] See especially *Report of the Immigration Commission*, vol. xix, *Immigrants in Industries* (Washington DC: GPO, 1911), ch. 7 'General Progress and Assimilation'.
[20] *Report of the Immigration Commission*, vols. xxxiv and xxxv, *Immigrants as Charity Seekers* (Washington DC: GPO, 1911).

medical examinations already in force played a significant role in identifying sufferers; these tests were less efficient in anticipating the development of such debilities. Legislation in 1882 and 1891 respectively excluded
the immigration of idiots and lunatics and of insane persons. In a key
section of its report, the Commission claimed immigrants were disproportionately represented in the asylum population: 'of the 150,151 insane
persons enumerated in hospitals on December 31 1903, 47,078 or 31.4 per
cent, were foreign-born whites. The proportion of native-born whites of
native parentage was 33.6 per cent and the proportion of native-born
whites of foreign parentage was 10 per cent. Only 6.6 per cent of all the
insane persons enumerated were colored.'[21] Combining the numbers for
the insane with the 'feeble-minded' produced a total of 47,934 'mentally
unsound persons of foreign birth' in US hospitals and institutions. These
data permitted the Commission to conclude that although significant
numbers of hopeful immigrants were excluded on mental health grounds,
nonetheless 'there are in the United States many thousands of insane or
feeble-minded persons of foreign birth'. Its own calculations suggested that
'insanity is relatively more prevalent among the foreign-born than among
the native-born, and relatively more prevalent among certain immigrant
races or nationalities than among others'.[22]

The Commission's data provided grist to the eugenists' mill. Its report
played an important role in reifying stereotypes about immigrants, roman-
ticizing the distinction between 'old' immigrants from northern and
western Europe and 'new' immigrants from eastern and southern Europe.
The latter were depicted as undesirable and unassimilable migrants in part
because of their alleged mental inferiority.[23] Congressman Albert Johnson,
who later cosponsored the major 1924 legislation on immigration,
remarked that the Dillingham Commission's study constituted the 'great
impetus' which culminated in the 1924 law.[24] However, the eugenist Harry
Laughlin, speaking in 1924, criticized the Dillingham Commission, despite
admiring the thoroughness of its method, for framing its researches, 'exclusively as an economic problem'; consequently, he maintained, the 'biology
of the task received relatively little attention'.[25] Notably, the dictionary of

[21] Immigration Commission, *Abstract of the Report on Immigration and Insanity*
(Washington DC: GPO, 1911), 9.
[22] Ibid. 22.
[23] It was a dichotomy rehearsed until the end of the 1920s: see e.g. the annual reports of
the Committee of Immigration, 1921–9, Allied Patriotic Societies, New York.
[24] 'Americanization of Adult Aliens', Hearings before a Subcommittee of the Committee
on Immigration and Naturalization, HR, 69th Congress, 2nd Session, 17 Feb. 1927, p. 17.
[25] 'Europe as an Emigrant-Exporting Continent; the United States as an Immigrant-
Receiving Nation', Hearings before the Committee on Immigration and Naturalization, HR,
68th Congress, 1st Session, 8 Mar. 1924, p. 1237.

race which Laughlin welcomed was not systematically integrated into the Commission's lengthy analyses. The findings of the anthropologist, Franz Boas, were also incongruous with the Commission's general approach, since they stressed environmental over hereditary factors, and were out of step with populist demands for restriction.

The Dillingham Commission recommended tougher assessment of potential immigrants in their country of origin, to find out about criminal records and mental suitability. Immigrants who became public charges within three years of arriving in the USA were to be deported. The continued exclusion of Chinese labourers was endorsed. Its major recommendations addressed the position of single, unskilled males migrating from southern and eastern Europe, whom the Dillingham Commission judged both uninterested and mostly unsuitable for assimilation. To effect a reduction in the number and type of immigrants, it proposed several measures: a literacy test, enacted in 1917;[26] a fixed quota by race 'arriving each year to a certain percentage of the average of that race arriving during a given period of years';[27] the exclusion of unskilled workers unaccompanied by dependents; annual limits on the number of immigrants admitted at each port; the specification of a fixed amount of money to be possessed by each immigrant on arrival; and an increase in the head tax, applied preferentially to men with families.

A single voice of dissent, that of Congressman William Bennet, from New York, argued strongly against a literacy test. Bennet maintained that the Commission's own research revealed that the problems of criminality, insanity, and pauperism amongst the new immigrants had been exaggerated (a view supported by the data[28]). Despite these protests the Commission's recommendations both structured discussion and informed the detail of immigration policy until 1929. Both the literacy test and the system of admission based on nationality quotas were adopted, a

---

[26] This was already a measure with considerable support in Congress (though not in the White House): see for instance, Hearings of the Committee on Immigration and Naturalization, HR, 60th Congress, 18 Feb. 1908, statement by Congressman John Burnett (Alabama) proposing a literacy test. It was supported by organized labour (fearful of cheap workers) and pressure groups such as the Immigration Restriction League. NA RG 233 Records of the US HR, 63rd Congress, Committee on Immigration, Box 455 Folder: HR63A-H8.1, letter to Congressman H. H. Dale from Samuel Gompers, President AFL, 22 Jan. 1915. NA RG 233 Records of the US HR, 62nd Congress, Committee on Immigration, Box 618 Folder: HR62A-H10.2, petition from the Immigration Restriction League, 24 May 1912. The League lobbied for a literacy test from the end of the nineteenth century. The League received support from the Bureau of Immigration at the Commerce Department, whose Commissioner-General endorsed a literacy test in 1900. NA RG 85 Records of the INS, Central Office, Subject Correspondence 1906–32, Box 56, Folder: 51762/21, letter from Commissioner-General, F. P. Sargent, to Prescott Hall, Secretary of the Immigration Restriction League, 21 June 1904.

[27] *Report of the Immigration Commission* i. 47.   [28] Fitzgerald (1996).

mechanism which effected selection by assessment of individual suitability. The 1917 literacy law—which exempted those who could demonstrate they were escaping from religious persecution (designed principally for Russian Jews) and an immigrant's dependents despite their illiteracy—marked a major revision of immigration policy. It substituted the principle of individual selection and suitability with one of group selection, thereby becoming a precursor for the 1924 law and 1929 regulations, as the historian Robert Divine explains: 'this concept of judging men by their national and racial affiliations rather than by their individual qualifications was to become the basic principle in the immigration legislation of the postwar period.'[29] The law's passage slowed down but did not end agitation for further restriction. The pressure for restriction by set nationality quotas intensified.

THE ENACTMENT OF THE JOHNSON–REED ACT 1924

Agitation for restriction of immigration grew from 1920. President Calvin Coolidge gave a restrictionist message—endorsing an 'America is for Americans' slogan—to the Congress in December 1923. It proved a prelude to the 1924 law. The Immigration Restriction League urged Coolidge to remain steadfast.[30] Congressman John Cable congratulated President Coolidge on his efforts 'to stop the seepage of aliens' entering the USA.[31] The US Department of Labor maintained that there were 'millions of unnaturalized, outside of the unnaturalizable races, immigrants' who lived undetected.[32] It wanted tougher enforcement laws and funding to increase the number of inspectors. The association of some immigrants with anarchism (manifest in the discovery of bombs in May 1919, including one outside the Attorney General's house) and labour conflict galvanized sentiments against immigrants. Alleged communists were arrested and deported.

Between 1917 and 1929, the shape of US immigration policy was set, with legislation in 1921, 1924, and regulations in 1929. In 1921, Congress, overturning a presidential veto, imposed a temporary limitation, organized in terms of nationality quotas, on new immigrants from Europe.

[29] Divine (1957: 5).
[30] LC MD Papers of Calvin Coolidge, File 133 (Reel 78), letter from W. Sanders, secretary Immigration Restriction League, to Coolidge, 14 Feb. 1924.
[31] LC MD Papers of Calvin Coolidge, File 133 (Reel 78) letter from Congressman John L. Cable to Coolidge, 22 Oct. 1923.
[32] Ibid., Department of Labor, Memorandum, 'In the matter of cooperation between officers of States and Municipalities with officers of the United States in connection with the enforcement of the Immigration Laws', 14 pp., Oct. 1923, p. 3.

Immigrants could constitute only 3 per cent of their country's extant population in the USA as measured in the census of 1910; total immigration was restricted to 357,000 per annum. The congressional leader of these restrictions was Albert Johnson.

Congressman Albert Johnson and immigration

Chairman from May 1919 of the House Immigration Committee, Albert Johnson responded to the restrictionist lobby by orchestrating the passage and enactment of legislation introducing nationality quotas and absolute limits for immigrants. Johnson, from Washington state, was the principal congressional actor both in the passage of the 1924 law and in shaping the final form of the national quotas arrangement established in 1929. Before entering Congress he made his reputation as a small town newspaper editor, opposed to organized labour.[33] Johnson was elected to Congress as a staunch restrictionist who, in May 1919, assumed the chairmanship of the House Committee on Immigration and Naturalization, a position he retained until 1933. By 1924, he dominated the seventeen-member House committee (only two members of which, Congressmen Samuel Dickstein from New York and Adolf Sabath from Chicago, ever opposed restriction).

As he made clear to his committee, Johnson harboured few doubts about restriction:

I have come to the conclusion through readings and studies of the situation in the larger cities that no matter who the members of this committee may be in the next few Congresses, or who will be the chairman, the [restrictionist] movement will keep on until there is just as complete suspension of immigration to the United States as is possible to be had.[34]

It was conflicts arising solely within white European groups that exercised Johnson. 'Becoming white' was a crucial aspect of assimilation for European immigrants, a process from which black Americans were excluded.[35]

Congressman Johnson formed the main conduit linking eugenists' arguments and research with immigration policy. His contacts with Prescott Hall of the Immigration Restriction League predated 1914. The League regularly provided information to the House Immigration Committee. Johnson corresponded steadily with Madison Grant, after the latter

[33] Higham (1988: 177–8).
[34] 'Americanization of Adult Aliens', Hearings before a Subcommittee on the Committee on Immigration and Naturalization, HR, 69th Congress, 2nd Session, 17 Feb. 1927, p. 17.
[35] On this process in respect of Irish Americans see the stimulating discussion in Ignatiev (1995). On the concept of 'whiteness' in the labour market see Roediger (1991); and on class and race see Nelson (1996), and Kelley (1993).

published his book (in 1916) on race decline. Johnson was elected President of the Eugenics Research Association in 1923.[36]

From nationality quotas to national origins

To constrict further the numbers of southern and eastern Europeans, activists lobbied Congress to restrict each nationality group already resi-dent in the USA to 2 per cent of its share of the population in the 1890 census.[37] This combination was enacted in the Johnson–Reed Immigration Act of 1924.[38] The new legislation reduced the annual total number of immigrants to 150,000. The 1924 law provoked enormous controversy. By accepting (in clause (*b*) of Section 11, see appendix to this chapter) that immigration should be regulated in terms of nationality quotas, derived from the 1890 rather than the 1920 census, it unleashed not only intense lobbying by various ethnic groups to enlarge or defend their likely posi-tion but opened up necessarily quarrelous and divisive debate about the suitability of different nationalities for membership of the US polity. President Coolidge was warned, in April 1924, by the Immigration Restriction League that failure to enact the law 'would be playing into the Democratic Candidate'.[39] In May of the same year, the President received a plaintive letter from Congressman Johnson warning him against vetoing the Bill: 'in my opinion, the House is likely to pass that bill over executive disapproval by a vote of at least 3 to 1. I think the Senate would show a similar proportion of votes to pass over a veto. I have examined the matter carefully and am in close touch with the great bulk of those favoring restriction.'[40] Presumably, committee chairmen could make such claims to the President rarely enough to retain the threat's credibility. In 1927, the quota system established in the 1924 Johnson–Reed Act was substituted by a national origins plan (implemented in 1929), calculated by a special executive board. Both the temporary quota system and the national origins plan replaced the principle of individualism as the basis of admittance to the USA with one of group selection.

Coolidge was also lobbied by congressional opponents of the legislation produced by the conference committee. Congressman Samuel Dickstein (D, NY), an unswerving opponent of the national origins quota, articulated the position of opponents:

[36] Higham (1988: 314).   [37] Archdeacon (1983: 171–2).
[38] It was passed by 323 to 71 votes in the House and 62 to 6 in the Senate, with the fol-lowing sectional pattern (cf. Divine 1957: 17), yes:no, House first: Northeast 53:56, 10:5; Midwest 125:15, 13:0; South 115:0, 21:0; Far West 30:0, 18:1.
[39] LC MD, Papers of Calvin Coolidge, File 133 (Reel 79), letter from George Rittings to Coolidge, 20 Apr. 1924.
[40] Ibid., letter from Congressman Albert Johnson to Coolidge, 13 May 1924.

the preference provided for in the bill is a camouflage and is discriminatory. It may work well insofar as England and Germany are concerned because of the greater number allotted them for their quota, but it practically bars the rest of the world; particularly so under the National Origins scheme to become effective on July 1, 1927, as incorporated by the Conferees. This is another section that is wholly discriminatory.[41]

In another letter, the same congressman claimed of the bill that 'it involves the reputation of millions of our citizens as to whether or not a stamp of inferiority is to be placed upon them'.[42]

Determining the national origins quotas

The 1924 Act postponed the implementation of the national origins quota, based on the 1890 census, until 1927, when it was again temporarily delayed. In January 1927, the Commission established by the 1924 Act[43] to set nationality quotas reported.[44] It was charged with determining the national origins of the American population as a basis upon which to make calculations about quotas. The analysis was focused exclusively on the white population. The committee basically attempted to distinguish two groups: first, using records from the 1790 census the 'original native stock', as documented in the government publication called *A Century of Population Growth* (published in 1909) which had categorized the estimated population in 1790 into nationality groups and whose more prosperous patrician descendants inhabited the turn-of-the-century world depicted in such Edith Wharton's novels as *The House of Mirth* and *The Age of Innocence*; and second the 'immigrant stock', who entered the country subsequently. On the basis of this dichotomy, 'of the 94,820,915 white population of the United States as enumerated in 1920, approximately 53,500,000 were of immigrant stock and 41,000,000 of original native stock'.[45] The smaller size of the later figure was bound to sound alarm bells amongst restrictionists: in 1890, the immigrant stock

[41] Ibid., letter from Congressman Samuel Dickstein to Coolidge, 17 May 1924.

[42] Ibid., letter from Congressman Samuel Dickstein to C. B. Slemp, Secretary to President Coolidge, 22 May 1924.

[43] Known as the Quota Board, with seven members overseen by the secretaries of Labor (James Davis), Commerce (Herbert Hoover), and State (Frank Kellogg). The three secretaries delegated the work to a committee composed of R. W. Flourney and S. W. Boggs (for State), Joseph A. Hill and Leon R. Truesdell (for Commerce), and W. W. Husband and Ethelbert Stewart (for Labor). Husband was a key architect of US immigration policy; Hill was the principal statistician.

[44] US Senate 69th Congress, 2nd Session, Document No. 190 'National Origins Provision of the Immigration Act of 1924', Message from the President of the United States, 7 Jan. 1927.

[45] Ibid., 3. Prepared by the three secretaries' committee.

TABLE 4.2 US White Population

Census	Total	Original native stock	Immigrant stock
1890	55,101,258	30,432,466	24,668,792
1900	66,809,196	34,272,951	32,536,245
1910	80,731,957	38,101,175	42,630,782
1920	94,820,915	41,288,570	53,532,345

numbered 24,668,792 compared with 30,432,466 original native stock (see Table 4.2).[46]

The debates after 1924 were complex and rebarbative, culminating a bitter few months before the scheme was finally accepted in 1929. First, the 1924 law returned temporarily to the 2 per cent quota system (based on the 1890 census) enacted in 1921 with a lower aggregate number of permitted immigrants. This system was opposed by advocates of open immigration and supporters of the interests of southern and eastern Europeans. Second, the 1924 law specified that the 2 per cent system should be replaced in 1927 (delayed until 1929) with a national origins scheme, according to which principles immigrants would be admitted in proportion to the quota of their nationalities determined to be present in the USA in 1890. This scheme upset descendants of the north-western Europeans— other than the British who gained substantially—since their quota, made public when the Quota Board reported in January 1927, fell precipitously. It was an argument based, furthermore, on a reading of the US nation as composed of certain 'stock'. Restrictionists were eager to retain the 1890 census base, their opponents seeking to substitute it with the 1920 census. The thirty-year alternative was much more than a quillet: it would make a considerable difference to the ethnic composition admitted after the quota regime commenced. Language was often emotive. Restrictionist sentiment was supported in the thousands of petitions and resolutions sent to members of the congressional immigration committees.[47] On 13 February 1929, the Senate Committee on Immigration ended its hearings on the quota issue and voted against postponing the date at which the National

[46] Figures derived from: National Origins Provision Immigration Act of 1924, Hearings before the Committee on Immigration and Naturalization, HR, 69th Congress, 2nd Session, 18 Jan. 1927, p. 12.

[47] NA RG 46 Records of the US Senate, 68th Congress, Committee on Immigration Box 237, Folder: Sen 68A-J27; contains many petitions, with multiple signatures—for example, petition to Senator Arthur Capper from Paradise, Kansas, 13 Mar. 1924. This collection contains many other examples, some sent to named senators and congressmen, others just to members of Congress.

Origins Clause became operational. President Hoover signed the law on 22 March and stipulated that the clause become law from 1 July 1929.

President Hoover, publicly an opponent of the clause, declared it would be in effect from 1 July 1929. Its enactment was a triumph for a view of the American people as racially homogeneous, whose racial integrity should not be compromised by unsuitable immigrants. This relatively narrow ethnic priority outweighed considerations of economic pressure. We now turn to the principal intellectual and political sources of such racial claims: eugenics research.

EUGENICS AND THE RESTRICTION OF IMMIGRATION

The national origins scheme represented the convergence of quotidian stereotypes about, and electoral hostility to, immigrants and the pseudo-science propagated by eugenists in the opening decades of the twentieth century. Attitudes and prejudices hitherto directed toward African Americans were now targeted upon the new immigrants. Patrician and 'old stock' American descendants feared the racial imbroglio posed by the new immigrants.

Eugenic arguments played a decisive role in transforming the immigration policy from a concern with absolute numbers to one about the suitability and assimilability of individual immigrants.[48] This was a crucial factor. As Garland Allen writes, using subjective criteria, eugenists 'classed as superior those people descended from Nordic or Aryan stock or those from wealthy classes. Conversely, inferior people were those from eastern European, Mediterranean, Asian, African, native American, or Jewish stock, along with the chronically poor.' He adds that 'to American eugenicists, the old Anglo-Saxon, Nordic stock was in danger of being swamped by a massive increase in the number of hereditary degenerates'.[49] From this, purportedly scientific, research, eugenists presented expertise about racial hierarchies, racial degeneracy, and the sources of mental competence. These findings were exploited by political advocates of immigration restriction, most of whom were already predisposed negatively to assess immigrants. This expertise—and the corresponding role played by eugenists—plainly had an instrumental value for policy-makers. It provided an apparently scientific gloss to the hard edge of populist anti-immigrant rhetoric. It was cited consistently and often decisively in congressional debate and law-making. It was rarely challenged in the 1920s and never successfully.

[48] Higham (1988: 151–7).   [49] Allen (1987: 172).

Eugenists favoured severe restrictions on immigration as part of a general programme to prevent dilution of the American 'race' or 'stock'. In 1914, both the Medical Society of New York State and the Massachusetts Medical Society complained to the House of Representatives Immigration Committee about the failure adequately to screen immigrants to exclude what each termed the 'mentally defective'. The second organization warned of the 'direful consequences of [immigrants] being allowed to marry and to propagate and so deteriorate the mental health of the Nation'.[50] Over a decade later, the president of the Eugenics Research Association warned Congressman Albert Johnson of the excessive fecundity of immigrants: 'it is necessary to protect—as far as possible—our best stock';[51] the Dillingham Commission's examination of this alleged fecundity of the new immigrants found higher average numbers of children born to women of foreign parentage than those born to white American women.[52]

Dr Harry Laughlin, eugenist[53]

The eugenist[54] with most influence on immigration policy during the 1920s was Dr Harry H. Laughlin, who worked at the Eugenics Record Office, located at Cold Harbor, Long Island (funded by the Carnegie Institution of Washington). The Office, established in 1910 by Charles Davenport, aimed to compile a dataset of the American population for eugenic research. Laughlin's expertise was solicitiously sought by Congressman Johnson, who praised one of his numerous congressional appearances as 'a fine presentation'.[55] Laughlin spoke often to the House Immigration Committee about the 'social inadequacy of aliens'.[56]

[50] NA RG 233 Records of the HR, 63rd Congress, Committee on Immigration, Box 458, Folder: HR63A-H8.1, petitions from the New York and Massachusetts Medical Societies.

[51] NA RG 233 Records of the HR, 69th Congress, Committee on Immigration, Committee Papers, Box 341, Folder: H69A-F20.1, letter from Frank L. Babbott, President Eugenics Research Association to Congressman Johnson, 31 Mar. 1927.

[52] Immigration Commission, *Abstract of the Report on Fecundity of Immigrant Women* (Washington DC: GPO, 1911).

[53] On Laughlin's papers see Bird and Allen (1981). They provide an introduction to the collection at Truman State University (formerly Northeast Missouri State University) at Kirksville.

[54] On the eugenic principles influential with Laughlin see the various memoranda in Laughlin Papers, Folder: Fundamental Biological Principles, C-4-4. Special Collections, University Archives, Truman State University.

[55] NA RG 233 Records of the US HR, 69th Congress, Committee on Immigration, Correspondence, Box 342, Folder: HR69A-F20.1, letter from Johnson to F. A. Kinnicutt, 27 Apr. 1926.

[56] NA RG 233 Records of the US HR, 69th Congress, Committee on Immigration, Committee Papers, Box 341, Folder: H69A-F20.1, referred to in a letter from Madison Grant to Johnson, 20 Apr. 1926; see also telegram from Laughlin to Johnson, 15 Apr. 1926.

Laughlin was employed from 1920, as Expert Eugenics Agent, by the House Committee to research and prepare data about the eugenic characteristics of immigrants and potential immigrants to the United States. As Laughlin wrote to one correspondent in 1922: 'Chairman Albert Johnson is much concerned with the new studies, and has recently designated me their agent with semi-official standing for the purpose of collecting and analysing data on the eugenical aspects of immigration.'[57] Some of the questionnaires gathering data for his studies were circulated under the Committee on Immigration's 'franking privileges' (an entitlement of his expert position).[58] In 1922 Laughlin produced an analysis of America's melting pot, in 1924 he reported his extensive field research (120 pages) in the main emigrant-exporting countries in Europe, and in 1928 discoursed on the 'eugenical aspects of deportation', building upon his earlier research. These studies were widely promulgated and discussed. Many sold out several print runs, as Chairman Johnson often reminded his colleagues. Laughlin continued to appear before the Committee after the enactment of the 1924 law, summoned, for instance, in 1928 to give his biological views on Mexican immigration;[59] he also journeyed to Europe on several occasions, sometimes as an accredited US Immigration Agent, and at personal expense to examine the so-called 'stock' of emigrants bound for the USA.[60] Working in the 1920s and 1930s, Laughlin was part of a burgeoning scientific profession whose members were drawn from a narrow social base, and who enjoyed social mobility and prestige. Thus, Kevles notes that the scientific professions provided a modest social mobility especially 'by which the children of middle- to lower-middle-class families, often from rural areas, migrated to the urban upper middle class, both in income and in social status.' Despite this mobility the 'American scientific professions remained overwhelmingly white, Anglo-Saxon, Protestant and male,' a milieu into which Laughlin fitted exactly.[61]

[57] Letter from Laughlin to Frank Babbott, 18 Feb. 1922, in Laughlin Papers, Folder: Letters, Frank Babbott, C-4-3.

[58] NA RG 233 Records of the US HR, 70th Congress, Committee on Immigration. Committee Papers, Box 240, Folder: HR70A-F14.6, a letter from Congressman Emanuel Celler to Harry Laughlin, 23 Jan. 1928 expressed some concern about one of the latter's surveys; the survey was eliciting information on the racial descent of American citizens who registered patents in a three-month period. Laughlin wisely referred the letter to Johnson who replied to Celler on 6 Feb.: 'this study is but one of several statistical studies designed to show statistics—the nationality of the ancestry etc, of those active in public and other affairs.'

[59] See letter from Congressman John C. Box to Laughlin 16 Feb. 1928, in Laughlin Papers, Special Collections, University Archives, Truman State University.

[60] He was appointed a 'dollar-a-year' representative from the Department of Labor on one occasion. See letter from Laughlin to Madison Grant 23 July 1930 suggesting a renewal of this arrangement, and a similar one with the State Department, in Laughlin Papers Folder C-4-1, Special Collections, University Archives, Truman State University.

[61] Kevles (1988: 116).

Mirroring British eugenists' work, Laughlin favoured pedigree studies on immigrants as he explained to one colleague: 'by doing pedigree work in the field abroad we can judge the family-stock of the immigrant but, if we let him come in without pedigree study we have to wait until his children and grandchildren come on before we can judge his worth'.[62] He told the Secretary of Labor, in 1930, that the aim of his trip was 'to throw some light upon the biological nature of the emigrants as breeding stock for future American citizens'.[63] Laughlin's Committee appointment ended in 1931.

Three closely interrelated themes dominate Laughlin's eugenic research for the House Immigration Committee: the problem of degeneracy; the fiscal burden of eugenically inferior immigrants; and the need for an immigration policy selection.

(i) Degeneracy and immigrants

Laughlin introduced a threefold categorization of the mentally ill, a schema paralleling that deployed in Britain by its Eugenics Society. He divided the 'feeble-minded' into three classes: 'the lowest are the idiots—the men can not attend to their own wants; they have to be clothed in dresses, and wear diapers. Then, above the idiots, there are the imbeciles, who can not be trained to do ordinary work; they, too, have to be placed in institutions. Then, above the imbeciles, come the morons. They are the borderline cases; they have the bodies of adults but the minds of 9 and 10 year old children; they can be trained to do useful pick and shovel work of a certain type, but they can not get along in school, no matter how long they attend. Nor do they acquire social responsibility.'[64] Laughlin warned the Congressmen that 'the moron is really a greater menace to our civilization than the idiot' since their deviousness enabled them to evade immigration inspectors; furthermore, the combination of fecundity and few inhibitions made moronic women 'highly fertile sexually'.[65] Laughlin cited Goddard's research at Vineland, New Jersey, as scientific evidence for these categories.[66]

---

[62] Letter from Laughlin to Captain John B. Trevor, 18 Aug. 1930, in Laughlin Papers Folder C-4-1, Special Collections, University Archives, Truman State University.

[63] Letter from Laughlin to James J. Davis, Secretary of Labor, 30 July 1930, ibid. He added: 'if I could have an appointment from the Secretary of Labor as "Immigration Investigator" or as "US Immigration Agent or Representative" I could conduct this work under the most favorable auspices and could, I believe, produce a study which would throw some first hand light upon the particular problem. This would involve no financial obligations on the part of the Government.'

[64] 'Biological Aspects of Immigration', hearings before the Committee on Immigration and Naturalization, HR 66th Congress, 2nd Session, 17 Apr. 1920, p. 13.

[65] Ibid.

[66] Dr H. H. Goddard published the study of the Kallikak family in 1912, and was the author of an influential general study, *Feeblemindedness: Its Causes and Consequences* (New York: Macmillan, 1914). He was a pioneer of IQ tests.

In respect of US immigration policy, Laughlin asserted that 'it is now high time that the eugenical element, that is, the factor of natural hereditary qualities which will determine our future characteristics and safety, receive due consideration'.[67] He wanted eugenic tests on immigrants in their home cities. Furthermore, immigrants had larger familes than nonimmigrants and would therefore contribute disproportionately to the growth of the US population.[68] Later in his testimony, Laughlin warned that, 'at present, not inferior nationalities but inferior individual family stocks are tending to deteriorate our national characteristics. Our failure to sort immigrants on the basis of natural worth is a very serious national menace.'[69]

To justify the eugenic approach of delving into family records and unearthing 'degenerate' forebearers, he cited the family histories of the Jukes, Ishmaels, and Kallikaks, all of whose dismal life narratives were aired widely by eugenists in the 1920s. Of the Jukes he observed that 'they are a worthless, mentally backward family or tribe . . . This backwardness is not all due to environment, because our field studies show that there is such a thing as bad stock . . . The lesson is that immigrants should be examined, and the family stock should be investigated, lest we admit more degenerate "blood".'[70] Similar studies of immigrants would prevent, Laughlin claimed, 'any deterioration of the American people due to the immigration of inferior human stock'.[71] In a subsequent appearance before the House Committee on Immigration, Laughlin reported that the Jukes and Ishmaels were simply the tip of what we might term the 'family degeneracy iceberg', since fieldworkers usually cncountered 'a great network of degenerate families'.[72] Unlike other students of immigration, eugenists were interested in the consequences for the American 'stock' of immigrants not their economic effects. Laughlin recommended that 'highly specialized and skilled' eugenists be employed at American consuls to examine immigrants and declare them mentally and physically fit for a visa. This proposal was rehearsed throughout the decade and, in part, implemented. Laughlin confidently informed the committee that there was, furthermore, a racial disparity in the distribution of morons: 'in reference to foreigners, one notices, by the names of individuals who are found in institutions, that the lower or less progressive races furnish more

---

[67] 'Biological Aspects of Immigration', hearings before the Committee on Immigration and Naturalization, HR 66th Congress, 2nd Session, 16 Apr. 1920, p. 3.
[68] Ibid. 4.   [69] Ibid., 17 Apr. 1920, p. 17.
[70] Ibid., 16 Apr. 1920, pp. 4–5. For one account and searing critique of the methodology deployed to study these families see Gould (1981), ch. 5.
[71] 'Biological Aspects of Immigration', hearings before the Committee on Immigration and Naturalization, HR 66th Congress, 2nd Session, 16 Apr. 1920, p. 4.
[72] 'The Eugenical Aspects of Deportation', hearings before the Committee on Immigration and Naturalization, HR 70th Congress, 1st Session, 21 Feb. 1928, p. 35.

than their quota.'[73] This latter characterization is difficult to reconcile with the claim that eugenists did not differentiate races as superior and inferior.

Overshadowing these eugenic investigations, like an incubus, was the spectre of 'racial degeneracy' (one conceived of in terms of 'the relative soundness of recent and older immigrant stocks'[74] the dichotomy formalized by the Dillingham Commission), identifying and excising its sources defined as the basic aim of immigration policy. For his melting pot study, Laughlin derived a set of predictions (termed quotas), from the 1910 census, about what number of each nationality should—on a normal distribution—be found in state institutions (about each of which data were collected for 1 January 1921).[75] This method was applied to a huge dataset compiled by the eugenists. Laughlin suggested that the 'outstanding conclusion' of his analysis was that 'making all logical allowances for environmental conditions, which may be unfavorable to the immigrant, the recent immigrants, as a whole, present a higher percentage of inborn socially inadequate qualities than do the older stocks'.[76] He singled out a number of European countries, from the data, who vastly exceeded their predicted quotas and were guilty of 'dumping' the socially inadequate on the United States. In respect of insanity these included Russia, Finland, Poland, Ireland, Bulgaria, and Turkey. Some results surprised the committee but were speedily explained by the eugenist. For instance, African Americans had the lowest measure of dependency, a finding counterintuitive to perceptions of this group's impoverishment. Chairman Albert Johnson's formulation—that 'in other words, their conditions of living are so low that dependence does not show itself'—was endorsed by Laughlin who added that 'the dependent or inadequate negro is taken care of by the plantation'. Such ad hoc explanation does not inspire confidence in this scientific framework, though curiously no sustained criticism was mounted by other scientists and the views were happily reproduced in news media. At the other extreme, the Irish in America were found to have an excessively high dependency ratio, again easily accounted for by stereotypes rather than evidence: 'the Irish have shown a quota fulfillment astoundingly high, 633.53 per cent. They are not thrifty, as a racial group in the

[73] 'Biological Aspects of Immigration', hearings before the Committee on Immigration and Naturalization, HR 66th Congress, 2nd Session, 17 Apr. 1920, p. 15.

[74] 'Analysis of America's Modern Melting Pot', hearings before the Committee on Immigration and Naturalization, HR 67th Congress, 3rd Session, 21 Nov. 1922, p. 731. Laughlin explained that the data compiled by him was designed to 'gauge the relative soundness and stability of the different racial and nativity groups in the United States, which gauge, in turn, would constitute a measure of their relative long-term value to the Nation, especially when viewed in the light of the inborn quality of future generations.'

[75] Ibid. 733.   [76] Ibid. 755.

United States; drink and dissipation were common, so that in many cases, especially in old age, their economic status was so low that many of them were thrown on the resources of the State.'[77]

In 1928, Laughlin compared the relative proportions of deportable and non-deportable foreign-born inmates, based on a survey of the 'socially inadequate' located in 684 state and federal prisons and asylums (of a total of 688 such institutions). Laughlin described deportation as the 'last line of defense against contamination of American family stocks by alien hereditary degeneracy'.[78] The 684 institutions disaggregated into: 53 for the 'feeble-minded'; 173 for the insane; 203 for criminals and delinquents; 12 for epileptics; 82 for TB sufferers; 1 for leprosy; 42 for the blind; 30 for the deaf; 5 for the deformed or crippled; and 87 for dependents. Collectively they held 74,170 foreign-born inmates in 1925 and 1926, a testimony to the failure of immigration policy, in Laughlin's view: 'if our immigration laws had worked as was intended, none of the present 74,184 inmates would have been admitted. But our first lines of defense were so broken by the alien attack that over 70,000 inadequates were found.'[79] Table 4.3 summarizes the findings. For Laughlin, the figures signalled an unacceptable failure of immigration policy, for which 'the principal remedy would seem to provide for more thorough examination into the individual and family histories of the would-be immigrant.'[80]

Laughlin's work was subject to remarkably little scrutiny, even by those favouring a more open immigration policy. One critic, a professor at Johns Hopkins University, H. S. Jennings, was sympathetic to eugenic research but alarmed about the political use of Laughlin's analyses. While the argument in favour of the 1890 census over the 1920 one seemed valid to Jennings, the case for it 'drawn from Laughlin's studies seem to me clearly illegitimate'.[81] As a consequence, Jennings tendered his resignation from the Eugenics Society, believing that 'this was not a good connection for me, as a worker in pure science'. Interestingly, Professor Irving Fisher, chairman of the Eugenics Society's committee on immigration, responding to Jennings, conceded the inaccuracy of Laughlin's statistical analysis[82]—excusing its use by the Eugenics Society as a result of tight

---

[77] Ibid. 748.
[78] 'The Eugenical Aspects of Deportation', hearings before the Committee on Immigration and Naturalization, HR 70th Congress, 1st Session, 21 Feb. 1928, p. 3.
[79] Ibid. 5.   [80] Ibid. 6.
[81] Letter from Jennings to Professor Irving Fisher, 27 Sept. 1924, in Laughlin Papers, Folder: Robert Ward, C-4-1. Jennings published his criticisms in *Science*, 59 (24 Mar. 1924), 256–7.
[82] Laughlin later addressed these criticisms before the congressional committee and rejected them: see his 'Europe as an Emigrant Exporting Continent and the United States as an Immigrant Receiving Nation.'

TABLE 4.3 Institutional Inmates 1925–1926

Type	Number of institutions	Native born		Foreign born		Total[a]
		No.	%	No.	%	
Feeble-minded	53	36,347	84.2	1,602	3.71	43,167
Insane	173	148,484	60.43	53,986	21.97	245,724
Criminalistic	200	85,057	78.76	11,224	10.39	107,996
Epileptic	12	7,391	72.52	749	7.39	10,192
Tuberculotic	82	13,478	74.85	2,608	14.48	18,006
Leprous	1	143	73.33	52	26.67	195
Blind	42	5,684	93.06	130	2.13	6,108
Deaf	29	6,382	91.84	57	0.82	6,949
Deformed & crippled	5	662	75.48	16	1.82	877
Dependent	87	21,254	54.28	3,746	9.57	39,155
Total	684	324,882	67.91	74,170	15.50	478,369

[a] Includes 79,317 (16.58%) for whom nativity was unknown.

Source: derived from 'The Eugenical Aspects of Deportation', Hearings before the Committee on Immigration and Naturalization, HR 70th Congress, 1st Session, 21 Feb. 1928, p. 6.

deadline—but retained faith in the organization's influence on immigration policy: 'our committee [of the Eugenics Society] did succeed in getting into the public consciousness the idea that an important or the important principle of sifting immigrants about eugenics. In the end, that idea however much it failed, in first trial, is more likely to win now that the thought is being held by millions of people who never thought of it before.' He dismissed Jennings's commitment to pure science: 'it is ridiculous for scientists on the one hand to keep aloof from the practical application of their work, and on the other hand, to express the hope that the work will proceed without them.' Fisher admitted that he had become what Jennings was 'inclined to dub a propagandist'.[83] Other criticisms were usually cavalierly dismissed.[84] And in the Progressivist 'age of the expert', eugenists flourished, especially when their research converged so easily with populist sentiments about immigrants upon which politicians such as Congressman Johnson had focused.

[83] Letter from Fisher to Jennings, 2 Oct. 1924, in Laughlin Papers, Folder: Robert Ward, C-4-1.

[84] In a letter from Charles Davenport, director of the Department of Genetics at the Carnegie Institution, to Laughlin, he writes: 'a review of your sterilization book appeared in "Nature" for September 15th. Dr Merriam [President of Carnegie] seems to take the criticisms involved somewhat seriously; tho he does not fail to recognize the excellence of the book.' 16 Oct. 1923, in Laughlin Papers, Folder: Field Workers, C-2-6.

(ii) The fiscal burden of immigrants

A theme of debates and analyses of immigration throughout the decades after 1900 was the fiscal burden posed by the disproportionately high percentage of immigrants in asylums, prisons, and poorhouses. In his presidential address to the American Medico-Psychological Association, in 1903, the psychiatrist and eugenist G. Alder Blumer called for 'stringent federal statutes' to exclude 'insane and other defective immigrants' because of the cost of monitoring them. He reported that in New York state 'fifty per cent of the inmates of State hospitals are of foreign birth', although the foreign born constituted only 25 per cent of the state's population.[85]

Such views were aired before congressional committees. Dr George Kline, commissioner of the department of mental diseases in Massachusetts, told Congress in March 1926 that out of 22,000 'defectives' and epileptics in state institutions 'approximately 40 per cent will be found to be foreign born, and perhaps 55 to 60 per cent will be found to be of foreign-born parentage'. At any given time, the state had about 130 such immigrants awaiting deportation.[86] Kline underlined the public expense posed by these inmates: 'the cost of maintenance of the insane, both alien and otherwise, is borne almost wholly by the State. Of course, an attempt is made to collect from the estate or whatever source we can, but the amount collected by the State institutions for the support of mental cases is relatively small. It is less than 11 per cent, and practically nothing from alien insane.'[87] Similar evidence was reported about the financial burden of the insane in New York and other States. The theme of the excessive cost of the so-called mentally unwell continued, the director of the New York State Hospital System complaining, in 1924, that of its '41,000 patients, 25 per cent, or over 10,000, are aliens with no legal claim upon the bounty of the State'.[88] The House Committee on Immigration heard about the cases of individual children classified as 'mental defectives' at another hearing and the burden they imposed.[89] Eugenists took solace from the national origins plan, believing it would result in immigrants of a quality and nationality apposite to the improvement of the American

[85] Cited in Dowbiggin (1997: 192).

[86] Hearings before the Committee on Immigration and Naturalization, HR, 69th Congress, 1st Session, 25–6 Mar. 1926, p. 129.

[87] Ibid. 130.

[88] Letter from C. Floyd Haviland to Professor Irving Fisher, 12 Jan. 1924, in Laughlin Papers, Folder: Robert Ward, C-4-1. The State asked the federal government for $18 million to support them.

[89] 'Admission of Mentally Defective Children', hearings before the Committee on Immigration and Naturalization, HR 67th Congress, 4th Session, 5 Dec. 1922 and 16 Jan. 1923; see esp. testimony by W. W. Husband, pp. 203–16.

race.[90] The 1924 Johnson–Reed Act imposed a deportation constraint on immigrants admitted to such publicly funded institution within five years of settling in the USA (a restriction aliens often proved able to sidestep).

When discussing the 'socially inadequate'—that is, 'a person is one who by his or her own effort, chronically, and regardless of etiology or prognosis, fails in comparison with normal persons to maintain himself or herself as a useful member of the organized social life of the State'[91] —Laughlin stressed the fiscal burden they presented. Indeed, he was mesmerized by the cost–benefit analogy: 'social inadequacy is a double debit: not only do the inadequates not pull their own weight in the boat, but they require, for their care, the services of normal and socially valuable persons who could well be employed in more constructive work.'[92]

One of Laughlin's studies, claiming to find an egregiously large percentage of foreign born in prisons and aslyums, received immense publicity in 1923.[93] He described the work thus to a colleague: 'we are studying, from first-hand sources, immigrant stocks by nationality and specific type of defect—the feebleminded, the insane, the criminalistic and the like. We are also comparing immigrant nationalities with the older American stock and with other alien races.'[94] The US Department of Labor made Laughlin's report the centrepiece of a memorandum on the enforcement of immigration laws. Describing Laughlin as 'one of the world's best known scientists', it reported his survey of state institutions: 'this expert finds that while the foreign born constitute 14.70 per cent of the nation's population, they furnish 20.63 per cent of the population of these institutions.' It added: 'one of the principal states of the union tells us that 47 per cent of the inmates in that state of institutions for the care of public dependents are foreign born, and that 27 per cent of them are still alien. We are further told that 30 per cent of the taxes of that state are devoted to the mainte-

---

[90] NA RG 233 Records of the US HR, 69th Congress, Committee on Immigration, Committee Papers, Box 341 Folder: H69A-F20.1; see letter from Henry Pratt Fairchild, 15 Jan. 1927.

[91] 'Analysis of America's Modern Melting Pot', hearings before the Committee on Immigration and Naturalization, HR 67th Congress, 3rd Session, 21 Nov. 1922, p. 730.

[92] Ibid. 731.

[93] A study was also undertaken in 1927, for the House Committee on Immigration, by the Department of Labor of the number of alien inmates in penal and public institutions in the USA. NA RG 233 Records of the US HR, 69th Congress, Committee on Immigration, Committee Papers, Box 345 Folder: HR69A-F20.3, letter from Robe Carl White, assistant secretary, to Congressman Albert Johnson, 9 Feb. 1927. It found a total of 111,673 alien inmates of whom *c*.40% were considered likely to be eligible for deportation.

[94] Letter from Laughlin to Frank Babbott, 18 Feb. 1922, in Laughlin Papers, Folder: Letters, Frank Babbott, C-4-3.

nance of public dependents.'[95] This theme of the excessive cost of the 'pauper insane and criminal classes' was pressed home by the Immigration Protection League which, in February 1928, proclaimed, without a source, that the USA had been 'expending approximately 27,000,000 dollars' on their maintenance.[96]

Table 4.4 reports estimates presented by Harry Laughlin to the House Immigration Committee in 1920 on the maintenance of what were crudely termed 'socially inadequate' aliens, composed of ten groups: '(1) Feeble-minded; (2) insane (including the nervous and psychopathic); (3) criminalistic (including the delinquent and wayward); (4) epileptic; (5) inebriate (including drug habitues); (6) diseased (including tuberculosis, the syphilitic, the leprous, and others with chronic infectious segregated diseases); (7) blind (including those with greatly impaired vision); (8) deaf (including those with greatly impaired hearing); (9) deformed (including the crippled); and (10) dependent (including children and folks in 'homes', ne'er-do-wells, tramps, and paupers).'[97] In case these data were not in themselves compelling, Laughlin gave an example to support his contention: 'in the census of 1900, the foreign-born [over 10 in age] population of the country was 19.5 per cent; and they contributed 34.3 per cent of the total insane population. Now, if that foreign stock was just as good as the stock already here, it ought to have contributed only 19.5 per cent.'[98] In 1920, the term 'constitutional psychopathic inferiority' was added to the reasons for non-admission to the USA, a modification winning Laughlin's full endorsement since, in his view, the category is a 'scrap-basket term, and it implies poor stock in the family; and in the particular individual, it implies degeneracy'. He also wanted the vague term 'general shiftlessness' given legal status; his definition rivalled the concept's generality: 'in every little Italian, or Scandinavian, or English, or Scotch town, there are village ne'er-do-wells who have not made good among their fellows. That is the type of immigrant which we want to exclude, even if he can stand up and get by the immigration officials and is able to pass the reading test, and can pay the head tax and may legally come into this country; we do not want him anyway. He is poor immigrant stock.'[99] The inexactness of this description (whose members were to be detected by local family history studies) and

---

[95] LC MD Papers of Calvin Coolidge, File 133 (Reel 78), Department of Labor, Memorandum, 'In the matter of cooperation between officers of States and Municipalities with officers of the United States in connection with the enforcement of the Immigration Laws', 14 pp., Oct. 1923, p. 2.

[96] LC MD Papers of Franklin MacVeagh, Box 31, Folder: Immigration Protection League 1905–28, Immigration Protection League Bulletin No. 28, Feb. 1928, 'Fake Economy'.

[97] 'Biological Aspects of Immigration', hearings before the Committee on Immigration and Naturalization, HR 66th Congress, 2nd Session, 17 Apr. 1920, p. 10.

[98] Ibid. 11.   [99] Ibid. 12.

TABLE 4.4 State expenses for Maintaining State Institutions for the 'Socially Inadequate', 1916

State	Total ($)	Rank among states	% of total state expenses for this purpose	Rank among states
Alabama	425,018	40	5.4	48
Arizona	255,922	45	12.7	37
Arkansas	743,372	28	18.5	16
California	3,228,827	6	15.4	24
Colorado	684,053	31	18.1	17
Connecticut	1,503,022	14	20.5	10
Delaware	91,782	49	10.8	45
DC	345,280	41	3.5	49
Florida	491,854	36	16.2	22
Georgia	836,225	26	13.4	33
Idaho	279,667	43	14.9	29
Illinois	4,665,459	4	23.7	5
Indiana	2,578,716	8	14.4	30
Iowa	2,000,997	12	22.6	7
Kansas	1,404,173	16	24.3	3
Kentucky	1,339,818	17	13.4	32
Louisiana	933,992	23	15.2	27
Maine	753,172	27	10.9	43
Maryland	1,113,561	18	16.4	19
Masssachusetts	6,322,275	2	30.5	1
Michigan	2,840,261	7	15.3	25
Minnesota	2,258,719	11	13.6	31
Mississippi	716,100	30	15.2	28
Missouri	1,885,125	13	20.0	11
Montana	589,940	34	16.4	18
Nebraska	976,516	22	23.4	6
Nevada	135,810	48	11.2	40
New Hampshire	456,840	39	22.2	8
New Jersey	2,344,680	9	13.3	34
New Mexico	186,453	46	11.6	39
New York	11,230,876	1	20.9	9
North Carolina	883,785	25	19.3	13
North Dakota	485,709	37	12.6	38
Ohio	3,966,756	5	24.6	2
Oklahoma	1,056,137	20	19.9	12
Oregon	624,676	33	16.3	21
Pennsylvania	4,772,212	3	15.2	26
Rhode Island	739,030	29	24.3	4
South Carolina	466,598	38	16.4	20
South Dakota	493,200	35	15.6	23

Table 4.4 (*Cont.*)

State	Total ($)	Rank among states	% of total state expenses for this purpose	Rank among states
Tennessee	1,058,595	19	18.7	14
Texas	2,285,383	10	12.7	36
Utah	265,194	44	9.4	47
Vermont	287,044	42	10.3	46
Virginia	968,329	24	11.2	42
Washington	998,286	21	11.2	41
West Virginia	683,983	32	18.7	15
Wisconsin	1,444,576	15	10.9	44
Wyoming	165,261	47	12.8	35
Average			17.3	

Source: Derived from 'Biological Aspects of Immigration', hearings before the Committee on Immigration and Naturalization, HR 66th Congress, 2nd Session, 17 Apr. 1920, p. 11.

consequent potential for dubious application is disturbing. All such decisions about exclusion and suitability were, in the eugenic scheme, to rest upon examination of family histories, of the sort popularized by Goddard and Dugdale, by trained experts.[100]

Laughlin believed his studies[101] influenced policy: 'I believe that these reports to the House Committee have done a great deal toward molding legislation and governmental policy in the direction of the eugenical basis for immigration control.'[102] Hubris no doubt encouraged an exaggerated sense of Laughlin's influence. In a rare admission of the difficulties of conducting his research, Laughlin observed that, 'I appreciate the fact that studies in population cannot be so definite as experiments in physics or chemistry. Still there are many important processes which govern the vicissitudes of races which can be analysed, and for which processes mathematical formulae can be found.'[103] Laughlin's caveats here were given added force in a letter from the Carnegie Institution's president to Charles Davenport. The president expected the eugenics research to take 'an important place' in the immigration debate, but cautioned that

[100] See Rafter (1988).
[101] See e.g. 'Crime and Race Descent', Oct. 1931, in Laughlin Papers, Special Collections, University Archives, Truman State University.
[102] Letter from Laughlin to Frank L. Babbott, 23 Jan. 1926, in Laughlin Papers, Folder: Letters to Babbott, C-4-3.
[103] Letter from Laughlin to President John C. Merriam, Carnegie Institution, 7 Nov. 1925, in Laughlin Papers, Folder: Letters—Immigration 1923–6, C-4-3.

interpretations should be 'exceedingly guarded lest conclusions go beyond the limits warranted by the facts and therefore ultimately diminish the effectiveness of our scientific work'.[104] One example perhaps of such unwarranted inferences was Laughlin's comparison of the racial composition of the delegates to the Constitutional Convention of 1787 with those of the members of the US Senate in the 69th Congress (1926–7). Finding that both were dominated by descendants of English immigrants Laughlin drew some firm conclusions: 'the lesson is that it behooves the American people to encourage the immigration and development of high political genius in our population. America must look forward toward raising the average intelligence of the whole people.'[105]

(iii) Selecting immigrants

Laughlin recommended tougher selection procedures for the admission of immigrants, procedures which would utilize eugenic 'family history' studies to identify signs of explicit or latent 'degeneracy' in migrants and to ensure the exclusion of potentially weaker 'members of the stock'. His judgement that modern institutional arrangements artificially sustained the lives of those who in earlier periods would have expired naturally aligns his analysis with the principles of early twentieth-century eugenic arguments about race, reproduction, and the biological sources of mental well-being and ability. Such views were commonplace among American intellectual circles and equally salient in other countries, including Britain and Germany. The comparable sort of language and allusion to the same studies (notably the classic American family histories) could be found in these other countries amongst intellectuals, experts, and enlightened figures. Expectations that eugenics held the potential for the more careful and selective breeding of races also coincided. As Laughlin explained, 'in our future immigration legislation it will be necessary to include the element of family history or biological pedigree, if we are to improve the American human stock by immigration'. The federal government had a pivotal role in such selective breeding since it controlled 'the hereditary quality of the immigration stream'.[106]

Laughlin[107] argued that the instrument of national origins quotas for

[104] Extract of letter from John Merriam to Charles Davenport included in a memorandum from Davenport to Laughlin, 26 June 1923, in Laughlin Papers, Folder: Letters—Immigration 1923–6, C-4-2.
[105] Material for Mr Frank L. Babbott, Notes on Immigration in Relation to National Fortunes, 1927, pp. 3–4, in Laughlin Papers, Folder: Immigration Commission, C-4-2.
[106] 'Analysis of America's Modern Melting Pot', Hearings before the Committee on Immigration and Naturalization, HR 67th Congress, 3rd Session, 21 Nov. 1922, p. 757.
[107] On the background to this study and Laughlin's preliminary findings from Europe see his long letter, written in Brussels, to Charles Davenport, 22 Nov. 1923, in Laughlin Papers, Folder: Field Workers, C-2-6.

admitting immigrants had to be combined with 'selection based on family stock quality'. This biological principle was much more important, he asserted, than either the USA's economic needs or its place as an asylum for the persecuted.[108] Laughlin urged, in unabashed terms, an extension of the eugenic principles first included in immigration policy in 1917: 'if "America is to remain American" we shall have to perfect the principle of selective immigration based upon high family stock standards. By national eugenics we shall have to correct the errors of past national policies of immigrants, but by new statutes which are sound biologically we can cause future immigration to improve our native family stocks.'[109] Laughlin remarked that only a proper eugenic policy avoided degeneracy of a race: 'institutionalization is the immediate palliative, but national eugenics is the long-term cure for human degeneracy.'[110]

Laughlin envisaged instituting a questionnaire requirement for potential immigrants to the United States, on which they would supply information about their individual history, physical examination, mental and educational examinations, and family stock values (secured by a 'eugenic study of 15 or 20 of the near kin'). He had high expectations about the value of this investigation into potential immigrants' family lineage:

by means of thcsc short pedigree studies, it is possible to throw some light upon the character of the individual, or enough to determine, much more surely than is done by personal examination alone, whether the individual is sound, whether he is likely to become a 'waster', whether he is of good stock, and from the soundness, initiative, natural intelligence, respect for law and order, industry, and the like, of his near kin, whether he would probably make a desirable addition to thc population of the United States.[111]

This proactive strategy was designed not only to preclude admission of the 'undesirable' immigrant but to establish a basis for selecting immigrants who would be 'a valuable addition to our national family stocks'.[112] He comfortably combined this advocacy with characterizations of the apolitical work of a scientist such as himself: 'a scientific study which has a bearing upon current political issues is always conducted under the greatest difficulty; but the scientist must, nevertheless, confine himself to facts and their analysis and must take into consideration only criticisms of

[108] 'Europe as an Emigrant-Exporting Continent; the United States as an Immigrant-Receiving Nation', Hearings before the Committee on Immigration and Naturalization, HR, 68th Congress, 1st Session, 8 Mar. 1924, p. 1237.
[109] Ibid. 1238.
[110] 'The Eugenical Aspects of Deportation', hearings before the Committee on Immigration and Naturalization, HR 70th Congress, 1st Session, 21 Feb. 1928, p. 23.
[111] 'Europe as an Emigrant-Exporting Continent; thc United States as an Immigrant-Receiving Nation', 1268.
[112] Ibid. 1269.

scientific work.'[113] This was a disingenuous juxtaposition of advocacy and impartiality. Asked explicitly whether the immigrant from northern Europe was more desirable than those from southern and eastern Europe, Laughlin declined to give an unequivocal response. It was difficult, as Laughlin's questioner, Congressman Dickstein, implied, not to draw this conclusion from the data presented and premises explicated in Laughlin's scientific research, however.

Laughlin identified some of the traits which these pre-admission questionnaires and tests would be designed to elicit. These were qualities of a 'biological order', about which it was 'possible to make biological studies ... and to make our sifting of the immigrant stream more effective by eliminating those applicants in whom the undesirable traits are disclosed'.[114] The traits were: 'truth-loving'; inventiveness and initiative; industry and common sense; the 'quality of responsibility'; and social instinct, the 'natural sense of a square deal'. Measuring these attributes certainly strikes the modern reader as ambitious. Mirroring eugenists in other countries, Laughlin wanted to move from a negative eugenic base in immigration policy—that is, one designed merely to 'eliminate the defectives'—to a positive and proactive one which selected desirable immigrants according to agreed eugenic criteria.[115]

From 1924, US inspectors played a significant role in vetting potential immigrants in their home country, a procedure Laughlin wanted strengthened, though how a questionnaire could predict accurately which individuals would become public charges was unclear. Improving these mechanisms was linked directly by Laughlin and the House Committee with the need to reinforce eugenic principles in immigration policy. Without strict controls upon immigrants, monitoring their mental conditions after arriving, and deporting those who fell victim to 'socially inadequate' flaws, Laughlin asserted that 'immigration will tend to work not toward the improvement but toward the degeneration of the American people'.[116] He told the American Eugenics Society that 'eugenical principles alone should constitute the basis for our future immigration laws and rules'.[117] Laughlin concluded that, 'unless the source of its immigrants be of a constant race and quality, no nation can suffer many such turnovers in population origin and retain its essential character.'[118]

---

[113] 'Europe as an Emigrant-Exporting Continent; the United States as an Immigrant-Receiving Nation', 1269.

[114] Ibid. 1273.　　　[115] Ibid. 1277–8.

[116] 'The Eugenical Aspects of Deportation', 46.

[117] Notes for the Fourth Report of the Committee on Selective Immigration of the American Eugenics Society, n.d., p. 1, in Laughlin Papers, Special Collections, University Archives, Truman State University.

[118] H. H. Laughlin, 'The Control of Trends in the Racial Composition of the American People', c.1928, p. 3, ibid.

Laughlin wanted three criteria, reflecting these eugenic imperatives, to be added to immigration policy: first, a higher intelligence level standard for immigrants; second, a rigorous family stock test; and third, a restriction to white races only.[119] Laughlin viewed the national origins scheme as a mechanism to make immigration consistent with the 'racial makeup of the entire people' which would 'keep America American'.[120] It was an agenda endorsed by Congressman Johnson, who concluded one committee hearing with the declaration: 'the task of our committee is to prepare proposed duties which will develop the American people along the racial and institutional lines laid down by the founders of the country, so far as the control of immigration can do it.'[121] Laughlin celebrated the passage of the 1924 law, since it committed the USA to the 'biological or eugenical basis for its immigration policy'.[122]

Laughlin's proposals were supported by the National Eugenics Society. Its subcommittee on selective immigration issued a report concerned with this topic. 'From the point of view of national eugenics', the Report's authors advanced the argument for inspection of immigrants.[123] Eugenists wanted the powers of examination of potential immigrants greatly expanded: 'we believe that it would be entirely proper to demand that he [the immigrant] produce reliable witnesses to support his own statements, even to the extent of demanding medical and other expert testimony to the effect that he is mentally and physically up to the standard required by our laws and that he belongs to sound family stock.'[124] They wanted to exclude immigrants who failed to equate with American physical, mental and moral attributes, an aim which necessitated a 'knowledge of his family as well we as his individual history'.[125] These ideas had been supported by Harry Laughlin who presented them on several occasions to the congressional committee on immigration.

Laughlin recommended a national registry of aliens, to 'follow up the

[119] 'Immigration from Countries of the Western Hemisphere', hearings before the Committee on Immigration and Naturalization, HR 70th Congress, 1st Session, 21 Feb. 1928, pp. 712–14.
[120] Notes for the Fourth Report of the Committee on Selective Immigration of the American Eugenics Society, p. 2.
[121] 'Immigration from Countries of the Western Hemisphere', hearings before the Committee on Immigration and Naturalization, HR 70th Congress, 1st Session, 21 Feb. 1928, p. 717.
[122] Letter from Laughlin to Professor Robert De C. Ward, 22 Nov. 1924, in Laughlin Papers, Folder: Robert Ward, C-4-1. See also Laughlin's later letter to Ward, 8 May 1925, ibid.
[123] NA RG 233 Records of the US HR, 69th Congress, Committee on Immigration, Committee Papers, Box 345, Folder: HR69A-20.3. Third report of the Subcommittee on Selective Immigration of the Eugenics Committee of the USA, 'The examination of Immigrants Overseas, as an Additional Safeguard in the Processes of Enforcing American Immigration Policy', 1926, 12 pp., p. 2.
[124] Ibid. 6.   [125] Ibid.

immigrant's process of naturalization and Americanization'.[126] Espousal of the need for such a national registry illustrates how the purported scientific interests of eugenists osculated with political or nationalist ends: a national registry of aliens 'would make the deportation of aliens who show certain anti-social qualities a feasible administrative possibility'. Aliens who suffered not only 'physical, mental or moral disorders' but committed crimes would be expelled; consequently, 'not only would an immediate social and economic service be performed, but the country would be protected against reproduction by these racially defective aliens'.[127] The mobilization of science for political judgements and ends is striking. Since the 'descendants of immigrants' would form the USA's 'future citizenry', Laughlin warned that 'we should therefore make the possession of desirable natural qualities one of the conditions for the admission of sexually fertile individuals'.[128]

Such themes dominated the discussion of immigration policy throughout this decade, to an extent hitherto neglected in the scholarly literature. Sufferers of mental illness (and other illnesses) were not treated as equal citizens. Eugenists also believed that, in respect to race mixing, certain groups were immiscible.

Laughlin continued to labour away at eugenic research and immigration through the next decade until his death in 1943. He prepared a report in 1939 on 'biological aspects of immigration', for the New York Chamber of Commerce's immigration committee. It echoed his earlier themes about racial qualities and marriage.[129] From the late 1920s he devoted his attention to the issue of aliens, and their registration, often finding support in the Immigration Service at the US Department of Labor.[130] In the 1930s increasing attention was given to immigration as a contributor to unemployment, though many of the so-called 'unemployables' were not immigrants.[131]

Harry Laughlin was the most energetic but not the only eugenist advising the House Committee on Immigration. Its chairman, Albert Johnson, solicited views from other eugenic scientists and developed routinized contacts with the eugenic community. He was sufficiently close to the eugenist

[126] 'Biological Aspects of Immigration', hearings before the Committee on Immigration and Naturalization, HR 66th Congress, 2nd Session, 17 Apr. 1920, p. 7.

[127] Ibid.	[128] Ibid. 8.

[129] 'Researches on the Biological Aspects of Immigration', summary, 12 pp., May 1939, in Laughlin Papers, Folder: Reports 1938–9, C-4-3.

[130] See, for example, the correspondence between H. G. Dunlap, Immigrant Inspector, and Laughlin, contained in Laughlin Papers, Folder: Registration of Aliens 1931, C-4-6. The folder includes Dunlap's memorandum on 'Registration and Deportation of Aliens'.

[131] See 'Shift in Responsibility for Inadequates', 1935, in Laughlin Papers, Folder: Immigration and Unemployment, 1935, C-4-4.

Francis Kinnicutt to request him to provide an administrative assistant for the Committee's work, and to ensure that the Eugenics Research Association's mailing list received committee papers.[132] As a keen supporter of the national origins plan, eugenists saw in Johnson a key and reliable ally. The American Eugenics Society established a Committee on Selective Immigration in the mid-1920s, whose membership included Laughlin and Kinnicutt. The Committee praised the national origins instrument, as the 'most scientific, soundest in principle and fairest to all elements in the population of any method of quota limitation which yet has been proposed'. The Society welcomed the plan's aim to treat immigrants descended from colonists and early settlers preferentially. The Committee wanted greater selectivity in the assessment of potential immigrants to ensure admission of 'only those who are superior to the median American in mental endowment as far as this is shown by approved psychological tests'.[133] Henry Fairchild, a fierce restrictionist,[134] and author of *The Melting Pot Mistake*,[135] the title of which conveyed his thesis, warned that 'indiscriminate blending' resulted in 'the mongrel type', a highly undesirable form: 'there is no question at all of the inferiority or superiority of the stocks. It is simply a question of a natural and inevitable throw-back to an earlier, more primitive generalized type. Every particular species or breed of plant or animal is produced by a process of careful selection which [intensifies] certain peculiar strains.'[136]

In 1924, the Harvard professor, Robert De C. Ward, wrote to President Calvin Coolidge to declare that, 'in signing the immigration bill you have approved one of the most important measures which has ever been put upon our statute books. You have lived up to the words of your Message of last December, that America must be kept American.'[137] The

---

[132] NA RG 233 Records of the US HR, 69th Congress, Committee on Immigration, Committee Papers, Box 341, Folder: H69A-F20.1, letter from Johnson to Kinnicutt, 28 Apr. 1926.

[133] NA RG 46 Records of the US Senate, 71st Congress, Box 172, Folder: 71A-J32. Letter from Edward T. Clark to Senator R. S. Copeland, 29 Nov. 1930, enclosing 'Immigration Programme' Committee on Selective Immigration of the American Eugenics Society, 11 Nov. 1930. The Committee members, who signed the programme, were: Madison Grant (chairman), Guy Irving Burch (Secretary), Charles W. Gould, Roswell H. Johnson, Francis H. Kinnicutt, H. H. Laughlin, John B. Trevor, Robert De C. Ward, Roy L. Garis, and Henry Pratt Fairchild.

[134] NA RG 233 Records of the US HR, 69th Congress, Committee on Immigration, Committee Papers, Box 345, Folder: HR69A-F20.3, Immigration Restriction Conference, under the auspices of the Clergy Club of New York and Neighborhood, New York, 21 Apr. 1924, proceedings, p. 4.

[135] Henry Pratt Fairchild, *The Melting-Post Mistake* (Boston: Little Brown & Co., 1926).

[136] Op. cit. n. 134 above, pp. 15, 17.

[137] LC MD, Papers of Calvin Coolidge, File 133 (Reel 79), letter from Robert De C. Ward to Coolidge, 26 May 1924.

Immigration Restriction Association assiduously maintained pressure not to abandon the national origins scheme enacted in 1924, circulating a thirty-page pamphlet, entitled 'National Origins and American Immigration', to all members of Congress in late 1928. It was written by Edward R. Lewis, a member of the executive committee.[138] Lothrop Stoddard, a eugenist in Massachusetts and author of *The Rising Tide of Color against White Supremacy*, wrote Johnson that the 'Immigration Act of 1924 is the second great turning point in America's national and racial destiny'.[139]

CONCLUSION

The making of American immigration policy in the 1920s arose from a concatenation of pressures, including economic interests, racism, ethnic cleavages, and eugenic propositions.[140] The close relationship established between the energetic proselytizer of eugenics, Dr Harry Laughlin, and the chairman of the House Committee on Immigration, Congressman Albert Johnson, demonstrates the direct representation eugenic research and arguments established in the legislative process. The national origins plan, together with the preceding quota scheme and literacy tests, were expressions of the eugenic position in that they differentiated between prospective immigrants in terms of mental or physical attributes. While the quota scheme established in 1921 can be interpreted as a reasonable policy response to a difficult question (and the resolution of which would inevitably upset some citizens), the shift to national origins appears in a different light since its premises were rooted unequivocally in issues of race and difference. Its formulation rested on judgements about who should be considered for full membership of the liberal democracy.

[138] NA RG 233 Records of the US HR, 70th Congress, Committee on Immigration, Committee Papers, Box 239, Folder: HR70A-F14.4, Edward R. Lewis, 'National Origins and American Immigration', 30 pp.

[139] NA RG 233 Records of the US HR, 69th Congress, Committee on Immigration, Correspondence, Box 342, Folder: HR69A-F20.1, letter from Stoddard to Albert Johnson, 14 Jan. 1927. The former was preparing his book *Re-Forging America*. Johnson replied obsequiously on 18 Jan., reporting that 'Captain Trevor and Francis H. Kinnicutt of New York, and J. H. Patten of Washington, are here and last night we held a conference at which I presented your letter.'

[140] This mix of factors is recognized in the major monographs, though the eugenic dimension is often underplayed. For instance, Robert Divine (1957: 9) argues of the 1921 legislation and the general shift to restriction that 'fundamentally, it was the transformation in American economic and political development that set the stage for restriction'. Divine does discuss eugenic ideas in respect of the 1924 law, however, about which he observes: 'the effect of racial theory on the Congressional mind was easily discernible', p. 14.

Several inferences germane to the book's thesis follow from this case. First, the analysis shows how eugenic arguments were unquestionably influential with immigration policy-makers; however, these propositions were employed instrumentally by restrictionists such as Albert Johnson. The eugenists' claims about racial calibrations, hierarchies, and inherited sources of severe learning disabilities were music to restrictionists' ears; had their message been less compatible with policy-makers' existing views it is improbable that eugenists would have achieved the salience they did in the legislative process. Expertise was important in this exercise in social policy but it rested upon other features of political process and was an instrument of political ends.

Second, the illiberality of the eugenists' arguments, and their violation of the equality of treatment principle celebrated in the Tocquevillian conception of American political culture, is plain.[141] Certainly, an immigration policy was both a sensible and a reasonable initiative for the US Congress but eugenic arguments enabled that policy to be constructed in terms of dubious pseudo-scientific categories with which to distinguish between individuals. Without this intellectual background, immigration restriction might have rested less obviously on such distinctions (though the existing exclusion of Chinese and Japanese immigrants implies that this conclusion would apply only to prospective European immigrants).

Finally, the close ties built between Johnson, Laughlin, and other eugenists and intellectuals parallels the policy links identified in respect of the British eugenic campaign for voluntary sterilization. This 'issue' or 'policy' network was far from immune to social and political pressures— in fact, it partially embodied them—but it was a crucial organizational mechanism through which expertise fed into policy choices, illustrating how electoral pressures and social engineering aims congeal. The eugenic network acquired a presence in Washington because of the compatibility of its members' views with prevailing policy sentiment.

Eugenics is now a discredited doctrine. The premises of eugenic arguments appear not just spurious but malevolent. Nonetheless, in the first decades of this century eugenics was a respectable area of scientific inquiry—linking anthropology with the techniques and methods of systematic scientific research—and its findings were widely circulated. Intellectual and policy-making elites in both the United States and other major western democracies (such as Britain, Canada, and some continental European polities) incorporated eugenics into their *bien-pensant* policy ambitions. Eugenic findings were applied to other public policy issues in the United States, notably the use of sterilization policy for certain

[141] Smith (1997).

categories of sufferers from mental illness.[142] Because of its categorization of members of a political community in terms of value and ability, eugenics is an anti-individualist doctrine, strikingly at variance with liberal democracy.

Debate about immigration policy in the United States during the period 1900 to 1929 (manifest in the Dillingham Commission's work, congressional committee hearings, and the national origins plan) is vitiated by a fear of inferior 'stock' or 'races' or 'nationalities' invading and commingling with the 'real American stock', that is, white descendants of the northwestern Europeans who first settled the New World colonies. African American descendants are considered as involuntary members of the US population, and basically as unassimilable. The ethos that immigrants should be assimilable with the dominant 'American race' underpinned the debates about immigration; assimilation occurred through a melting pot but the ingredients needed to be predetermined. This debate is significant for what it reveals about the notion of equality within a liberal democratic polity. In essence, immigration policy-makers were determining who would be entitled to become members of the polity and thereby have the opportunity to exercise such equal rights. In 1952, President Harry Truman characterized the law as 'a slur on the patriotism, the capacity and the decency of a large part of our citizenry'.[143]

The discussions ineluctably affected perceptions of and attitudes to those already present in the community: new immigrants—Europeans from southern and eastern Europe—were treated as less than equal in the eyes of the preceding generations of immigrants, the 'old immigrant'. This fundamental division between two sorts of potential immigrants from Europe—those consistent and easily assimilable with extant Americans and those from a distinct background (allegedly burdened with an array of imperfections and flaws)—structured the formulation of the 1924 Johnson–Reed Act and the system of quota-based admission it initiated. Consequently, US immigration policy compromised the doctrine of equality supposedly at the centre of the polity's ideology and political institutions; Congressman Adolph Sabath, a member of the House Immigration Committee, remarked that the 1924 law 'would be the first instance in our modern legislation for writing into our laws the hateful doctrine of inequality between the various component parts of our population,'[144] a view, however, which itself exposed an ignorance of segregation laws. It was an

---

[142] See Reilly (1991).

[143] Quoted in US Senate, Committee on the Judiciary 96th Congress, First Session, May 1979, *U.S. Immigration Law and Policy: 1952–1979*.

[144] 'Restriction of Immigration', HR House report No. 350, 68th Congress, 1st Session (Washington: GPO, 1924), Part II, p. 4.

inegalitarian and discriminatory decision based on notions of worth and desert incompatible with a political ideology constructed from classical liberal sources or with the principle that oppressed peoples could find refuge in the USA. It was dismantled fully in the mid-1960s.

The arguments about the true or genuine 'stock' making up Americans had malign implications for African Americans. By defining these citizens, if only *en passant*, as in essence unassimilable, the debates and decisions about immigration policy contributed powerfully to the definition of the place of black Americans as lacking full rights of citizenship in the US polity.[145] It exposed the enmity with which these citizens were viewed by the dominant white population, specifically those describing themselves as eugenically superior and direct descendants of the pure stock of colonial settlers. Individualism is now presented unproblematically as an American constitutional and ideological convention; yet its formulation in this period of eugenic-inspired debate about immigration was far from race-neutral.[146]

The importance of immigration policy in the study of the United States as a political community deserves restatement. Both the historical origins of the polity—as a society based on the resilement of an external colonial power—and the ideology of liberty and rights promoted for the new country placed individual self-worth and equality at its centre. Immigration policy broke both these precepts, settling upon group rather than individual selection for its admission choices and, amongst individuals, distinguishing desirable and undesirable types. The historical and political significance of these distinctions in the composition of the USA's individualist liberal political culture should not be overlooked.

APPENDIX

The relevant part of the Immigration Act 1924 stated:

Section 11 (*a*) The annual quota of any nationality shall be 2 per centum of the number of foreign-born individuals of such nationality resident in continental United States as determined by the United States census of 1890, but the minimum quota of any nationality shall be 100.

(*b*) The annual quota of any nationality for the fiscal year beginning July 1, 1927, and for each fiscal year thereafter, shall be a number which bears the same ratio to 150,000 as the number of inhabitants in continental United States in 1920 having that national origin (ascertained as hereinafter provided in this section) bears to the number of inhabitants in continental United States in 1920, but the minimum quota of any nationality shall be 100.

---

[145] This point is elegantly developed by Glazer (1997). See also Smith (1997).
[146] A theme of Smith's (1993) important essay. See also Fitzgerald (1996).

(*c*) For the purpose of subdivision (*b*) national origin shall be ascertained by determining as nearly as may be, in respect of each geographical area which under section 12 is to be treated as a separate country (except the geographical areas specified in (*c*) of section 4) the number of inhabitants in continental United States in 1920 whose origin by birth or ancestry is attributable to such geographical area. Such determination shall not be made by tracing the ancestors or descendants of particular individuals, but shall be based upon statistics of immigration and emigration, together with rates of increase of population as shown by successive decennial United States censuses, and such other data as may be found to be reliable.

(*d*) For the purpose of subdivisions (*b*) and (*c*) the term 'inhabitants in continental United States in 1924' does not include (1) immigrants from the geographical areas specified in subdivision (*c*) section 4 or their descendants, (2) aliens ineligible to citizenship or their descendants, (3) the descendants of slave immigrants, or (4) the descendants of American aborgines.

PART III

Liberal Amelioration and Collectivism

Introduction

COLLECTIVISM is the antithesis of the individualism celebrated by theorists and practitioners of liberal democracy. Its employment by governments in the USA and Britain posed huge political challenges if it was to be made consistent with liberal precepts. The chapters in Part III examine how these challenges were met, if not fully resolved, taking the example of work camps in the 1930s.

Social policies which violated liberal principles were defined by three features: a broad ideological appeal, a basis in expertise, and a compatibility with liberal democracy. This last characteristic is manifest in the liberal democratic tradition commitment to both social reform and individual moral improvement. They provide a consistent political stimulus for social policies designed to ameliorate the circumstances of the least well-off in society. The British doctrine of New Liberalism and the USA tradition of Progressivism were both expressions of this position. The historian of the former, Michael Freeden, explains that liberalism 'alone realized the complexity of society by encompassing within its scope both collective organization and individual incentive'.[1] Of the American context, Richard Hofstadter writes more broadly: Progressives belong to the liberal tradition in American politics which functions 'at first to broaden the numbers of those who could benefit from the great American bonanza and then to humanize its workings and help heal its casualties'. Without such ameliorative inclinations, Hofstadter concludes, the American polity would have been 'as in times and places it was, nothing but a jungle'.[2]

These national liberal ameliorative impulses were rarely as tested or mobilized as during the 1930s when the problems posed by the economic depression and mass unemployment were formidable. In the United States, the employment of collectivist institutions in the New Deal was part of the formulation, shrewdly orchestrated by Democrat President Franklin Roosevelt, of an interventionist government significantly distinct from earlier policy; nonetheless, the ideological and political problems of

[1] Freeden (1978: 161). Daniel Rodgers argues that the CCC was based in part on the plans developed between 1918 and 1920 to resettle soldiers on federal reclamation land (Rodgers 1998: 415).

[2] Hofstadter (1955a: 18).

reconciling collectivist social policy with a political culture premised on individualist liberalism were real ones which had to be confronted and resolved. British anti-unemployment policy in the 1930s was, in comparison, tepid and on a modest scale (since the movement to a social democratic welfare state and Keynesian economic policy was a post-1945 phenomenon); this modesty makes the apparent incompatibility of work camps and political tradition less visible but did not obviate the need for some such justification.

The chapters in Part III of this book examine in detail a case study from the United States and Britain of their respective experiments with work camps in the 1930s: the Civilian Conservation Corps (CCC) and Instructional Centres. The chapters examine how the idea of collectivizing the unemployed was initiated and implemented, and examine how its potential illiberalism was averted. Several sorts of rationale were formulated to justify the use of collective institutions to aid the unemployed. These included: their provision of an opportunity to 'recondition' or physically toughen up victims of long-term unemployment, making them prepared to take work were it available; that participation in a rigorous three-month camp work regime would improve the morale of the unemployed and rekindle (or instil) work habits; and that work camps could be used as a discipline, enforced to impose a work requirement upon the unemployed in receipt of benefits no longer paid from accumulated insurance contributions. The relative salience of these factors differs between the two cases strikingly. This introduction discusses some of the precursors of the interwar collectivist experiments.

CAMPS AND EXPERTISE BEFORE 1930

The idea of using camps or colonies to deal with social problems such as vagrancy, unemployment, and various forms of illness, including mental ones,[3] was popular in the closing decades of the nineteenth century. Camps (or colonies) were advocated as institutions in which to concentrate sections of the unemployed or other marginal groups such as vagrants. They were also used for people suffering from mental illnesses, such as the Epileptic Colony at Lynchsburg, Virginia, or equivalents in Britain.[4] From an empirical point of view, many of the problems confronting western societies in the nineteenth and twentieth centuries arose from groups of citi-

---

[3] For instance, camps were used in parts of Britain and the United States for the confinement of epileptics, and for people with some sorts of mental illness. For the European origins of this strategy see Pick (1989).
[4] Thomson (1998), ch. 3.

zens either lacking productive work or gathering together idly in large numbers. It was hardly surprising therefore that, in the inter-war decades, some intellectuals and policy-makers should propose confining or collectivizing groups of such citizens to deal with their specific problems. Such proposals were advocated by a range of individuals and groups interested in addressing unemployment and the related sores of vagrancy and idleness, including philanthropists, politicians, social reformers, and clergymen.

Speaking in the House of Commons in 1903 the Liberal MP, Herbert Samuel, enthused about colonies to lock up vagrants. He cited, approvingly, European practice: 'if such institutions were established in this country they would do much to prevent these deliberate idlers and wastrels becoming burdens on the ratepayers in workhouses or on the taxpayers in prisons.'[5] From the 1880s, support for 'labour colonies' to alleviate unemployment grew in Britain.[6] In several continental European countries, confinement was promoted as a solution to the problem of marginality: tramps, vagrants, and more generally the unemployed were identified as apposite candidates of camps.[7] In Britain this strategy complemented proposals to set aside farm land to be worked by unemployed people. Speaking in Parliament in 1903, the Labour leader, Keir Hardie, urged his parliamentary colleagues to 'devise some means whereby to provide every willing Englishman with an opportunity of working for his living.'[8] Hardie identified land reclamation schemes—a common activity in labour colonies—as suitable work for such publicly funded programmes: 'the Haarlem Lake was reclaimed and 46,000 acres were added to the arable land of Holland, and now the Government of Holland propose to reclaim from the Zuyder Zee a million acres by the same means. If that can be done in Holland it can also be done in England.'[9] Reforestation was instanced by Hardie as a suitable task for public works schemes (a theme he repeated in later sessions[10]). As centres of sustained work, labour colonies periodically gained supporters, especially when unemployment grew. Their deployment was on occasion linked with a punitive component. Thus the English Poor Law Commissioners, reporting in 1909,

[5] *Hansard*, vol. cxviii [Fourth Series] House of Commons, 19 Feb. 1903, cols. 317–18. Samuel represented Yorkshire West Riding, Cleveland. He also cited the colony at Merxplas in Belgium.
[6] See Freeden (1978) for the intellectual background amongst the opinion-forming elite and, for details of policies, Harris (1972).
[7] For details see *Report on Agencies and Methods for Dealing with the Unemployed*, PP vol. lxxxii (London: HMSO C-7182; 1893–4), Part IV.
[8] *Hansard*, vol. cxviii [Fourth Series] House of Commons, 18 Feb. 1903, cols. 252–3.
[9] Ibid. cols. 253–4.
[10] *Hansard*, vol. cxxx [Fourth Series] House of Commons, 19 Feb. 1904, cols. 458–9.

recommended establishing labour camps for malingerers. The principal models were German and Dutch ones.

The nineteenth-century model

German labour colonies were established in the 1880s, with twenty-six in place by 1892. The Germans established labour colonies for three reasons: first, for economic motives, principally the dislocation of industry prompted by the 'commercial collapse succeeding the inflation of trade due to the payment of the war indemnity by France'; second, philanthropic Conservatives wished to tackle poverty to 'counterbalance the propaganda of the Social Democrats', a strategy exemplified by Bismarck's social reforms; and third, colonies were set up in a 'spirit of humanitarianism'.[11] The colonies were funded with grants from the government and charitable donations. The colonies were a form of 'Christian charity', to which 'all able-bodied men who are willing to work are admitted without distinction of character or religion as there is room'.[12] Most colonists were 'able-bodied, and most past middle age', and while some were plainly alcoholic, many others were victims of misfortune: 'a typical sort of case was that of a clerk who had got into some trouble, lost his situation, and could not get another, till at last his clothes became so bad that no one would employ him. By working in the colony he will be able to buy new ones, and in the meantime the manager is trying to find a place for him.'[13] The colonies' welcome did not extend to 'dipsomaniacs', despite aiming 'to secure the permanent moral elevation of the colonists'. Board and lodging and, importantly, pay was to be lower than prevailing local wages, a measure ensuring that the camps accommodated rather than distorted the labour market.[14]

Of the German labour colonies, twenty-three were agricultural ones, and only two were located in cities (Berlin and Hamburg); the final colony was a 'Home colony,' a place of resort for families, at Friedrich-Wilhelmsdorf, near Bremerhaven.[15] In total, the colonies provided 3,044 places. In the ten years ending in 1893, 63,394 persons entered the colonies, of whom 61,334 had been discharged. The mean residency was a period of over 100 days. Administrators endeavoured to shift people through the colonies quickly. The maximum period of residence permitted was two years. This stipula-

---

[11] *Report on Agencies and Methods for Dealing with the Unemployed*, 269.
[12] Ibid. 270.
[13] *Report on German Vagrancy and the Workmen's Colonies*, *PP* vol. lxxx (London, 1888), 47.
[14] *Report on Agencies and Methods for Dealing with the Unemployed*, 270.
[15] Ibid. 271.

tion was often evaded, with some of the colonists becoming 'practically permanent residents'.[16]

Discharges from colonies reflected several reasons. Thus, 2,623 obtained employment or 'situations' during this period though of these 814 were subsequently readmitted to the labour colonies. Of 8,564 who left of their own wish, almost 40 per cent—3,117—returned within two years of their discharge. Some colonists made a practice of enrolling in several camps sequentially, earning the German sobriquet 'colony-bummler' from the German verb *bummel*, to loaf.[17] Overall, in twenty-two colonies between 1889 and 1891, 46.3 per cent of the enrollees had enrolled more than once.[18] These data imply that labour camps were acting as temporary residential institutions for parts of the German population unable to manage their own lives.

The most common previous condition for colonists in the German labour colonies was that of prisoner: a startling 76 per cent of the colonists had been in prison, a history which exacerbated the difficulty of finding employment.[19] There was a seasonal bias to the camps' population size, with winter months a favoured time for enrollees needing to escape harsh climatic conditions. Eighty per cent of the enrollees were single.[20]

Work in the labour colonies did not affect local labour market wage rates adversely since its scale and character were both modest. Anticipating twentieth-century trends, the principle of conservation, or in this case land reclamation, as suitable employment for the able-boded unable to find work determined the activity undertaken in the camps. Since most of the German colonies were located in rural regions, agricultural reclamation was an intelligent option, even if in some of them the level at which it was conducted was primitive: 'hand labour' was used when 'mechanical appliances might be adopted with advantage'.[21]

Under Pastor von Bodelschwingh's direction, the Wilhelmsdorf colony expanded its living area and constructed a network of roads, superseding the single route initially available for access. The camp included meadow land, forest, and plantings of potatoes, rye, maize, buckwheat, wheat, lupis, vegetables as well as beet for fodder. In common with most colonies, including twentieth-century imitators, Wilhemsdorf was quite remotely situated, five miles from a town and nine from the nearest inn.

No wages were paid for the first fourteen days of enrolment though enrollees were supplied, if needed, with clothes (on credit). Wages were not paid until enrollees left the colony permanently, at which point many

---

[16] Ibid. 272. [17] Ibid. 281. [18] Ibid. 282. [19] Ibid. 274.
[20] Ibid. 280. [21] Ibid. 289.

TABLE III.1 Timetable and diet at Wilhemsdorf colony

Routine:	Winter	Late Spring	Summer
Rising: weekdays	5.0–5.30	4.30	4.0
Sundays	6.0–6.30	6.0	6.0
First breakfast	5.20–5.50	4.50	4.20
Morning Service	5.40–6.10	5.10	4.40
Second breakfast	9.0	8.30	8.30
Dinner	12.0	12.0	12.0
Afternoon meal (in the fields)	—	3.30	3.30
Supper	5.50	7.0	8.0

Menu:	
First breakfast	Coffee, black bread, beet jelly.
Second breakfast	Lard or butter or cheese, black bread.
Dinner	Vegetables with potatoes, pig's fat three times a week.
Afternoon meal	Coffee, bread, and lard.
Supper	Milk (or rice or peas), soup, potatoes, herring occasionally.

Source: derived from Parliamentary Papers (1893–4), *Report on Agencies and Methods for Dealing with the Unemployed, PP* vol. lxxxii HMSO C-7182, pp. 294–5.

were apparently in debt and received no cash. This fiscal condition raised issues at the heart of the camp experiment:

what occurs is simply that men come for a few weeks to the colonies, get clothes on credit, and then go off on the tramp. If, on the other hand, the colony were permitted to detain a colonist until his clothes had been paid for, there would at once be an infringement of the principle of liberty of movement which the colonies hold sacred, and the door would be open to some of the incidents of the sweating system which might, in spite of the philanthropic character of the colonies, work to their disadvantage.[22]

Commitment to the 'principle of liberty of movement' is instructive of the constraints upon such collectivist experiments.

Once at the colony, enrollees adhered to a standard routine and diet, as Table III.1 summarizes. The majority worked as fieldworkers, with a small number able to work at the trade in which they were skilled such as shoemaker, joiner, smith, or mason.

The principal work activity was land reclamation, achieved through the method of trenching. In the summer time all the men were assigned to harvest work.

[22] *Report on Agencies and Methods for Dealing with the Unemployed*, 293.

Dutch labour colonies began in 1818, founded at Frederiksoord by a charity, the Society of Beneficence. There were two types, one known as 'free colonies', the other 'beggar colonies' at which the regime was close to a penal one, and to which some of the inmates were sentenced: begging was punishable by imprisonment in Holland, and those convicted could opt instead to spend 'a certain number of years in the forced or pauper colonies'.[23] Unlike German colonies, the Dutch free colonies were populated by families, and residence was often permanent. At the colony at Willemsoord, there were, in 1892, twenty-two families engaged in agricultural work. The education of children was attempted: 'attendance at the day or evening school is compulsory. There are five elementary schools on the colony lands maintained at the expense of the Government, and, in addition, the colony has established (a) a School of Forestry, (b) a School of Agriculture, (c) a School of Horticulture. In these institutions the children of the colonists are trained and sent out at from 20 to 22 years of age to situations.'[24] However, permanency of residence, admission of families— who lived together—and provision of educational services in the Dutch free colonies not only boosted their cost but ran the danger of 'producing a class of workers who tend to become quite dependent—tend, indeed, to produce *a permanent race of paupers*'.[25] The camps did not inculcate self-sufficiency or independence. Charged with assessing the scheme's suitability for Scotland, Sir John McNeill concluded that few Dutch families—after three decades of the colony—had progressed toward self-sufficiency. McNeill's conclusions were unpromising: 'the free colonies, after an experience of thirty-four years, are not only a complete failure, but there is no reason to believe that the scheme could possibly have succeeded.'[26] McNeill was equally despairing about the children of free colonists who, despite acquiring reasonable educations, '*had not learned to trust to their own exertions for a livelihood*, and there are few of them who were able to maintain themselves'.[27] The failure of agricultural toil to extract a decent return from the colonists seemed, to McNeill, to arise from inevitable human attributes and follies: thus the 'principle of demanding a present sacrifice for the sake of a distant benefit', which he believed informed the colony, was regrettably 'precisely the kind of virtue that the improvident classes are least capable of exercising'.[28] McNeill was equally gloomy about the effects of training upon colonists' capacity to acquire

---

[23] For an early assessment see Report by Sir John McNeill, Dec. 1853, on Free and Pauper Colonies in Holland, Appendix A to Eighth Annual Report of the Board of Supervision for Relief of the Poor (Scotland), *PP*, vol. xxix (1854), 8.

[24] *Report on Agencies and Methods for Dealing with the Unemployed*, 314.

[25] Ibid. 316, emphasis added.

[26] Report by Sir John McNeill, Dec. 1853, on Free and Pauper Colonies in Holland, p. 7.

[27] Ibid. 8.   [28] Ibid. 11.

gainful employment after leaving, concluding that 'the training in the colonies is not more effectual than the measures resorted to in other countries for reclaiming a class which, from peculiarities of constitution and of circumstances, appear to be born only to live upon the labour of others'.[29]

Britain was not alone in looking to experience and policies in other countries as ways of addressing unemployment. The same phenomenon is apparent in the United States, as the historian Udo Sautter observes: 'from the 1890s a search for inspiration from overseas was quite evident.'[30] The Massachusetts Bureau of Labor Statistics published a report in 1894 documenting in great detail the use of labour colonies in Germany, Holland, Belgium, Austria, Switzerland, England, and New Zealand.[31] Proposals to shift the unemployed back to the land were also aired in the late nineteenth century, including bills in Congress federally to finance such initiatives. Farm colonies, as rural equivalents of poor houses, were also discussed as a serious policy option in several states but not acted upon.

Twentieth-century camps

Camps were also established as voluntary institutions to assist the unemployed acquire skills for labour market participation. This approach was adopted by the Salvation Army in Britain and the United States; and, in another variant, by Franklin Roosevelt through his New Deal agency, the Civilian Conservation Corps. A prototype of this approach was formulated and implemented in New York State in the years immediately prior to the Roosevelt New Deal administration. Camp Bluefield, was established by NYC's Department of Public Welfare. The Department selected 200 unemployed men, previously accommodated in the Municipal Lodging House in the city, paid them $6.00 a week (funded by the state's Temporary Emergency Relief Administration), and put them to work on conservation tasks. This novel collectivism yielded promising results: 'there has been a decided improvement in the morale of the men, and an average gain of 7 pounds per man in their weight. They have satisfactorily done forestry and landscape work under the supervision of the Palisades Interstate Park Commission.'[32] Camp Bluefield became a model for the CCC.

In California, a gubernatorially appointed committee recommended

[29] Report by Sir John McNeill, Dec. 1853, on Free and Pauper Colonies in Holland, p. 11.

[30] Sautter (1991: 31).

[31] Massachusetts Bureau of Statistics of Labor, *24th Annual Report 1894* (Boston: Massachusetts Bureau of Statistics of Labor, 1894), 4–77, cited in Sautter (191: 32).

[32] NARA RG 35 Records of the CCC, Division of Selection General Correspondence 1933–42, Box 4, File: Camps and Projects. Ralf Astrofsky, 'Work Relief Camps in Present Emergency', 20 Mar. 1933, 4 pp., p. 1.

using camps for unemployed citizens. The first state work camp was opened on 31 December 1931, heralding the state-wide labour camp scheme. It was another influential forerunner of Roosevelt's Civilian Conservation Corps. By the middle of 1932, California had established 28 forestry and 2 highway work camps, absorbing in total 3,532 men, of which total 1,593 were located in camps in Southern California and 1,759 in camps in Northern California. There was no payment, with only food, clothing, shelter, and tobacco provided. Enrolment was voluntary: 'no drones were tolerated. Every man had to work or quit, but every man had the alternative of quitting if he did not want to work. No man was under obligation to stay, provided he did not try to sneak off with the clothing given to him. Indeed, if he wouldn't work he was put out.'[33] Another influence upon the 'camp for unemployed' strategy was the work of the Economic Conservation Committee of America, based in California. This voluntary organization proposed creating 'Guest Camps' to provide industrial training for transient, homeless youth.[34] The Californian initiative was inspired in particular by the palpable wastage of surplus fruit and vegetable products at a time when many Americans were emaciated with hunger. The Committee wanted not simply to prevent hunger and to house transient young Americans but aimed ambitiously to lay 'a foundation for future citizenship' in these latter through the camps. It recommended that the 'Guest Camp Plan be set up in the Department of Labor, as a national program, under the administration of a Federal Director at Washington'. Confinement of the unemployed was not an end in itself:

it is clear that the "Guest Camp" program is not intended as a mere "Camp" to simply feed these youths and keep them out of the cities and off the highways and freight trains, but a semi-long range constructive program, covering perhaps one to three years, to provide these youths with suitable industrial training, certain phases of schooling, together with a part time work program, recreation, etc. but all bent toward the one purpose of equipping them for employment and a useful life. . . . [I]n addition to providing a form of semi-self government, it will also serve as a laboratory study of citizenship.[35]

This theme of residential camps as places for inculcating citizenship values is one which recurs throughout the 1930s. Labour colonies illustrate the concern of nineteenth-century welfare reformers to siphon off the

---

[33] Samuel G. Blythe, 'Camps for Jobless Men', *Saturday Evening Post*, 27 May 1933, p. 9.
[34] NARA RG 35 Records of the CCC, Division of Selection General Correspondence 1933–42, Box 4, File: Camps and Projects. Economic Conservation Committee of America, 'Skeleton Outline of Proposed Plan of "Guest Camps" for Industrial Training for Unemployed Homeless Youths', n.d. 4 pp. The Committee's Executive Secretary for J. B. McCleskey. See his article 'Economic Conservation Made Practical', *Plant Flower and Fruit Guild Magazine* (May 1932). [35] Ibid. 3.

undeserving or vagrant—always an ambiguously defined category—from the benefits of any government intervention in the labour market.

At the Salvation Army farm colony established in Essex in 1890, the work consisted of farm labouring and brickmaking. The Farm Colony idea was promoted in General Booth's proclamation for the Salvation Army: he declared that 'there is any amount of waste land in the world, not far away in distant Continents, next door to the North Pole, but here at our very doors.'[36] Booth envisaged recruiting unemployed able-bodied men from cities for the Farm Colony. The Army purchased 3,000 acres at the village of Hadleigh in the face of some local hostility: the local villagers feared a 'colony of rascals'. 'Able-bodied' was defined as willingness to work regardless of previous destitution. This specification enabled the Army to discriminate amongst applicants: 'very few men who are not willing to work come to the Colony—a fact which says much for its value as a sifter of loafers.'[37] In the 1890s, the Army frequently received applicants from workhouses. Work was the Colony's rationale: 'the Colony is intended only for those who cannot obtain occupation elsewhere, and who are prepared to work, having shelter and maintenance only provided in exchange for their labour.'[38] Each colonist had to sign an agreement with the Salvation Army, before joining the Colony, which included a commitment to the rules, abstinence ('I understand that any departure from this rule may be followed by my instant dismissal'), avoiding profane language, and submitting to 'sole Arbitration of the Governor' to solve conflicts.[39] Similar farm colonies were established in the United States during the 1890s by the American branch of the Army—in Romie (California), Amity (Colorado), and Herrick (Ohio).[40]

Charles Booth's scheme was criticized by the philosopher and Charity Organization Society (COS) officer, Bernard Bosanquet. Bosanquet published a pamphlet attacking Booth's colony scheme, as the historian McBriar reports: 'Bosanquet was willing to allow that a "very carefully dis-

[36] Branwell Booth, *In Darkest England and the Way out* (London: Salvation Army, 1890), 124. In 1890 the Army opened a labour exchange in London which within six months had received applications from 2,462 men and 208 women; ibid. 113.

[37] *Hadleigh: The Story of a Great Endeavour* (London: International Heritage Centre, Salvation Army, 1902), 14.

[38] *The Darkest England Social Scheme: A Brief History of the First Year's Work* (London: International Heritage Centre, Salvation Army, 1891), 59.

[39] By the end of 1894, 1,616 men had spent time at the Colony, of whom 128 left immediately; of the remaining 1,488, 51 were restored to friends, 283 were sent to jobs obtained for them through the Colony, 51 enlisted in the armed forces, 602 left with jobs in prospect, 6 left as satisfactory cases but with no positions in view, 146 left without giving notice, and 349 were discharged as unsatisfactory. Branwell Booth, *Working Darkest England* (London: International Heritage Centre, Salvation Army, 1894), 49.

[40] Spence (1985).

criminatory small scheme" of a farm colony might serve as a "healthy open air workhouse" for the few cases who slipped through the COS's fingers and who might be restored to industry, but he was sure that a big scheme would prove disastrously unsuccessful'.[41] The COS's individualist approach to poverty—whereby each pauper was treated as an individual case and a strategy designed for him or her—was superior, Bosanquet believed, to that proposed of lumping together sufferers in a farm or labour colony.

In Britain, the principle of providing some activity for unemployed men was commonly presented to investigative committees. Farm and labour colonies were proposed to the 1905–9 Royal Commission on the Poor Laws. George Lansbury, from the Poplar district in London, recommended that 'all able-bodied men applying for Poor Law relief should be sent to colonies or institutes in the country, where the entire work shall be reclamatory and in no way penal'.[42] Writing to the 1905–9 Royal Commission on the Poor Laws, Lansbury outlined his plan for three types of labour colonies, which McBriar characterizes as his 'hobby-horse':[43] first for vagrants; second for 'ordinary able-bodied paupers applying regularly for relief'; and third, colonies for the ordinary unemployed.[44] As late as 1931, Beatrice Webb argued before a Royal Commission that the provision of publicly funded training should be undertaken irrespective of whether jobs existed, since its purpose should be to fill the time of the unemployed. She stated:

the experience of the Ministry of Labour has been that they hesitate to put people into training unless they feel that there is some good prospect of employment afterwards. I think that this is a mistaken feeling. The provision of training is for the purpose of preventing deterioration by idleness. It has nothing to do with preventing future unemployment. The question is what effect it has on the person, and in preventing unnecessary claims.[45]

Logically this view, presented by a respected expert on unemployment and relief, would support the principle of reconditioning institutionalized in the instructional centres established in the 1930s in Britain (discussed in Chapter 5).

What did these nineteenth- and early twentieth-century experiments suggest about the utility of work camps as a solution to unemployment and what problems did they pose to liberal democratic values? First, the Dutch

[41] McBriar (1987: 60–1).
[42] Jackson and Pringle Report to the Royal Commission on the Poor Laws, Cd. 4795, p. 22, cited in McBriar (1987: 51).
[43] McBriar (1987: 220).
[44] Quoted ibid. from a letter from George Lansbury to Beatrice Webb, 23 Apr. 1907.
[45] Minutes of Evidence to the Royal Commission on Unemployment Insurance, 12 Nov. 1931, p. 1336.

and German system were clearly dominated by the problems of ex-prisoners and vagrants rather than of the unemployed. German and Dutch experience suggested that work colonies were appropriate for suppressing beggars, clearing the highways of tramps, or housing discharged prisoners. As solutions to the problems of bona fide workmen, the parliamentary report in 1893 doubted their contribution: 'a labour colony open to all comers would speedily be occupied by the vagrant and the discharged prisoner ... The hard working man of reputable life who seeks the colony because he is out of employment is exceedingly rare, if he exists at all. The classes will not mix, to admit the one is to exclude the other.'[46] This generalization prompted the recommendation that, if such collective measures were deployed, two types of camps be established: one for the 'vagrant and the loafer' open to all comers, and an alternative selective system for the 'worthy unemployed on the principle of "selection" or at least "investigation" '.[47] The administrative problems associated with such a selective system were, however, immense and likely to delay the dispensation of urgently needed relief. With the mass unemployment of the 1930s neither the British nor the US governments could choose to disregard any possible remedies, including work camps, though the way in which this scheme was implemented differed significantly between the two polities in terms of voluntariness, public visibility, and the morale of the recruits. Furthermore, the selection criteria employed in the USA were designed to exclude the undesirable from admittance.

Nineteenth-century labour camps were pragmatic and experimental responses to poverty, vagrancy, and unemployment. While some of their advocates pontificated rather grandly about the physical and spiritual virtues accruing from life in the outdoors and 'honest toil', that these benefits would in fact be forthcoming lacked a compelling evidential basis, and evaluation of collectivist experiments revealed modest results. As such, they were quintessential pragmatic responses to social problems in a liberal democracy: mostly voluntary and well intentioned, work camps nonetheless rather lacked decisive intellectual rationales as policies, a deficiency rendered all the more glaring by their establishment in liberal democracies committed to individualism and market sovereignty. Beatrice Webb's advocacy (and that of others in the 1909 Poor Law report) rested in speculative hope about the potential for 'reconditioning' rather than in well-formulated argument rooted in evidence. To be made democratically acceptable, two points stand out: entry to camps was voluntary and departure could be effected at any time; and second, few of these experiments identified satisfactory work activities with which to occupy their residents,

---

[46] *Report on Agencies and Methods for Dealing with the Unemployed*, 337.
[47] Ibid.

falling back instead upon manual toil and hence posed no threat to regular labour market participation. Both features apply to the cases examined in Chapters 4 and 5, though far more so in respect of the British than the American experiment.

CAMPS AND THE POLITICS OF HARD TIMES

In the 1930s, the pressure on British and American politicians to respond imaginatively and creatively to that decade's unemployment and misery was intense. In both countries, policy advice was divided between traditionalists' (for instance, at the British Treasury) reluctance to take novel economic steps, and other economists and experts who urged the adoption of new government policies to stimulate economic activity and fund employment (by, for instance, permitting the public sector deficit to rise) or alternatives to employment (such as public works schemes or work camps). The porousness of the US polity permitted the latter sorts of proposals to have a greater influence there. Retrospectively, the most significant aspect of new ideas for economic and social policy in the 1930s was the nascent forms of Keynesianism implemented, even if the influence of Keynes was indirect in the way Peter Hall notes: 'the reflationary programs of the interwar period often owed little to Keynes' own ideas but could be described in more general terms as Keynesian.'[48] It was what we now think of as Keynesian-type ideas which provided the principal alternative to the economic orthodoxy present in the inter-war decade. Public works projects plainly fitted with this approach, one sufficiently broad to include the USA's Civilian Conservation Corps (CCC). British work camps have a more nebulous origin, however.

Although the British Labour Party had long talked about settlement and small holding schemes, work camps were less commonly advanced. The National Government, in place from 1931, was inherently cautious about policy innovation, a caution matched amongst senior civil servants in the Bank of England and especially the Treasury, about which Weir and Skocpol declare: 'the key to bureaucratic inertia in the 1920s and 1930s can be found in the organizational and intellectual stranglehold that one ministry, the Treasury, had gained over all other government departments inside the British civil service.'[49] Post-First World War administrative reforms in the British civil service induced, according to Weir and Skocpol, 'a profound bias against policy innovations contravening economic orthodoxy', throughout the 'entire British state apparatus'.[50] Despite the

---

[48] Hall (1989: 7).   [49] Weir and Skocpol (1985: 127).   [50] Ibid.

existence of a separate Labour Ministry potentially open to policy ideas and proposals in respect of unemployment, it was the Treasury which took the decisions. The Labour Ministry's historian, Rodney Lowe, confirms this view observing that in the inter-war decades the 'Ministry's least developed role . . . was that of an economic department'.[51] It singularly failed, in Lowe's judgement, to establish itself, 'in rivalry to the Treasury, as a centre of "alternative" economic advice'.[52] Nonetheless, officials at the Labour Ministry did not lack for diagnoses of the causes and consequences of unemployment. They formed the view that it was structural and that those parts of the country most adversely affected required regional policy, both in terms of greater industry and provision of training for the unemployed. The Labour Ministry argued, in the 1930s, that the market was not clearing spontaneously and that some effort to alleviate the regional correlation of high unemployment and few jobs was imperative. The policy of transferring unemployed men to areas where jobs were available (originally a Liberal Party proposal) was developed in the late 1920s by civil servants in the Ministry partly to address this need. This measure was applied to the so-called 'distressed areas'. These 'distressed areas' were also the principal target of the scheme of 'reconditioning' work camps initiated in 1930, the subject of Chapter 5.

The collectivist ethos of the New Deal programmes and agencies, which extended to the CCC, ran counter to American political culture.[53] Both the idea of publicly funded work and the principle of providing unconditional relief were incongruous with prevailing values. Nonetheless, the scale of the crisis in the 1930s compelled the federal government, galvanized by Franklin Roosevelt's New Deal, vastly to expand its relief of hardship. Massive work relief projects, orchestrated under the Works Progress Administration (WPA), put millions of unemployed men to work.[54] Other initiatives such as the National Youth Administration (NYA), the Public Works Administration, and the CCC were also animated by the principle of work—getting unemployed men into physical activities to train them for work. Most of the workers on these public schemes were taken from relief rolls. These projects—some of which produced valuable public buildings and notable works of art—were principally means of occupying the unemployed, as Patterson rightly notes: New Dealers 'never claimed to be doing much more than keeping people busy. Anxious to relieve unemployment in the here and now, they . . . concentrated on tiding workers over until the emergency disappeared.'[55]

---

[51] Lowe (1986: 191).   [52] Ibid. 192.
[53] For an influential statement of the USA's individualist tradition, see Hartz (1955).
[54] For excellent analyses see Amenta (1998), Kesselman (1978), and Leuchtenburg (1963).
[55] Patterson (1981: 65).

Roosevelt and his close adviser Harry Hopkins were keen that recipients of assistance should do something in exchange for it, an aim which prompted founding the Public Works Administration (PWA): 'from his earliest days as Governor of New York Roosevelt had consistently maintained that relief was normally a local responsibility and had expressed his dislike of anything approaching a dole.'[56] Kesselman records 'Roosevelt and Hopkins's distaste for providing a dole to persons able to work. They justified the higher cost of work relief by the increased worker morale and the additional useful output.'[57] Politically, Roosevelt justified such measures as consistent with the USA's commitment to individual rights. In one address, the President defined the role of modern government as that of assisting 'the development of an economic declaration of rights, an economic constitutional order'.[58] Political scientist Daniel Tichenor comments of Roosevelt's statement that the 'recasting of American liberalism in fact demanded a sense of communal responsibility, one in which citizens share in, or at least support, the enterprise of attaining a basic standard of economic integration for all members'.[59] The historian Alan Brinkley argues that although Roosevelt instinctively recoiled from 'deep ideological commitments', he was 'not without beliefs', and from his wife's uncle, Theodore Roosevelt, Franklin Roosevelt 'derived a lasting commitment to a highly nationalistic view of government, a belief that Washington had an important role to play in the life of the nation'.[60] This view was on display once he entered office during the Great Depression.

The desire to help the unemployed was cultivated within certain basic principles about work. Work programmes cost close to 40 per cent more than providing direct relief.[61] The value of the work undertaken on 1930s federal relief schemes increased, however, as the decade advanced. The WPA was responsible for heavy construction jobs undertaken on contracts. Its political status was vulnerable, as Kesselman correctly stresses; many members of Congress remained unpersuaded of the value or acceptability of such a large public programme: 'political pressure reduced the WPA to a scale below that desired by many advisers to the President . . . It is notable that the WPA appropriations acts up to mid-1939 specified that funds could be used for direct relief as well as for work relief. Moreover, the Taber amendment to the 1942 appropriations act—which aimed to replace the WPA with direct relief—was just narrowly defeated.'[62] Thus,

---

[56] Brock (1988: 270).   [57] Kesselman (1978: 161–2), and see Brinkley (1998: 22).
[58] Cited in Milkis (1993: 42).   [59] Tichenor (1995: 270).   [60] Brinkley (1998: 8).
[61] An estimate of 37% in respect of the WPA is provided in E. W. Gilboy, *Applicants for Work Relief: A Study of Massachusetts Families under the FERA and WPA* (Cambridge, Mass.: Harvard University Press, 1940).
[62] Kesselman (1978: 164).

the public works programmes of the 1930s were always contested and this absence of broad ideological appeal differentiates ameliorative liberalism from the other two examples examined in this study. Supporters wanted them tied to traditional American values of self-sufficiency and work. Critics disputed their economic utility, feared their effect on private economic activity, and charged that such collectivism was a breach with American political values.[63] Such opinions usually coincided with the view that work relief should be more concerned with extracting an activity from recipients of assistance, than with serving a defensible economic purpose. As a consequence, by the end of the 1930s, 'the whole idea of work relief was under attack from increasingly conservative critics',[64] and even its defenders rarely cited the WPA retrospectively as an argument in favour of public employment schemes.

Setting aside these criticisms, the new collectivist measures differed from workfare schemes. The ethos of participation in these New Deal programmes differed fundamentally from nineteenth-century schemes: it was voluntary, with little punitive or disciplinary content. It was bandage work rather than social engineering or constructivism, a point Patterson makes fairly, and which he appropriately contrasts with the ethos of Lyndon Johnson's Great Society in the 1960s, in which programmes the aim was significantly to enhance the labour market prospects of participants by education and training; for the most part, the New Deal programmes had no such ambitions: 'during the Depression public officials were coping with an emergency situation and did not have time for social engineering. They were relatively free of paternalistic notions about changing people.'[65] Nevertheless, as in the British reconditioning camps, the work ethic held centre-stage in the measures, a point underlined by William Brock in respect of the WPA programme: 'the philosophy of the right to work could be criticized as being no more than a restatement of the work ethic. It was the individual's function to work, and if private business was unable to provide employment, it was the duty of government to do so. Though WPA administrators often criticized business behavior, it could be argued that their function was to keep the labor force occupied and content until industry was ready to take up the slack.' Crucially, 'the right to work did not imply a right to refuse work.'[66] New Deal works projects embodied an unresolved dualism, between their role as a part of the relief process, in which men worked for benefits, and their part in a more ambitious approach to economic planning. Brock suggests that Harry Hopkins and other administrators such as Aubrey Williams, were 'prudent social engineers'[67] within the limited potential of the WPA projects. They were

---

[63] See Hoover (1938) for instance.   [64] Patterson (1981: 67).
[65] Patterson (1981: 65).   [66] Brock (1988: 353).   [67] Brock (1988: 354).

undoubtedly prudent and pragmatic, cognizant of cultural and democratic limits to any expansion of the federal government's role. By stressing that work was not being offered to everybody, New Dealers attempted to bolster its value. Harry Hopkins, Roosevelt's close associate and key architect of the New Deal, declared that 'the purpose of the Works Progress Administration is to provide useful work for particular groups of people in their particular skills. It was not our purpose to provide work for everybody.'[68] It was not, therefore, a workfare scheme rooted in liberal contractarianism. WPA workers had to come from the relief rolls, targeting the long-term unemployed, and penalizing men recently made redundant.

One exception, nonetheless, to this general pattern was the Civilian Conservation Corps (CCC) programme, which did have ambitions to train participants to improve their employment prospects, and aimed also to 'tone up' or 'toughen' recruits. It had a mild social engineering ethos, its administrators eager to inculcate patriotism and citizenship. The CCC also seems to have succeeded in an aspect which most other New Deal public works projects did not, that of sustaining or restoring the morale of participants. Many WPA jobs were much less successful in this respect.

Federal works programmes marked a significantly new initiative in the labour market and as such required ideological justification. This was undertaken through strikingly transparent propaganda. In 1940, the Corps's Director described the camps in this programme in fulsome terms to the American public: 'have you visited a CCC camp? If not, you should. There are no fences around the camps. As a taxpayer you should go and see how your "CCC" dollar is spent . . . If there is a camp near you, visit it. There is no surer way of understanding the nature of this new institution.'[69]

Roosevelt himself lauded the Corps, employing the language of national pride to conceal the political novelty of the camps' collectivism. The President declared, 'this kind of work must go on. I believe that the nation feels that the work of these young men is so thoroughly justified and, in addition, the benefits to the men themselves are so clear that the actual annual cost will be met without much opposition or much complaint.'[70] Attendance was voluntary and proposals, such as the fingerprinting of new arrivals, were implemented cautiously. Characterized by voluntary

[68] Speaking to the 74th Congress; cited in Brock (1988: 278).
[69] NARA RG 35 Records of the CCC, Division of Selection: Records relating to organization and operation of Selection Work, 1933–42, Box 15, Folder: 'Now They are Men'. Typescript of James J. McEntee, 'Now They are Men: The Story of the CCC' 1940, preface.
[70] NARA RG 35 Records of the CCC, Personal Correspondence of the Director, Box 2, File: A–Z 1934. Letter from Roosevelt to the CCC Director Robert Fechner, 6 Oct. 1934.

enrolment and non-military organization, the CCC is nonetheless a major exception to the American individualist approach to societal problems. To accommodate this exception the camp philosophy was integrated into mainstream politics. Once the period of crisis abated, the Corps was rapidly wound down.

5

'Reconditioning the Unemployed': Work Camps in Britain

THE scale of unemployment in Britain in the 1920s and 1930s could not be ignored politically. It seemed to demonstrate the inability of the labour market unproblematically to achieve an equilibrium of supply and demand. Particularly in those areas of highest and most persistent unemployment, the so-called 'distressed areas', life was miserable. As part of its strategy to cope with unemployment, the government opened Instructional Centres (dubbed 'labour camps') and instituted physical training classes. Described as the '"slave camps" of Labour's first New Deal' in a recent newspaper article, these collectivist experiments have been the source of controversy and interest, with their detractors viewing them as malevolent mandatory work institutions, attendance at which was only notionally voluntary for the affected unemployed workers.[1] One recruit, William Dunseath, describes how he joined a work camp after a period of unemployment: '"I had been working in a spinning mill in Accrington, and been out of work for six months, on the Means Test, not receiving any benefit because we'd got one person in a family of five working." He was summoned to the employment exchange: "I received a card asking me to call and see the Manager of the Labour Exchange. He asked me if I'd go to a training centre. Well, I agreed to go, with three pals of mine; we'd worked together." '[2] Dunseath proved to be one of many unemployed workers directed to the instructional centres for physical reconditioning.

In this chapter, the establishment and operation of British Instructional Centres is documented. The competing negative and positive assessments of these collective institutions are rehearsed and assessed. Several issues are pursued. First, the question of whether camps constituted illiberal institutions is considered. As an experiment in social policy, camps were a dramatic response to the problem of unemployment. Their novel character feeds into the second theme of the chapter: what was the expertise or

---

[1] M. Austin, 'Revealed: "slave camps" of Labour's first New Deal', *Sunday Times*, 9 Aug. 1998; and see D. McKie and M. Wainwright, 'Jobless "hardened" in labour camps' *Guardian* 12 Aug. 1998.

[2] Quoted from an interview in Field (1992: 80).

knowledge basis for this experiment in collectivization? I argue that there was little expertise cited or marshalled in the formulation of this strategy and that work camps were not dissimilar to other ad hoc, short-term responses to mass unemployment. Rather, the idea rested upon a perception amongst senior civil servants (supported at the Ministry of Labour) that the long-term unemployed required physical 'reconditioning' successfully to enter the labour market (though the shortage of jobs meant few did so). In pursuing this strategy, both the civil servants and Minister acted independently of social or political forces: in fact, a Labour Party minister initiated this policy despite hostility from parts of the labour movement. Striking is the absence of compelling evidence in favour of such an approach: as a consequence, work camps differ significantly from eugenic measures and from workfare by the paucity of expert knowledge supporting their establishment.

ESTABLISHING WORK CAMPS

Transfer Instructional Centres (renamed Instructional Centres in June 1932) were opened in May 1929 by the Ministry of Labour, the first at Blackpool. Ten years later there were thirty-five such centres functioning. Participants were directed to the centres by labour exchange officials. The centres or 'labour camps' were designed, through vigorous outdoor work, to 'recondition' the unemployed; they were focused on long-term unemployed men living in the areas with highest unemployment, and in greatest 'distress'. The Industrial Transference Board estimated that close to a quarter of million men lacking work were located in these, mostly mining areas.

With civil service support, the Minister of Labour, Margaret Bondfield (a trade union sponsored Labour MP), promoted the idea of work camps. The stimulus for creating Instructional Centres originates in a concern amongst senior policy-makers at the Treasury and Ministry of Labour about a 'class of men' resistant to government employment schemes, principally those schemes necessitating transfer to elsewhere in the country; this concern predated the election of the Labour government in 1929. In a memorandum from F. G. Bowers at the Ministry of Labour to A. W. Hurst at the Treasury on 12 December 1928, this rationale was explained:

I think I ought to warn you that we have under consideration here a proposal to deal with the class of men to whom our existing training schemes do not apply. I refer to those, especially among the younger men who, through prolonged unemployment, have become so 'soft' and temporarily demoralised that it would not be practicable to introduce more than a very small number of them into our ordinary training centres without danger to the morale of the centre on which the effect of the training depends. Nor could they be sent to a labouring job in London or elsewhere. It is essential to the success of the transference policy, which already has many difficulties to contend with at the receiving end, that only the best material available be sent forward for any given job. It is obvious, therefore, that the class of whom I am speaking cannot be considered by our local officers for transfer until they are hardened.[3]

The evidential basis for this assessment is unclear: whether it reflected direct interviews or inspection of the 'unconditioned' unemployed men or mere speculation is unstated. Nor is there a group of policy experts advocating such a programme (although several voluntary organizations advanced the use of land settlements for the unemployed); the proposal is compatible with a 'public works' approach and work camps are perhaps logical as part of an anti-unemployment policy. By the end of the 1920s, Keynes supported public works schemes as part of a response to the problem of unemployment.[4] Rodney Lowe characterizes the Instructional Centres as a 'social measure' introduced to 'prevent the demoralization of the unemployed'.[5] However, the grounds for assuming that unemployed men were demoralized were partial as Ross McKibbin argues. McKibbin concludes that, in the inter-war years, 'tiredness was often mistaken for apathy', and furthermore that the psychological disintegration commonly imputed to unemployed persons was unproven: there is little 'evidence to support the then fashionable social-psychological theories which suggested that the unemployed progressed in stages to a state of personal and social disintegration'.[6] In support of this interpretation is the ease with which the unemployed returned to the labour market at the end of the 1930s, pointing to the temporary character of any 'demoralization' arising from the absence of work.

Some of the rationale for the initiative is suggested by the Ministry of Labour's annual report describing the establishment of the ICs:

the Department's experience in transferring men from depressed areas to work in other parts of the country has shown that, in those areas, prolonged unemployment has robbed many men both of the physical fitness and of the attitude of mind which would enable them to undertake heavy work under ordinary industrial conditions without having some opportunity, in circumstances under which their progress could be carefully watched, of accustoming themselves once more to regular hours and steady work.[7]

---

[3] PRO T/161/902. Letter from F. G. Bowers, Labour, to A. W. Hurst, Treasury, 12 Dec. 1928. And see Colledge (1989: 5–6 where this document is cited without reference), Colledge and Field (1983: endnote 13, where the date is given as 12 Dec. 1929 and the author identified as F. G. Briers) and Field (1992: 66–7) where the citation is correct.
[4] Clarke (1988: 77); see also Weir and Skocpol (1985).   [5] Lowe (1986: 224).
[6] McKibbin (1998: 152, 160), and McKibbin (1990).
[7] Ministry of Labour, *Annual Report for the Year 1929* (London: HMSO, 1930), 37.

This view is the opposite of McKibbin's who provides an account of the highly structured routines assumed by unemployed men in the 1930s, routines organized around the pursuit of work.[8] Bowers's memorandum simply reported 'an intimation' not a fully formulated plan; he proposed market gardening work or manual forestry work as tasks suitable to 'hardening' the targeted groups. The Ministry of Labour's annual report in 1929 set out a similar view. It concluded that 'prolonged unemployment' had denuded men in distressed areas 'of the physical fitness and of the attitude of mind which would enable them to undertake heavy work under ordinary industrial conditions without having some opportunity, in circumstances under which their progress could be carefully watched, of accustoming themselves once more to regular hours and steady work'.[9]

Margaret Bondfield, the Minister of Labour, submitted a minute to the Cabinet in February 1930 about the need to recondition these 'hardened' unemployed: 'there are a number of young men in the distressed areas who are very unlikely to obtain work either locally or elsewhere without some course of reconditioning, but who refuse to avail themselves of the offer of training.'[10] Bondfield's contention that these unemployed men refused training implies a disciplinary motive for the proposed camps, a measure only partially enforced.

The Treasury and Ministry of Labour collaborated[11] to produce a set of proposals for the establishment of 'reconditioning centres' targeted on unemployed men in the distressed areas.[12] These workers were ineligible for existing training programmes and unqualified for immediate transfer to an area with jobs. They had allegedly 'become so "soft" and temporarily demoralised,' that they were implausible as applicants for employment. Reconditioning work (such as reforestation or building recreation grounds) would help such individuals, it was argued, to prepare for work by enhancing their skills and, through strict discipline, rekindling the work ethic. Removal from their local community was deemed essential: 'the progress of re-conditioning will be quicker and more effective, if carried out away from the distressed areas, so that men live away from the depressing atmosphere of the coalfields under more favourable conditions.' Attendance at camps was proposed for twelve-week periods, with efforts

---

[8] McKibbin (1998: 152–60).   [9] Ministry of Labour, *Annual Report 1929*, 37.

[10] Cabinet, Distressed Areas. Withdrawal of benefit from men refusing to attend a training centre. Memorandum by the Minister of Labour, 3 Feb. 1930, CP 37 (30), in PRO Folder: CAB 24/209.

[11] PRO T/161/902. Letter from F. W. Reith Ross, Treasury to the Permanent Secretary, Labour, 28 Dec. 1928.

[12] PRO T/161/902. Proposal No. 3225. Ref 2/F. 966/1928. Labour Emergency Expenditure Committee. Proposal. To commence a scheme of 'Reconditioning' Centres to fit men for transfer in the distressed areas who have been long unemployed.

to place trainees in jobs initiated after eight weeks. Trainees would receive an allowance 'dependent on good behaviour and progress', in addition to their unemployment benefit, and expenses to cover lodgings, and the cost of transport. Clothing was to be provided gratis: 'in so far as it is to be found directly to be necessary it is proposed to issue free of cost a pair of boots, overalls and oilskins, at an estimated cost of 35/- per man.' Some of the men would be permitted to transfer from the reconditioning centres into Government Training Centres.[13]

The government, a Labour administration with Ramsay MacDonald as Prime Minister, wanted a tough line taken with those refusing to attend training courses. Thus, the Minister of Labour declared in February 1930 that: 'I think the stage has been reached . . . when such men should have their benefits disallowed if they refuse without good reason to take a course of instruction when it is offered to them.' She cited union support for such a tougher line: 'I have consulted the Trades Union Congress General Council on the point and they fully agree in principle. They make the reservation that the procedure proposed should not be applied to attendance at Handyman centres but only at the Transfer Instructional Centres.'[14] The TUC's social insurance committee discussed this proposal in January 1930 and agreed 'to the principle laid down in the [Ministry of Labour] memorandum, that acceptance of training or reconditioning should be made a condition for the receipt of unemployment benefit, subject to the individual's right of appeal to the Board of Assessors.'[15]

Bondfield outlined the formal mechanism she envisaged to preclude unjust treatment:

the procedure which I contemplate is that if a man for whom a course of instruction at a transfer instructional centre is thought to be necessary refuses without good reason to take it, he should be brought before the local Board of Assessors, and, if they agree, he would be told that unless he takes the course, benefit would be with-held. If, after going to the centre, he leaves it without a good reason before the end of the course, he will again be brought before the Board of Assessors and if they approve, benefit will be disallowed. This procedure should provide sufficient safeguard against any risk of harsh treatment.[16]

[13] PRO T/161/902. Proposal No. 3225. Ref 2/F. 966/1928. Labour Emergency Expenditure Committee. Proposal. To commence a scheme of 'Reconditioning' Centres to fit men for transfer in the distressed areas who have been long unemployed.

[14] Cited in Colledge (1989: 14).

[15] MRC Warwick TUC Records, Folder: MSS.292/131.3/4; 131.3 (1), included in an internal memorandum from J. L. Smyth to Mr H. V. Tewson, 18 Mar. 1940, p. 4.

[16] Cabinet, Distressed Areas. Withdrawal of benefit from men refusing to attend a training centre. Memorandum by the Minister of Labour, 3 Feb. 1930, CP 37 (30), in PRO Folder: CAB 24/209.

Bondfield's proposal to establish TICs was discussed at the Cabinet in February 1930. Although the term 'reconditioning' provoked anxiety amongst some of those present, the Cabinet agreed 'to approve the Minister of Labour's proposal to lay on the Table of the House of Commons a formal Regulation as to attendance at courses of instruction, amending certain existing Regulations under the Unemployment Insurance Acts'.[17]

By 1933, nine instructional centres were functioning. Each provided '10 to 12 weeks reconditioning for over 8,000 men in all'.[18] Unemployment remained high, however. In October 1932, 2,858,000 persons were registered as unemployed, of whom the vast majority (2,303,000) were men aged over 18 years.[19] The instructional centres absorbed about 10,000 men a year, a modest number.[20] In 1934, new legislation provided for temporary summer camps:[21] tent accommodation, occupied only for the summer months, was attached to permanent Instructional Centres. They were first set up in 1933, when five tented camps were operating with places for 1,100 men.[22] Temporary camps were popular: 'the tented camps are based upon the centre, and are under the general supervision of the Manager.' The camps reproduced 'many of the conditions of a pioneer camp, the site chosen being usually in a remote spot where the men must improvise for themselves their amenities and recreations. These conditions have an immediate appeal to the men, and the camps have secured the friendly interest of the neighbouring villages and landowners.'[23] 'Reconditioning' camps were probably more agreeable in the summer than winter. By 1937, there were twenty-two centres (Table 5.1), including permanent and temporary summer ones, housing about 21,000 men a year,[24] of whom few were placed in jobs. Each work camp took trainees from a designated area. Initially trainees came only from distressed mining areas but, from 1934,

[17] Cabinet Minutes, 5 Feb. 1930, p. 4, in PRO CAB 23/63.
[18] Cabinet. Training and Occupation for the Unemployed Next Winter. Memorandum by the Minister of Labour (Margaret Bondfield), 21 July 1933, CP 189 (33) 7 pp. p. 3 in PRO Folder: CAB 24/242.
[19] Cabinet. Unemployment Committee (chairman: De La Warr), Interim Report, 24 Oct. 1932, 25 pp., p. 2, CP 307 (32) in PRO Folder: CAB 24/233.
[20] Cabinet. Unemployment Committee (chairman: De La Warr), Interim Report, 24 Oct. 1932, 25 pp., p. 3, CP 307 (32) in PRO Folder: CAB 24/233.
[21] Unemployment Insurance Act 1934.
[22] Cabinet. Training and Occupation for the Unemployed Next Winter. Memorandum by the Minister of Labour (Margaret Bondfield), 21 July 1933, CP 189 (33) 7 pp., p. 3. in PRO Folder: CAB 24/242. See also Ministry of Labour, *Annual Report for the Year 1933* (London: HMSO, 1934), 37–8.
[23] Cabinet. Training and Occupation for the Unemployed Next Winter.
[24] Official Report, 5th Series, Parliamentary Debates, House of Commons 1936–7, vol. 326, col. 211, 6 July 1937.

TABLE 5.1 Instructional Centres (Labour Camps), 1935

Non-residential
Carshalton (St Helier Estate, Selby Green, Carshalton, Surrey)
Rheola (Resolven, Glamorganshire)

Residential
Bourne (Lincolnshire)
Fermyn Woods (Brigstock, near Kettering, Northamptonshire)
Shobdon (near Leominster, Herefordshire)
Weeting (near Brandon, Suffolk)
High Lodge (near Brandon, Suffolk)
West Tofts (Mundford, Norfolk)
Cranwich (Cranwich Heath, Mundford, Norfolk)
Carstairs (Lampits Farm, Carstairs Junction, Lanarkshire)
Glenbranter (near Strachur, Argyllshire)
Kielder (Northumberland)
Allerston (Low Dalby, Thornton-le-Dale, Yorkshire)
Hamsterley (Bedburn, Hamsterley, Witton-le-Wear, Co. Durham)
Kershopefoot (Newcastleton, Roxburghshire)
Nrechfa (Treglog, Llansawel, Llandeilo, Carmarthenshire)

Summer camps
Kirkby Underwood, Pickoworth Woods and Aslackby, attached to Bourne Centre,
    Lincolnshire.
Wigmore Forest and Presteigne, attached to Shobdon Centre, Herefordshire
Drayton Woods, attached to Fermyn Woods Centres, Northamptonshire
Harling, attached to High Lodge Centre, Norfolk
Lynn Road attached to Weeting Centre, near Brandon, Suffolk
Cynarth, attached to Brechfa Centre, Carmarthenshire
Ballemeanoch, attached to Glenbranter Centre, Argyllshire
Whickhope, attached to Kielder Centre, Northumberland
Hockham Heath, attached to West Tofts Centre, Norfolk
Glangwili (Alt-Walis Road, Carmarthen) unattached
Redesdale Summer Camp (Low Byrness, Otterburn, Newcastle-on Tyne), unattached
Gilling (Brandsby, Yorkshire) unattached

Source: derived from Statement by Mr Oliver Stanley Minister of Labour, 2 May 1935, in Official Report, 5th Series, Parliamentary Debates, Commons, 1934–5, vol. 301 cols. 561–2.

recruitment was broadened to cover any area in the country with high unemployment.[25]

Attendance was voluntary, a point underlined by several Ministers of Labour in the Commons.[26] Several commentators dispute this feature and

[25] Ministry of Labour, *Annual Report 1934*, 33.
[26] Official Report, 5th Series, Parliamentary Debates, House of Commons 1936–7, vol. 325, col. 1350, 24 June 1937. The Minister was Ernest Brown. See also 1933–4, vol. 291, col. 591, 21 June 1934, when Sir Henry Betterton, then Minister for Labour, made a similar declaration.

journalistic accounts continue to question just how voluntary attendance was.[27] The ICs were included as an approved course of instruction for the purposes of Section 7 (v) of the Unemployment Insurance Act 1920, under which section insurance officers were empowered to require attendance at such a course as a condition for the receipt of unemployment benefit. The Ministry of Labour itself recognized the damage of compulsion not least in the suitability of trainees for any job placements available under the scheme: 'there may be a case for "compelling" the transitional payment applicants to enter the Centres, but it would be regrettable if it were necessary to give a preference to such men, apart from their industrial merits, in filling the limited number of "prize" vacancies.' It concluded that 'no compulsion should be used at the recruiting stage at any TIC or Occupational Centre, at any rate in the early days of the experiment.'[28] The Unemployment Assistance Board's (UAB) openness to a more compulsory approach found little political support, particularly as the mandatory Nazi labour system became better known. Although retrospective comparisons with this system are somewhat odd it is one, however, which some of those attending the camps now provide. Thus, Willie Eccles is now reported as saying that his treatment in the camp at Glenbranter mirrored 'the way the Nazis treated people'.[29] Writing at the time, Wal Hannington of the National Unemployed Workers' Movement described the centres as 'compulsory labour camps and task work centres' which constituted a 'big step nearer by the National Government to fascist administration in Britain'.[30]

Instructional Centres received a substantial number of participants. Between 1928 and 1938, over 120,000 unemployed men spent time in them (and another 7,000 were enrolled at the GTCs).[31] Training centres were also provided for women, under the aegis of the Central Committee on Women's Training and Employment, funded and regulated by the Ministry of Labour. 'Training' for women meant principally preparation for domestic work: at both residential and non-residential centres, 'instruction in cookery, housewifery, laundry and needlework on practical lines' was provided.[32] Predating the depression, these centres received over 60,000

---

[27] See the articles in *Sunday Times*, 9 Aug. 1998 and *Guardian*, 12 Aug. 1998, the authors of neither of which produce evidence to support the mandatory claim but nonetheless each makes it. See also Colledge (1989).

[28] Draft: Area of Recruitment, 20 Apr. 1932, cited in Field (1992: 73–4). The archival source is PRO LAB 2/1280.

[29] In *Sunday Times*, 9 Aug. 1998.   [30] Quoted in Field (1992: 87).

[31] Numbers reported in Whiteside (1991: 102).

[32] Cabinet. Training and Occupation for the Unemployed Next Winter. Memorandum by the Minister of Labour (Margaret Bondfield), 21 July 1933, CP 189 (33) 7 pp., p. 6. in PRO Folder: CAB 24/242.

women between 1921 and 1933, and by 1933 were able to provide places for 4,400 women and girls per year. Eighty per cent of trainees were placed in domestic employment.

Young unemployed men were to be restored physically and toughened up mentally at the work camps. The Ministry of Labour reported that work was designed at a level judged appropriate for individual cases: 'when the men first entered the centres they had not done any steady work for some time and they were often under-nourished. They were therefore started gradually, the nature and amount of work which each man was required to do being governed by his physical strength and general condition.'[33] Early in the programme, selection was increasingly limited to men capable of physically heavy work.[34] The camps consisted of Nissen hut colonies located on land controlled by the Forestry Commission. The participants attended for three-month periods 'of military-style discipline and pick-and-shovel labour'. Work began at 6.00 a.m., and the working day was a long ten to twelve hours. The work was manual—digging ditches, cutting down trees or building roads—and former police officers or sergeant majors were employed to oversee the workers. Camp life was austere: 'the living conditions were spartan and in the evenings and weekends there was little to do as the camps were deliberately built in remote spots like Brechfa in Carmarthenshire or Glenbranter in Argyllshire, far from the temptations of the pub and the dance hall. For their trouble the inmates received two or three shillings and a packet of Woodbines per week.'[35] A Ministry of Labour memorandum elaborated further upon arrangements for the camps:

all these centres are residential, unemployed single men being brought to the centres from the depressed areas. They receive their board and lodging and in addition a small sum weekly for pocket money; against this expenditure is set off the amount of unemployment pay to which they are entitled. Where necessary working kit is served out to them. The residential centres provide the most effective method of improving the employability of the men because the corporate activities of the centre after working hours are not the least important part of the course, and the general policy will continue to be based upon residential centres.[36]

A short-lived residential centre for married men was opened in South Wales in 1933.

The sort of work undertaken at the centres was dictated by location in rural areas: it consisted of 'instruction in elementary woodwork and metal work, trenching, shoring and timbering, road making, quarrying etc'.[37] In

[33] Ministry of Labour, *Annual Report 1929*, 38.
[34] Ministry of Labour, *Annual Report for the Year 1930* (London: HMSO, 1931), 36.
[35] Humphries and Gordon (1994: 116).
[36] Cabinet. Training and Occupation for the Unemployed Next Winter.   [37] Ibid.

common with both the comparable US experiment—the CCC—and later workfare programmes, work was concentrated on manual activities with no particular training component.

LIBERAL OR ILLIBERAL? THE CAMPS AT WORK

Assessment of British labour camps has been divided. Contemporary views included both favourable and hostile evaluations. Thus, one MP told the Commons, in 1935, that 'the workers in the country are up against these training camps entirely. They do not call them training camps; they call them conscription camps, and they look upon them with very great disfavour.'[38] However, the *Daily Herald* ran a series of articles praising the 'concentration camps', and indeed the camps were established by a Labour government with union support. Historical accounts are generally unsympathetic: for instance, recent assessments describe them as Labour's first New Deal or, somewhat bizarrely, as equivalent to Nazi labour camps.[39]

The instructional camps took unemployed men receiving benefits who 'volunteered' to attend. Volunteer was a euphemism in the opinion of critics and observers, since labour exchange officials were accused of pressuring recipients to attend them. Earning the sobriquet 'slave camps',[40] the centres were harsh according to some scholars. Government ministers defended them robustly, the Minister of Labour dismissing the description 'slave camps' as 'so grotesque as hardly to merit contradiction . . . I do not believe that anyone who has ever visited one of these camps . . . could ever repeat a statement of that kind.'[41] Some MPs did indeed approve of them.[42]

Noel Whiteside portrays the camps as grim places, in which the participants worked rigorously on tedious tasks, and were denied much privacy because of the dormitory sleeping arrangements. She reports that the IC 'initiative was very unpopular among the unemployed themselves, who earned no allowance but whose families' unemployment assistance was docked five shillings while they were away, ostensibly to pay for their

[38] Official Report, 5th Series, Parliamentary Debates, House of Commons 1934–5, col. 1495, 1 Mar. 1935; the speaker was George Griffiths.
[39] Colledge (1989) and Colledge and Field (1983). M. Austin 'Revealed: "slave camps" of Labour's first New Deal', *Sunday Times*, 9 Aug. 1998; and see D. McKie and M. Wainwright 'Jobless "hardened" in labour camps', *Guardian*, 12 Aug. 1998.
[40] See, for example, W. Hannington, *The Problem of the Distressed Areas* (London: Victor Gollanz, 1937), ch. 7, and Humphries and Gordon (1994), ch. 4.
[41] Official Report, 5th Series, Parliamentary Debates, House of Commons 1934–5, col. 1508, 1 Mar. 1935; the Minister was Oliver Stanley.
[42] Official Report, 5th Series, Parliamentary Debates, House of Commons 1933–4, col. 604, 21 June 1934, where MP Miss Ward offers 'warm congratulations' to the Labour Ministry arising from a visit to the camp at Kielder.

keep'.[43] In Colledge's view, the camps were militaristic both in physical layout and in the maintenance of discipline: 'the camp manager stood at the head of the camp. He was invariably ex-army or navy or airforce officer material representing a ruling clique';[44] below the commander was the camp steward who supervised clerks and the head ganger who organized a team of gangers supervising the men at work. With his co-author John Field, Colledge argues that 'the prevalance of ex-military personnel among the camp hierarchy' was disliked by many members of the camps.[45] For these recruits, the camp leader was a remote figure rarely encountered during residence in the Instructional Centre, the physical layout of which reinforced distinctions of rank. Camps were deliberately placed at a distance from the nearest village or town, though the Ministry of Labour's 1930 annual report noted that 'all reasonable measures are taken to ensure the men's comfort and well being and to help them withstand the pull of former ties and associations'. This comfort did not prevent desertion, as the Ministry conceded: 'nevertheless, a substantial proportion of the men, on one pretext or another, leave the centre to return home.'[46] The remoteness of the camps was justified by the Labour Ministry as a necessary feature of reconditioning. Colledge offers the figure of 24,264 from total admissions of 103,672 as leaving the camps.[47] According to Ministry of Labour figures, over 20,000 trainees either left or were dismissed before the end of their designated stay in 1936, 1937, and 1938. The charge of militarization can be overdrawn. Thus, although John Field reports the presence of ex-servicemen at the camps, he qualifies the significance of this factor: 'despite the selective borrowing of symbolic and organizational forms from the military, the primary function of the camps—physical and moral "reconditioning"—required an intrinsically civil, voluntary socialization into the desired attributes of the "free" labourer'.[48]

In his judicious study, John Field writes of the camps that 'here as in no other training institution the emphasis upon reintegration into the work-based social order was at its most clear, crystallised as it was through the potential for comprehensive domination which a residential institution allows.'[49] Field views the camps as institutions designed principally to instil the value of work:

whether for paupers, prisoners and ill-behaved soldiers, or for the long-term unemployed, structured work was in itself held to have therapeutic power. From it, you learn not only how to work—the main ulterior objective—but also acquire or

[43] Whiteside (1991: 102).   [44] Colledge (1989: 9).
[45] Colledge and Field (1983: 159).   [46] Cited in Colledge (1989: 13).
[47] Ibid. 13, though no source is provided.   [48] Field (1992: 87).   [49] Ibid. 2.

reinforce other valued characteristics: dignity, responsibility, self-respect, membership of a wider community . . . in short, work is part of the reordering of identity.[50]

Field commends the Goffmanian 'total institution' framework for analysis
of the camps—since the camps were 'closed, remote and residential . . .
devoted to the observation, education, classification and control of their
inmates' behaviour'.[51] This approach is overly elaborate, however, and
unjustified by the voluntariness of attendance and the freedom to leave
open to trainees in the British camps. Indeed, Field finds himself struggling
with the approach, conceding that 'remarkably little effort was made to
control the trainees' lives outside of working hours', and that social life
'was left largely to the trainees'.[52] Strictly 'total institutions', such as prisons
or asylums, are much more regimented. Where Field's analysis is more
useful is in recognizing how the sort of liberal amelioration represented
by camps was associated with ambitions about 'improving' the individuals
concerned by sharpening their sense of the work ethic. Help was combined
with centrally planned ends.

Writing together, Colledge and Field stress further the punitive function
of the work camps: 'the purposes of the labour camps were less directly
economic than disciplinary.' They adduce evidence for this thesis: 'the
camps were there first and foremost to discipline the long-term unemployed, in a way that had to be spoken of with terms that were intentionally impersonal and even brutal: to "recondition human material", one had
to look to the physical and moral degeneration wrought by long-term
unemployment.'[53] This emphasis on the labour camps' disciplinary role
sees them as exercises in social engineering aimed at shaping those attending them into better workers. The aim was to recondition by exposing
the unemployed men to 'regular, tough, menial, manual labour.'[54] And, as
Colledge and Field underline, an emphasis upon reconditioning through
manual and routinized work rather obviated the scope for training or
skills acquisition. ('Reconditioning' proved a troublesome term when
these centres were approved by Cabinet but it nevertheless garnered a
majority.) They also report that complaints about the standard of food
were commonplace amongst inmates. Field contends that the fact the
camps continued to operate—and even to expand—after 1932, when
unemployment began to decline in some regions, indicates that the 'centres
proved a considerably more significant policy innovation than they might
have seemed in 1929'.[55] Compared with similar institutions in the United
States—notably the US Civilian Conservation Corps and the National

---

[50] Field (1992: 3–4).   [51] Ibid. 17.   [52] Ibid. 79.
[53] Colledge and Field (1983: 156).   [54] Ibid. 157.   [55] Field (1992: 75).

Youth Administration—the British centres functioned on a modest scale, relatively cheaply and it is therefore difficult to demonstrate Field's view.

Voluntary or mandatory attendance?

As noted, the power mandatorily to direct unemployed men to work camps was approved in legislation. It had modest effects—resulting in 1800 claimants being sent to centres—and was abrograted after nine months. Noel Whiteside claims that labour exchange officials manifested an enthusiasm for compulsion and provided a springboard for dispatching unemployed men to the new Instructional Centres, 'under the impression that their "availability for work" would be questioned and their benefit disallowed if they refused'.[56] The use of labour exchanges to select men to attend camps is a crucial aspect of the British work camp policy, differentiating it from the United States. It complemented other monitoring aspects of exchange officials' work.[57] The Ministry of Labour itself commented that while 'many men declined to leave home on grounds which must be regarded as reasonable', others, 'including many for whom the centres afford the only reasonable hope of re-employment, have declined to take advantage of these courses for reasons which cannot be regarded as sufficient'.[58] In fact, the record on employment did not justify the claim that the ICs were a route to jobs. A year later, the Ministry commented that 'when the scheme was instituted, attendance at the centres was voluntary, but it was found that a large number of men on the registers of the Employment Exchanges for whom a course at one of the centres would obviously be beneficial declined to go forward for reasons which could not be regarded as adequate.'[59] This recalcitrance led the Labour Minister to encourage activating the 1920 powers to require attendance at the centres.

The discretionary power granted employment exchange officials by the Unemployment Act of 1934 (legislation which increased their power in respect of the long-term unemployed who had exhausted benefits) was opposed vigorously by the National Unemployed Workers' Movement (NUWM). Its leader, Wal Hannington, objected to the provision that the Ministry of Labour could direct unemployed men to Instructional Centres.[60] The NUWM's journal, the *Unemployed Leader*, voiced these concerns, and its organizers attempted to agitate trainees in camps with very limited success, hampered not least by the camps' remote locations

---

[56] Whiteside (1991: 102). No evidence is supplied for this assessment.
[57] McKibbin (1990).   [58] Ministry of Labour, *Annual Report 1929*, 39.
[59] Ministry of Labour, *Annual Report 1930*, 36.
[60] For the NUWM and work camps see the discussion in Croucher (1987: 162–71).

and the uninterest of the trainees. In his book *Problems of the Distressed Areas*, Hannington criticized the labour camps, characterizing them as an undesirable form of militarization.[61] John Field also argues, in his study, that compulsion was a 'transparent' factor in attendance at the Centres,[62] though he also comments elsewhere that 'compulsion was shortlived [between 1930 and 1932]; with increasing sophistication, the authorities took to using the novel techniques of advertising'.[63]

Labour and the camps

A far less bleak view of the camps is contained in other contemporary records. The *Daily Herald*, sympathetic to labour and unions, published a series of laudatory articles in 1934 on the centres, under the byline of 'concentration camps'.[64] The five pieces, by H. R. S. Phillpott,[65] were based on a tour of most of the camps and unmonitored interviews with the participants. Phillpott reported that, unremarkably, officials preferred the description 'reconditioning centres' to 'concentration camps', though it was under the latter by-line that his newspaper articles appeared.[66] He visited numerous camps and recorded his conversations with administrators based in Norfolk and Suffolk. The latter painted a dismal portrait of the unemployed: 'when the trainees come into the camps many of them are in very, very poor physical and mental condition, caused by the prolonged distress they have undergone. Their morale is low. They have a hangdog, downtrodden expression. A sort of paralysis seems to have gripped them.'[67] Phillpott gave a description of the camps' *modus vivendi* and operation:

young, unemployed single men (very few married men are taken) agree on the advice or the invitation of their local Unemployment Exchange to go to a camp for an 'instructional' or a 'reconditioning' term of 12 weeks. They are fed and housed, work 44 hours a week, and are given 3s a week pocket money. The allowance was 4s a week before the unemployment benefit 'economy' cut.[68]

Phillpott's terms, 'advice' and 'invitation', as exercised by Labour Exchange officials, clashes with retrospective claims about compulsion. Non-claimants, those unemployed who had exhausted their benefits, also got invited to the camps.

At the camps Phillpott visited, the men rose at 6.30, had breakfast at 7.15, worked from 8.00 until noon, and then after a meal worked from 1.00

---

[61] Hannington, *The Problem of the Distressed Areas*.
[62] Field (1992: 68).   [63] Ibid. 82.
[64] *Daily Herald*, 15, 16, 17, 19, 22 Mar. 1934. On the *Daily Herald* see Richards (1997).
[65] See also his piece 'Those "Concentration Camps"', *Labour: A Magazine for all Workers*, 1/8 (Apr. 1934).
[66] *Daily Herald*, 15 Mar. 1934.   [67] Ibid.   [68] Ibid.

until 5.00, the working day peppered with numerous 'smoke' breaks. Phillpott expounded the virtues of the camp at Weeting Hall near Brandon in Suffolk, a mansion owned by the Ministry of Labour: 'around the mansion, in what were once the gardens, are blocks of red-painted, corrugated iron huts, also spacious and centrally heated. Seven of them accommodate 250 trainees who are served out with corduroy trousers, a jacket and working boots, knife, fork, spoon and enamel cup when they arrive for their 12 weeks' course. There is a dining-room with wooden forms and tables covered with oilcloth on which are served wholesome and plentiful meals, handed out from the adjoining kitchen through hatches to the trainees as they file in. There is also the recreation room, the sick bay and so on.' Some of the trainees wanted to return home, but had no 'specific complaints', while others told Phillpott that the camp was 'champion' and that they put on weight and were indeed ready for work.[69] At the camp at Cranwich Heath in Norfolk, heat was maintained in the huts by wood fires since there was no central heating but, again, Phillpott judged the accommodation salubrious: 'its unpainted corrugated iron huts and administrative offices branch away from each side of a great, well-kept lawn surrounded by weedless gravel paths. The term "huts" should not be misunderstood. They are big and well-built, weatherproof, well-lighted and comfortable.' He found other features to admire: 'here also are the customary recreation hut, the sick bay, the school, the little library, the ablution hut where men wash themselves and what few clothes they possess and have shower baths. Admittedly, the shower baths have cement floors instead of marble ones, but the showers do shower and there is plenty of hot and cold water.'[70]

Phillpott did not share in the complaints about the dominance of ex-servicemen amongst the camp personnel. Instead he reported that, 'I found nothing to suggest that there is, at present, anything in the nature of militaristic discipline or official bullying. On the contrary.'[71] He regularly praised the administrators in his series: 'one of the things that has impressed me during this tour of the camps [is] the interest of the officials. They work to a system, of course, as they are bound to do—a system of times and regularity, but my experience is that they work to it humanly and understandingly.'[72] This is a rather different view to Field's 'total institution'. Phillpott attributed the success of the camps to the quality and dedication of the managers, attributes which explained why 'these young men are reacting so grandly despite the years of hopelessness and physical and mental impairment have imposed on them'.[73] The managers were closer to

[69] Ibid.   [70] *Daily Herald*, 17 Mar. 1934.   [71] 'Those "Concentration" Camps'.
[72] *Daily Herald*, 17 Mar. 1934.   [73] *Daily Herald*, 19 Mar. 1934.

'social workers' than to 'officials', composed of a 'fine type' dedicated to the reconditioning task: 'they see the human problem, and they do a very noble best to cope with it'. Furthermore, 'they worry when, having "reconditioned" a man they have to send him back to the conditions out of which, for twelve weeks, he had been lifted.'[74]

The trainees worked in gangs of 20 to 24, overseen by a ganger. At Weeting Hall, they laboured on sawing and splitting wood, trench-digging, clearing and levelling ground. Phillpott observed the gangs working 'away steadily', the 'majority of them cheerfully. They shouted "chat back" as the logs fell from the teeth of the saws and as the axes clove into the logs. They were in the "hardening-up" stage and most of them were on the smallish size.'[75] That such toughening up was necessary was plain to the camp managers, one of whom, in Kettering, told Phillpott: 'the trainees are in such bad condition when they arrive that it is impossible to build up their physique or restore a partly deadened mentality in less time than [seven to eight weeks].'[76] Phillpott had no doubt about the success of this reconditioning: 'I have by now seen hundreds of the young men [and] would like to say this. There is a remarkable difference between the rather frightened trainee who has been in a camp for a week and the axe-swinging, pick-wielding trainee who after nine or ten weeks re-conditioning has found both his strength and his confidence grow, and who says, as many of them have said to me: "now I'll take on any job because I think I can do it—if only one comes." '[77] After talking with one group of trainees, Phillpott mused, 'think of it, These youths not only cannot get jobs but without "reconditioning" they probably would not be able to do them even if they could get them.'[78] The trainees 'have been made fit for jobs, but the jobs are not there for men to have'.[79]

Placement statistics underlined this conclusion: of 1,165 trainees entering the Suffolk camp at Brandon in 1933, a mere 91 were placed in work and 23 others found work on their own; 110 left the camps voluntarily, a euphemism for dismissal (and whose 'unemployment benefit is brought before their Court of Referees'[80]); and 941 completed the three month course without being placed in work. At the Kettering camp in 1933 a mere 20 per cent of trainees (who totalled 967) were placed in jobs.[81]

Phillpott stressed the voluntary ethos of the camps, and dismissed charges that labour exchange officials forced attendance: 'attendance at the camps is entirely voluntary, and the trainees are practically all single men of not more than twenty-five years of age. They are given the opportunity

[74] 'Those "Concentration" Camps'.   [75] *Daily Herald*, 16 Mar. 1934.
[76] *Daily Herald*, 17 Mar. 1934.   [77] Ibid.   [78] *Daily Herald*, 19 Mar. 1934.
[79] 'Those "Concentration" Camps'.   [80] *Daily Herald*, 15 Mar. 1934.
[81] *Daily Herald*, 19 Mar. 1934.

of going to the camps by their local Employment Exchanges, but a man who refuses to go is not penalised in connection with his unemployment benefit.' Sanction did follow dismissal, however: 'if, on the other hand, he goes to a camp and is dismissed for misconduct (this is rare), or voluntarily goes home, his case for benefit comes before his local Court of Referees.'[82] The TUC also believed attendance to be voluntary, describing the process by which trainees were selected for the instructional camps in 1938: 'under both the Unemployment Insurance Scheme and the Unemployment Assistance Scheme there is power to withhold benefit or assistance from people who refuse to undergo training or instruction, but I do not think that the Scheme is worked that way at present. The Ministry prefer to get volunteers, and having got them, an order is then formally made requiring them to go to the centre. This is done so as to enable the allowances to be legally paid at the centres.'[83] Misinterpretation of this procedure would appear to explain many charges about mandatory participation. The Minister of Labour had the power, from 1920, to make training a condition of receiving benefit but it was rarely exercised. Even the labour exhanges were reluctant to compel potential trainees, according to the TUC's knowledge: 'the Employment Exchanges have, so far, merely encouraged the unemployed persons to attend at these centres, and cases of compulsion to attend are very rare indeed.'[84]

The common theme amongst trainees was their overwhelming desire to get a job, as Phillpott concluded from his interviews: 'they give the impression that a job is the great but (as far as their experience has one) the unattainable thing.'[85] Phillpott conceded that most of the trainees were eager to complete the three months' stay and to get home, though he had difficulty unravelling the precise reasons, alighting upon a less than wholly plausible one:

I asked them how they had fared at the camp, and got the replies:
'All right,' 'Fine,' and 'Champion.'
Was the food good? Yes.
Were they bullied? No.
Were they fitter and heavier than when they came? Yes.
Had they any grouses? No.
What were they going to do when they went back? They didn't know but they wanted jobs.

[82] 'Those "Concentration" Camps'.
[83] MRC Warwick, TUC Records Folder: MSS.292/131.3/4; 131.3 (1), letter from J. L. Smyth, Social Insurance Department to Mr R. Morrow, Belfast & District Trades Union Council, 17 June 1938.
[84] MRC Warwick, TUC Records Folder: MSS.292/131.3/4; 131.3 (1), memorandum. Research & Economics. G. Woodcock and H. Croft, 27 Nov. 1936 'Training and Instructional Centres'. [85] *Daily Herald*, 16 Mar. 1934.

Nevertheless many of them wanted to 'go home.' I searched for the reason and presently, I think, found the general one. They are town-bred and have never been away from home before. The quiet of an isolated countryside is something new and something hard to understand. And when a young man's physique and mental outlook has been affected by malnutrition and unsought idleness the strange things are disturbing things.[86]

Perhaps Phillpott was naive in assuming how open the men would be with him. Alternatively, the men were simply bored and homesick.

Phillpott stresses the quality of food provided and the recreation facilities. He particularly enjoyed a concert given for trainees at the Kettering camp, concluding his third article with a colourful description:

I have just returned from an evening concert in one of the recreation huts. The programme was supplied by a group of people from a neighbouring township. I was at the back of the hut mixing with the 'chaps' and they revelled in the old melodies that the singers gave them. There they were in their corduroy trousers and their hob-nailed boots, drinking in the music and enjoying every moment of it. One of them turned to me and said: 'Fine. It takes your thoughts off things.' Rough diamonds perhaps, but diamonds all the same.[87]

Phillpott's syrupy prose aside, his reports on the camps were positive.

Support for Phillpott's positive assessment comes from other contemporary sources. Although the TUC received many casual complaints about the workings of the work camps these were never substantiated, and as Runciman has pointed out, organized labour was capable of mobilizing against unpopular government measures in the 1930s as it did in respect of the revised scales of benefit enacted under the Unemployment Act of 1934.[88] One academic wrote that compared with the government training centres 'there is less criticism of the instructional centres' by organized labour.[89] Unions feared that the government training centres placed workers in skilled positions without sufficient training and that employment exchange officials gave preferential treatment to these trainees over those trained traditionally. The TUC's principal concern at this time was the alleged use of workers on training schemes or in labour camps to perform work for which unemployed men, payable at full wages, were available. The secretary of the Congress's Social Insurance department explained: 'we object to the kind of training given in many cases, both because of its nature and of its inadequacy, and we also object to the trainees being used, as they have been in some instances, to threaten the

---

[86] *Daily Herald*, 16 Mar. 1934.
[87] *Daily Herald*, 18 Mar. 1934.   [88] Runciman (1966: 65–7).
[89] D. Christie Tait, 'Unemployment of Young People in Great Britain', *International Labour Review*, 31 (Feb. 1935), 177–89, p. 187.

wage standards of workers in industry.'[90] A similar letter was sent to many local councils who enquired about training on government schemes. The TUC assiduously filed complaints about such usages, though the material was rarely decisive as it conceded to one correspondent: 'the Government contend that the employment of these trainees does not displace skilled labour, and whilst we contend the opposite, we have not been able up to now to obtain any proof that it is so.'[91] It responded to all letters complaining about the camps by asking for detailed statements, but received no further accounts from the complainants. For instance, in March 1934 a letter was sent to Mr Frank Day in Brighton thanking him for his 'letter of 13th of March regarding men sent to training camps having to parade each morning and salute the Union Jack and also being marched through the town and district all in fours on Saturday afternoons. We have no knowledge of these points, and if you have any further information we will be much obliged if you will further it on.'[92] Nothing further was heard from the correspondent, as was commonly the pattern with other correspondents complaining about the ICs.

A TUC delegation to an instructional centre at Presteigne, in 1930, came away favourably impressed by its work: 'we have to report that the spirit of the men generally appeared to be one of happiness and contentment. In our opinion the facilities at the Camp are satisfactory and successfully fulfil the programme intended—reconditioning and preparation of men for re-engagement in industry.'[93] The delegation arrived unannounced. Writing in the ILO's journal, Christie Tait provided a detailed account of the work camps.[94] Tait stressed the voluntariness of attendance at the camps and the absence of military overtones: 'the discipline is strict but quite informal. There is nothing which suggests military training in the remotest degree. On the contrary, everything is done to avoid the least suspicion of anything military throughout the course. There are no uniforms, there is no marching to and from work, there is no saluting either when the manager speaks to the men or at any other time.'[95] The trainees at the camps Tait visited

[90] MRC Warwick, TUC Records, Folder: MSS.292/131.3/3; 131.3 (1), letter from J. L. Smyth, Social Insurance Department, TUC to William Lorimer, General Secretary Associated Blacksmiths' Forge and Smith Workers' Society, 22 Aug. 1933.

[91] Ibid., letter from J. L. Smyth, Social Insurance Department, to Mr Alex Gossip, National Amal Furnishing Trades' Association, 3 Oct. 1938. See also letter from J. L. Smyth, Social Insurance Department, to Mr R. Morrow, Belfast & District Trades Union Council, 17 June 1938.

[92] Ibid., letter from J. L. Smyth, Social Insurance Department, TUC to Frank Day, Brighton Trades Council & Labour Party, 14 Mar. 1934.

[93] Ibid., Report of the Sub-Committee appointed to visit the Ministry of Labour, Transfer Instructional Centre at Presteign, 8 Oct. 1930, p. 2

[94] Tait, 'Unemployment of Young People in Great Britain'.   [95] Ibid. 185.

'looked happy' and 'pleased' to be there. Reconditioning was effective: 'as an example of the benefit which the men derive from the course I was shown a record of their weights on entering the centre and on subsequent dates. There were cases in which a man had gained as much as two stone after a period of eight weeks in the centre.'[96] The TUC also noted that trainees attended labour camps voluntarily, informing one correspondent that 'attendance at these centres is not compulsory, and we understand that there are large numbers of unemployed who are anxious and willing to accept the course.'[97] It cited Phillpott's articles in the *Daily Herald* in support of its favourable evaluation. The TUC liked the camps in part because of the generality of the 'training' provided, meaning that no threat to existing training schemes was posed: 'these centres are for people who have been unemployed a very long time and, in many cases, who have never had employment at all, the object being to give them a short course so as to fit them for employment if any should be offered to them, as it is contended that through their long unemployment they would not be able to do a job if it were offered to them.'[98]

The conflict in historical assessments of labour camps, such as Colledge's or Field's, and contemporary perceptions, such as Phillpott's, turns more on the interpretation of these institutions than on disagreements about their operation. Admittedly, Colledge's account finds serious deficiencies in the food and standards available, and Field bases his criticisms in part on interviews with some former trainees, but otherwise their analyses are not inconsistent with much of Phillpott's. The differences seem rather to arise from alternative readings of the same material. Both acknowledge the fundamental problem of reconditioning men for work in the absence of jobs, a deadening effect for the trainees; the grinding boredom of life in often remote camps looms larger in Colledge's account than in Phillpott's but is still present in the latter's pieces. Memories of the work camps is also presumably influenced by the time of year spent there: winter in a remote, poorly heated labour camp must have been rather less pleasant than three months in the Suffolk countryside in spring or summer. Such differences were probably amplified by the genuine homesickness that affected many of the trainees, away from their home and local community for the first time, and the quality of the camps may have deteriorated by the end of the 1930s. On balance, being a trainee was probably not much fun but nor was it as relentlessly grim as recent descriptions contend, the

[96] Tait, 'Unemployment of Young People in Great Britain'. 186.
[97] MRC Warwick TUC Records, Folder: MSS.292/131.3/4; 131 (1), letter from J. Smyth, Secretary of Insurance Department TUC to John Walker, Secretary Middlesbrough Trades and Labour Council, 28 June 1934.   [98] Ibid.

better camps combining decent food with physically tiring work. No amount of reconditioning, however, produced jobs.

After serving three months in an Instructional Centre, unemployed men were supposed to be placed in jobs. High unemployment made this improbable. Colledge argues that placement in employment was integrated into a reward and sanction system: jobs 'were "given away" as prizes to the more "conscientious trainees". It was also developed as a method of camp discipline.'[99] Given the general shortage of jobs available at the time, camp managers had a rather small number of places to award or withhold, somewhat limiting this mechanism as a general instrument of discipline. Phillpott puts it differently but recognizes the same problem: 'Are the "concentration camps" or the "instructional centres" or the "reconditioning centres", as they are variously called, making a real and lasting contribution to the solution of the problem of unemployment? I have visited most of them, and have come to the conclusion that the answer to that question is in the negative.'[100] In terms of benefiting the trainees, however, Phillpott was, contrary to later views, unreservedly laudatory: 'are the camps fulfilling a useful social work of human reclamation and rebuilding? The answer to that is certainly in the affirmative. No unbiased person visiting the camps, talking to the young men in them, watching the system of administration, and noting the difference between new trainees and those who have had a few weeks' experience of the camp life, could come to any other conclusion.'[101]

PHYSICAL TRAINING CLASSES

The need to maintain 'employability' was an enduring concern of civil servants and politicians in policy toward the unemployed. Mental or physical deterioration was viewed with alarm and frequently identified as a spectre hovering over the unemployed. This led to pressure, in the words of one civil servant, to extend 'what is being done in the training centres' to a larger proportion of the unemployed. The concerned official, J. A. Barlow, concluded that the regulation of the numbers admitted 'by the expectation of placing' was an inadequate response to this pressure even if logically it seemed sensible:[102]

we have always resisted this, not only on the grounds of expense, but also because we are satisfied, as the result of considerable experience, that the efficiency of the training centres essentially depends upon the prospects of placing at the end of

---

[99] Colledge (1989: vi).   [100] *Daily Herald*, 22 Mar. 1934.   [101] Ibid.
[102] Memorandum to Deputy Secretary, Ministry of Labour, from J. A. Barlow, 12 Nov. 1931, in PRO LAB 18/25.

the course, and that vocational training for adults is likely to be at best futile unless a high proportion of the men trained are placed.[103]

If the criterion for an expansion of training was the guarantee of a job for trainees then the prospects for an enlarged programme were unpromising. Nevertheless, the Ministry accepted the value, confirmed 'both by some of our own officers and by a number of independent observers' of offering occupation to those unemployed more than six months, 'even if at the end of it he must still remain unemployed'.[104] Barlow reported support for some form of 'physical instruction' especially for the younger unemployed: 'several of us have visited the training courses provided by the London Public Assistance Authority and have been much impressed by the value and possibilities of the physical training given in them by expert instructors. Physical training has also been a very successful item in many of the Junior Instructional Centres.'[105] An initial, modest, arrangement was sketched out by Barlow. He proposed an 'experiment' under which 'for (say) six months or a year, in (say) half a dozen selected areas, suitable young men between the ages of (say) 18 and 25 who have been unemployed for (say) not less than three months or six months would be invited to attend a course of physical instruction, to be provided by the Ministry for (say) three hours a day one day a week, or an hour a day on three days a week, for 10 weeks or three months.' The experiment would require modest expenditure by the Ministry of Labour: 'the Ministry would obtain premises (if possible rent free) and would provide an expert instructor, who would have to be paid, a small amount of equipment, consisting mainly of a few mattresses, and a simple outfit for each man. The outfit would consist of a singlet, shorts and a pair of gym shoes.'[106] Barlow did not anticipate very high costs for the scheme: £400 a year to provide training for 450 individuals; £4,000 to run six courses with 2,700 participants. In Barlow's view, obviously a keep fit enthusiast, British citizens neglected the 'possible attractiveness of modern physical training as an athletic amusement', in contrast to other polities: 'movements of this kind have developed on a very large scale in other countries such as Sweden, Czecho-Slovakia and Germany, and though there the organisations have often been captured for political ends, their beneficial effect on physique and morale is undoubted.'[107] The scheme was initially to be voluntary, to test whether enthusiasm was sufficient to warrant compulsory attendance. An optimistic statement of aims explained the purpose of physical exercise: '(1) to develop character, (2) to produce alertness of mind and (3) to create bodily fitness.'[108]

[103] Memorandum to Deputy Secretary, Ministry of Labour, from J. A. Barlow, 12 Nov. 1931, in PRO LAB 18/25.
[104] Ibid.   [105] Ibid.   [106] Ibid.   [107] Ibid.
[108] 'The Objects of Physical Training', 6 pp., n.d., in PRO LAB 18/25.

The scheme was adopted. Physical training classes were established in areas with high unemployment—Glasgow, Liverpool, Pontypridd, and Middlesbrough.[109] Sessions were for three months. Eligibility was restricted to 'young men between 18 and 30 years who are wholly unemployed'. Crucially, it was voluntary: 'no compulsion is placed on men to attend nor is any penalty imposed on those who drop out during the course.'[110] In a survey in October 1933, Barlow reported good progress in the development of the centres. The programme was organized in four divisions (North-East, Midlands, Scotland, and Wales), each with two centres.[111] The Ministry aimed to have these centres taken over by voluntary organizations and extended throughout the country. Funding for physical training centres remained problematic,[112] and the standard of training provided varied greatly between centres: 'although the position looks tolerably satisfactory on paper [there are] misgivings as to a good many of the centres which are of a very amateurish character. In some, the instructors are definitely bad and accidents are happening, to the consequent prejudice to the movement.'[113]

The eight training centres, called demonstration centres, in place in 1934, were intended as centres for the unemployed. However, as the UAB had to determine whether the 'extent to which physical training provides a cheap and satisfactory means of maintaining the employability of those applying for public assistance,'[114] attendance was not always popular.

CONCLUSION

Several conclusions arise from this analysis of British labour camps operative in the 1930s. First, it is difficult to sustain the highly critical interpretations of them offered by several scholars. Granted they were probably not terribly congenial places (with some much worse than others) and many of us would prefer not to be resident in one, the camps hardly constituted Goffmanian total institutions or functioned according to a martinet militaristic code. While there was the odd fracas in some camps and a proportion of trainees left before the end of their three months, on the whole most trainees stuck with it. Furthermore, the accounts of the benefits to physique and health are not entirely negative. As disciplinary institutions, their role appears modest, even though the Labour Party Minister

---

[109] Ministry of Labour, *Annual Report for the Year 1932* (London: HMSO, 1933), 34.
[110] 'Physical Training Classes', n.d., in PRO LAB 18/25.
[111] 'Physical Training Centres. Present Position', 27 Oct. 1933, 3 pp., in PRO LAB 18/25.
[112] Memo to Mr Allen, 3 Jan. 1934, in PRO LAB 18/25.
[113] Memo to Mr Humbert Wolfe from Barlow, 18 Jan. 1934, in PRO LAB 18/25.
[114] Memo to Mr Humbert Wolfe from Barlow, 18 Jan. 1934, in PRO LAB 18/25.

of Labour, Margaret Bondfield, plainly had ambitious plans in this direction. The exclusively male focus of the centres might warrant some support for a disciplinary view (women were not seen by policy-makers as central to the labour market) but such a gender composition is hardly startling in the inter-war years.[115] The initiatives for unemployed women in this period provided activities reflecting such views, with instruction in domestic management and tasks common. The work camps were limited strictly to those at the core of the labour market.

Second, the paucity of expertise employed by the key civil servants is striking. There were clear views about the need to 'toughen up' or 'recondition' the unemployed but this rested more on anecdotal sources than systematic data collection. Decision-making was restricted to senior civil servants (at Labour and the Treasury) with some input from the Labour Party's Minister of Labour, but there is remarkably little evidence of these policy-makers examining other camp experiences, whether the nineteenth-century European prototype or voluntary efforts in Britain such as that of the Salvation Army (consideration of which was available in several government reports), though they may have been aware of earlier support for camps for the unemployed such as that expressed by Beatrice Webb. They plainly did know about comparable schemes established in the same decade in other European countries. Ministers and civil servants were petitioned with those advancing land reclamation and settlement schemes rather than work camps. This absence of expertise must have informed the simplicity of the work schedules and routines established in the camps: training was basic or minimal (and certainly well below the standards sought by the TUC), and the emphasis solely upon physical reconditioning. Thus the camps did not fundamentally modify the men's ability to enter the labour market in terms of the jobs they could take. They simply attempted to restore their physical powers and morale. This leads John Field to characterize them as focused upon inculcating a work ethic: however, since all the men (and indeed administrators) interviewed by Phillpott indicated nothing but an eagerness to obtain work, Field may be overinterpreting this aspect of the camps.

Finally, although the historical record does not give these camps a salient position, and a modest historiography has developed centred on their perniciousness, in fact there is little evidence that the government attempted to keep them secret or invisible: they were discussed in parliament and included in the Ministry of Labour's annual reports. The accounts of Phillpott, under the byline 'concentration camps', suggests exactly the reverse, as do reports in the Ministry of Labour's annual reports. They were

---

[115] See the discussion in McKibbin (1998: 164–76).

conceived of as part of an ameliorative initiative, collectivist experiments which governments composed of different parties were willing to justify at the time as part of a concerted response to the unemployment crisis. They were pragmatic experiments, implemented with strikingly little knowledge. The camps' voluntary character—even though the extent of this feature varied at times—made this collectivist arrangement compatible with liberal democratic precepts. However, in contrast to the United States, the extent of this compatibility was much less adequately stated or integrated into national politics—indeed, it is remarkable how little effort was made in this regard. That work camps in Britain flirted with, rather than being subsumed in, an illiberal framework reflects the embeddedness of the country's liberal democracy.

6

'They Have Been Given a Chance': The US Civilian Conservation Corps

THIS chapter examines the United States' use in the 1930s of work camps, in the Civilian Conservation Corps (CCC), as a mechanism to address unemployment. It begins with a brief account of the origins and establishment of the CCC, and in the main part of the chapter provides an account of the Corps at work. The exposition is structured by two issues: the ways in which the Corps was made compatible with traditional US political values; and how attempts to make the CCC permanent were thwarted. I argue that the Corps encountered pressures arising from the liberal political culture in the United States, as interpreted and manipulated by President Roosevelt, which precluded its becoming a permanent collectivist institution. As a government programme, it fitted well with a liberal ameliorative agenda but only on a short-term basis.

As an exercise in social policy, the Corps rested on a modest informational basis. Policy-makers were familiar principally with state-level experiments in collectivist solutions to unemployment, which combined a concern with conservation with the needs of large numbers of unemployed persons. These examples came directly to Roosevelt's White House with his key administrators such as Harry Hopkins; and they were part of the overall New Deal initiative in which competing and varied ideas and proposals were articulated amongst senior policy-makers. As Weir and Skocpol show, in the 1930s, the US federal government was open to new proposals, which could help address unemployment.[1] Upon assuming office, Roosevelt quickly brought his famous 'brains trust' to the White House, academic experts (such as Raymond Moley and Rexford Tugwell) to advise him on policy.

The CCC is part of the general public works programme which characterized the New Deal response to misery and unemployment. However, as a programme the Corps is distinct from other New Deal publicly funded initiatives. First, it was residential, with participants allocated to camps in

[1] See Weir and Skocpol (1985).

often remote areas, unlike participants on work relief schemes under the Civil Works Administration, the Federal Emergency Relief Administration, or the Works Progress Administration, all locally administered and based. Second, sending participants off to remote camps, some of whom had not previously spent time away from home (and the Corps specifically selected young men from families on relief), opened up the potential for it to be a punitive institution. Third, the training component offered in the Corps was modest compared with other New Deal agencies such as the National Youth Administration (open to young women as well as men unlike the Corps), though the stipend received from the former was greater.[2] Finally, although established as a temporary agency, an ambition to make the CCC permanent was soon pursued by its administrators. Whether such an institution should become permanent or remain short-term was an issue of significance against the background of Franklin Roosevelt's efforts to reforge American liberal values through his New Deal programmes.

Combined, these four characteristics indicate how a programme such as the CCC might have broken decisively with the USA's individualist liberal values. How this was avoided can be explained in two sorts of ways. First, in the context of the New Deal initiatives, when politics was dynamic and occasionally volatile, policy innovative, and there was an openness to new schemes which could plausibly contribute to reducing unemployment, any reasonable scheme would be assessed seriously by policy-makers, and attention given to its potential excesses. Both Roosevelt and Hopkins brought their experiences from New York state to the White House, which included conservation projects. Alan Brinkley remarks that the CCC, because of its work content, was 'a plan the president particularly liked'.[3] More generally, the Corps was protected by the prestige increasingly attaching to the New Deal as the 1930s unfolded. Second, the way in which programmes such as the CCC were implemented could be designed to ensure that illiberal dangers were deflected, both by rendering it politically compatible with liberal democracy (in this instance as reflected in Roosevelt's stated ambition to broaden American liberalism to include government responsibility for economic security); and by making it compatible with key aspects of contemporary US society. Both sorts of factors are germane to an explanation of the CCC's operation, and after briefly describing its establishment, I turn to the four ways through which the Corps compatibility was inured.

[2] Amenta (1998: 156).
[3] Brinkley (1998: 21).

ESTABLISHING THE CCC

The CCC was established in the midst of the New Deal.[4] Eligibility was strictly regulated. Participation was limited to young men between 18 and 25 whose families were registered on the relief rolls, excluding married men, women, and young men in work. Enrollees received $30.00 a month, $22.00 of which was intended for the enrollee's dependents.

The organizational principle informing the CCC was uncomplicated. First, there were large numbers of able-bodied young men unable to find work. Second, the United States' natural resources included major conservation projects going unattended, such as reforestation. The Corps was designed to 'kill two birds with one stone. Put the young men to work conserving the soil and planting trees. Save the soil, save the forests and by that process save the young men. It was really quite simple, as are most great ideas.'[5] Camps were established throughout the United States in which enrollees (initially limited to six-month periods though some were permitted to re-enroll) undertook vigorous outdoor activity (winningly portrayed in the CCC's newsletter, *Happy Days*). Organizational simplicity did not render the CCC problem free, however. The Corps was accused of inadequately addressing the needs of young Black Americans seeking to enrol (in the segregated camps established for them); it was under pressure to militarize; and its most ardent supporters wanted to make it a permanent organization. Each of these pressures was countered.[6]

Conservation work for the unemployed

The CCC was a new experiment for the US federal government. One Labor Department official characterized the new experience it offered young American men: 'life in the out-of-doors in a well-managed camp, work in the conservation of natural resources, guidance and supervision by officers and foremen who desire to grow men as well as trees, and to develop personality as well as parks—all these factors contribute to make membership in the Corps an experience of great significance to eager and

---

[4] The CCC—or Emergency Conservation Work to give it its formal title—was created by Act of Congress approved 31 Mar. 1933; the authorization for its extension to and including 30 June 1937 was included in the Emergency Relief Appropriation Act 1935 and the first Deficiency Act of 1937. Roosevelt's Executive Order No. 6101, issued on 5 Apr. 1933, gave organizational effect to the original bill. It was part of the Emergency Relief Administration.

[5] NARA RG 35 Records of the CCC, Division of Selection: Records relating to organization and operation of Selection Work, 1933–42, Box 15, Folder: 'Now They are Men'. Typescript of James J. McEntee 'Now They are Men: The Story of the CCC' (1940) 10.

[6] For the best scholarly study see Salmond (1967). The CCC receives obligatory reference but litte detailed consideration in most accounts of the New Deal.

baffled youth.'[7] There was a clear rationale: 'their purpose is to save the natural resources of the United States.'[8]

There was no federal precedent in the country's preceding 150 years, though some states had instituted comparable experiments on a small scale. To succeed, three necessary conditions were identified: first, camps had to be established on 'public lands where there is no competition with regular paid labor'. Trade unionists were doubtful that this condition would be achieved: the president of the American Federation of Labor (AFL), William Green, at first criticized the proposed scheme for offering too low wages and because of, in Edwin Amenta's phrase, the 'seeming regimentation of workers',[9] precisely the sort of criticism of the New Deal in general marshalled by critics such as Herbert Hoover and Friedrich Hayek.[10] One Detroit local declared that the 'Roosevelt plan of relief, the so-called Labor Camps, are nothing else but an insult to the working class'.[11] Politically, this view remained a marginal one, however, and indeed the Corps's Director, Robert Fechner, was a former vice-president of the AFL. Second, the type of work most suited for the camps was forestry, landscaping, and reclamation of lands in public park reservations. And, third, 'if additional work projects should be needed to care for the number of men applying, it is recommended that industrial agricultural colonies be established on arable lands,' a location which would make the camps self-sufficient.[12] These recommendations informed the CCC programme.

The Corps's ideology, which rapidly developed, stressed the principles of preserving natural resources and of preserving the self-esteem of unemployed young 'men of character and fitness'[13]—as Figure 6.1, reproducing an illustration from 1935 depicts. In the official history of the CCC, the language used to describe the Corps was extravagant. Characterizing unemployment as an 'epidemic' and 'plague', the study's author, James McEntee,

[7] NARA RG 35 Records of the CCC, Division of Selection, Records relating to organization and growth of Selection Work 1933–42, Box 1, Folder: W. Frank Persons, Speeches and Statements. Remarks by W. Frank Persons at the Conference of State Directors and Supervisors of CCC Selection, Washington, 4 Apr. 1938, p. 6.
[8] Ibid., Box 1A Folder: Papers. 'The Purposes, Requirements and Opportunities of the Civilian Conservation Corps', memo December 1940, p. 2.
[9] Amenta (1998: 74).
[10] Hoover (1938) and Hayek (1944).
[11] NARA RG 35 Records of the CCC, Division of Selection General Correspondence, Box 11, Folder: Resolution of Protest, passed on 25 Apr. 1933, by 200 members. Detroit branch of the AWU.
[12] NARA RG 35 Records of the CCC, Division of Selection General Correspondence 1933–42, Box 4, Folder: Camps and Projects. Ralf Astrofsky, 'Work Relief Camps in Present Emergency' 20 Mar. 1933, 4 pp., pp. 1–2.
[13] NARA RG 35 Records of CCC, Division of Selection, Records relating to the Organization and growth of Selection Work 1933–42, Box 1, Folder: Secretary of Labor. 'The Selection of Men for the Civilian Conservation Corps' 5 Apr. 1933–5 Apr. 1935, p. 2.

declared that, 'it is the mission of this generation to find these means of control before these plagues destroy us. It is upon that mission we, in the United States, are embarked. Only in a land of free men is it possible to embark on such a mission.'[14] Liberal democracy permitted collectivist experiments, though within strict limits.

The Corps was allowed to recruit 250,000 men for the camps it established in the national forests, the national parks, and on the public domain;[15] (an additional 25,000 older men, knowledgeable of local conditions, were recruited later). Enrolment was voluntary, as the Selecting Handbook underlined: 'no coercion or pressure should be used to induce any man to enroll. No one is being "drafted" or "conscripted" for this work ... Only applicants who are anxious to have a part in this project are wanted.'[16] Nor could a recruiting agency threaten to withhold relief from a recipient unwilling to enroll, since such a practice amounted to 'coercion' and would be 'contrary to the whole spirit of this enterprise.'[17] This celebration of the Corps's voluntary character differentiated it from comparable British policy, whose critics accused of being coercive. In fact, the Corps was oversubscribed.

That only 'suitable' men should be selected was stressed by the CCC's senior administrators. They wanted the 'best qualified of this needy group'.[18] Selection criteria were clear, and were not dissimilar to those for British camps:

it was decided that the new work program would be reserved primarily for those physically fit, unmarried men, 18–25 years of age, who were then unemployed. They were required to be citizens of the United States. Priority was given to those who wished to allot to their needy relatives the major portion of their monthly $30 cash allowance. These young, unmarried men were selected partly because of the type of work and the camp life involved, and partly because this age group had met

[14] NARA RG 35 Records of the CCC, James J. McEntee, 'Now They are Men: The Story of the CCC', pp. 1–2. McEntee continued with the disease metaphor likening unemployment to tuberculosis, a standard analogy: 'economic depression and war are diseases of society which are somewhat analogous to tuberculosis in human beings. There is no simple vaccine against them. The approach of each is insidious. To reduce their toll we must be on guard in many different ways.'

[15] NARA RG 35 Records of the CCC, Reference Files 1933–42 Box 1, US Department of Labor, National Emergency Conservation Work: What it is—How it Operates, 20 Apr. 1933.

[16] NARA RG 35 Records of the CCC, Reference Files 1933–42 Box 1, US Department of Labor, 'Handbook for Agencies Selecting Men for Emergency Conservation Work', revised 25 Sept. 1933, 10.

[17] Ibid.

[18] NARA RG 35 Records of the CCC, Division of Selection, Records Relating to Conference 1936–42, Box 6, Folder: Mr Persons' Speeches. Remarks by W. Frank Persons at the Conference of State Directors and Supervisors of CCC Selection, Washington DC, 4 Apr. 1938, p. 3.

great difficulty in securing either work or relief. Some of them had never found a job since leaving school.[19]

Since the focus was upon aiding those individuals and families who lacked earned income, the names of eligible men were first taken from those of families in receipt of public aid.[20]

Finally, 'moral character' was a criterion for selection. Although it could 'not be compressed into formal eligibility requirements', nonetheless, it 'pervaded the whole enterprise': 'those selected were to be young men of character—clean-cut, purposeful, and ambitious,' since it was deemed to be a 'privilege' to participate in the Corps.[21] After listing physical fitness, unemployment, unmarried, the age requirement, citizenship, dependents, and allotment of income to dependents, the Department of Labor also emphasized 'character' as 'basic to the success of the whole undertaking'. It explained: 'this peace-time "forest expeditionary force" should be made up of young men of *character*—men who are clean-cut, purposeful and ambitious—the finest young men that can be found in all the eligible group.'[22] These criteria implied grounds for exclusion: 'unattached, homeless, transient men were not selected because it was believed that the enterprise would be of more benefit to whole families than to single individuals. The requirement of physical fitness was an obvious necessity for strenuous outdoor work.'[23] The objection to transients[24] was restated at the CCC's Advisory Council, to whom James McEntee reported that 'the President does not want the transients—only boys who have dependents. He did not want boys without dependents mixing with those that have

---

[19] NARA RG 35 Records of CCC, Division of Selection, Records relating to the Organisation and Growth of Selection Work 1933–42, Box 1, Folder: Secretary of Labor. 'The Selection of Men for the Civilian Conservation Corps', 5 Apr. 1933–5 Apr. 1935, p. 5.

[20] NARA RG 35 Records of the CCC, National Emergency Conservation Work: What it is—How it Operates, 20 Apr. 1933.

[21] NARA RG 35 Records of CCC, Secretary of Labor, 'The Selection of Men for the Civilian Conservation Corps', 5 Apr. 1933–5 Apr. 1935, p. 6. See also Ibid. Box 1, Folder: W. Frank Persons, Speeches and Statements; remarks by W. Frank Persons at the Fifth Anniversay Banquet of the CCC, Washington, 5 Apr. 1938.

[22] NARA RG 35 Records of the CCC, Reference Files 1933–42 Box 1, US Department of Labor, 'Handbook for Agencies Selecting Men and Emergency Conservation Work', 1 May 1933, p. 5. Emphasis in original text.

[23] NARA RG 35 Records of CCC, Secretary of Labor, 'The Selection of Men for the Civilian Conservation Corps', 5 Apr. 1933–5 Apr. 1935, p. 5.

[24] NARA RG 35 Records of the CCC, Division of Selection, General Correspondence 1933–42, Box 4, Folder: Camps and Projects. For an early discussion of transients see US Department of Labor Children's Bureau, 'Memorandum on the Transient Boys', Washington 1932, 7 pp. This document reported both the scale of the problem and the breakdown of pre-Depression mechanisms to address it: 'most of the communities through which this hungry, tired, and dirty horde passes are no longer able to meet the needs of their own unemployed adequately. They have no choice but to spend as little as possible on nonresidents' (p. 3).

dependents.'[25] This is a revealing political calculation by the Democratic President about who voted and whose votes mattered.

Recruitment was rapid. By 10 June, two months after its establishment, the CCC had accepted 240,577 men. A week later the national quota of 250,000 was either in conditioning camps preparing for the work camps or at the camps (of which 1,330 were established). Reflecting on this early period, Frank Persons recalled that local recruitment offices were 'literally inundated by waves of the unemployed asking for this new work'.[26] The contrast with Britain is marked. By 1937, 1,651,523 Americans had been enrolled in the CCC and $1,557,900,679.79 allocated to dependents.[27] According to Persons, the enrollees were paragons of American virtues:

rightly considered, the Corps is not a stop-gap agency. . . . young men do not seek enrollment merely in order to escape idleness for a time or because the CCC offers a haven for those who lack ambition. They apply in large numbers, now many times greater than can be enrolled, because they want the chance to contribute an honest day's labor on useful projects and through that effort to gain health, the habit of work and useful skills; and, at the end of the work-day, to engage in activities of educational or recreational nature as the means of self-improvement.[28]

Joining the CCC did not reflect poorly on an individual's character but simply the tragedy of adverse circumstances: 'membership . . . is in no sense a badge of destitution. Rather, these young potential workers are unwilling victims of a vicious circle: being unable to get jobs without experience and unable to get that experience without jobs.'[29]

At its foundation, the CCC decided against camps for unemployed women although unemployment was not an exclusively male phenomenon. Persons explained this policy to a female enquirer in 1938. Because the founding legislation specified young unemployed men, 'there is no legal authority for the CCC organization to extend aid to any other group'.[30]

[25] NARA RG 35 Records of the CCC, CCC Advisory Council Minutes, Box 1, Meeting, 18 June 1935, p. 8.

[26] NARA RG 35 Records of the CCC, Division of Selection, Records relating to the Organization and Growth of Selection Work 1933–42, Box 1, Folder: W. Frank Persons, Speeches and Statements. Remarks by W. Frank Persons at the Conference of State Directors and Supervisors of CCC Selection, Washington, 4 Apr. 1938, p. 2.

[27] Hearings before the Committee on Labor, House of Representatives, Seventy-fifth Congress, First Session on HR 6180, 'To Make the Civilian Conservation Corps a Permanent Agency', 14 and 15 Apr. 1937 (Washington, DC: GPO), 12–13, 16–17.

[28] NARA RG 35 Records of the CCC, W. Frank Persons, Speeches and Statements. Remarks by W. Frank Persons at the Conference of State Directors and Supervisors of CCC Selection, Washington, 4 Apr. 1938, p. 5.

[29] Ibid. 6.

[30] NARA RG 35 Records of the CCC, Division of Selection, General Correspondence Box 21, Folder: Women's Camps. Letter from Frank Person to Miss Agnes Butterby, 18 Aug. 1938.

The National Youth Administration, another New Deal agency, took the initiative regarding unemployed women, establishing camps in thirteen states in the mid-1930s.[31] The camps imitated those of the Corps, enrolling up to 5,000 women in total for periods of three to four months and placed them to work in outdoor environments supplemented with some education.[32]

There were problems in filling the number of CCC places in later years, especially because of the disinclination to recruit men from families not on relief. The selection criteria were modified extending the eligible age upperwards.[33] And, in 1937, the CCC was allowed to consider juniors and veterans who were on probation or parole,[34] an innovation Director Fechner hailed enthusiastically to his colleagues: 'the very nature of these camps, I think, offers a splendid opportunity for unattached men or men who have become involved in some controversy with the law, to be given a chance to rehabilitate themselves.'[35] The Corps founding legislation had excluded such enrollees. Full-time employment was preferred by participants; rumours of job openings prompted speedy departures from the camps.[36]

Created on 5 April 1933 (a mere sixteen days after the President's inauguration), a report from the commander of one conditioning camp on 23 April suggested that the CCC's selection criteria were operating successfully (see Figure 6.1): 'we have had 1500 men for 12 days, and during that period I have had only ONE disciplinary case. I had him on the carpet and he is a cheerful, willing worker now. I have not had a single case of drunkenness, fighting or refusal to work. The men are a fine, eager lot of boys.'[37]

[31] The key figure at the NYA was Ella Ketchin, Director, Division of Educational Camps; for an overall view see NARA RG 119 Records of the National Youth Administration 1936–7, Records of the Division of Educational Camps, Correspondence of the Director, Box 1, Folder: Education Committee, NYA 'Report of Educational Camps for Unemployed Young Women', Jan. 1936 to July 1937, Aug. 1937, 65 pp.

[32] 'NYA Establishing Camps for Women', *Baltimore Sun* 30 Nov. 1936.

[33] NARA RG 35 Records of the CCC, CCC Advisory Council Minutes, Box 1, Meeting of 9 Sept. 1935. From June 1940, enrollees needed simply to be unemployed, rather than part of a family household on welfare.

[34] The CCC's founding legislation in 1933 explicitly stated that no person under conviction for crime or serving sentence therefore could be employed; or persons on probation or parole.

[35] NARA RG 35 Records of the CCC, Report of Conferences Box 1, Report of Conference concerning the enrolment in the Civilian Conservation Corps of Juniors and Veterans who are on probation or parole, Department of Justice Building, Washington DC, 12 Nov. 1937, p. 4.

[36] The Advisory Council was informed in September 1935 that 'all the States are beneath their quotas' because of job rumours. NARA RG 35 Records of the CCC, CCC Advisory Council Minutes, Box 1, Meeting of 9 Sept. 1935, p. 4.

[37] NARA RG 35 Records of CCC, Secretary of Labor, 'The Selection of Men for the Civilian Conservation Corps', 5 Apr. 1933–5 Apr. 1935, p. 7.

FIG. 6.1 Shall we continue this? Or change to this?

Source: NARA RG 35 Records of the CCC, Reference Files 1933–42, Box 1, 'Conservation of Natural Resources, Unemployment and Crime: One Solution for All Three' (Riverside, Calif.: Tr-Counties Reforestation Committee, 1935).

The Department of Labor pressed the CCC director, Robert Fechner,[38] systematically to include vocational and education training in the pro-gramme of enrollees, maintaining that the ultimate purpose of the Corps was to 'prepare the young men who are seeking the avenue of escape from

[38] Fechner was vice-president of the International Association of Machinists and a lec-turer on labour at Harvard University. Franklin Roosevelt appointed him director of the CCC (officially titled the Emergency Conservation Work) in 1933.

unemployment'.[39] Labor's representative, Persons, wanted training to be substantial. An education programme was included from 1934. CCC camps gave considerable attention to education and training as the following table list shows reports: 89 per cent of all enrollees were engaged in some sort of educational activity (November 1938).

1. Total number of enrollees studying academic subjects: 104,284.
    a. (1) No. of illiterate enrollees: 7,494.
       (2) No. studying literacy courses: 7,331.
    b. (1) No. on elementary level: 95,268.
       (2) No. attending elementary courses: 50,104.
    c. (1) No. on high-school level: 144,791.
       (2) No. studying high-school courses: 47,338.
    d. (1) No. on college level: 37,903.
       (2) No. studying college courses: 2,580.
2. Number of enrollees attending vocational courses: 128,195.
3. Number of enrollees attending all informal activities: 46,785.
    a. No. enrollees attending arts and crafts: 26,437.
    b. No. enrollees attending music groups: 17,067.
    c. No. enrollees attending dramatic groups: 4,728.
4. Number of enrollees receiving training on the job: 177,346.
5. Number of individuals attending foreman, teacher, and leader training: 36,063.

Total: Number of individual enrollees participating in educational activities: 255,262.

Percentage 89.3.

(*Source*: 'To Make the Civilian Conservation Corps a Permanent Agency', Hearings before the Committee on Labor, House of Representatives, Seventy-sixth Congress First Session on HR 2990 9, 23, and 24 Feb. 1939 (Washington DC: GPO), 55.)

These data suggest a considerable educational programme within the CCC camps; they reveal also the educational deficiencies of many enrollees, including about 80,000 illiterate boys.[40]

CCC administrators soon boasted about the accomplishments of their camps. In July 1933, after 250,000 men had been selected and enrolled in

---

[39] Ibid. 9.
[40] 'To Make the Civilian Conservation Corps a Permanent Agency', hearings before the Committee on Labor, House of Representatives, Seventy-sixth Congress, First Session on HR 2990, 9, 23, and 24 Feb. 1939 (Washington DC: GPO), 69. It was proposed by Graham Barden, a Democrat from North Carolina.

CCC work camps,[41] its director, Robert Fechner assured President Roosevelt that mobilization for the CCC had 'gone a long way toward breaking the back of the depression'. He stressed the gains to the enrollees: 'these young men have been benefited, their families have been given important assistance at a time when such assistance was desperately needed . . . Young men who never had had a job and whose morale was at a low ebb have been taken from the distress of the family circle and the perils of the street corner to the helpful environment of the forest camp, and given the satisfaction of being well fed, and doing an honest day's work. They have been given a chance.'[42]

Camp organization and life

Each CCC camp had about 200 members. The young male enrollees worked eight-hour days, five days a week. Upon arrival at their camp, enrollees were given a Government Issue (GI) set of clothing, assigned to a tent (later replaced by barracks), and given a vigorous medical examination. The camp had a 'town centre' and was designed physically to emulate a community. It had its own 'store, usually a small newspaper, a library, a school building, a community dining room ("mess hall") for which the CCC members do the cooking and take care of the kitchen, a recreation hall, athletic contests, a small hospital, and facilities for adapting the camp assembly room as a church for religious worship. . . . Each camp has a leisure time program of education and training.'[43] Camps were, in effect, small towns. Camps were run by a civilian officer appointed as the Commanding Officer, and each camp of 200 men was designated a company. The War Department was responsible for constructing camps, housing, feeding, and clothing the men, making payments and supervising the work undertaken by Corps camps. The Labor Department selected the men. The Departments of Interior and Agriculture identified conservation projects which were under the supervision of Camp Superintendents appointed to each camp: 'each day the Commanding Officer turns over to the Camp Superintendent the work crew consisting of most of the enrollees in the camp. The enrollees work for eight hours under the direction of the Camp Superintendent and his staff of

[41] NARA RG 35 Records of the CCC, Reference Files 1933–42 Box 1, letter from Fechner to Roosevelt, 1 July 1933, p. 1.

[42] Ibid. 3.

[43] NARA RG 35 Records of the CCC, Division of Selection, Records relating to the Organization and Operation of Selection Work, 1933–42, Box 1A, Folder: Papers. 'The Purposes, Requirements and Opportunities of the Civilian Conservation Corps', memo Dec. 1940, p. 3.

foremen; there are usually from five to nine project foremen in each camp.'[44]

The young trainees signed an agreement accepting the rules of camp life.[45] Enrollees agreed to serve in whatever part of the country they were assigned to. The terms of enrolment reminded recruits that they were entering a contractual arrangement with the government: 'the Government is ready to spend considerable money to give you a decent uniform, to feed you, to pay you for your work, house you, give you medical attention, provide for your recreation and possibly give you the benefit of a trip to the West. It does expect you to do your part.' Failure to fulfil this agreement could 'result in your receiving an administrative or dishonorable discharge. This may appear to be unimportant now but you will find that a discharge of either type will make it very difficult for you to secure employment in the future.'[46] (This contractual obligation had echoes of the agreement signed by recruits to the Salvation Army camp at Hadleigh.) New CCC members took an oath of enrolment and were encouraged to obey the rules associated with their new status. They were urged to strive for the 'one thing which every CCC boy should attain—an honorable discharge'.[47] The same speaker gave the new recruits two pieces of advice about camp life: first, 'find out what the regulations of the CCC are, what the regulations of the particular camp to which you are assigned are, and follow those rules and regulations to the letter'; and second, a further admonishment, 'to always do what you're told, and do what you're told when you're told to do it'.[48]

Speaking in Congress, Robert Fechner often emphasized the routinized nature of camp life and its similarities with military arrangements: 'the men get up at the same time, eat at the same time, go to work at the same time, and go to bed at the same time. All enrollees get the same basic rate of pay; all assistant leaders are paid identical amounts, as are the leaders.'[49] Thus like the famous French Minister of Education who could look at his watch and know what every French schoolchild was studying, the Director of the Corps could know what enrollees at the thousands of camps were

[44] Ibid. 5.

[45] NARA RG 35 Records of the CCC, Division of Selection Policy Files 1933–42, Box 16. See 'Places and Conditions under which Enrollees Selected from the First Corps Area may Serve', 5 pp.

[46] Ibid. 3.

[47] Ibid., 'A Typical Talk given by the Connecticut State Selecting Agent to each group of newly enrolled members of the CCC at the reception center immediately after the applicants have taken the oath of enrollment', 25 Jan. 1939, p. 1.

[48] Ibid. 1.

[49] 'To Make the Civilian Conservation Corps a Permanent Agency', hearings before the Committee on Labor, House of Representatives, Seventy-sixth Congress, First Session on HR 2990, 9, 23, and 24 Feb. 1939 (Washington, DC: GPO), 38.

doing according to the time of day or night—a very unAmerican phenomenon! Director Fechner also emphasized the few disciplinary problems in Corps camps: 'the C.C.C. has discipline and I believe it is the finest
type of discipline in the world, because it is effective and conforms to
American ideals and the American way of living.' He elaborated further:
'Our C.C.C. discipline is established almost entirely through moral suasion
and through superior leadership.'[50] Overall, the collectivizing effect of the
camps diminished individuality, though Fechner presented this effect as a
virtue:

the entire pattern of the Civilian Conservation Corps life teaches men to live
together, work together, and exert their energies as a team instead of solely as individuals. I have been informed by many high-ranking military and naval professional men that the job of teaching men to live together and work together is one
of the most difficult jobs which arises in connection with the creation of a large
military force for defense purposes.[51]

Such a celebration of collectivism over individualism is incongruous with
the values normally identified as foundational to US political culture and
reflect the contingencies presented by the 1930s.

The friendly atmosphere of CCC camps did not prove irresistible to all
enrollees. From the Corps's inception in 1933 there were discharges and
dropouts. Most commonly these arose because of employment opportunities of which enrollees wished to avail; others deserted. Table 6.1 gives a
breakdown of reasons for departure during the first three years of the
CCC. Perusing the statistics, Director Fechner observed that the 'two items
of disciplinary discharges and desertion together', was 'pretty high'.[52]

The camps were commonly remote from towns, limiting recreation and
the opportunity to get away from the camp. They shared this geographic
characteristic with British camps. In those camps for African Americans,
quite often the closest towns were unwelcoming, particularly in northern
states.[53]

Some Corps camps were poorly run. Members of Company 1287 petitioned various federal administrators and Black American interest groups
to remove its commanding officer, Lieutenent Landy J. Hames. The
men accused Hames of alcoholism, as a consequence of which the 'camp
has experienced a complete degeneration'.[54] Most camps functioned

---

[50] 'To Make the Civilian Conservation Corps a Permanent Agency', 39.   [51] Ibid.
[52] NARA RG 35 Records of the CCC, CCC Advisory Council Minutes Box 1, Minutes
20 Apr. 1937, p. 2.
[53] LC NAACP I Box C 223, Folder: CCC, 1937. Letter to Walter White from enrollee at
Camp Co. 246 S-106, Salamanca, New York, 26 Nov. 1937. And see Salmond (1965: 80–1).
[54] LC NAACP I Box C 233, Folder: CCC Eugene Boykin, Jan.–Mar. 1939. Statement from
Company 1287, 22 Jan. 1939, 6 pp., p. 2.

TABLE 6.1 Discharges from the CCC April 1933–28 February 1937

Type of Discharge	Number	%
Physical disability	40,864	2.67
To accept employment	392,946	25.71
Disciplinary reasons	119,582	7.82
Desertion	177,419	11.6
Other causes (90% = expiration of term of enrolment)	798,208	52.2
Total	1,529,019	100.0

Source: NARA RG 35, Records of the CCC, CCC Advisory Council Minutes Box 1, Minutes 20 Apr. 1937, pp. 1–2.

efficiently. Black Americans often complained of relatively worse conditions in their camps compared with those for whites, as in this report from Texas about Camp Bullis, in 1933:

they are not fed as well as the white soldiers, and are jim crowed in every respect. I found that the Colored boys are compelled to wait until the white men have had their fill of every thing before the Colored men are considered. The writer visited the dining room while the soldiers were being served apples which had been worm eaten and rat bitten, the very cheapest apples and the white men were served delicious apples while the Colored men looked on.[55]

THE CAMPS AND COLLECTIVISM

In some countries, collectivist solutions to social problems became a common response applied in a range of policies. This did not occur in the United States, where the CCC was a conspicuous exception. As an exercise in collectivist social amelioration, the CCC was precariously placed. It had to balance the urgent need to address mass unemployment through collective conservation and training measures, with historical political anxieties about the infringement of American democratic values symbolized by such an approach. Consequently, its social radicalism was diluted and the CCC stands, retrospectively, much more with the stop-gap of conventional government policy in a market democracy, in this instance a form of pragmatic illiberalism, than with socialist collectivism. The way in which the CCC developed and the failure of attempts to make it a permanent

[55] LC NAACP I Box C223, Folder: CCC, 1933. Memorandum from George Duncan, Houston Texas to the NAACP New York, 8 July 1933.

organization illustrate how political and ideological factors determined the outcome.

Camps and american politics

The use of camps by the CCC depended upon conceptualizing them positively as part of the mainstream of society and government policy. Thus, despite taking its enrollees almost exclusively from relief rolls, the Civilian Conservation Corps was celebrated and lauded as emblematic of American political values. Franklin Roosevelt himself adroitly emphasized the non-material gain of the CCC camps: 'more important . . . than the material gains will be the moral and spiritual value of such work . . . We can take a vast army of these unemployed out into healthful surroundings.'[56] Frank Persons grew rhapsodic about the idyll of CCC camp life: 'life in the out-of-doors in a well-managed camp, work in the conservation of natural resources, guidance and supervision by officers and foremen who desire to grow men as well as trees, and to develop personality as well as parks.'[57] The canonizing strategy won public support for the CCC:

both the public and Congress liked the results so well that there was no hesitation in appropriating more funds for the CCC after the first funds were exhausted. The Corps dug in to stay awhile. Wooden barracks replaced tents. Machinery was purchased to speed up the work production. Supervisors settled down to a program of training their men carefully. An educational program was introduced. Baseball teams were organized.[58]

Thus in contrast to collectivist solutions in other countries, the CCC was widely advertised and indeed celebrated; and it was voluntary. It is also significant that the Corps failed to become a youth movement given its potential to assume this role. Indeed, one observer detected such a tendency: 'the C.C.C. is today outstanding as a school of citizenship in this broad but decidedly vital and liberal sense . . . It is developing habits of work in its members while at the same time it is meeting their employment problem and that of their families.'[59] Inculcating 'habits of work' and

[56] NARA RG 35 Records of the CCC, James J. McEntee, 'Now They are Men: The Story of the CCC', p. 12.

[57] NARA RG 35 Records of the CCC, Division of Selection, Records Relating to Conference 1936–42, Box 6, Folder: Mr Persons' Speeches. Remarks by W. Frank Persons at the Conference of State Directors and Supervisors of CCC Selection, Washington DC, 4 Apr. 1938, p. 6.

[58] NARA RG 35 Records of the CCC, James J. McEntee, 'Now They are Men: The Story of the CCC', p. 12.

[59] LC NAACP I Box C223, Folder: CCC Eugene Boykin 1937–8. 'A Discussion of the Educational Program of the C.C.C. in New Jersey', Dec. 1937, p. 4.

attributes of citizenship, while worthy tasks, could too easily slip into over-bearing direction, a temptation resisted.

Measures which deviated from the positive conception of the CCC programme were handled gingerly. The decision, in May 1935, to take finger-prints of CCC enrollees was reached reluctantly. The memorandum announcing the decision warned that 'in view of the bias against finger-printing prevalent among many people in the United States care must be exercised by company commanders to present this subject in a tactful and patient manner that misunderstanding may be removed and unfavorable publicity be avoided.'[60] The policy had been discussed at the CCC's Advisory Council in April 1935 when the President's support for finger-printing was reported, though Roosevelt 'felt that it should be commenced on a voluntary basis. He feared that if it were made immediately compulsory, there might be considerable public reaction against the move.'[61] The Army's wish for fingerprinting to be mandatory was realized on 1 October 1937.[62] The instructions for this process were elaborate and designed to prevent abuse of the system;[63] public disquiet about the new policy was, however, not stilled: and Persons had to explain that there would be no intermingling of fingerprints gathered from CCC enrollees for the FBI's civil file with those on the FBI's criminal file.[64] To stem the anticipated hostility, the memorandum advised Corps commanders to begin fingerprinting on a 'voluntary basis in order that the reaction of enrollees may be observed, and decision made as to whether or not it should later be made mandatory'.[65]

African Americans and the CCC

One mechanism for diluting collectivism is to assimilate the prevailing societal assumptions about marginality in access to the new institutions. In

[60] NARA RG 35 Records of the CCC, Reference Files 1933–42, Box 2, Memorandum from Adjutant General's Office, War Department to All Corps Area Commanders 'Fingerprinting of C.C.C. Enrollees', 1 May 1935, p. 1.
[61] NARA RG 35 Records of the CCC, Division of Selection, General Correspondence Box 6, File: Fingerprinting. Report of Advisory Council in memorandum from Dean Snyder to Frank Persons 30 Apr. 1935, p. 2.
[62] NARA RG 35 Records of the CCC, Division of Selection, General Correspondence Box 6, File: Fingerprinting. War Department, the Adjutant General's Office, memorandum to All Corps Area Commanders 'Fingerprinting, Civilian Conservation Corps', 14 Sept. 1937, p. 1.   [63] Ibid.
[64] Ibid. See letter from Frank Persons to William Ellis, Commissioner Department of Institutions and Agencies, New Jersey, 12 Nov. 1937. Persons alludes to alarmist newspaper reports of the fingerprinting practice.
[65] NARA RG 35 Records of the CCC, Reference Files 1933–42, Box 2, Memorandum from Adjutant General's Office, War Department to All Corps Area Commanders 'Fingerprinting of C.C.C. Enrollees', 1 May 1935, p. 1.

the United States, this strategy was effected straightforwardly by limiting the opportunities for Black Americans to join CCC camps or to serve in supervisory capacities in the Corps. The Corps thus reproduced the segregated race relations prevalent in the federal government and in American society. Black Americans complained about the failure to appoint blacks to the position of educational counsellor in segregated camps.[66] One visitor remarked on the 'notable absence of Negro officers' in the Corps: 'here and there a line or staff officer has been appointed but in the main, the obvious advantages of this practical experience in dealing with human beings have been denied to Negro Reserve Officers.'[67] Walter White, Secretary of the NAACP, supported the Corps's continuing but not as a permanent organization. He had one reservation, singling out the 'timidity' which Corps officers had 'exhibited regarding the appointment of qualified Negroes to administrative and other posts in the CCC camps'.[68] This pattern endured throughout the Corps's existence: 'ever since the advent of the C.C.C. we have had complaints about discrimination, in the personnel of the Camp, in the number of men recruited for service, etc.'[69]

Although the Department of Labor extolled non-discrimination,[70] African Americans formed a different view. And in 1935, Director Fechner, a southerner, acknowledged that although the CCC's founding legislation prohibited discrimination by race, a policy of segregated camps was pursued:[71] 'at the very beginning of this work, I consulted with many representative individuals and groups who were interested in the work, and the decision to segregate white enrollees, negro enrollees, and war veter-

[66] LC NAACP I, Box C-223, File: Civilian Conservation Corps May–Nov. 1934. See enclosed correspondence about this problem.

[67] LC NAACP I, Box C233, File: Eugene Boykin 1937–8, 'Negro Leadership in the Civilian Conservation Corps', Dec. 1937, p. 1.

[68] LC NAACP I Box C 223, File: CCC 1936, letter from Walter White Secretary, NAACP to United States News, 16 Dec. 1936, p. 2.

[69] LC NAACP I Box C 223 File: CCC 1938/39. Letter from E. Frederic Morrow, Branch Coordinator NAACP to Clifton E. Davenport, 28 July 1938. He added: 'Our office has taken these matters up with Mr Fechner in Washington, and he has been very cooperative with us in an attempt to iron out these difficulties.'

[70] NARA RG 35 Records of the CCC, Reference Files 1933–42 Box 1, US Department of Labor, 'Handbook for Agencies Selecting Men and Emergency Conservation Work', 1 May 1933, p. 6.

[71] LC NAACP I, Box C 223, File: CCC, July–Dec. 1935. In a letter from James McEntee, Assistant Director of the CCC to William Carter, Secretary Fact-Finding and Inter-Racial Commission, LS Inter-Denominational Ministers' Alliance, Los Angeles, 18 Oct. 1935, additional justification for segregation is offered: 'from experience it appears that segregation is desirable for the happiness, contentment and general welfare of the colored enrollees. We have received numerous complaints from the colored enrollees themselves, who have been assigned to companies wherein the strength was largely composed of white enrollees, that they would much prefer being sent to a camp composed entirely of colored men.' McEntee may rather be confusing the reasons for this latter request.

ans, was generally approved.'[72] He tendentiously rehearsed the familiar *Plessy* v. *Ferguson* (1896)[73] legitimated defence of this peculiar arrangement: 'this segregation is not discrimination and cannot be so construed. The negro companies are assigned to the same types of work, have identical equipment, are served the same food, and have the same quarters as white enrollees.' He added: 'I have personally visited many negro CCC companies and have talked with the enrollees and have never received one single complaint.'[74] In correspondence with the NAACP, Fechner refused to budge on this issue, declaring: 'I am confident the negro enrollees themselves are thoroughly satisfied with the arrangement.'[75] The NAACP petitioned President Roosevelt and administrators in Washington about the segregated camps. A rather brusque letter from Fechner in February 1936 (prompted by a communication from the President's Assistant Secretary) reveals the tenacity of segregation in the federal administration: 'I am convinced that from every point of view it is desirable to segregate white and negro Civilian Conservation Corps enrollees.' His reassurances about equality within this invidious framework rang hollow: 'there is absolutely no discrimination in this segregation. The same quarters are provided for all enrollees.'[76] The most glaring feature of this arrangement which might have been 'pointed to as indicating discrimination' was the segregation itself, of course, implying as it did inequality. Fechner marshalled a mendacious account of Black American enrollees requesting to leave white camps.[77]

As early as June 1933, the NAACP protested about discrimination in the selection of Black Americans, particularly in the South: 'despite the efforts of the Department of Labor to make known to recruiting officers that there should not be any discrimination in this enlistment, instances are cropping up of absolute refusal of colored people.'[78] In October 1933,

---

[72] Ibid., letter from Robert Fechner to Thomas L. Griffith Jr, President NAACP Los Angeles, 21 Sept. 1935.

[73] *Plessy* v. *Ferguson* 163 US 537 (1896).

[74] LC NAACP I, Box C 223, File: CCC, July–Dec. 1935, letter from Robert Fechner to Thomas L. Griffith Jr, President NAACP Los Angeles, 21 Sept. 1935.

[75] Ibid., letter from Robert Fechner to Thomas L. Griffith Jr, President NAACP Los Angeles, 7 Nov. 1935.

[76] LC NAACP I Box C 223, File: CCC, 1936. Letter from Robert Fechner to Thomas L. Griffith Jr, President NAACP Los Angeles, 18 Feb. 1936.

[77] Ibid.: 'I think you must know that last summer it was apparently necessary to assign about thirty negro enrollees from Los Angeles to a Civilian Conservation Corps camp in which the remainder of the enrollees were white. I quickly received an appeal from a number of these negro enrollees, as well as letters from other individuals, urging that the negro enrollees be withdrawn from the camp, and this was done.'

[78] NARA RG 35 Records of the CCC, Division of Selection, Policy File 1933–42 Box 14, File: Negro Question, General J–Z. Letter from Roy Wilkins, Assistant Secretary NAACP to Frank Persons, 27 June 1933.

one group complained to Frank Persons that, 'during the first encampment of the Civilian Conservation Corps, the Negroes did not receive the same opportunities as other groups. We should like to believe that this happened more through carelessness than through deliberateness.'[79] Disregarding the Corps's founding legislation, Black Americans were selected on a quota basis, that is, only as vacancies arose in the camps for African Americans.[80] Praising the CCC's aims, another African American observed that the 'Negro youth, who has found it much more difficult to find gainful employment than the white youth of the country is just as much in need of this opportunity to maintain his morale and build his character as the white youth'.[81] The National Urban League complained that Black American youths received inadequate 'opportunity to avail themselves of the camp facilities'. It hoped that 'the Department of Labor will be able to register a larger number of Negro men'.[82] In response, Persons asserted that 'each State Director has been specifically informed that negroes have as much right to the places now vacant as have the whites'.[83] Complaints were received by the NAACP from Arkansas and Texas also, which it took up with the Secretary of Labor.[84] In Alabama, the Director of the State Relief Administration complained about the allocation for Black Americans: 'one difficulty in Alabama has been in not having a sufficient colored quota. In several of our black belt counties as high as 80% of the case load is colored . . . Since July, 1934, we have been asked, by the Corps Area Commander, for only 70 colored men.'[85] In fact, over 2,000 African American men on relief were eligible. The problem of a small quota persisted in Alabama and was reproduced in some other southern states, notably Arkansas. In pursuing the question in the latter state in 1934, Persons discovered that only one camp (after much delay) was established

[79] NARA RG 35 Records of the CCC, Division of Selection, Policy File 1933–42 Box 14, File: Negro Question, General A–H. Letter from J. Gordon Baugherd Secretary, the Philadelphia Council of the Emergency Advisory Council for Negroes to W. Frank Persons, Director USES, 31 Oct. 1933.   [80] Salmond (1965: 83–4).

[81] Op. cit. n. 79 above. See also Baugh's further letter of 31 Oct. and Persons' reply 6 Nov. 1933.

[82] Ibid., letter from T. Arnold Hill, National Urban League to Frank Persons 25 Oct. 1933.

[83] Ibid., letter from Frank Persons to T. Arnold Hill, National Urban League 30 Oct. 1933.

[84] LC NAACP I Box C223, File: CCC 1933. See correspondence between Roy Wilkins NAACP and Frank Persons Department of Labor, particularly Persons' letter to Wilkins, 2 June 1933.

[85] NARA RG 35 Records of the CCC, Division of Selection, Policy Files 1933–42 Box 14, File: Negro Question—Alabama. Letter from Thad Holt, Director Alabama Relief Administration to Frank Persons, 9 May 1935, p. 2. See also Persons's reply 15 May 1935, in which he wrote: 'I am concerned about the fact that the Army enrollment officers have not given you opportunity to present more qualified colored men. I have abstracted the paragraph in your letter referring to this situation and transmitted same to Colonel Duncan K. Major, who is the War Department Representative on the Advisory Council for Emergency Conservation Work.'

in the state for African Americans.[86] In 1938, a near riot in a CCC camp—between Black American enrollees at the CCC and white WPA workers—in Forrest City (Arkansas) exposed the tensions of race relations. A decision to relieve the company commander after this incident harmed relations with the local civilian population.[87]

In a long letter to Frank Persons in May 1933, Will Alexander of the Commission on Interracial Cooperation, warned him that failure to stamp out discrimination in recruitment would reverbate widely, and encourage Communist agitation amongst Black Americans. Although African Americans were registered for CCC camps in Georgia, few were enrolled and malevolent obstruction ensured that this was the status quo. Referring to Fulton County, Georgia, Alexander reported that although, 'nearly two hundred Negroes had been registered' it was unlikely that the 'state director would ever call for them'. According to Alexander, 'if this situation was allowed to take its own course without interference, no Negroes would be recruited in Georgia.'[88] The reasons for this egregious treatment of Black Americans rested in prejudice and their electoral irrelevance: 'the facts are that in most of these communities Negroes are a long way from the center of things. Committees that are handling this, in many cases at least, are composed of men who are primarily interested in politics. *Negroes, of course, have no political significance.*'[89]

In Georgia, special relief measures were administered by 'men whose experience has been largely in rural politics. Many of them are of limited experience,'[90] presumably a euphemism for local racism. Alexander reminded Persons of the key role open to the federal government. It was perceived as autonomous from local and state racism: 'Negroes have always had faith in the federal government. They have been held loyal to

[86] Ibid., letter from Colonel Duncan K. Major to Persons, 2 Nov. 1934.

[87] NARA RG 35 Records of the CCC, Division of Selection, Policy Files 1933–42, Box 14, File: Negro Question—Arkansas. Memorandum from Headquarters CCC, District of Arkansas, Little Rock, 15 Mar. 1940 to Commanding General, Seventh Corps Area, Omaha, Nebraska. The memo noted: 'the project superintendent was a native of long standing at Forrest City and the former camp commander who was discharged as a result of this investigation has taken up his abode and is in business with one of the leading commercial houses of that city. It is believed that the influences of the former project superintendent and company commander are constantly alert and as a result thereof, the present camp personnel will never be given an opportunity to return to the friendly relationship that existed prior to the above cited incident.'

[88] NARA RG 35 Records of the CCC, Division of Selection Policy Files 1933–42, Box 14, File: Negro Question General A–H. Letter from Will Alexander, Commission on Interracial Cooperation to Frank Persons, 19 May 1933, p. 1. See also letter from Secretary of Labor Frances Perkins to President Roosevelt 1 June 1933 confirming lack of enrolment of any Black Americans in Georgia.

[89] Ibid., emphasis added.

[90] Ibid., letter from Will Alexander, Commission on Interracial Cooperation to Frank Persons, 19 May 1933, p. 1.

the country by the fact that the federal government has always dealt justly with them. Any real discrimination in relation to these government funds would undermine this faith in the federal government, which, in view of all the past history, would seem to me to be a great tragedy.'[91] Frank Persons summarized the unpromising Georgian situation: 'the attitude of the county committees generally is this: (a) there are few negro families whose boys apply who need an income as great as twenty-five dollars a month in cash; and (b) such families are more appropriately helped through the relief agencies and the work relief opportunities that those agencies provide.'[92] Although Governor Talmadge promised, in a telegram to President Roosevelt, that 600 Black Americans would be enrolled in Georgia, Persons judged 200 a more probable figure.[93]

Complaints of discrimination were common.[94] At the Advisory Council, the issue surfaced powerfully in November 1934. Persons reported the difficulties:

I wish to state that I have before me now two letters in which the Army officers advised selecting agencies how many whites and how many negroes to send. In one State, they were told to send all whites, and our selecting officers did this. The Department of Labor is responsible for the enforcement and observance of the law. The law definitely states that there must be no discrimination, and it cannot be put in the position of discriminating against the negro race. I would like to have it known that I will give advance notice to the selecting agencies that no limitations are to be made as to race, creed, or color.[95]

A year later, the Department of Labor had to reply to complaints submitted by Mrs Eleanor Roosevelt[96] about the failure of the CCC to provide equal opportunities to Black Americans. Persons retorted that 'it has not been our policy to establish arbitrary colored quotas in any State. Nothing

---

[91] NARA RG 35 Records of the CCC, 2.

[92] Ibid., memorandum from Frank Persons to Secretary of Labor Frances Perkins, 1 June 1933, p. 1.

[93] Ibid. 2. Secretary Perkins received a letter from Arnold Hill at the National Urban League, dated 24 May 1933, complimenting Persons for his 'quick and efficient handling' of the discrimination about Black American enrollees.

[94] Kelley (1990: 70), Salmond (1965).

[95] NARA RG 35 Records of the CCC, Minutes of the Advisory Council to the Director, Box 1, Minutes 1 Nov. 1934, p. 10.

[96] NARA RG 35 Records of the CCC, Division of Selection Policy Files 1933–42, Box 14, File: Negro Question, General A–H. Letter from Garth H. Akridge, Julius Rosenwald Fund, to Frank Persons 30 Mar., 1935. Akridge wrote: 'as much as you or we may like to think otherwise, the plain facts indicate beyond the remotest possibility of doubt that in many, yes in practically all, sections of the south Negroes are not being placed in Civilian Conservation Corps on anything like an equitable basis. We make this statement without fear of successful contradiction and we are prepared to defend it with authentic data on any reasonable basis of equitability.' The complaint originated with an investigation by Gareth Akridge for the Julius Rosenwald Fund.

is more certain than that such action on our part would provoke opposition in these Southern States.'[97] However, as Salmond notes, despite these repeated warnings by Persons, 'local authorities were using a definite quota system in the selection' of African American enrollees to the Corps.[98]

The percentage of African American enrollees and the number of black American camps were both fixed, and the CCC demonstrated no flexibility about these quotas or about segregation. Director Fechner refused requests from the CCC's Advisory Council to increase the number of places for African American enrollees, as the following exchange reveals:

Mr Fechner: I think we can easily defend and justify a policy of making replacements in accordance with the color of the vacancy existing. The practical thing is to maintain the organization we've got. Every time we make a change, it constantly brings up more friction.

Mr Persons: I have never been told I must limit negro enrollments.

Colonel Major: Mr Persons, this same subject came up about some companies in Tennessee, and I think Mr Fechner made the decision that these black companies would only be filled by the color of the vacancy existing.

Mr McEntee: There certainly is a problem in placing these camps. Quite a controversy exists between the Park and Forest Services. Many of the States protest against having negro companies in their State, but they are people nevertheless.[99]

Persons's ambition to get more Black American enrollees into the CCC was defeated. Fechner supported a policy of only selecting African Americans as vacancies arose in African American camps. By October 1935, Black Americans constituted about 10 per cent of the CCC's enrollees, totalling 49,000 out of 506,000. In January 1937, the CCC issued a press release in which it again defended its service for young Black Americans.[100] By 1939, 200,000 young Black Americans and 30,000 Black American men and veterans had served.[101] There were 147 Black American educational advisers in CCC camps, 600 Black American cooks and 2,000 project assistants, leaders, and assistant leaders. Fourteen African Americans served as medical officers.[102] Against this advance, however, of 150 camps for Black Americans in 1939 only two had Company

[97] Ibid., memorandum from Frank Persons to Secretary of Labor Frances Perkins, 26 Apr. 1935, p. 2.

[98] Salmond (1965: 83).

[99] NARA RG 35 Records of the CCC, Minutes of the Advisory Council to the Director, Box 1. Minutes 1 Nov. 1934, p. 11.

[100] LC NAACP I Box C-223, File: CCC 1937. Emergency Conservation Work, Washington, 'What the Civilian Conservation Corps is doing for Colored Youth', 4 Jan. 1937. By that date 150 Black Americans had served in the Corps.

[101] Civilian Conservation Corps, Office of the Director, *The Civilian Conservation Corps and Colored Youth* (Washington, DC: CCC, 1939), p. 1.

[102] Ibid. 2–4.

Commanders who were African Americans and 'we have not more than five Technical men out of a total of some 25,000 foremen and 1500 Camp Superintendents'.[103]

The CCC's director, Robert Fechner (a Democrat from Tennessee), informed the NAACP in 1935 that: 'I am satisfied that the negro enrollees themselves prefer to be in companies composed exclusively of their own race.' He added, deploying an argument widely articulated by senior federal officials, that 'this segregation is not discrimination and cannot be so construed'.[104] By 1940, Persons noted, the War Department had 'adopted a policy prohibiting the assignment of colored enrollees to white camps in all except the First Corps Area. It is my recollection that Mr Fechner approved the policy.'[105] These arrangements resulted in considerable geographic movements for some Black Americans: thus the Minnesota Urban League complained, in 1940, that because of 'gross discrimination against Negroes by the C.C.C. in Minnesota, it is necessary for the young men of the Negro group to go to camps in Missouri, even though there are vacancies in the camps of this state when they make application.'[106]

Despite repeated demands from the NAACP and other groups Director Fechner resolutely declined to weaken the segregationist principle. He stated that: 'I am convinced that from every point of view it is desirable to segregate white and negro Civilian Conservation Corps enrollees.'[107] The CCC assured a black Americans' committee that 'segregation is desirable for the happiness, contentment and general welfare of the colored employees'.[108]

[103] LC NAACP I Box C 223, File: CCC 1939. Letter to Walter White from the Washington DC Branch of NAACP, 17 June 1939.

[104] LC NAACP I, Box C 223, File: CCC 1935 July–Dec., letter from Robert Fechner to Thomas L. Griffith President NAACP, 21 Sept. 1935. See also King (1998a).

[105] NARA RG 35 Records of the CCC, Division of Selection Policy Files 1933–42, Box 14, File: Negro Question, General J–Z. Memorandum from Frank Persons to Charles H. Taylor, 23 Aug. 1940, p. 1.

[106] Ibid., letter from Clarence Mitchell, executive secretary St Paul Urban League to Paul McNutt, Commissioner Federal Security Administration, 16 Aug. 1940. Mitchell noted the particular distress in moving black Americans from Minnesota to Missouri: 'aside from the disadvantages of a southern environment which these young people face when they are sent from Minnesota to Missouri, this is also a practice directly opposite to the customs of our state. Here we do not have a separate school system, our recreational facilities are for all citizens and we have even gone to the trouble of passing a civil rights law to protect the minorities living here.'

[107] LC NAACP I Box C 223, File: Civilian Conservation Corps 1936. Letter from Robert Fechner to Thomas Griffith President, NAACP LA Branch.

[108] LC NAACP I, Box C 223, File: Civilian Conservation Corps, 1935 July–Dec. Letter from J. J. McEntee, Assistant Director, Emergency Conservation Work, to William R. Carter Secretary, Fact-Finding and Inter-Racial Commission Los Angeles Inter-Denominational Ministers' Alliance, 18 Oct. 1935.

When the CCC provided four companies to participate in the inaugu-ration parade in Washington DC in 1937, three were white and one was composed of Black Americans. This publicly demonstrated the segregated arrangements. In common with most aspects of the US federal govern-ment, Black Americans were rarely promoted to positions of authority; consideration was given to using the, by then, single black CCC company with Black officers but this proposal was dropped.[109] Fechner rightly antic-ipated complaints about this arrangement from black American groups.[110]

An expansion in the number of places allocated to Black American enrollees was resisted by the CCC's director. Fechner's implacability caused great bitterness amongst Black Americans, alienated by the New Deal's second-class treatment of their needs. In its maintenance of segre-gation and discriminatory treatment of Black Americans, the Corps proved similar to other New Deal agencies. As the historian Tony Badger, observes, 'the New Deal specifically sanctioned discrimination against blacks.' Badger singles out Fechner as a federal official, unwaveringly com-mitted to segregation, and who consequently 'made little effort to open up CCC opportunities to blacks'.[111] The correspondence above between Fechner and Persons confirms this assessment, though as Salmond reports, Fechner's intransigence enjoyed presidential support.[112] Whereas in other agencies discrimination was an unavoidable feature of local administra-tion, at the CCC it was embraced at the federal level.

The militarization of the CCC

Although the US Army played a substantial role in administering in CCC camps, any extension of their military character was nipped in the bud. Expressing a common view, the NAACP's president announced, as early as 1936, that 'I do not think military training should be introduced in the camps.'[113] In January 1937, the CCC director Fechner anticipated com-plaints about the drilling required by the four CCC companies selected to participate in the inauguration parade. He asserted that 'just as soon as this parade is over there will not be any more drilling'.[114] The founding regulations for the CCC made explicit that despite being under the super-vision of the United States Army officers, military rules did not apply: 'the men will not be under military discipline in these camps nor will they

[109] NARA RG 35 Records of the CCC, CCC Advisory Council Minutes, Box 1, Minutes 8 Jan. 1937, p. 2.
[110] Ibid. 3.   [111] Badger (1989: 253).   [112] Salmond (1965: 85, 87).
[113] LC NAACP I, Box C223, File: Civilian Conservation Corps 1936. Letter to the United States News, 16 Dec. 1936.
[114] NARA RG 35 Records of the CCC, CCC Advisory Council Minutes Box 1, Minutes 8 Jan. 1937, p. 3.

engage in any military drill.'[115] A call from the Veterans of Foreign Wars to train CCC enrollees as an adjunct of the Army was robustly rejected by the Corps: 'the Veterans seem to have the CCC confused with Herr Hitler's Labor Corps. The Reich's Labor Corps, like most other Hitlerian organizations, have a military purpose in their background, maybe in their foreground. Not so the CCC. This never was, is not now, and the Nation does not want it to be military in any sense.'[116]

In the first months of the CCC's establishment, some of the commanding officers in the camps were regular Army officers. These were replaced with reserve officers. President Roosevelt issued an order placing all camp commanding officers on civilian status: 'their Army uniforms were replaced by a new green CCC uniform. Officially, they were no longer to be Captains or Lieutenants; they were plain "Misters".'[117] The wearers of the new uniform bore a striking resemblance to their predecessors. Militarization was also averred by the absence of weapons and of military drill from CCC camps. Nonetheless, the daily routine, held at 4.45, known as 'retreat', had militaristic overtones: 'retreat is a simple formation of the men before the flag. They are all clean. They have shed their blue denim work clothes and have donned their neat green uniforms. Their hair is combed and they stand erect. The C.O. inspects them. They like it. It is a formation which makes the men feel good.' Indeed, this activity sublimally articulated the Corps ethos, as part of an American ethos: 'it seems to symbolize unity among them. During the moments while they stand at attention, they know that they are more than individuals; they are a part of that camp, they are a part of a big organization working to preserve the health and wealth of America; they are citizens of the United States.'[118]

One member of Congress identified aspects of camp life beneficial to national defence preparedness. Although there was 'no military discipline', the CCC camps were 'building up a splendid morale and these young men have developed physically and mentally'. The trainees put on weight, and imbibed a national ideology: 'after enrolling in the camps they get a different viewpoint of life, and of the Government. They realize what this program is doing for the young men of the Nation. I could give you many instances of what the C.C.C. has done for individual enrollees. Results

---

[115] NARA RG 35 Records of the CCC, Reference Files 1933–42 Box 1, US Department of Labor, National Emergency Conservation Work: What it is—How it Operates, 20 Apr. 1933, p. 9.

[116] NARA RG 35, Records of the CCC, Division of Selection, General Correspondence Box 9, File: Military Aspects of the CCC 1934–7, n.d. 'CCC Not Military'.

[117] NARA RG 35 Records of the CCC, James J. McEntee 'Now They are Men: The Story of the CCC', p. 24.

[118] Ibid.

count; they go back home loyal to the Government and better fitted to earn a living.'[119]

Within Congress it was not uncommon to find expressions of support for the Corps's militarization. Director Fechner told the Advisory Council that one supporter of the CCC in the House, wanted to 'have military training made compulsory in CCC camps'.[120] At one congressional hearing, Fechner was asked directly for his opinion about some 'type or form of military training in the C.C.C.', to which he responded:

I do not believe it would be desirable to introduce compulsory military training in the CCC camps. This organization was set up as a work organization; the boys are required to devote 40 hours each week to work on the actual projects.

If anything like a worth-while military program were introduced into the camps, it would necessarily mean a reduction in the work program. I doubt whether the value of any military training that could be had in the camps would be worth the reduced efficiency of the work projects.

Fechner also thought it unfair to 'single out' this one group of Americans for military training. Most enrollees joined the CCC to help out their families. The director considered it unjust to 'require these boys, as a prerequisite for the opportunity to earn their way and to help their unfortunate families . . . to take military training'.[121] Interest in military training was understandable in 1939, the year of the hearings. To placate such sentiments, Fechner suggested that CCC camp life was already analogous, peripatetically, to military life: 'they go into these camps under a degree, we might say, of military discipline and control. They are taught proper respect for constituted authority; they are taught the necessity for discipline in the camps; and they are built up physically to a splendid standard.'[122]

Republican Bruce Barton (New York) suggested to Fechner that 'some type of training similar to what we ordinarily term military training would not be amiss in these CCC camps',[123] a view from which the director demurred. Fechner was keen to stress that aspects of CCC work contributed to defence concerns, even if the camps did not constitute military organizations: 'I think we should recognize that at present—even though

[119] Hearings before the Committee on Labor, House of Representatives, Seventy-fifth Congress, First Session on HR 6180, 'To Make the Civilian Conservation Corps a Permanent Agency', 14 and 15 Apr. 1937 (Washington, DC: GPO), 7. The speaker was Representative Jed Johnson of Oklahoma, a Democrat.

[120] NARA RG 35 Records of the CCC, CCC Advisory Council Minutes, Box 1, Minutes 15 Oct. 1936, p. 13.

[121] 'To Make the Civilian Conservation Corps a Permanent Agency', hearings before the Committee on Labor, House of Representatives, Seventy-sixth Congress First Session on HR 2990 9, 23, and 24 Feb. 1939 (Washington, DC: GPO), 8–9.

[122] Ibid. 9. Such views were aired by Representative Albert Thomas, a Texan Democrat.

[123] Ibid. 10.

civil in character, the Corps contributes measurably to the ability of the Nation to defend itself in case of emergency.' 'Disciplined men' learned how 'to take orders, carry them out, and [were] also taught how to give orders and see that they are carried out'.[124] He generously praised the CCC's military potential: the CCC had established a 'remarkable discipline' based on 'moral suasion and leadership instead of through fear of punishment'; the enrollees were 'very fine physical specimens'; and, in a final surge of encomium, Fechner declared that as a result of CCC work, the 'War Department is today better versed in the complex economic problems of procurement and supply than ever before during the peacetime history of our country'.[125]

The pressures to militarize intensified rather than receded. Rumours about military training had an adverse effect on recruitment to the Corps.[126] The CCC had to repudiate proponents of militarization: 'if it is desired to set up an enlisted reserve, let it be entirely free from any relief undertaking. What difference is there between this plan for military training in the Civilian Conservation Corps and the practice of Nazi Germany which, before the European War, attempted to solve its unemployment problem by regimenting its youth into the Army?'[127] The speaker, James McEntee, reminded listeners that the voluntary enrollees already worked eight-hour days on top of which it was proposed to add military training. McEntee wondered what the 'country might expect from such training?' He added: 'apparently the military minded group is content to allow the public to draw the mistaken conclusion that the addition of a few hours of drill per week to the CCC's regular program would present the nation with first class fighting reserves, ready for instant call in an emergency. Nothing could be further from the truth.'[128] Again, McEntee spelt out the dangers of imitating other countries, if compulsory military training was imposed in the camps: 'wouldn't forced military training in the CCC camps be the opening wedge to general conscription of all youth for peacetime military duty as is done by Germany? I am certain that such a course would be so hateful to the American people that it would never be adopted short of war.'[129] McEntee stressed a point iterated above that routinized camp life, by instilling a form of discipline and communal living,

---

[124] 'To Make the Civilian Conservation Corps a Permanent Agency', 38–9.
[125] Ibid. 39.
[126] NARA RG 35 Records of the CCC, Division of Selection, General Correspondence, Box 9, File: Military Aspects of CCC 1939. Memorandum from Commissioner Ellis, New Jersey State Director of CCC Selection to Dean Snyder, 19 Dec. 1939.
[127] Ibid., Address by James J. McEntee, Acting Director CCC, 17 Dec. 1939, Mutual Broadcasting Company Radio Forum, 9 pp., pp. 1–2.
[128] Ibid. 5.   [129] Ibid. 6.

imbued qualities constitutive of the 'backbone of military discipline'.[130] Finally, McEntee saw no reason for encumbering Corps enrollees with a military discipline from which the remainder of American youth would be exempt: 'if we are to have conscription in peace time, let us conscript your boy and my boy, as well as the boys in the CCC camps. Let us refrain from trying to do it by making the Corps part civilian and part military.'[131]

Persons also opposed the introduction of voluntary military training into camps because of its administrative cost and deflection from the Corps's conservation role. The values of patriotism and loyalty already inculcated through camp life would themselves constitute a form of military preparedness: 'both by the work and the influences of the camp, and in the preservation of natural resources, the Corps now constructively prepares the Nation for any crisis which may be occasioned by need for military defense of this country.'[132] Both McEntee and Persons were fighting uphill battles. Although military training was excluded from the Corps, enrollees, after their period of service, were often immediately contacted by army recruiting agents. This practice, plainly legal, fostered the public impression that service in the CCC led ineluctably to Army service.[133] Nonetheless, military training—voluntary or mandatory—was kept out of the Corps' camps.

The United States' entry into the Second World War transformed the context within which the CCC operated. Politically, it was to the CCC administrators' advantage to stress the camps' value in preparing potential recruits for the armed forces. Thus by the middle of 1941, Frank Persons—who had assiduously fought off efforts to militarize—now chose to emphasize how compatible Army life and Corps camp life were: in the CCC camps, 'enrollees learn "at least 75%" of the school of the soldier'. Furthermore, 'ex-enrollees who have entered the Army by volunteering or by operation of the Selective Service Act, have promptly shown their fitness for advancement and for responsibility.' Compared to those lacking Corps experience, 'they are far ahead in physical fitness'.[134] Such a speedy reverse in administrators' attitudes to militarization does not inspire confidence.

---

[130] Ibid. 7.   [131] Ibid.

[132] Ibid., memorandum from Frank Persons to Guy D. McKinney, 12 Dec. 1939, p. 2.

[133] Ibid., memorandum from Frank Persons to J. J. McEntee, 25 Nov. 1939, in which this issue is discussed at length.

[134] NARA RG 35 Records of the CCC, Division of Selection, General Correspondence, Box 9, File: Military Aspects of CCC 1941. Letter from Frank Persons to George Keith, Director, Division of Public Assistance, State Department of Public Welfare, Wisconsin, 24 May 1941, p. 1.

A permanent Corps?

Attempts to make the CCC permanent proved protracted and ultimately unsuccessful. Soon after its establishment, some Corps administrators dedicated themselves to this task. Their ambition began to infuse characterizations of the Corps. Unlike militarization, which was an initiative imposed from the outside, the advocates of permanency were the Corps's own administrators (a finding consistent with theories of bureaucratic budget-maximizing). Frank Persons remarked to the Secretary of Labor, Frances Perkins, that the CCC 'combined the features of an employment program and a relief program. It was the first large work-relief program launched by the Federal Government. It was hardly anticipated that this might eventually develop into a permanent enterprise.'[135] In fact, this aim quickly pervaded the senior Corps administrators and was well entrenched by the time of Persons' memorandum, as he recognized: 'there has been a very significant change of attitude toward the Civilian Conservation Corps.' According to a newspaper poll, '82% of the public is in favor of continuing the CCC enterprise'. This popular support implied, in Persons' view, that the 'public is ready to accept the Corps as a continuing agency'.[136]

In Persons' view, the source of the Corps's popularity lay not only in its positive effects upon young unemployed males but in the fact it was *not* 'work-relief'. He explained: 'it accomplished useful public work, but the emphasis has rather clearly shifted to the individual and social value of the program for the young men involved and for society as a whole.'[137] Evidence of this important shift in perceptions of the CCC consisted in, according to Persons, the strong urge to relax the relief status criterion of enrollees. The CCC's educational and vocational programmes could be expanded and emphasized more forcefully in an enduring agency. Persons' aims here were rather pious and seem remote from the average young person's interests; he thought a 'Camp Counselor' could promote four aims: '(1) cultivating reading interests and habits; (2) stimulating and developing hobbies; (3) providing some systematic instruction; and (4) providing vocational guidance.'[138] Given the modest literacy of many enrollees, Persons' ambitions were premature. Five changes were necessary to make the CCC permanent: first, ending the relief status enrolment requirement; second, ending the mandatory allocation of part of an enrollee's wage to his family; third, reducing the monthly pay from $30 to $20 to stress the educational and vocational dimension of enrolment;

---

[135] NARA RG 35 Records of the CCC, Division of Selection, Records relating to legislation: Permanent CCC Legislation, Box 5, File: Permanent CCC, Memoranda to the Secretary of Labor, 1936, 1937. Memorandum from Frank Persons to Secretary of Labor 27 Aug. 1936, p. 2.
[136] Ibid. 3.   [137] Ibid.   [138] Ibid. 6.

fourth, lowering the age of recruitment; and fifth, establishing an eighteen months' maximum term of service, a measure which would 'emphasize that the CCC program is a preparation for future employment and that it is an opportunity to be coveted'.[139]

Fechner informed the Corps's Advisory Council[140] that the 'President is very desirous of having the CCC made permanent'.[141] Director Fechner convened a special session of the Advisory Council to discuss this topic,[142] and it was discussed again in 1937.[143] In a letter to Fechner and (presumably drafted by the indefatigable Persons), the Secretary of Labor outlined some twenty features which her department would consider crucial to a permanent Corps. A key point was to make a permanent CCC 'work-centered', linked systematically to cyclical unemployment patterns: 'it should take up the slack in normal private employment opportunities for the out-of-school, youth age groups. It should promote physical fitness and educational and cultural experiences. It should be a stimulus to ambition and to the development of desirable qualities as character and citizenship.'[144] This strategy suggests an effort to link the Corps's role intellectually with the developing principles of Keynesian demand-management macroeconomics. A permanent Corps would drop the recruitment requirements that enrollees be on relief (and other criteria such as age and maximum term of service) and would expand the training provisions.

The first legislative effort to achieve permanent standing for the CCC came in 1937 in the Senate. Director Fechner made the case for permanence, stressing the number of enrollees successfully participating in CCC camps. Although he rehearsed the Corps's benefits for the USA's natural resources he laid greatest stress upon the non-material gains: 'I feel that the creation and preservation of human values has been and continues to be the signal service of the CCC to the nation'.[145] Fechner identified mass

[139] Ibid. 14.

[140] NARA RG 35 Records of the CCC, CCC Advisory Council Minutes, Box 1, Minutes 15 Oct. 1936. The discussion became quite heated between Fechner and Persons, the former opposing the latter's proposal that a commission should be appointed to examine the grounds for a permanent CCC and the best way to realize it.   [141] Ibid. 13.

[142] NARA RG 35 Records of the CCC, Division of Selection, Records relating to legislation: Permanent CCC Legislation, Box 5, File: Permanent CCC, Memoranda to the Secretary of Labor, 1936, 1937. Memorandum from Frank Persons to Secretary of Labor 13 Oct. 1936.

[143] NARA RG 35. Records of the CCC, CCC Advisory Council Minutes Box 1, Minutes 9 Apr. 1937.

[144] NARA RG 35 Records of the CCC, Division of Selection, Records relating to legislation: Permanent CCC Legislation, Box 5, File: Permanent CCC, Memoranda to the Secretary of Labor, 1936, 1937. Letter from Frances Perkins to Frank Persons, 13 Oct. 1936, p. 2.

[145] NARA RG 35 Records of the CCC, CCC Advisory Council Minutes Box 1, Minutes 12 Apr. 1937: Statement of Mr Robert Fechner, Director of Emergency Conservation Work with regard to the proposed bill for making the Civilian Conservation Corps permanent, Senate 13 Apr. 1937, pp. 3–4.

unemployment as the principal rationale for the Corps, warning of the 'very bad social results which we could expect if we permitted a large group of young men to be condemned to idleness'.[146] He added that this 'enforced idleness' arose 'through no fault of their own'.[147] The same point was made with equal force by a Democrat Congressman before the Labor Committee in 1937:

you saw a great army of young men go to the White House a few weeks ago to camp on the doorsteps. There is a growing sentiment in the country, especially with the young men of the country, that they are the forgotten men. We are turning out thousands of high school and college graduates yearly, many of whom are unable to find jobs. We must find a place for these and other young men. Idle hands you know is the devil's workshop.[148]

Fechner extolled the CCC's 'work program' character as superior to the dole. It instilled education and training: 'the work program of the Corps . . . has in fact already given to many thousands of young men practical education which has fitted them to become self sustaining productive members of society.'[149] The diversity of the Corps's work implied a 'great deal of training'.[150] Fechner understandably emphasized the educational dividends of the CCC: 'the total average enrollment in all academic courses during the year 1936 was 146,352 enrollees. For job training courses this figure was 185,726 enrollees; for vocational courses 176,082 enrollees, and for foreman, teacher, and leader activities the average enrollment during the year 1936 was 54,578.'[151] A skilful bureaucrat, Fechner assured the Senate committee that the CCC did not duplicate or replicate the 'functions of already existing departments'. On the contrary, the CCC 'through coordination makes possible the fuller and more effective use of the specialized facilities of many government agencies'.[152]

In 1937, legislation to create a permanent CCC (defined as extending it for three years) progressed to a congressional conference committee formed of members from the House and the Senate; it was reported out of the committee and returned to the floor in each chamber.[153] The Bill

---

[146] NARA RG 35 Records of the CCC, 4.   [147] Ibid.

[148] Hearings before the Committee on Labor, House of Representatives, Seventy-fifth Congress, First Session on HR 6180, 'To Make the Civilian Conservation Corps a Permanent Agency', 14 and 15 Apr. 1937 (Washington, DC: GPO), 9. Jed Johnson, Oklahoma Representative speaking,

[149] NARA RG 35 Records of the CCC, CCC Advisory Council Minutes Box 1, Minutes 12 Apr. 1937: Statement of Mr Robert Fechner, Director of Emergency Conservation Work with regard to the proposed bill for making the Civilian Conservation Corps permanent, Senate, 13 Apr. 1937, p. 5.

[150] Ibid. 6.   [151] Ibid. 10.   [152] Ibid. 11.

[153] Hearings before the Committee on Labor, House of Representatives, Seventy-fifth Congress, First Session on HR 6180, 'To Make the Civilian Conservation Corps a Permanent Agency', 14 and 15 Apr. 1937 (Washington, DC: GPO). This bill (HR 6180) was discussed in hearings before the House Labor Committee.

which passed relaxed eligibility requirements for enrollees to the Corps, but failed to make the CCC permanent.

Another bill to make the CCC permanent was considered by the House Committee on Labor in February 1939.[154] Director Fechner warmly endorsed the proposed legislation.[155] He identified several reasons to place the CCC on a permanent footing, rehearsing those advantages aired in earlier sessions. First, he cited the 'great need for employment and training on the part of a very large number of young men in this country'.[156] CCC work camp projects instilled such skills. Mass unemployment justified a permanent CCC; it had succeeded in 'converting a large number of unfortunate, unemployed young men from possible or probable public charges to self-respecting citizens'.[157] Second, Fechner alluded to the continuing need for conservation work,[158] which private industry would not undertake. Third, permanent status was required efficaciously to stabilize and routinize the CCC as an organization, and to discourage 'key employees' from seeking permanent jobs elsewhere.[159] Fechner rebuffed, if not wholly cogently, a charge that the CCC was simply one of many New Deal programmes whose administrators covetously sought to make permanent, maintaining that 'the work of the CCC could be substantially improved and probably be conducted more economically if those in charge of the works projects could plan in a more orderly way for the development of the necessary conservation program over a longer period and not merely for 2 or 3 years'.[160] This argument no doubt applied to other agencies. He found support for a permanent CCC amongst some Committee members, though unsurprisingly from Democrats not Republicans. Democrats Lawrence Connery (from Massachusetts) and Frank Fries (Illinois) gave staunch support, the latter adumbrating: 'I honestly believe that the C.C.C. has done more to restore a number of young men to society and to rehabilitate some of our young people who have been denied employment through no fault of their own then any other organization we have or ever have had.'[161] Congressman Connery dubbed the CCC 'outstanding'.[162] Congressman William Norrell (a Democrat from Arkansas) was also laudatory: 'of all the New Deal projects we have, I think that the C.C.C. has been operated in the most satisfactory manner.'[163]

---

[154] 'To Make the Civilian Conservation Corps a Permanent Agency', hearings before the Committee on Labor, House of Representatives, Seventy-sixth Congress, First Session on HR 2990, 9, 23, and 24 Feb. 1939 (Washington, DC: GPO).
[155] A key issue at these hearings was whether the employees of the CCC should be placed under the civil service, a provision provided for in the Bill but treated with scepticism by several committee members who did support making the CCC permanent. Since this issue of civil service status is secondary to the principle of permanency and tied in with issues of civil service reform (represented partly by Robert Ramspeck on the Committee) I do not deal with it.
[156] Ibid. 2.   [157] Ibid. 3.   [158] Ibid. 2.   [159] Ibid. 5–6.
[160] Ibid. 12.   [161] Ibid. 15.   [162] Ibid. 16.   [163] Ibid.

Nebraskian George Heinke, a Republican, was sceptical about permanence for the CCC, observing irritably that, 'in our county we have more people engaged in administering relief than were formerly engaged in conducting the affairs of our courthouse.'[164] Heinke enquired irascibly of Director Fechner whether 'this emergency has become a permanent condition?'[165] Fechner's affirmative reply allowed Heinke to record his objection to a permanent CCC. Gerald Landis, a Republican from Indiana, praised the CCC but opposed making it permanent, commenting, 'how would it affect the morale of our people, especially the youth of America, to say that the Civilian Conservation Corps is going to be a permanent organization, and we are going to show them that it affords the future they will have to look toward?'[166] Formulated in economic terms, this hostility to a permanent Corps conveyed a fear of liberal amelioration slipping into socialism. Landis's hostility to a permanent CCC was counterbalanced by the opinion of Reuben Wood, a Democrat from Missouri, who anticipated continued immiseration amongst the workforce: 'there is not any question in my mind about the necessity for a Civilian Conservation Corps during the next 10 years. There is not any possibility of discontinuing the C.C.C.' Wood thought it likely that the CCC would have to serve the needs of older workers displaced by technology—or as he phrased it 'consigned to "no-man's land"'.[167] Without an unemployment crisis, it is hard to see how the proposal to make the Corps permanent would ever have arisen, however.

Republican Representative Barton of New York pressed one issue of concern shared by opponents of a permanent CCC: the relative cost of the work completed under its auspices compared either with private sector alternatives or other public agencies.[168] In defence of the practices, F. A. Silcox, Chief of the US Forest Service, Department of Agriculture argued that 'there is a definite disciplinary and training value in having the men together. They perform the work almost as efficiently as adults. On many types of work I would rather have a camp of C.C.C. workers than the usual adult laborers.'[169]

Fechner's desire for a permanent CCC was an ambition shared by several other New Deal organizations. His appeals to Congress for permanency were weakened by this context. As one Republican representative exclaimed, 'what we have to face is the fact that one by one the so-called emergency operations are coming to us to demand that they be placed on a permanent basis.'[170] This made special pleading for the CCC

---

[164] 'To Make the Civilian Conservation Corps a Permanent Agency', hearings before the Committee on Labor, House of Representatives, Seventy-sixth Congress, First Session on H.R. 2990, February 9, 23, and 24 1939 (Washington, DC: GPO) p. 18.
[165] Ibid.   [166] Ibid. 21.   [167] Ibid. 29.   [168] Ibid. 59.   [169] Ibid. 60.
[170] Ibid. 22. The speaker was Bruce Barton of New York.

harder and, indeed, it was difficult to demonstrate why its needs were more compelling, despite the undoubted popularity its advocates could cite. As a Californian Republican remarked, 'while I have no particular objection to placing the C.C.C. on a permanent basis, I know when once we establish one of the new agencies permanently it is extremely difficult to dispense with it. All these new creations want to become permanent.'[171]

By 1942, defending the Corps's existence had become increasingly problematic. The number of enrollees dropped precipitately and the CCC was under pressure to demonstrate its 'definite usefulness to the Nation', since 'otherwise the Corps would be abolished by Congress'.[172] The Corps concentrated upon junior enrolments, and further reductions in the number of camps and enrollees was anticipated. Some members of the CCC wanted the Corps reorganized and integrated with the whole country's war mobilization effort. As one of its Advisory Council member adjured: 'the thing to do is to put the Corps on a war-time basis. Go before the public and the youth of this country and say to them this is a real war effort—we are protecting those things which are important to the nation.'[173] The same speaker maintained that if the CCC failed to 'convert into a National Defense project', then Congress would abandon it: 'it is the thought of the day and we may as well be practicable and face it.'[174] The writing was soon on the wall for the CCC and the atmosphere, at the Advisory Council, one of resignation. James McEntee solemnly announced, in June 1942, that the Senate would not appropriate funds for the Corps, and he recommended discussing its dissolution: 'I think we should talk over, frankly, the best method to be adopted for winding up the activities of the Corps... because the Corps has taken such a battering within the last month, its morale is low.'[175] Legislation terminating the CCC was passed by Congress and signed by the President in July.[176]

CONCLUSION

The CCC was an experiment in social amelioration, employing federal resources and authority on a substantial scale. By its completion it had inducted tens of thousands of trainees. These enrollees arrived voluntarily

[171] Ibid. 27. The speaker was Congressman Richard Welch.
[172] NARA RG 35 Records of the CCC, CCC Advisory Council Minutes, Box 2, Minutes 9 Jan. 1942.
[173] Ibid. 4. The speaker was Mr Wirth.
[174] Ibid. The speaker was Mr Wirth.
[175] NARA RG 35 Records of the CCC, CCC Advisory Council Minutes Box 2, Minutes 26 June 1942, p. 1.
[176] Eight million dollars was appropriated for the costs of liquidating the Corps.

(in fact, there was initially oversubscription) but as a collectivist institution the Corps had to be rationalized in terms consistent with American political values. Expertise featured modestly in this exercise, a characteristic of other New Deal initiatives according to Weir and Skocpol: 'the early New Dealers married wide popular support—achieved by channeling "temporary" spending for relief and public works through locally rooted congressmen and Democratic politicians—with low-cost, Progressive-style extensions of federal regulations in the national interest.' They continue: 'without having to fashion any political program explicitly recognizing class interests, the New Dealers could offer something to individuals or groups in all classes. They put the federal government in the role of an active umpire ensuring common efforts for national recovery by regulating against "uncooperative" elements in all groups.'[177] Pragmatism and electoral pressure compelled the federal government to act and gave policy-makers precious little time to formulate, insulated from society, coherent policy responses. Both the federal public works and the CCC illustrate these practices. The Corps is an instance of government policy used for amelioration, within the strictures of liberal democracy.

I have also explained how the potential illiberalism of the Corps was avoided: most obviously by making it a voluntary institution imbued with American values and by deflecting efforts to make it a permanent agency. And although the New Deal agencies always faced criticisms in Congress, especially from fiscal conservatives, nonetheless the general prestige of the New Deal in US society was a considerable bulwark against any casual slippage into involuntarism. The distinct treatment of enrollees in the CCC was willingly acceded to: most Americans, certainly those suffering from hardship in the 1930s, welcomed a stronger role for the federal government designed to address economic depression. Indeed the so-called New Deal electoral coalition, in place until the 1960s and 1970s, articulated this priority. Within the US political system, however, mobilizing a consensus and electoral coalition to underpin a permanent shift in favour of massive federal government activism—in respect of public works—was immensely difficult. (The experience of President Carter's initiative, the Comprehensive Empolyment and Training Act (CETA), demonstrates these enduring obstacles. It was a major public employment programme generally judged a failure because of poor local implementation.)[178] The failure of Corps administrators to garner support for a permanent institution is perhaps cogent evidence of this conclusion and it is unlikely that the objection to this proposal would have been received more sympathetically even without the outbreak of war. While President Roosevelt will-

---

[177] Weir and Skocpol (1985: 136–7).   [178] See King (1996) and Weir (1992)

ingly defended the Corps as part of his administration's short-term, pragmatic reponse to economic crisis, supporting its transition to a permanent status was rather a different matter. As a temporary institution, whose members were recruited voluntarily, the Corps's collectivisim could be made acceptable to an individualist political culture. Within this latter context, however, its prospect of becoming an entrenched programme seemed slim.

It is important to underline the racial dimension of the Corps's organization and activities, for two reasons. First, by employing prevailing segregationist arrangements, the Corps's conventionality was enhanced and any perception of it as an unacceptably radical collectivist experiment further diminished. Second, the Corps's restriction of African Americans to unpromoted positions and confinement to a rigidly enforced allocation of camp places contributed further to their political marginalization. In these effects, the Corps did not differ from other New Deal agencies but rather converged with them. Thus although the CCC was promoted and defended in decidedly liberal individualist terms, for African Americans their experience of a federal government agency as discriminatory and segregationist was little different from the treatment they encountered with its other agencies.

PART IV

Liberal Contractualism

Introduction

THE two chapters in this section examine one of the oldest issues in social policy: programmes to alleviate the plight of the unemployed or, in an older period, of paupers. Alarm about poverty, unemployment, and malingerers paralleled the diffusion of industrial capitalism. Such problems exposed weaknesses in market forces and prompted a variety of government responses, mostly centred upon ways to improve the participation of these unemployed individuals by modifying the incentives stimulating or preventing their entering the labour market. Policies for the unemployed have consistently taken a social engineering form: that is, they have attempted to modify the behaviour of individuals or to direct their activities and they have frequently been advanced on a strong evidential basis. Thus the New Poor Law, the ideas of scientific charity and twentieth-century workfare measures all aim to change the behaviour of the unemployed and welfare recipients (as do companion schemes such as penalizing single mothers who have children while receiving public benefits). The most common mechanism, historically, is to make life on benefits unattractive. These schemes have been advanced for a variety of reasons. A constant theme is how obligations fall upon welfare recipients as a consequence of the contractualism at the core of liberal democracy. The state's commitment to the poor or unemployed (most recently articulated as the social rights of citizenship) carries with it duties and obligations, falling upon the supplicant. Historically, obligations were the more dominant aspect: social rights are a twentieth-century invention (though one consistent with a basic definition of liberalism) and recent policies are marked by a return to the obligations side of the contract.

As Chapters 7 and 8 demonstrate, modern workfare schemes have their historical origins in nineteenth-century debates and policies. This historical embeddedness is conveyed by two examples, the first drawn from the Poor Law Commission preceding the 1834 reform which pronounced that 'in proportion as the condition of any pauper class is elevated above the condition of independent labourers, the condition of the independent class is depressed . . . The converse is the effect when the pauper class is placed in its proper position below the condition of the independent labourer. Every penny bestowed, that tends to render the condition of the pauper more eligible than that of the independent labourer, is a bounty on indolence and vice.'[1] The second quote is from an eminent journalist's column in the *Sunday Times* in October 1997: 'the only sure way of making work relatively more attractive is to make benefits relatively less attractive, by keeping them quite a bit lower than wages and by setting fairly rigorous qualifying tests. There is no entirely pain-free alternative.'[2] Sandwiched between these two claims are over 150 years of policies which view unemployment as, in significant part, a consequence of individual indolence and choice, a perspective which requires that public policy be used to modify the behaviour and incentives of the unemployed. This historical continuity well illustrates the interweaving of the liberal and illiberal dimensions of social policy. The belief in the excessive costs posed by the unemployed for the rest of society has been a recurring one since the nineteenth century. As we will see, both New Labour's and the New Democrats' approach fit with this inherited orthodoxy.

In both the United States and Britain in the twentieth century a dominant aspect of policy toward the unemployed has been to move them into the labour market. This principle has been relaxed only in the relatively prosperous 1945–75 decades when high employment made the problem of unemployment politically insignificant; and when the prevailing welfare state consensus took a benign view of individual unemployed persons, embracing them in the universalist framework (in principle if not in practice) and according more importance to structural sources of unemployment than to individual fecklessness (as in the Great Society). The warnings about the negative consequences of long periods spent on the dole, issued by such public policy eminents as William Beveridge,[3] intellectual founder of the British welfare state, were disregarded (to the point of their appearing politically unimportant). Likewise, in the United States discussions of unemployment in the 1950s and 1960s were dominated by concerns about the consequences of technological development and the danger of leaving behind those concentrated in urban ghettos.[4] The Great Society put these concerns at the centre of the political stage, powerfully influenced by the agenda of civil rights activists, but, from the late 1970s, a more historically conventional view of the inability of welfare programmes to function effectively gained credence amongst Washington policy-makers. This negative position culminated in the 1996 welfare

---

[1] *Report from His Majesty's Commissioners for Inquiring into the Administration and Practical Operation of the Poor Laws, Published by Authority* (London, 1834), 228.

[2] Ferdinand Mount, 'Let a tight fist rule in the Giving Age', *Sunday Times*, 5 Oct. 1997.

[3] See the excellent discussion in Deacon (1996).

[4] See King (1995: 133–7) and Weir (1992).

reform act signed by President Clinton which ended the federal government's direct role (acquired in 1935) in welfare provision. How this position was attained is examined in Chapter 8 below.

If the movement to collectivist solutions to unemployment examined in the previous section was characterized by a modest evidential basis, a striking feature of welfare policy has been an abundance of expertise and well-established policy networks but considerable disagreement about what constitutes the apposite reform. This characterization is true of the welfare debate in both Britain and the United States. And, in both countries, the government's decision to pursue various forms of workfare has privileged and validated a particular line of argument, amongst several available, in the germane expertise.

Both countries inherited, at the beginning of the twentieth century, a New Poor Law approach to misery, that is, that some sort of deterrence system centred on a poorhouse or work system should function. But they have developed along separate trajectories, with different attitudes to welfare and welfare recipients. There are distinctive intellectual and political cultural traditions about welfare policy manifest in the two countries. Despite these dissimilarities both countries increasingly approximate what the sociologist Gosta Esping-Andersen terms the 'liberal' welfare state type, and in fact he identifies the USA as one of the 'archetypical' examples of this model. A liberal welfare state is defined as one in which 'means-tested assistance, modest universal transfers or modest social-insurance plans predominate'. He adds that in such systems, 'the progress of social reform has been severely circumscribed by traditional, liberal work-ethic norms: it is one where the limits of welfare equal the marginal propensity to opt for welfare instead of work. Entitlement rules are therefore strict and often associated with stigma; benefits are typically modest.'[5] Two points are worth making about this characterization. First, although the British welfare state of the 1960s would not have obviously fitted this liberal type, it did in fact include means-tested benefits and contained, if only nascently, the basis for a tougher enforcement of eligibility rules, a potential activated in the 1980s. Second, while such a characterization overstates certain features—for example, the importance of universal health care in Britain and the presence of public pensions in the USA—it accurately captures the essence of a liberal system. Specifically in respect of welfare benefits (that is, income maintenance programmes in both countries) and the relationship between receiving assistance and participation, however indirectly or desultorily, in the labour market the description of liberal is apt.

[5] Esping-Andersen (1990: 26).

The British experience is differentiated first by a decisive shift to national welfare programmes in the policies of the 1906–11 Liberal administration, which conceded government responsibility for general welfare and the alleviation of unemployment. The politically most popular system of alleviation was one based on the unemployment insurance principle, which had two consequences: first, a parallel system, initially of pauperism and then of means-tested relief under the National Assistance Board developed. This dichotomy—between insurance and non-insurance assistance—was retained in the post-1945 mature welfare system institution. It was politically an insignificant element until the 1970s when mounting unemployment, particularly youth and long-term unemployment, financially strained the non-insurance component of relief. Second, rights and membership of the polity were defined in part to complement this dual system: the insurance-based model of unemployment relief was one rooted in industrial employment (with members of a male earner's family defined in relation to that position), and historically paupers forfeited political rights. These assumptions had implications for issues of dependency, gender, and social citizenship.[6] In an important paper, Jane Lewis has examined how certain gender assumptions—for instance, taking no account of unpaid work in the home, discharged overwhelmingly by women—have structured typologies of welfare programmes. Lewis describes how the male breadwinner model was institutionalized in post-1945 British welfare arrangements:

under the post-war Beveridgean settlement, women continued to be treated as dependants for the purposes of social security entitlements. Beveridge wrote at length of the importance of women's role as wives and mothers in ensuring the continuance of the British race (at a time of fears about population decline) and insisted on marriage as a "partnership" rather than a patriarchal relationship. It was, however, a partnership in which the parties were to be equal but different. Hence women were defined as wives and mothers and therefore as dependent on a male wage.[7]

In the United States, the welfare debate (that is, discussions about the Aid to Families with Dependent Children, AFDC, programme) have revolved around an implicit or, on occasions, explicit presentation of it as a single mother's benefit.

Intellectually, Britain enjoys a distinct approach to social policy. Institutionalized in university departments of social administration and policy in the post-1945 decades this tradition was one imbued with a Marshallian view of the social rights of citizenship (of the sort described in Chapter 1) and universalism in service delivery. Alan Deacon correctly

---

[6] See Lister (1990, 1993, 1997), O'Connor (1996), and Orloff (1993*a*, 1993*b*).
[7] Lewis (1992: 163).

notes that in terms of instruction and values within the social administration community, it was above all the work of the LSE academic Richard Titmuss which dominated the prevailing views and practices in the post-war mature welfare state;[8] a dominance complementing T. H. Marshall's intellectual framework of social citizenship. Titmuss's views influenced both a generation of university lecturers and the values of the Labour Party administrations of the 1960s (and lingeringly, of the 1970s too). Titmuss embraced universalism because of the stigma attached to means-tested benefits and the judgemental character of social services distributed by discretion.[9] Together, the work of T. H. Marshall and Titmuss constituted the dominant framework in the formulation of British social policy until the 1980s. The sociologist, A. H. Halsey, records how his LSE experience informed his development of the discipline at Oxford: 'Richard Titmuss was a remarkable figure ... My own conception of [Oxford University's social policy department] was to be based on Richard Titmuss's reform of the department at LSE.'[10] It also facilitated the development and influence of policy or issue networks based on a particular sense of appropriate welfare policy. In contrast to other issue networks (of the sorts identified by political scientists) the social policy network was defined by a particular conception of what the content of welfare policy should include.

In common with Britain, the major federal welfare system enacted in the 1930s embodied a dichotomy between insurance-based unemployment assistance and means-tested benefits for those outside the insurance system. It is the descendant of this latter branch (AFDC) which prompted controversy in the 1970s and 1980s, and was terminated as a federal entitlement programme in 1996.

The political cultural framework of the US welfare system is distinct from others. Numerous scholars have argued that the American public's sensibility in respect of welfare recipients is jaundiced: there is a generosity toward the individual apparently helping him or herself but a hostility toward those allegedly making no sustained effort to enter the labour market, the able-bodied unemployed, or more recently single parents.[11] It is this latter bias which has fuelled the electoral appeal of the 'ending welfare as we know it', rhetoric adopted by both Democrats and Republicans. It was used by both President Reagan, in 1988, and President Clinton, in 1996.

A fundamental difference between the welfare policy context of the

---

[8] Deacon (1996).   [9] See Titmuss (1967, 1968, 1974, 1976) and Timmins (1996).
[10] Halsey (1996: 58).
[11] For an influential formulation of this dualism see Heclo (1986). For the normative background see Goodin (1988).

United States and Britain is the role of racial divisions in the former polity. The origins of the federal welfare system in 1935, its expansion and consolidation in President Lyndon Johnson's Great Society programmes, and excoriation and contraction in the last fifteen years have each been seared with racial implications, whether stated overtly or acknowledged indirectly.[12] The 1935 founding legislation devolved administrative responsibility for non-insurance-based relief to the states, some of which discriminated against African Americans.[13] The Great Society had as part of its agenda the need to address grievances articulated by the civil rights movement, leading to a further populist identification between race and welfare programmes. Finally, the debates about welfare reform in the last twenty years have been deeply affected by race; thus the political scientist Martin Gilens concludes, in a recent article, that 'racial attitudes are a powerful influence on white Americans' welfare views. . . . racial considerations are the single most important factor shaping whites' views of welfare'.[14] Gilens adds that an explanation of this pattern based simply on the 'demographics of poverty cannot fully account for whites' tendency to think about welfare in racial terms'. Instead, 'beliefs about blacks in general, and black welfare mothers in particular, are substantially more important in shaping whites' welfare views than are beliefs about the poor or perceptions of white welfare mothers.' In the United States, he argues, it is 'blacks' overrepresentation among the poor' which 'acquires an exaggerated salience for white Americans'.[15]

These issues—the resonance of historical debates and values, the tenacity of institutional arrangements for relieving unemployment and need, the shifting role of expertise—are addressed in this Part of the book.

Finally, it is worth underlining that the abundance of issue and policy networks in welfare policy in the two countries hides a difference between them, as the ensuing chapters illustrate. In Britain, the dominant intellectual thrust of the social policy community has been to increase universalist benefits and reduce means-tested stigmatizing programmes. This community, based principally in university social policy and administration departments, has opposed workfare, whether advanced for moral and economic reasons, and urged the expansion of government intervention in universalist welfare measures. Advocates of workfare have either been mavericks in think tanks, such as the Institute for Economic Affairs[16] (until

---

[12] See, amongst others, Sugrue (1996), Katznelson (1981), Massey and Denton (1993), Quadagno (1994), Lieberman (1995, 1998), Skocpol (1992), and Gilens (1996).

[13] Lieberman (1998).   [14] Gilens (1996: 601).   [15] Ibid. 602.

[16] The subtitle of a 1987 IEA publication by Ralph Harris and Arthur Seldon is revealing: *Welfare without the State: A Quarter-Century of Suppressed Public Choice* (London: IEA, 1987). However, the IEA has enjoyed prominence in the last ten years, acting as a crucial forum for bringing American neoliberal and conservative ideas to Britain: see Murray (1990) and Mead (1997*b*)

the 1980s considered marginal to policy debates), or a small minority of academics; crucially, external influences, specifically US expertise, have been used decisively in the formulation of workfare policy, as Chapter 7 explains. It is the latter view which gained most influence with civil servants and politicians in the 1990s. In the United States, the absence of a dedicated university discipline has meant that the welfare policy network has been based in think-tanks (for instance, the Urban Institute or American Enterprise Institute). It has, historically, been divided between punitive and liberal approaches to workfare with, as Chapter 8 illustrates, an increasing convergence intellectually around the principle of work and its appropriateness for welfare recipients (a convergence which has not obviated important differences between policy advocates, however). Which of these approaches has influenced policy content has depended upon politicians' choices.

These contrasting intellectual traditions have affected the introduction of workfare. Although both countries adopted a form of *deterrent* work-fare in the nineteenth century (based in the Poor Law), in the twentieth century, British policy seemed to break more directly with this approach, especially after 1945, as did the USA though in a more limited way. What has happened in the last twenty years has been the revival of workfare but in what I term its *contractualist* form, rooted in the liberal contractual tradition. Common to both forms of workfare and to both the nineteenth and twentieth centuries is the emphasis upon individual failing. The aim of this policy is the traditional one of modifying welfare recipients' behaviour. Crucially, it is a policy which has found political support across the left–right political spectrum.

7

'Aroused like one from sleep': From New Poor Law to Contractual Workfare

IN April 1998, the Labour administration, led by Tony Blair, introduced a massive 'welfare to work' programme or more grandly a 'New Deal', a workfare scheme targeted on the young and long-term unemployed designed to facilitate their entry to the labour market. Intellectually and historically this initiative, which consolidates significant reforms undertaken by the preceding Conservative administration, was characterized by Frank Field (the minister charged with 'thinking the unthinkable' about the welfare system[1]), as the third stage in a fourfold vision of welfare provision. In this schema, stage one consists in the nineteenth-century Poor Law relief of pauperism and destitution; stage two, both the Lloyd George Liberal administration of 1906–11 and the 1945–51, Beveridge inspired, Attlee government's attack on poverty and need. Stage three will be the welfare to work programme (combined with education reforms) intended to prevent poverty; and stage four envisage welfare state programmes transmogrified into 'well-being not welfare' measures.[2]

Absent from this stepwise framework is an appreciation of the historical dominance of a liberal contractarian approach (manifest, for example, in the New Poor Law and in the Conservatives' welfare programme) which has been used to justify treating the unemployed or welfare recipients in highly directive ways. This chapter supplies both this historical perspective and an analysis of the intellectual sources of workfare programmes. I argue that workfare is best thought of as taking one of two forms: first, as an institution to *deter* potential paupers seeking relief, an aim dominant in the nineteenth-century New Poor Law; and, second, as schemes designed *contractually* to oblige recipients of benefits to undertake an activity or to participate in a training programme in exchange for that assistance.[3] Although

---

[1] For this description see 'Analysis: Welfare Reform', *Guardian*, 21 Oct. 1997.

[2] As set out in Field's Keith Joseph Memorial Lecture at the Centre of Policy Studies on 15 Jan. 1998. For a formal statement of this fourfold model see Department of Social Security, *New Ambitions for our Country: A New Contract for Welfare* (London: HMSO 1998, Cm. 3805), esp. p. 80 where a table Summarizes the respective duties of government and of individuals in the new welfare contract.

[3] Deacon (1997) distinguishes three justifications for workfare: deterrence; utilitarian; and paternalistic arguments. I think the first two categories overlap.

expressed in different ways, both deterrence and contractualism share the basic assumption of workfare: those receiving assistance from the state through public funds should, as a condition of that benefit, be subject to some sanction or requirement aimed at modifying the behaviour which has produced the individual's condition of need (an approach recently advanced as the core of New Labour's 'Third Way'). Both forms of workfare constitute significant social engineering experiments in the sense that each has a theory of the sources of hardship—locating these principally in the failings of individuals—which the programme is designed to remedy. Expertise has been central to both workfare initiatives. Data was collected for the New Poor Law by the commissioners, and since the 1970s welfare policy has been the subject of copious research and debate, if rarely of consensus about the meaning of this material.

THE BIRTH OF DETERRENT WORKFARE: THE 1834 POOR LAW

The nineteenth-century approach to the unemployed was punitive. The seminal Poor Law Commissioners' Report of 1832–4, the basis for the New Poor Law, identified two key elements to guide policy. First, the workhouse should act as a deterrent institution to which the poor, if they searched for work too casually, would be dispatched. According to the commissioners, the experience of the Workhouse, or the prospect of entering it, infused 'new life, new energy into the constitution of the pauper; he is aroused like one from sleep, his relation with all his neighbours, high and low, is changed; he surveys his former employers with new eyes. He begs a job— he will not take a denial.'[4] Crowther observes that the new law was 'based on the hard belief that the deserving and the undeserving poor could be distinguished from each other by a simple test: anyone who accepted relief in the repellent workhouse must be lacking the moral determination to survive outside it.'[5] This principle fits with one of the justifications for modern workfare identified by Alan Deacon: because recipients of assistance have won some respite against the plight of unemployment and are therefore less inclined diligently to seek work, they must be deterred from entering the benefit system.[6] Charles Murray's book *Losing Ground*, published in 1984, and influential amongst welfare reformers especially in the United States, takes a strikingly similar line of analysis. He advocates abolishing welfare systems—what Murray calls the 'Alexandrian solution:

---

[4] *Report from His Majesty's Commissioners for Inquiring into the Administration and Practical Operation of the Poor Laws, Published by Authority* (London, 1834), 247–8.
[5] Crowther (1981: 3).　　[6] Deacon (1997).

cut the knot, for there is no way to untie it'—because they create 'per-verse incentives' for their participants.[7] In common with the Poor Law Commissioners' Report preceding the 1834 law, Murray provides detailed statistical data which he claims to provide support for his proposition.

Second, the principle of 'less eligibility' was established in the New Poor Law. Less eligibility meant ensuring that assistance to the unemployed person maintained that person at a lower income than that of the lowest paid member of the labour force. In the administration of relief, the commissioners wrote, the 'public is warranted in imposing such conditions on the individual relieved, as are conducive to the benefit either of the individual himself, or of the country at large, at whose expense he is to be relieved . . . Every penny bestowed, that tends to render the condition of the pauper more eligible than that of the independent labourer, is a bounty on indolence and vice.'[8] Work should, in this perspective, always be more attractive than idleness or relief. The requirement that those receiving relief be placed in the workhouse operationalized the less eligibility principle: the able-bodied poor were to receive relief only through the workhouse. This measure was supposed to encourage participation in the labour market. As Derek Fraser observes: 'employing the apparently faultless logic of "less eligibility", reformers such as Edwin Chadwick assumed that voluntary paupers would now quit the class of pauper for the more rewarding condition of independent labour. To strengthen that incentive and to provide adequate institutional care for those labelled "impotent" all relief would be channelled into a workhouse, and outdoor relief (the bane of the old system) would cease.'[9] The reformers therefore had a firm idea about the type of incentives to be created for the indigent and unemployed.

That the 1834 legislation sought to modify the behaviour of the poor and unemployed, by holding up the prospect of a strict life in a workhouse as a condition of assistance, implied a particular understanding of the source of emiseration. It arose from individual failing. The commissioners presented this thesis explicitly:

whatever inquiries have been made as to the previous condition of the able-bodied individuals who live in such numbers in the town parishes, it has been found that the pauperism of the greater number of them has originated in indolence, improvidence, or vice, and might have been averted by ordinary care and industry. The smaller number consisted of cases where the cause of poverty could not be ascertained rather than of cases where it was apparent that destitution had arisen from blameless want.[10]

[7] Murray (1984: 228).
[8] *Report from His Majesty's Commissioners for Inquiring into the Administration and Practical Operation of the Poor Laws*, 228.   [9] Fraser (1976: 1).
[10] *Report from His Majesty's Commissioners for Inquiring into the Administration and Practical Operation of the Poor Laws*, 264.

Ensuring that these tendencies toward indolence were controlled and excised was thus made a premiss of relief. The historian Crowther concludes that, although the Poor Law commissioners did not intend to 'pander to employers', their strong commitments to 'individualism' and to 'forcing labourers to make their own way', meant that the report 'underwrote some of the worst excesses of laissez-faire'.[11]

The intellectual arguments for the New Poor Law were developed in particular by the commissioner Nassau Senior (then Drummond Professor of Political Economy at Oxford University) and the assistant commissioner, Edwin Chadwick. They rested on a substantial database. The Commission distributed two questionnaires to all rural areas and a further one to towns (receiving a 10 per cent return), and the team of twenty-six assistant commissioners visited over 3,000 poor law authorities. Senior and Chadwick personified an increasing faith in both the market system's inherent efficiency and appeal, and a utilitarian trust in modifying individual behaviour through the structuring of their incentives to enter the labour market. Thus, Checkland and Checkland conclude that 'the Benthamite and the economists' view of the Poor Law largely converged; both saw it as in need for reform both in terms of efficiency and the reduction of outdoor relief. For the Benthamite the great need was to reassert control over a chaotic system.'[12]

Although the discrepancy between theory and practice in the New Poor Law, and the tension between central administration and local practices was a constant one,[13] nonetheless the principles formalized in the 1834 legislation had a lasting effect on British policy for the unemployed. Able-bodied men who asked for relief were referred (with their families) to the workhouse; they were denied outdoor relief. If able-bodied men undertook some work for the local parish it was to be recompensated in kind, not in cash. In this last measure are found the historical origins of a workfare principle, that is, the condition that in exchange for receiving assistance recipients must undertake some work activity. The development of this principle was driven partly by economic contingency. Unemployment and economic hardship in the early 1840s was so extensive that workhouses could not accommodate all the able-bodied men (and their families) pressing for assistance. Hence 'Labour Yards' were established, as Karl de Schweinitz describes: 'here men were employed at various tasks—picking oakum, cutting wood, and breaking stone. They and their families continued to live in their own homes. The amount and character of the work required differed according to the particular [Poor Law] unions involved.'[14]

[11] Crowther (1981: 19).   [12] Checkland and Checkland (1974: 22).
[13] See Crowther (1981) and Fraser (1976).   [14] De Schweinitz (1943: 135).

This Labour Yard system was intended to be a short-term measure, resorted to only during economic crises or emergencies. However, it quickly acquired a permanent status. Labour Yards enabled recipients to circumvent the workhouse. Local authorities obviously liked them too, since by the 1870s the ratio of indoor relief (that is, in a workhouse) to outdoor relief (that is, some form of labour) was 1 to 6.[15] Fraser concludes that 'outdoor relief survived because it was a logical way of dealing with a labour demand which was necessarily seasonal. Exploiting loopholes in the regulations, rural guardians pragmatically looked to outdoor relief to solve the problem of underemployment.'[16] It persisted also in urban areas, with considerable variation between cities. Thus Fraser, again, remarks that 'variety was the essence of the New Poor Law as of the old,' and, that 'at no time in the nineteenth century did the poor relief system achieve even the semblance of uniformity.'[17]

This 'labour test' or 'test work' system, as it became known, was regulated by the Outdoor Labour Test Order which ordered that half of the relief to able-bodied recipients of the Labour yard should be in kind— food or clothing etc.—and that employment for such beneficiaries was restricted to that specified by the responsible local poor law guardians. In London and other urban areas, the practice of specifying work in exchange for assistance quickly replaced confinement to the workhouse as the preferred poor law guardians' response to indigency (a trend of which the Poor Law Central Board's commissioners, devotees of the workhouse but who could not disregard local preferences, intensely dispproved). Labour yards increased, overseen by a regulation in 1852, as a later Royal Commission described: 'in towns in which the Regulation Order is in force, it is always open to the Guardians, without any special relaxation, to grant out-relief to the able-bodied, provided that, in the case of males, half of it is given in kind and that the recipients are kept at work.'[18] This potential was exploited in 1886, when Joseph Chamberlain (at the time president of the Local Government Board[19]), issued a circular empowering local

---

[15] Ibid. 157; see also Jones (1971) especially ch. 13.

[16] Fraser (1976: 14).   [17] Ibid. 17.

[18] *Report of the Royal Commission on the Poor Laws and Relief of Distress* (London: HMSO, 1909, Cd. 4499), 203. De Schweinitz (1943: 136) writes: 'under this instruction at least one-half of the relief to the able-bodied must be in food or fuel or in other articles of necessity. The guardians were not permitted to set up a relief applicant in business or to purchase tools for him or to pay his rent. Every able-bodied male receiving relief must be put to work by the union.' The Out-door Relief Regulation Order, 10 Dec. 1852.

[19] The administration of the New Poor Law changed four times: (i) 1834–47: Poor Law commissioners, and secretary (Edwin Chadwick), and 9 clerks. Assistant commissioners undertook local inspection; (ii) 1847–71: Poor Law Board, created by Act of Parliament, with permanent secretary and inspectorate; (iii) 1871–1919: Local Government Board, poor law administration was a department of the Board; and (iv) 1919–29: transferred to the newly created Ministry of Health.

authorities to use recipients of out-relief in municipal public works such as building recreation grounds, cemeteries, or new streets.[20] The circular stated:

What is required to relieve artisans and others who have hitherto avoided Poor Law assistance, and who are temporarily deprived of employment, is—(1) work which will not involve the stigma of pauperism; (2) work which all can perform, whatever may have been their previous avocations; (3) work which does not compete with that of other labourers at present in employment; and lastly, work which is not likely to interfere with the resumption of regular employment in their own trades by those who seek it.[21]

This measure not only reduced the role of the workhouse but facilitated the greater involvement of local governments in addressing unemployment and labour market imbalances. Chamberlain's innovation was aimed at the deserving or genuine poor,[22] but demarcating this category precisely from others in need of assistance was never easy. It also implied assigning workers on assistance to tasks that might ordinarily have gone to waged workers, a source of future conflict.

The Poor Law commissioners, in place after 1834, were critical of the test-work system, but their preference that the principle of deterrence embodied in the workhouse should dominate the relief framework enjoyed only limited success. Some poor law districts amalgamated the two systems to create 'the able-bodied workhouse', in which work was undertaken within the curtilage of the workhouse. Such institutions quickly deteriorated into places in which the non-able-bodied paupers were forced to labour, as the category for whom it was designed avoided entering them. However, the Royal Commission of 1909 underlined the diffusion of the Labour Yard system, regretting its embeddedness. Labour Yards were appropriate responses to the 'genuine and temporary crisis'. However, the Yards often became permanent fixtures: 'when this is the case there grows up a nucleus of loafers, who have found the stoneyard under lax supervision an easy way of earning a scanty living, and who act as a centre of corruption when the crisis does come and the respectable workers are forced to have recourse to the Poor Law.'[23] The Commission articulated a distinction between the 'genuine worker', requiring assistance during hard times, and the 'good-for-nothing loafer', irresistibly attracted to the soft life of a labour yard, who thereby devalued the system for the former group. There is a consistent assumption of the moral inadequacy or failing of the able-bodied idler, while a policy's adequacy is assessed by its ability to

---

[20] Local Government Board, *Sixteenth Annual Report 1886–87*, Circular letter to Boards of Guardians, 15 Mar. 1884, pp. 5–7.

[21] Circular, 15 Mar. 1886, cited in McBriar (1987: 48).   [22] Crowther (1981: 72–5).

[23] *Report of the Royal Commission on the Poor Laws and Relief of Distress*, 203–4.

drive such individuals into the labour market. Poor Law policy, therefore, has both a moral and an economic rationale.

The monumental study of the Royal Commission undertaken between 1905 and 1909 (which issued Majority and Minority reports) recommended a significant shift in language from that of 'Poor Law' to 'Public Assistance'. It retained, however, the commitment to individual improvement and well-being: 'the general aim will remain . . . the independence and welfare of the people, but as a means towards that end we desire to introduce into all branches of the work a spirit of efficiency and hopefulness.'[24] Reformers were reluctant to abandon the assumption of the 1834 Poor Law that pauperism was an individual responsibility and a condition reflecting personal failing (certainly the view of Edwin Chadwick, secretary to the earlier study), a conception which justified designing an incentive system of assistance focused on individual behaviour. The emphasis upon personal inadequacy and indolence was muted, however, by a recognition of the unavoidable effects of a market system upon an individual's opportunities in the labour market. The workhouse as a test of diligence was dropped. Instead, the 1909 commissioners replaced the idea of 'test' with that of 'treatment'. The commissioners wanted to reform individuals' behaviour to preclude their becoming paupers, with outdoor relief a key instrument of this ambition. The desire to accommodate relief with the market persists but the government's role in this process is directive rather than solely punitive.

CONTRACTUALIST WORKFARE: FROM SOCIAL RIGHTS TO OBLIGATIONS

The modern workfare initiative has been successfully marshalled as a reclaiming of the 'obligations' of social citizenship, neglected by social policy theorists of the welfare state's rights.[25] On this premiss, government policy toward the unemployed and welfare recipients, since the mid-1980s, has purposefully and adroitly integrated the receipt of benefits with labour market participation, often through training requirements.[26]

Modern workfare—applicable in respect of those in receipt of non-insurance-based benefits and unemployment assistance—is different in character from its nineteenth-century precursor but certain essentials persist. These include: first, it is rooted fundamentally in market democracy, that is, a political system in which policy is designed to complement and accommodate rather than disrupt or control market forces, particu-

---

[24] *Report of the Royal Commission on the Poor Laws and Relief of Distress*, Part IV, p. 96.
[25] Mead (1997c). [26] See King (1995).

larly labour market processes is the norm. Second, it assumes that individuals need to modify their behaviour. Increasingly, this position is tied to a critique of existing welfare benefits which, it is argued, create undesirable incentives regimes; this view is commonly articulated in terms of the 'dependency culture' allegedly fostered by welfare and unemployment systems, in journalist Melanie Phillips's phrase 'slums are not the problem—people are'.[27] Third, implicit assumptions about the demoralization believed ineluctably to arise from prolonged periods of unemployment prevail, though the evidential basis for this view is not overwhelming. And, finally, there is a considerable emphasis upon the obligations which should rightly fall upon beneficiaries as a condition of their assistance.

In this perspective, benefits are damaging because they foster instead of erode dependency; furthermore, simply providing assistance without helping recipients acquire the skills to re-enter the labour force is ultimately soul destroying and demoralizing. In the hands of a modern welfare reformer, such as the influential American Lawrence Mead, these defects become the basis for a strong paternalistic approach to benefits regimes, one justified philosophically by the contractual obligations accruing from membership of the polity.[28] It is this contractual argument which is most powerfully invoked in both the American and British versions of modern workfare. Frank Field, the Labour Party minister supposed to formulate a plan to reform the welfare state (before his departure from the office in July 1998), has endorsed these views.[29] Workfare represents a fundamental challenge to the dominant intellectual tradition in British social policy and administration, that of the social rights of citizenship formulated by T. H. Marshall.[30] In place of rights, or at least in tandem with rights, advocates of modern contractual workfare have discovered and ardently embraced obligations.

The rediscovery of obligations has also prompted careful re-readings of the work of seminal figures in the formation of the British welfare state, notably that of William Beveridge. As Alan Deacon has pointed out, Beveridge's blueprint for the post-1945 British welfare state was acutely sensitive to the dangers of demoralization for individuals confined to long periods of unemployment. Beveridge's original report advocated attendance at a training course as a condition of receiving unemployment assistance,[31] an arrangement consistent with the type of social democratic

---

[27] The title of her column in the *Sunday Times*, 20 Sept. 1998.
[28] Mead (1985). Mead's arguments have been influential in Britain: see Mead (1997*b*).
[29] Field (1997).
[30] Marshall (1964), King and Waldron (1988). For a critique see Mead (1997*c*).
[31] *Social Insurance and Allied Services*, by William Beveridge (London: HMSO, 1942, Cmd. 6404).

welfare system he seems to have favoured. Lacking evidence in his support Beveridge worried about the demoralization of the unemployed and declaimed about what would now be called the perverse incentives of remaining in a benefit regime, since 'men, as creatures who adapt themselves to circumstances, may settle down to them'.[32] The evidence for this view, commonly articulated, is incomplete. For instance, writing about inter-war unemployment, the historian Ross McKibbin identifies poverty rather than unemployment per se as the principal cause of demoralization and psychological decay.[33]

It was the Beveridgean view which was dominant amongst policy-makers after 1945, however, as Deacon illustrates with a quotation from wartime Minister of Labour (and Labour Party member), Ernest Bevin. Bevin maintained that:

a man who remains compulsorily unemployed for many months gradually adjusts himself to a lower level of mental and physical activity. He does so in self protection and often he develops a protective ailment: he loses heart, and the better man he is the more he deteriorates, for the chief sufferers in this respect are those to whom it is morally intolerable to be one of the unwanted.[34]

To preclude abuses of the system, a time limit was placed upon drawing unemployment insurance in the post-1945 regime, at which point the recipient shifted to non-insurance assistance. However, the time limit was substantial: 180 days of insurance-based benefit could be extended by a further 130 days; and during a five-year transition period successful appeal to a tribunal could allow benefits to continue beyond the time limits (Clause 61 of the 1946 National Insurance Act), appeals which were almost always granted. Low unemployment in the post-war decades permitted this arrangement to routinize without any serious political consequences or its close scrutiny.

Research evidence suggests that people mostly dislike being unemployed. Daniel reports, from a survey asking the unemployed to rank the experience from 'don't really mind' to 'worst thing that ever happened to me', that just under 50 per cent opted for the latter view and only 5 per cent selected the first option.[35] Michael White examined the stigma of unemployment (without indicating his sample size) and from survey responses found that: 'more than one in 10 felt that they were "treated differently" by others because they had been unemployed for long periods.' He concludes that the evidence 'confirms that feelings of stigmatization

---

[32] *Social Insurance and Allied Services*, 58.   [33] McKibbin (1990).

[34] E. Bevin memorandum, 'Sanctions Applicable to the Recalcitrant or Workshy', PRO, PR (43) 64, cited in Deacon (1996: 196).

[35] Daniel (1990: 82); the sample size is not reported.

have been quite widespread among unemployed people, but not as dominant as some might have expected'. White speculates that 'it may be that after a decade of high unemployment, these feelings are wearing off.'[36] Such findings appear, unsurprisingly, to reveal that unemployment is not a condition enjoyed by those who experience it. They do not provide a sufficient basis, however, for drawing robust conclusions about demoralization. Nonetheless, reform, premissed on this effect, continues.

Deacon argues, correctly I think, that both the wartime Coalition and 1945–51 Labour governments were cognizant of the dangers of creating a welfare state which provided benefits without any time limits, even though these themes were dormant until the 1970s. Deacon writes that post-war legislation was designed to 'ensure that those who benefited from [the welfare state] still had a powerful incentive to seek work and to accept responsibility for their families. Moreover, even amongst those most closely identified with the values which underpinned the 'classic welfare state' there remained a residual concern with the impact of welfare upon individual behaviour and attitudes, and with the limitations of providing only cash benefits for the unemployed. Such concerns were to be expressed less often in the post-war years.'[37] These concerns have resurfaced powerfully since the 1970s, however, under both Thatcherite conservatism and Blairite New Labour as the twin claims about a dependency culture and the need to enforce contractual workfare have gained increasingly wide acceptance (even with some members of the old social policy and administration discipline). Policy advocates of this tougher line, for long at the margins of the welfare reform debate and marginalized in the social policy intellectual community, have found themselves increasingly at its centre.

The intellectual case for workfare

Amongst policy advocates Lawrence Mead has perhaps pushed the new paternalist rationale for workfare the furthest, presenting it in the contractualist framework. He argues that a cultural explanation of poverty or of growing welfare rolls is the most powerful, and that to overcome the misery and demoralization of welfare or unemployment, work must be required of recipients. This work requirement will break the dependency culture, foster self-esteem, and equip welfare recipients to enter the world of work permanently and thereby become self-sufficient functioning individuals. Mead argues that 'more important than any economic factor as a cause of poverty . . . is what used to be called the culture of poverty'. Surveys find, he tells us, that 'poor adults want to work and observe other

---

[36] White (1991: 41).
[37] Deacon (1996: 196–7); see also Addison (1975).

mainstream values. Many, however, resist taking the low-paid jobs that are most likely to be available to them. A greater number are simply defeatist about work or unable to organize their personal lives to hold jobs consistently.'[38]

Three key points of this analysis are worth stressing: first, Mead's preferred remedy requires the state in a market democracy to intervene directly and forcefully in the unemployed individual's or welfare recipient's circumstances, a strategy which does not necessarily imply diminishing the role or size of the state despite the alleged failure of existing programmes; second, it places a good deal of emphasis upon individuals' attitudes and responses to incentive structures; and third, consistent with the dominant values and beliefs of a market democracy, full participation in the labour market is deemed to constitute a key source of self-esteem, worth, and entitlement to equal membership of the polity. Work, not wealth, is promoted as key to individuals' sense of self-worth.[39] This model has had considerable influence, certainly in the 1996 welfare reform enacted by President Clinton and in recent British policy. Mead's views and analyses have constituted one of the most significant sources of expertise in welfare policy choices, influential with welfare reformers in both countries.

The propensity toward contractualist workfare among the British policymakers has marginalized the traditional source of expertise, academic social policy specialists. As a profession they have historically been loyal to a Marshallian and Titmuss framework. For example, there is now conflict about welfare policy between experts about the issue of benefit payments,[40] and the abandonment of income redistribution (a concern voiced by an eminent group of social policy experts[41]). These issues have arisen because of the planned major overhaul of the welfare state, an overhaul promising to be as significant as Beveridge's plan.

Underpinning New Labour's welfare to work reforms is a willingness to employ a strong state to restructure the welfare system and labour market, and crucially, to impose sanctions and compulsion upon reluctant or recalcitrant participants. These measures epitomize a moral liberal approach to welfare. Thus, Frank Field, until July 1998 a minister at Social Security, characterizes the American contractual workfare approach, based on a theory of the culture of poverty and welfare dependency, as a 'compelling analysis'.[42] He welcomes the 'corrective' to both the right-wing and left-

[38] Mead (1997b: 12).   [39] Arneson (1990b).
[40] See the debate between Julian Le Grand and Ruth Lister *Guardian*, 28 Jan. 1998. The LSE professor, David Piachaud, argues that New Labour's policies will increase rather than reduce poverty. 'Millions more face poverty under Labour', *Guardian*, 5 Jan. 1998.
[41] See the letter of Professor Ruth Lister et al. in the *Financial Times*, 1 Oct. 1997.
[42] Field (1997: 59).

wing analyses of the unemployed's behaviour: these latter accounts, Field argues, 'have crippled thinking on British social policy for so long—on the right that the poor deserved to be so because they are lazy, on the left that the poor are immune from the faults of laziness or dishonesty'.[43] As part of the reform of welfare, and following logically from his critique of existing assumptions about the motivations of the unemployed, Field endorses a compulsory workfare system underpinned with sanctions:

I believe that the majority want to get off welfare but need active help to do so ... Sanctions need to be part of the New Deal. The threat of penalisation begins to affect the culture in which people consider how they should respond and, indeed, what their responsibilities are. They are, then, more a teaching agent (for they will only ever directly affect a small minority) than a great engine for social change.[44]

Field's views resonate historically, I would argue, with the New Poor Law assumption that, without a deterrence, unemployed people will slip onto benefits and, because of perverse incentives, opt to remain there rather than find work. (They are rather different to conclusions Field himself reached in 1994, with his co-author Matthew Owen, that 'all regulations that use attendance at training schemes as a condition of receiving benefit' were undesirable.)[45] It may be that this new position is an appropriate response to the working of the welfare state but its historical echoes are striking and warrant consideration by policy-makers.

Alan Deacon disentangles the arguments for and against compulsion in the administration of workfare programmes by distinguishing between two issues: first, the philosophical or normative question of whether compulsion is acceptable in a liberal state; and, second, whether it is a practicable policy. In its favour, Deacon argues, is the contractual workfare framework: that is, because the state's provision of benefits is increasingly premissed on a contractual exchange with the recipients, enforcing sanctions should be part of this package.[46] Logically this is accurate. In policy terms, it constitutes a shift to contractualist workfare.

The intellectual and political movement to contractualist workfare has been a steady one in the 1990s and, for the most part, bipartite. Thus, John Major remarked in February 1993 that, 'I increasingly wonder whether paying unemployment benefit, without offering or requiring activity in return serves unemployed people or society well.'[47] A year before the Conservatives' (1997) electoral defeat, the House of Commons Select Committee on Employment issued a substantial report on workfare.

---

[43] Ibid. 62.   [44] Ibid.   [45] Field and Owen (1994: 1).
[46] See Deacon (1998: 8–10) and Deacon (1997).
[47] House of Commons Sessions 1995–6, Employment Committee Second Report, *The Right to Work/Workfare* (London: HMSO, 13 Feb. 1996), p. vii.

Entitled 'The Right to Work/Workfare', the report's authors urged a 'fundamental rethinking of the system by which the unemployed are supported in the UK'.[48] Intellectually, the Committee's report marks an unequivocal shift to contractualist workfare, despite the illiberal implications of such measures. The report's authors criticized the omission of Beveridge's recommendation to make the receipt of unemployment benefit conditional upon either discharging a work or training activity: 'instead, payment of unemployment benefit has been unaccompanied by a requirement to work or train'.[49] It cited comments made to the Committee by Frank Field: 'we have the old Poor Law tradition still in that people are paid to be idle.'[50] Field's observation provoked a set of general observations by the report's authors:

Paying people to be idle is not just a waste of the country's money: it is a waste of human resources. . . . The payment of unemployment benefit without the provision of suitable training or work tends to undermine people's capacity to work at all. Skills are neither maintained nor updated; separated from the practice and discipline of employment individuals quickly find they are excluded from jobs because of demoralisation, lack of skills or experience or by employer discrimination. Furthermore, the benefits system can distort economic behaviour in unintended and damaging ways. Some people may be better off (though still poorly-off) on benefit than in a job, and therefore perfectly rationally decide not to work.[51]

In this context, the Committee addressed itself to the question of whether a system of contractual workfare based on conditionality should be implemented, hearing and receiving comments from a range of experts on social policy and labour market economics.

The Committee stressed the historical commonality of conditionality as a requirement of benefits: not only did the New Poor Law employ this element but so had the 1601 Elizabethan Poor Law. It cited the Labour Yard work system, encountered above, and Joseph Chamberlain's efforts to 'encourage local Government to provide work outside workhouses to the unemployed poor';[52] and of course Beveridge's treatment of this issue in his 1942 Report. The Select Committee detected a trend toward workfare, citing the Conservatives' forceful measures implicitly to establish conditionality in the Restart and Jobseeker's Allowance system, as evidence of a general trend toward this element in the unemployment benefits regime.

Expertise seemed to support this move to contractuality, on grounds not

---

[48] House of Commons Sessions 1995–6, p. v. An interesting document, some of its factual grasp—for example, its dating of the US AFDC scheme in the 'early 1930s', when it was enacted in 1935 and operative in 1936—does not inspire confidence in its scholarly foundations.
[49] Ibid.   [50] Ibid., p. vi.   [51] Ibid.   [52] Ibid., p. xix.

incompatible with nineteenth-century views. Thus, several expert witnesses argued that paying unemployment benefits simply stoked indolence. The LSE economist Richard Layard informed the Committee that unemployment benefits constituted 'a subsidy to idleness, and it should not be suprising if they lead to an increase in idleness'.[53] The long-term unemployed were poor choices for employers, and the longer they remained unemployed the less appealing a prospect they became. This conclusion implied special treatment for the long-term unemployed if their chances of entering employment were to become realistic. Benefit recipients needed customized programmes to get them into jobs or to prepare them for employment. In the Committee's terminology, a shift from 'passive' unemployment measures to active schemes was imperative. However, its enthusism for workfare schemes was tempered by two caveats: first, work schemes 'should not be regarded as a permanent solution to the problem of long-term joblessness. They should be seen as an avenue back to work,' accompanied by measures such as jobsearch help, remedial education, training, and help with childcare. Second, its members were anxious about compulsion: 'though compulsion may not affect the attitude to the work offered for many people, for some it will, and these people will be capable of disrupting the opportunities for many others.'[54] Thus, the Employment Committee firmly rejected a mandatory system of contractual workfare, though it seemed to accept that the benefits system created so-called perverse incentives. It praised programmes (such as the WISE group in Glasgow) which combined training and jobs by paying a proper wage while allowing individuals to acquire or improve skills.

In respect of workfare, the Employment Committee rehearsed three common arguments in its favour: morally, it was appropriate to expect reciprocal activity from benefit recipients on contractual grounds; fiscally, it might deter some false claimants; and psychologically, it would revive the unemployed suffering from Beveridge's classic demoralization who, without hope or motivation, have abandoned attempts to enter work, and for whom 'a compulsory system of unpaid work . . . will prepare [them] for the labour market by teaching them good work habits and skills, and restore their motivation'.[55] It is the first and third rationales which find expression in the contractualist workfare framework: improve the unemployed's morale and instil the responsibilities associated with contractual obligations. Nonetheless, the Committee also received plenty of evidence suggesting that enforced or mandatory attendance at training programmes was the least desirable recipe for either participants or their trainers. Moving unemployed persons straight into employment rather than

---

[53] Ibid., p. xii.   [54] Ibid., p. xlvii.   [55] Ibid., p. xxvii.

training schemes was considered a solution to this conumdrum: 'we accept the case for programmes of work experience as a way of helping long-term unemployed people back into work—but stress that the best outcomes are likely to be had from programmes which mix work and training,'[56] a view with which the architects of inter-war reconditioning camps would have concurred. It approved of the Conservatives' Workstart programme in this context, adding weight to the pro-contractualist workfare shift.

WORKFARE IN OPERATION

The intellectual arguments for workfare having been examined, in this section the experience of deterrent and contractualist schemes is studied, beginning with the test-work system established by the New Poor Law before turning to the schemes implemented in the 1990s.

Test work in the inter-war years

The system inaugurated under the Poor Law Labour Yard persisted into the twentieth century. The scheme's appeal arose principally from the need to have a deterrent during periods of economic adversity, specifically in respect of work in workhouses, as Crowther suggests: 'the type of work done in many workhouses soon assumed a penal character; it was done not for profit or use, but because it was irksome. Stone breaking, stone pounding and oakum picking were most frequently associated with workhouses, though a few unions encouraged local industries.'[57] Stone breaking was used for road building while oakum was sold to the navy for caulking ships. Neither was profitable, and stone breaking was an activity which ironically, as McBriar notes, 'required a good deal of skill that most unemployed did not possess'.[58] In urban areas, the work required by paupers was neither profitable nor even useful, according to Crowther: tasks were assigned 'purely for deterrence'.[59] In the decades before 1914, some task or test work was administered through colonies set up by poor law unions, such as those in London (the Belmont Industrial Colony, Hollesley Bay, and the Dunton Farm Colony, near Brentwood).[60]

Conditions of application and levels of benefits varied significantly across parts of the country according to poor law union practices. Systematic complaints about abuses of the test-work system grew from the early 1920s,[61] when depressed economic conditions prompted an increase

---

[56] House of Commons Sessions 1995–6, p. xxxii. [57] Crowther (1981: 198).
[58] McBriar (1987: 40). [59] Crowther (1981: 199). [60] Field (1992: 24).
[61] MRC Warwick, TUC Records, Folder: MSS.135.82/1. *History of Case: Test and Task Work*, 8 pp.; documents complaints between Mar. 1924 and Sept. 1933.

in outdoor relief rolls and the burden on local taxpayers.[62] As Crowther observes, the system reached crisis in the late 1920s when mass unemployment 'threw ever-increasing numbers of people on to the Poor Law'. The appropriate administrative response—offering the 'workhouse or the labour yards as a test of destitution'—was, in this context, 'patently unworkable'.[63] In London, one poor law inspector, C. F. Roundell, proposed, in 1928, a special test-work institution, with a broader remit than the labour yards, since in these latter the 'old corn mills are now regarded as museum pieces and stone-breaking is, I think, only done in one institution i.e. Westminister . . . Discipline in the ordinary workhouse to-day is not strict.'[64] The workhouse test was demoted in the Poor Law Act of 1930, with other forms of outdoor relief for the able-bodied permitted. The Local Government Act of 1929, introduced by Neville Chamberlain, initiated the systematic dismantling of the New Poor Law but its extinction occurred only in 1948. Consequently, in the 1930s the system of 'less eligibility' remained, and 'governments tried to keep the level of the dole below the lowest independent wages, though as in previous times, large families were hardest hit'.[65] In 1934, the Unemployment Assistance Board was established with national responsibility for unemployment.

For trade unions, the most important objection to test work was the competitive threat to waged workers posed by the unemployed compelled by local authorities to undertake work. This problem was highlighted, in 1909, by the Royal Commission: 'we think it is advisable that in organising the work of the able-bodied, the Public Assistance Authorities should aim at as great a variety of occupations as possible in the interests of minimising the disturbance to the labour market.'[66] It cited woodcutting in the Paddington Union (London), which allegedly forced private employers out of business. Test work was used as a pretext, the TUC maintained, to set the 'able-bodied unemployed to work in ordinary wage earning occupations for the amount of relief which they receive'.[67]

From the 1920s, the TUC provided detailed accounts of cases of test-work abuses throughout the country: for example, at Portsmouth, men were put to work in parks and open spaces. In this instance, the Ministry of Health conceded that they had been given work which might reasonably have been done for wages; and that the test-work men were set to

---

[62] In 1921 over £5 million were spent on the relief rolls, a figure which rose to over £15 million a year later: Ministry of Health, *Ninth Annual Report* (London, 1927–8), 142.

[63] Crowther (1981: 101–2).

[64] Memorandum by C. F. Roundell, 17 Jan. 1928, cited in Crowther (1981: 108).

[65] Crowther (1981: 109).

[66] *Report of the Royal Commission on the Poor Laws and Relief of Distress*, 206.

[67] MRC Warwick, TUC Records, Folder: MSS.135.82/1. TUC General Council, *Test Work*, Deputation to the Minister of Health, Sir E. Hilton Young MP, from the Trades Union Congress General Council, 14 Nov. 1933, Private and Confidential, p. 2.

labour with normal waged workers.[68] Cases were submitted from Dudley, Shipley, Oxford, Stapleford, Gateshead, Derby, Bermondsey and Rotherhithe, Dalton, Carlton and Netherfield, Retford, Crayford, Shrewsbury, Kent, East Suffolk, Stockport, Bromley, Lowestoft, Cornwall, and Sunderland, in all of which the TUC maintained the work was that which would have normally been performed for wages and that the test workers often laboured side by side with ordinary wage earners. These were not the only cases. However, the Conservative Health Minister,[69] Sir E. Hilton Young, rejected many of the complaints, stating: 'I make it a condition of my approval that test work shall not be of such a nature as to displace regular wage-earners. The amount of relief paid in any case is governed by the needs of the applicant's household, and bears no necessary relation to the rates of wages paid for ordinary employment.'[70]

Even when local authorities claimed that such work would not be done without assistance schemes, the TUC argued that bona fide employees should be employed for it. The TUC was anxious to prevent local authorities from paying test-work men wages 'below the market rate for such work'.[71] Parliamentary questions reporting abuses of test work were tabled annually by concerned MPs. One MP claimed that men on test work were assigned tasks irrespective of their physical well-being—'there is no medical standard of physical requirement to which all relief must conform'—and, ironically, inappropriate work rendered relief workers *less* employable: test work is 'tending steadily to worsen the physical condition of those people, and all the time it tends to confirm them, not only in their unemployment, but in their unemployability'.[72] But the employability defence was routinely deployed by ministers to justify test work. Thus, the Health Minister's Parliamentary Secretary told the Commons that 'the main object of the requirement that able-bodied men should be set to work or trained or instructed, is to maintain the employability of applicants for relief by, at the least, providing them with some regular occupation during what must otherwise be a period of enforced idleness.'[73]

By 1929 there were 70,000 able-bodied men on outdoor relief. One

[68] MRC Warwick, TUC Records, appendix, p. 2.

[69] The Local Government Board was replaced by the Ministry of Health in 1919, which assumed responsibility for this legacy of the Poor Law.

[70] Official Report, 5th Series, Parliamentary Debates, Commons, 1932–3, vol. 274 col. 1889, 23 Feb. 1933.

[71] MRC Warwick, TUC Records, Folder: MSS.135.82/1. TUC General Council, *Test Work*, 3.

[72] Official Report, 5th Series, Parliamentary Debates, Commons, 1930–1, cols. 110–11, 14 Apr. 1931.

[73] Official Report, 5th Series, Parliamentary Debates, Commons 1934–5, vol. 300, cols. 514–15, 4 Apr. 1935; the speaker is Geoffrey Shakespeare, Parliamentary Secretary to the Minister of Health.

hundred and ninety-five unions required test work of 29,014 men, 13 unions had cooperative schemes affecting men on relief, and 146 unions, with 25,347 men affected, had no test-work schemes.[74] Of the last figure, the majority of the able-bodied men were concentrated in a very few unions. From a survey of every union, the Ministry of Health identified fifteen types of test work, ranging from gardening work (123 cases) and woodcutting (100), general maintenance work (90), to stone breaking and quarrying (21), road making (50), road scavenging (13), work in public cemeteries (11), and boot repairing (2). A mere five cases of enrolment in educational and training schemes were found.[75] The unions varied in the work assigned to test workers, the degree of assessment of the men's physical abilities, and in provision of opportunities to find permanent work (with one union giving test workers Monday off for such searches).

The 1930 departmental report on test work came after over a decade of complaints about the system, aired annually in the Commons by its opponents. In 1924, John Wheatley, the Minister of Health, rejected a request in the Commons to abolish 'all forms of test work at present being operated in Britain by Poor Law authorities'.[76] This position was defended by his successors, Conservative and Labour. Arthur Greenwood, a senior Labour minister in MacDonald's administration, justified the system in the late 1920s.[77] The sorts of abuses perpetrated under test work were described by one MP to the minister: the Hellesdon test ground, Norwich, was 'nearly four miles from the centre of the city; consequently a tramp of nine miles or more is necessitated in many cases; the exposure of the test workers in wet weather has led to physical deterioration in many cases.'[78] Stone breaking was detested by test workers and its abolition regularly sought.[79] Pure stone breaking was proscribed by the Health Ministry from 1 April 1931, but it continued in quarrying districts which did not require ministerial approval.[80] Oakum picking was ended in June 1925 by the Minister of Health, Neville Chamberlain.[81]

[74] Ministry of Health, *Report of a Special Inquiry into Various Forms of Test Work* (London: HMSO, May 1930, Cmd. 3585), 5.

[75] Ibid. 8.

[76] Official Report, 5th Series, Parliamentary Debates, Commons, 1924, vol. 173, col. 937, 12 May 1924.

[77] Official Report, 5th Series, Parliamentary Debates, Commons, 1929–30, vol. 232, cols. 1608–9, 28 Nov. 1929.

[78] Ibid. The MP was Geoffrey Shakespeare, later a Parliamentary Secretary for Health.

[79] It was specified as appropriate work in the Casual Poor (Relief) Order of 1925. Official Report, 5th Series, Parliamentary Debates, Commons, 1929–30, vol. 231, col. 598, 27 Mar. 1930; see answer by the Minister of Health, Arthur Greenwood.

[80] Official Report, 5th Series, Parliamentary Debates, Commons, 1931–2, vol. 265, col. 1909, 11 May 1932; the Parliamentary Secretary to the Minister of Health, Ernest Brown, provided this information.

[81] Crowther (1981: 263).

Other criticisms of test work were unearthed in the 1930 departmental inquiry. They included: the unsuitability of work tasks required, the shortage of work as the numbers on relief grew, excessive journeys to the test-work sites, and exposure to bad weather. One inspector told the inquiry that: 'the old-fashioned form of test in a workhouse is too crude for modern conditions, and the work should be varied, educative and calculated to tone up physical and mental slackness.'[82] The inspectors unanimously rejected the charge that test work was demoralizing or degrading. The inspector responsible for London told the inquiry that 'our inquiries are quite definite on one point—when men are questioned as to the test work they are performing, and whether they consider it hard or degrading, the invariable answer has been that they appreciate it, that it is far better than loafing around the streets, and that they have felt more fit than when they were doing nothing and merely hanging about.'[83] Significantly, the inspectors were uniformly agreed that this early form of workfare, test work, succeeded as a deterrent: it prevented those not genuinely unemployed seeking assistance. They included some statistics contrasting the higher numbers seeking relief in unions without test work as grounds for this inference. As a deterrence, it worked.

One hundred and three local authorities did require test work of able-bodied men in receipt of outdoor relief.[84] The 1930 Order[85] gave wide discretion to local authorities about test work, as a subsequent Minister of Health, Sir E. Hilton Young, conceded in the Commons: the Order 'does not specify the nature of the work, and allows considerable latitude to local authorities in making the necessary arrangements'. He added: 'I see no reason for withdrawing the Order,' and rejected the claim that test workers felt, in the words of one MP, that 'the work is placed upon them as a punishment for crime, their only crime being that they are poor'.[86] It was the Ministry of Health section dealing with relief which advocated most keenly the use of test work.[87] Especially under the Conservative Neville Chamberlain, the Ministry of Health adopted a severe position toward paupers but was unable comprehensively to control the decisions and policy of every set of locally elected poor law guardians. The resulting

[82] Ministry of Health, *Report of a Special Inquiry into Various Forms of Test Work*, 13.

[83] Ibid. 16; Mr Roundell quoted.

[84] Official Report, 5th Series, Parliamentary Debates, Commons, 1930–1, vol. 248, cols. 2276–7, 26 Feb. 1931, Greenwood reporting.

[85] The new Relief Regulation Order succeeded the Relief Regulation Order of 1911, which directed that 'except as hereinafter provided, the Guardians of a Poor Law Union shall not afford relief other than institutional relief to any person who is within a union'. Cited in De Schweinitz (1943: 215).

[86] Official Report, 5th Series, Parliamentary Debates, Commons, 1931–2, cols. 1999–2000, 30 June 1932. Smedley Crook MP speaking.

[87] Ministry of Health, *Ninth Annual Report*, 144–7.

variations stimulated the creation of the Unemployment Assistance Board as a mechanism for enforcing central directives and reigning in local deviation.[88]

In 1934, the TUC argued that the 'whole question of test work' required a 'fundamental change'.[89] The TUC led a delegation to the Minister of Health to press their case. It argued that the tasks undertaken on test-work schemes were systematically integrated with that of ordinary waged workers employed by local authorities. This arrangement violated a condition of test work whereby the 'work should not be such as would ordinarily be performed for wages'.[90] The TUC submitted cases illustrating how this rule was regularly transgressed. The delegation asked the minister to 'take a strong line in this matter', since it had become a 'general practice throughout the country in dealing with test work'.[91] It presented a series of individual cases of injustice.[92]

The Minister for Health, Sir E. Hilton Young, responded to these complaints by first reiterating the principle of deterrent workfare: 'the principle of requiring work as a condition for relief was one continually upheld by successive Governments.' He underlined the value of such a condition for worker employability: 'indefinite continuation of out relief without condition was not good for the recipient'. It was necessary to maintain 'the physical and moral condition through the performance of suitable work'.[93] Young accepted the inappropriateness of test workers being assigned positions alongside regularly waged workers. He did acknowledge, however, disagreement or 'honest differences' in determining 'whether work was, or was not, such as would ordinarily be performed for wages'.[94] He denied that test-work abuses were as widespread as the deputation maintained. Young did promise to continue to investigate each complaint submitted by the TUC.

The TUC's deputation to the Minister of Health led to improvements in the test-work system, including redress in several local cases.

[88] See the discussions in Briggs and Deacon (1974) and Deacon and Briggs (1974).

[89] MRC Warwick, TUC Records, Folder: MSS.292/131.3/3, letter from J. Smyth, Secretary Social Insurance Department to John Walker, Middlesbrough Trades and Labour Council, 11 July 1934.

[90] MRC Warwick, TUC Records, Folder: MSS.135.82/1. TUC General Council, *Test Work*, Deputation to the Minister of Health, Sir E. Hilton Young MP, from the Trades Union Congress General Council, 14 Nov. 1933, Private and Confidential, p. 1.

[91] Ibid., Minutes of the meeting, p. 4.

[92] At Willenhall, Young was informed, 'several ex-servicemen, employees of the Council, had been discharged and test workers retained doing their work . . . these men were put on work for a 5/3 grocery ticket for which they previously received 45/—wages per week.' Ibid. 6. This case was raised by a representative of the National Union of Local and Metal Workers. Similar charges were marshalled by the Furnishing Trades' Association, whose members' work was being undercut by woodworkers in test work centres.

[93] Ibid. 8.   [94] Ibid. 9.

Nonetheless, the system remained in place throughout the 1930s. The TUC monitored its implementation, seeking rectification of repeated cases of abuse: 'the General Council have never lost sight of the matter and pressure has been maintained by means of questions in the House, letters to the Minister and so on, with the result that further complaints in many districts have been rectified.'[95] The Unemployment Assistance Board, established in 1934, took over the functions of public assistance authorities, constituting a national body for what was previously a local affair, but did not put an immediate end to all test work.[96] Its termination came after 1945.

Contractualist workfare

The post-1945 welfare state social democratic consensus lasted, broadly, from 1945 to the mid-1970s.[97] During this period the commitment to full employment was largely untested by adverse circumstances, and the ambiguous position of those unemployed persons who exhausted their insurance-based benefits was politically irrelevant. The coincident growth of unemployment from the late 1970s and the diffusion of a liberal individualist ideology provided a fertile framework for a modern version of workfare.

The 1945–75 welfare state period—which the historian Rodney Lowe terms the 'classic welfare state'[98]—was conceived in what appear, retrospectively, to be narrow terms. The dominant intellectual rationale was one based in T. H. Marshall's essay about the social rights of citizenship (which Marshall considered twentieth-century corollaries to early civil and political rights[99]). This framework complemented that of the dominant social policy academic and expert, Richard Titmuss, who made his opposition to means testing and celebration of universalism the central plank of his discipline, social policy.[100] This theoretical lacuna has been highlighted by José Harris who notes that paradoxically, in this post-1945 period, when the British state's activities were expanding at their most rapid, there was a 'widespread silence . . . on the theme of the underlying nature, powers and purposes of the state'.[101] In social policy, the combined effect of little systematic theoretical reflection and the uncritical adherence to Marshallian assumptions rendered discussion vulnerable to the neoliberal critiques

[95] MRC Warwick, TUC Records, Folder: MSS.292/135.82/5, letter from Secretary, Social Insurance Department to Councillor L. C. Gray, Bridgwater & District Trades Council, 2 Mar. 1939.
[96] See the discussion in Pedersen (1993: 294–304), Fulbrook (1978), and Gilbert (1970).
[97] For an excellent overview see Lowe (1993).
[98] Ibid., Part II.   [99] Marshall (1964).
[100] See Deacon (1993).   [101] Harris (1996: 15).

engineered by the New Right in the late 1970s. In fact, Harris underestimates the prevalence of a Marshallian theory of the social rights of citizenship (a nice complement to the pleasing teleological account of British history taught in political science classes), as evidenced in the huge literature generated on the topic of citizenship since the 1970s. It was the uncritical embrace of the social *rights* argument, as the basis for the political relationship between citizens and the state, which proved damaging intellectually since its theorists de-emphasized (or entirely ignored) the responsibilities or obligations dimension of citizenship; and thereby induced a complacency in a particular form of state-based social policy. The rise of contractualist workfare restored the focus upon obligations.

The Conservatives' welfare reforms induced a decisive shift toward contractual workfare, culminating in the experimental workfare Project Work schemes. The relationship between income maintenance recipients and the state (represented by the Employment Service) is now a contractual one.[102] In 1986, the Restart programme[103] was introduced for those receiving contributory non-means-tested national insurance benefits: a set of compulsory interviews at the employment service office at which 'back to work' plans were completed. In October 1996, this scheme was reformulated into the 'jobseeker's allowance', an agreement between recipients and the service whereby the jobseeker signs a document outlining the measures he or she will take to look for work each week.[104] The Restart programme required jobcentre staff to offer help to all interviewees at their offices. One study of the Restart programme concludes that it had 'made a difference at the individual level'. From their research, the authors concluded that 'those passing through Restart, compared with the control group, spent less time in claimant unemployment, made their initial movement off the register more rapidly, entered jobs more rapidly . . . and, at the end of the study period, were more likely to be in employment and ET and less likely to be on the register.'[105]

Within six months of the passage of Restart, the Employment Secretary, Kenneth Clarke, reduced the period before being invited for an interview

[102] From a substantial literature see especially Ainley and Vickerstaff (1993), Ashby (1989), Peck (1991*a*, 1991*b*, 1996).
[103] Dolowitz (1996) characterizes this programme as explicitly workfare.
[104] Employment Department, *Jobseeker's Allowance* (London: HMSO, Oct. 1994, Cm. 2687). For commentaries see I. Murray and P. Convery, 'Jobseeker's Allowance White Paper', *Working Brief* (Nov. 1994), I. Murray, 'Jobseekers Bill Starts Commons Passage', *Working Brief* (Feb. 1995), and I. Murray, 'Jobseeker's Allowance: Six Month Delay', *Working Brief* (June 1995). See also 'Workfare: Ministers adopt US-style scheme to replace "something for nothing" benefits', *The Times*, 25 Oct. 1994, *Turning up the Heat: Will the Jobseeker's Allowance get the jobless back to work?* (London: Unemployment Unit, Sept. 1994), and R. Taylor and J. Blitz, 'Paying for the Jobseeker's Bill', *Financial Times*, 23 Mar. 1995.
[105] White and Lakey (1992: 158).

from twelve to six months; and introduced a job-seeking questionnaire administered during Restart interviews, to determine whether jobseekers were unduly limiting the types of jobs they would take. The 1989 legislation also reintroduced the 'actively seeking work' requirement,[106] directing each recipient of state assistance to undertake a specified activity each week in exchange for their benefits. The 1989 Act required recipients to take suitable employment and to show 'good cause' for refusing a position; furthermore, refusing part-time employment was no longer acceptable. These changes modified a regime in place since the 1920s.[107]

Under the British jobseeker's allowance, failure to attend fortnightly interviews or to comply with the jobseeking measures ('actively seeking work') can result in the loss of benefits; the agreement permits the jobseeker's mandatory participation in a workfare programme. The jobseeker's allowance gives considerable discretion to the employment advisers in the employment service. The advisers can require jobseekers to attend certain job interviews. This is an interventionist system, focused mostly on the long-term and young unemployed, and likely both to push some people out of the claims system and to direct others into the bottom end of the labour market. The employment service must administer the increasingly conditional work-welfare programme which has developed since the 1980s.

Historically, the jobseeker's allowance system is the biggest change in the dole system since 1948: it has replaced unemployment benefit and income support for the unemployed, cutting means-tested state support from twelve to six months. Its significance was recognized by the House of Commons Employment Committee Report:

although it may fall short of a formal Workfare programme, the Jobseekers Act marks the culmination of a policy which has approached the problem of mass unemployment as essentially one whose cause is the lack of sufficient jobseeking skills amongst jobless individuals. The degree to which unemployed people must satisfy their availability and readiness for work through the formalised contract with the taxpayer through the Jobseeker's Agreement are the most demanding conditions to be imposed on jobhunters so far.[108]

The Labour Party retained the jobseeker's programme after entering government in May 1997.

[106] Social Security Act 1989, Section 10 (1).
[107] Deacon (1976).
[108] House of Commons Sessions 1995–6, Employment Committee Second Report, *The Right to Work/Workfare* (London: HMSO, 13 Feb. 1996), p. xxiv.

In December 1995, the Conservatives committed themselves to workfare programmes,[109] a commitment complementing the Jobseeker's Allowance. Commencing in April 1996, experimental workfare programmes, known as Work Project, were targeted on areas with high unemployment.[110] Selected unemployed persons between the ages of 18 and 50, categorized as long-term unemployed (out of work for two or more years), were required to join work schemes, receiving an additional £10 a week for participation, and if they declined faced consecutive reductions in their unemployment benefits; (on the first occasion of refusing to participate unemployed people lost two weeks' benefits, the second time a month's benefits, and on the third occasion the right to benefit was abrogated).[111] Before losing the election in 1997, the Conservative government had proposed to extend Work Project from its initial clientele of 8,000 people to tens of thousands. 'Project Work' broke with Marshallian social rights of citizenship.[112] According to the then Secretary for Education and Employment, the scheme was aimed at the 'recalcitrant few' who were disinclined to return to employment.[113] The logic and analytical assumptions

[109] J. Hibbs, 'Jobless will have to work for dole', *Daily Telegraph*, 2 Dec. 1995. See 'Labour invited to back "workfare" ', *Financial Times*, 2 Dec. 1995 and 'Major Defends "workfare" plan', *Guardian*, 2 Dec. 1995. Such draconian US-style policies had been predicted on many previous occasions: see e.g. ' "Work or lose dole" Bill for autumn', *Observer*, 31 July 1994 and 'Workfare plan to make jobless earn dole money', *Sunday Times*, 22 May 1994—both front-page headline stories. See also 'Behave well—or lose the dole', *Observer*, 4 Dec. 1995, and 'Compulsory workfare plans for dole blackspots', *Daily Telegraph*, 3 Apr. 1995. See also 'Workfare by any other name marks new departure', *Working Brief*, No. 70 (Dec. 1995–Jan. 1996).
The debate about adopting workfare programmes has carried on for several years in the government, with the Treasury long a staunch opponent on the grounds of the costs of such schemes. A pilot scheme with mixed results was implemented in North Norfolk in late 1992, the constituency of the Commons' main advocate of workfare, Tory MP Ralph Howell (who published a pamphlet with the Adam Smith Institute entitled *Why Not Work?* advocating workfare). In early 1993 the then Secretary for Employment Gillian Shephard expressed scepticism about workfare principally on grounds of cost, though in February 1993 the Prime Minister John Major told the Commons that a compulsory work programme remained under ministerial consideration; A. Smith, 'Major defends workfare', *Financial Times*, 5 Feb. 1993. In a speech on 3 Feb. Prime Minister Major was quite fulsome about US workfare programmes and made explicit his interest in their adoption in Britain.
[110] Preceding this measure, in July 1995 Frank Field and Sir Ralph Howell sponsored a bill, 'The Right to Work Bill', which was in effect workfare. House of Commons, Right to Work Bill 158, July 1995. And see House of Commons Sessions 1995-6, Employment Committee Second Report, *The Right to Work/Workfare* (London: HMSO, 13 Feb. 1996).
[111] Of the pilot scheme's 2,481 participants, 20% left the register after 13 weeks and 37% at the stage of entering compulsory work schemes, figures which suggest that the programme as a whole acts as a deterrent to claiming benefits.
[112] 'Workfare by any other name marks new departure', *Working Brief*, No. 70 Dec. 1995/Jan. 1996.
[113] J. Hibbs, 'Jobless will have to work for dole', *Daily Telegraph*, 2 Dec. 1995. The incumbent was Gillian Shephard.

of this statement mirrors the views of Beveridge and Bevin discussed above but accords them greater prominence and reveals that workfare programmes are intended to defray such perverse incentives.

New Labour has pushed these schemes further along the liberal contractarian path. In a speech entitled 'The rights we enjoy reflect the duties we owe', Tony Blair proclaimed: 'in the 1970s and 1980s, the Conservatives regarded the notion of duty as their own. Now, in the 1990s, they seem neither to understand it nor to act upon it. In fact, duty is an essential Labour concept. It is at the heart of creating a strong community or society.'[114] A 'strong society' was not be confused with a 'strong state', however. He elaborated further, in the new contractual language: 'the distinctive contribution of the Left is to ground the notion of duty within society itself . . . There is a covenant between society and each of its citizens within which duty must be set; and it involves duties from society to citizen as well as the other way about.' Thus although the state had a duty to house the homeless, 'equally, those who are housed by the state have a duty to behave responsibly. *That is the contract.*'[115] The same contractual argument was propounded by the Labour MP Chris Smith, when shadow minister for social security: 'we need a new relationship between the welfare state and the individual who turns to it for help: a relationship that treats them as a citizen, not as a supplicant, and with the combination of rights and responsibilities that flow from citizenship.'[116]

In office, the Labour government has adhered to these principles, and consolidated the work project scheme. The massive 'welfare to work' programme targeted on the long-term unemployed,[117] with twelve pilot programmes (called 'pathfinder areas') was set up in April 1998;[118] (the government has also discussed measures for those on disability benefits, young unemployed, and single parents, particularly mothers). Its design is the remit of a task force chaired by Sir Peter Davis, recruited from the Prudential insurance company.[119] The five-year, £5.2 billion budgeted welfare to work programme provides four options for unemployed people,

---

[114] Tony Blair, 'The rights we enjoy reflect the duties we owe', Spectator Lecture, 22 Mar. 1995.

[115] Ibid., emphasis added.

[116] Chris Smith, 'Social Justice in a Modern World', Institute for Public Policy Research Lecture 1996.

[117] For details see Paul Convery, 'Details of New Deal options announced', *Working Brief* (Aug./Sept. 1997), 4–6; id., 'The New Deal gets real' *Working Brief* (Oct. 1997), 7–14; M. Nimmo, 'Welfare to Work and incentives to work', *Working Brief* (Nov. 1997), 8–12, and the discussion in *Working Brief* (Dec. 1997).

[118] These were in Tayside, Swansea and west Wales, Sheffield and Rotherham, Eastbourne, Lambeth, Harlow and Stevenage, Cumbria, Wirral, south Derbyshire, the black country, Newcastle, Gateshead, and south Tyne and Cornwall.

[119] 'Prudential chief leads team to find work for jobless', *Financial Times*, 5 June 1997.

one of which they must select in exchange for taking their benefit. These are: first, a job with the private sector. The plan offers private employers subsidies of £60 a week per worker for six months, to recruit under-25-year-olds who have been out of work for six months or more. A subsidy of £75 is provided to employers who take on workers out of work for more than two years.[120] Second, enter full-time education or part-time education. Young unemployed persons lacking educational qualifications are permitted to study full time while on benefit, provided the course is approved by the Employment Service. Third, the unemployed can take a job in the voluntary sector with one day per week used for formal education or training. The voluntary organizations will receive a fee for participating in the training. Fourth, join the environmental task force in which a young unemployed person's employability is supposed to be enhanced by work on community benefit projects concerned to address energy needs.[121] Some system of accreditation for the work will be provided.

This fourfold 'New Deal' for the unemployed is integrated with the sanctions regime established by the Conservatives' Jobseeker's Allowance.[122] Refusal to take one of the options, without good cause, will result in immediate suspension of the unemployed person's benefit for two weeks, and for a further four weeks if they continue to reject the options.[123] There is no fifth option. Thus the programme includes a disciplinary element,[124] with refusal to undertake some activity—in New Labour language, to reject the contractual obligations attaching to citizenship—resulting in the forfeiture of benefits, or the loss of a social right of citizenship in old-fashioned Marshallian language. One minister describes the regime as 'tough but fair' and balancing 'rights and responsibilities'.[125]

Welfare to work is the cornerstone of New Labour policy, particularly its emphasis upon the work component. In one of his earliest speeches as Prime Minister, delivered on a housing estate in Southwark, south London, Tony Blair proposed a 'new bargain' for the unemployed: 'the basis of this modern civic society is an ethic of mutual responsibility or duty. It is something for something. A society where we play by the rules. You only take

[120] The danger of employers using these subsidized workers in place of routine recruitment is a real one, and the government has indicated it will monitor and sanction abusers. 'Employers warned on welfare-to-work rule', *Financial Times*, 18 July 1997. The use of the funds to hire graduates by private companies has been stopped too.
[121] In addition to their normal benefits, participants will get £400 in total for the period of attendance on the programme.
[122] See Finn, Blackmore, and Nimmo (1998) and Tonge (1998).
[123] 'Welfare to work sets tough terms', *Guardian*, 4 July 1997.
[124] A point made by the Employment Policy Institute report authored by Alan Deacon in July 1997: Deacon (1997).
[125] Andrew Smith, Employment Minister, quoted in 'Tougher conditions for young in "welfare-to-work" scheme', *Financial Times*, 4 July 1997.

out if you put in. That's the bargain'.[126] To another audience, the Prime Minister concluded that the inherited system of welfare was responsible for 'encouraging dependency, lowering self-esteem and denying opportunity and responsibility in almost equal measure'.[127] The Labour leader made welfare reform a major plank of his first party conference address as Prime Minister. He declared that 'the modern welfare state has to encourage work not dependency . . . The new bargain for welfare will mean something for something', a sentiment echoing the earlier quotations.[128] It also echoed the language of Frank Field, speaking as minister for welfare reform at the Department of Social Security: the government wants 'people to take more responsibility for their own welfare' and to dissipate the 'welfare equals state' mentality.[129] This rhetoric of contract found its way into the government's Green Paper on welfare, issued in March 1998, whose authors proclaimed: 'at the heart of the modern welfare state will be a new contract between the citizen and the Government based on responsibilities and rights'.[130] New contractual arrangements would enhance, the Green Paper's authors argued, trust, transparency, responsiveness, responsibility, and empowerment but not, notably, rights. The Green Paper's proposals were also part of Labour's formulation of a 'third way' in public policy, and indeed one architect of this framework, the sociologist Anthony Giddens, defines its prime motto as 'no rights without responsibilities,' continuing: 'unemployment benefits, for instance, should carry the obligation to look for work, and it is up to governments to ensure that welfare systems do not discourage active search.'[131]

The New Deal welfare to work programme is influenced directly by American experience. The US model also guided work-welfare policy as developed by the Conservatives. Mirroring the influence of American welfare experts with British policy-makers, the language of contractual workfare is reproduced from the United States[132] and increasingly the delivery of employment services, by private companies, within the welfare

---

[126] Quoted in 'Blair offers jobless a new "bargain"' *Guardian*, 3 June 1997.

[127] Speech entitled 'The 21st Century Welfare State', to the Social Policy and Economic Performance Conference, Amsterdam, 24 Jan. 1997.

[128] *Financial Times*, 29 Sep. 1997; the text is what the FT expected in the leader's speech.

[129] Quoted in 'Government seeks shift from welfare to self help', *Financial Times*, 25 July 1997.

[130] *New Ambitions for our Country: A New Contract for Welfare* (London: HMSO, 1998, Cm. 3805). And see MacGregor (1998) and Oppenheim (1998).

[131] A. Giddens, 'We're in the family way', *The Times Higher Education Supplement*, 18 Sept. 1998.

[132] See the accounts in King (1995) and Dolowitz (1997), and see Lawrence Mead's testimony included in House of Commons Sessions 1995–6, Employment Committee Second Report, *The Right to Work/Workfare* (London: HMSO, 13 Feb. 1996), Appendix 8.

to work scheme are imitative of American arrangements.[133] Private sector companies emphasize the acquisition of so-called 'soft' skills (rather than the 'hard' ones acquired through lengthy training programmes) and the development of 'job-readiness'. Similar patterns are likely in Britain and indeed New Labour's reforms may well include a much greater role for private sector companies (though a proposal to devolve budgets to local employment service and benefit offices has been dropped[134]). Private companies have also been brought in to hire welfare dependents in the USA, a strategy copied in Britain.

Welfare to work breaks with the dominant intellectual tradition of the Labour Party to welfare, according to some of its critics.[135] However, the Secretary of State for Education and Employment, David Blunkett, rejects this charge, recently arguing that 'welfare-to-work draws directly on Labour's deep traditions. "Work not dole" was the cry 60 years ago, and that's exactly with the New Deal is all about.'[136] The proposed reform of the welfare state has divided the Labour Party, partly exposing the cleavage between old Labour members and New Labour (though in terms of willingness to employ a strongly interventionist state there is little difference). Attempts to retain the legacy of Beveridge continue, however. In a pamphlet from the Department of Social Security, entitled *The Case for Reform*,[137] three principles are imputed to the founder of the post-war welfare state which New Labour wishes to respect. These are: society has a continuing responsibility to people with genuine needs and unable to care for themselves; whenever possible individuals have a responsibility to provide for their own needs; and poverty is best avoided and escaped by employment for those able to work. Work is the mainstay of New Labour's workfare plan, welfare to work.[138]

The New Deal welfare to work programme, together with some of the

---

[133] A presently fadish approach in the USA is to use private contractors to provide the employment service support for welfare recipients compelled to enter the labour market. The Maximus company has received a good deal of publicity in its role as a private sector company apparently making a profit from helping welfare recipients prepare for work, and gain a job. See the account in Nicholas Timmins, 'Welfare-to-work Inc', *Financial Times*, 22 Dec. 1997.

[134] Field wrote in 1997 that 'the UK government is looking at ways of giving our local benefit offices greater autonomy of actions, more scope for innovation, and more incentive to reduce their caseloads by helping people back into work.' Field (1997: 63).

[135] For one strand of opposition within the Labour Party see Brown (1998).

[136] D. Blunkett writing in the *Observer*, 1 Nov. 1998.

[137] Published on 15 Jan. 1998.

[138] Critics of this system charge that without parallel amendments to the benefits and tax systems the incentives to push people willingly into the labour market will fail to materialize. The economist Edmund Phelps argues that only an employment subsidy will reduce unemployment on the scale required by this workfare scheme. Edmund Phelps, 'Quids in if you work', *Financial Times*, 31 Oct. 1997.

benefit cuts proposed by the Labour Party, has incensed some of the party's backbenchers. Driving single parents into the labour market and cutting their benefits (and the proposal to cut disability benefits) has provoked votes against the government and criticisms of the Secretary of State for Social Security, Harriet Harman (until July 1998). One Labour MP told Harman that 'there are significant sections of the population who receive benefits but for whom work is neither a practical nor an appropriate response. Welfare to Work cannot be part of the fundamental solution for them.'[139] This view is plainly unacceptable to New Labour's policy-makers. A more significant critic of the benefit cuts, particularly those proposed in disability benefits, was the Education Secretary, David Blunkett, whose objections were revealed in another leaked memorandum. Blunkett wrote to the Chancellor, Gordon Brown, expressing 'some serious concerns about some proposals for reform of the benefits system for disabled people.'[140] The departure of Frank Field from the government, in July 1998, was attributed in part to hostility at the Treasury to some of his proposals.[141]

For the present, it is the pro-contractualist workfare supporters who have set the terms of the debate and defined policy. From the political right, the Tory MP David Willetts attacks the New Deal scheme for its inevitable fanning of public expenditure, and disputes the anticipated benefits of increased training levels in the workforce.[142] Furthermore, the concentration of New Deal spending in a number of areas with high unemployment constitutes a significant challenge to the programme. Nonetheless, buoyed by early successes,[143] the New Deal welfare to work

[139] See the memorandum from Labour MP Charles Clarke to Harman (10 Dec. 1997), leaked in the *Observer*, 4 Jan. 1998.

[140] Leaked in the *Sunday Telegraph*, 21 Dec. 1997; the date of the letter is not given.

[141] See 'Field puts blame on Brown', *Independent*, 30 July 1998 and 'Chancellor betrayed me says Field', *Guardian*, 30 July 1998. Field himself stated: 'welfare reform is a central issue for this government and I believe I can support the prime minister more effectively from the backbenches,' quoted in *Financial Times*, 28 July 1998. See also *New Ambitions for our Country: A New Contract for Welfare* (London: HMSO, 1998, Cm. 3805). For Field's thinking before the Green Paper see his piece 'The tests that will show we've got welfare right,' *Sunday Times*, 22 Mar. 1998.

[142] D. Willetts, 'New Deal is no way to cut the bills', *Guardian*, 20 Apr. 1998; and see Willetts (1998).

[143] 'Ministers set to claim signs of success for New Deal', *Financial Times*, 25 May 1998, and report in *Financial Times*, 28 May 1998. By the end of July 1998, 92,500 people aged 18 to 24 had started on the New Deal programme, and an additional 1,950 were in the scheme's full-time education or training options, 610 were in work experience in the voluntary sector, and 540 were on the environmental task force; in total 20,000 employers had signed New Deal agreements; 243 young people had suffered benefit sanctions, and 11,000 had moved from welfare to work. *Financial Times*, 31 July 1998. The Secretary of State for Education and Employment, David Blunkett, wrote fulsomely about welfare to work's accomplishments in November 1998: 'thirty thousand 18 to 24 year olds have already found work

scheme is set for expansion: in June 1998 it was extended to the over-25 age group (who have been without a job for two or more years)—a substantial group with over 200,000 eligible, for whom the threat of benefit sanctions also holds;[144] lone parents have been included (and are likely to be required to attend interviews at Jobcentres[145]), and from October 2000 it is proposed to include the disabled and the childless partners of the 18–24-year-olds.[146] At an estimated subsidy of £4,000 a year per position, New Deal is an expensive and ambitious programme.

CONCLUSION

This chapter has used historical and contemporary evidence to demonstrate how major themes of government policy toward the unemployed in Britain have recurred in the last 150 years. They reflect upon the content of the polity's liberal democracy, its relationship to the market system, and the continuing influence of a liberal contractarian framework. Liberal democracy necessitates government intervention in many respects since not all members of the polity succeed equally. The liberal contract defines the form of this intervention: rights are juxtaposed with obligations.

Persistent themes of the workfare measures include: first, workfare-type policies attempt to accommodate and not to modify the workings of the

through the New Deal and nearly 20,000 more are on a New Deal training or voluntary sector option. This is practical intervention with practical results', *Observer*, 1 Nov. 1998.

A key test will be how many remain in work after the employer subsidy ends. And by October cracks were beginning to appear: see 'Drop-out rate of 40% hits New Deal jobs', *Sunday Times*, 25 Oct. 1998. And there have been reports of discontent within the British Chambers of Commerce about the failure to supply young people for job openings: see the leaked letter from Chris Humphries, director of the British Chambers of Commerce to Sir Peter Davids, chairman of the New Deal Task Force quoted in 'Business blasts Labour over New Deal fiasco', *Independent on Sunday*, 1 Nov. 1998. And see 'Minister claims New Deal is cutting long-term jobless rate', *Financial Times*, 27 Nov. 1998, and 'New Deal shows signs of success', *Guardian*, 26 Nov. 1998. These stories, based on a statement by the Minister of Employment, Andrew Smith, indicated that from its launch in April 1998, 167,400 young people had entered the New Deal scheme by 30 September 1998, of whom just over 40,000 had left. Of the participants over 50 per cent were in the education and training option, a quarter in subsidized employment, 10 per cent were working in the voluntary sector, and 9 per cent were on the environmental task force. For a less sanguine view see Foyer Federation, *Foyer and the New Deal: Six Months On* (London: Foyer Federation, Nov. 1998).

[144] 'Over-25s warned on New Deal', *Financial Times*, 26 May 1998. See also P. Convery, 'New Deal for the over 25s', *Working Brief*, June 1998.

[145] 'Lone parents face benefit cuts', *Independent*, 27 Oct. 1998, reporting the view of the Secretary of State for Social Security Alistair Darling. This plan was acted upon in the Welfare Reform and Pensions Bill, February 1999, and justified by Secretary of State Darling in 'We make no apologies for our tough benefits regime,' *The Independent* 10 Feb 1999.

[146] 'Labour to extend compulsion to work', *Financial Times*, 31 Mar. 1998.

market, a claim consistent with the specification of the 'liberal' welfare model presented by Esping-Andersen.[147] The unemployed or welfare dependent are subject to policies designed to push them into the labour market, even if at low wages. Second, workfare policies have a social engineering component: the intention is to modify the behaviour and attitudes of the targeted populations. After 1834, the threat of confinement in the poorhouse was supposed to deter the unemployed from seeking assistance, as was the inter-war test work requirements; New Labour's welfare to work places its deterrence in a set of forced options, refusal of which results in forfeiting benefit. The aim to reform recipients' behaviour gives workfare its moral character. Third, the policies are Janus-faced, weighed down with an unavoidable dualism combining the desire to assist the needy with a fear of undercutting market forces. This latter concern is commonly identified as the disciplinary element of welfare policy. Fourth, vitiating policy toward the unemployed is an ill-defined distinction between the deserving poor and undeserving scrounger, with a reluctance to assist the latter unduly influencing decisions. Although these historical continuities are observable the new definition of the state's role in welfare should not be underestimated. Government policy accepts both the appropriateness of benefit sanctions and the conditionality of income assistance, two elements redefining social citizenship.

The movement to a contractual workfare system of welfare assistance in Britain is of fundamental importance. It accords the government a new role in this liberal democracy and restructures the relationship between some members of the polity and the state. While I have suggested that modern workfare shares some traits and characteristics of earlier programmes—both nineteenth-century relief and aspects of the institutional framework established in the twentieth century—nonetheless the sharpness of the new initiative is striking as is its break with the 1945–75 universalist welfare state. Contractualist workfare retains the concept of social citizenship but emphasizes the obligations and responsibilities of the individual over the rights enjoyed by that person: it treats some people unequally. It embodies also a particular view of human nature, that individuals will choose to avoid work if the benefit regime is of comparable value.

The new role functions in two ways. First, conditionality is explicitly built into the welfare to work contractual framework. Previously, even under the Conservatives, this conditional element remained implicit and indirect, the shift to a mandatory system handled gingerly. Second, sanctions are part of the regime: failure to meet conditions will result in benefit reduc-

---

[147] Esping-Andersen (1990).

tion or eventually in their withdrawal. In principle it relegates unemployed persons, and some other recipients of assistance, to second-class status in the polity, and this is a serious weakness. It is certainly a new phase in the British state's responsibility for the welfare of its citizens and forcefully illustrates how the development of the polity's liberal democracy is a dynamic process.

8

'A Second Chance, Not a Way of Life': Welfare as Workfare in the USA

DESPITE the massive economic growth and vast physical resources available to the United States, its economy has not been immune to economic depressions or mass unemployment. The 1870s and 1930s are two well-known examples of these periods, both provoking policy responses for the destitute unemployed—in the former decade local and poorhouse-oriented strategies, in the latter through federal intervention. More recently, unemployment policy has become entangled with that for welfare recipients, as the perception of the existence of a welfare dependency culture has gained widespread, if not complete, acceptance.[1] Running through these policies—which stretch over a 150-year period—are certain constants about the problem. With the brief exception of parts of the New Deal in the 1930s[2] and the Great Society in the 1960s[3] (during which periods the country's major welfare programmes were enacted: Social Security, Medicaid, Medicare, food stamps, supplementary security income, unemployment insurance, and AFDC), unemployment and welfare dependency have been viewed as problems of individual indolence rather than as structural manifestations of an industrial economy. This is particularly the case for able-bodied unemployed men, and more recently single mothers who find themselves definitionally equated with the former group (a categorization not without racial connotations). This assumption has generated a hostility to policies which subvert or distort the market system: with appropriate diligence and application, it is commonly supposed that any able-bodied person should be able to get work.

The discussion in this chapter concentrates upon the history and politics of workfare in the USA, the practice of requiring a work activity in exchange for relief. I analyse the late nineteenth-century Poor Law deterrent tradition and the post-1960s shift to modern contractualist workfare, which culminated in the 1996 law, the Personal Responsibility and Work Opportunities Reconciliation Act (PRWORA). This extremely important

---

[1] Fraser and Gordon (1997), Etzioni (1995a).
[2] See Berkowitz and McQuaid (1992), chs. 5, 6, Berkowitz (1991), Patterson (1981), chs. 3–5, Noble (1997a). For a highly critical view see the essays in Mandell (1975).
[3] Davies (1996), Lemann (1991). On the Johnson presidency see Bowles (1987).

act dilutes federal responsibility for welfare significantly, returning much greater control to states: to receive the federal contribution the states must implement tough work requirements for adult recipients of welfare assistance.

Policy towards the unemployed shows certain common elements across these historical stages. First, the work ethic is to be instilled amongst the unemployed or welfare dependent. Second, there is an assumption that indolence is a preferred lifestyle amongst the unemployed, particularly amongst a hardened group of malingerers or welfare dependent, though defining this group precisely has invariably proved problematic. And third, workfare, in its various guises, is promoted as a mechanism which will best accommodate the market system. As in Britain, the content of workfare has varied over time. Nineteenth-century fiscal anxieties about outdoor relief prompted a policy response of a principally deterrent character. In the 1970s and 1980s, workfare was more consistent with a contractual approach: obligations accrue to the recipients of welfare, the discharge of which will improve their self-esteem and foster their re-entry to mainstream society. This contractarian perspective differs from Britain in the relatively weak status achieved by social rights. As I explain below, one of the salient features of the 1996 reform is its attempt to combine these deterrent and contractual elements.

That workfare forms part of social amelioration strategies is well conveyed by one journalistic summation of the 1996 law: for the states, 'the goal is always the same: not just to reduce the rolls, but to transplant the values of mainstream society into the welfare underclass. It is a grand social engineering project in behavioural change, and one that could have a big impact on the lifestyle and culture of a large chunk of the population.'[4] As the political scientist Charles Noble observes, the act is 'an unprecedented experiment in institutional re-engineering'.[5] Consequently, the workfare thrust of federal social policy since the 1980s differs from the values and aims inspiring both the New Deal and the Great Society, whose architects held a more generous conception of the attitudes of, and incentives confronting, poor people unable to get into the labour market. The post-1980s view sees a welfare system created for good motives becoming unwittingly a limiting framework: it has institutionalized perverse incentives. Its construction has fostered the need for new social policy, though the aims and assumptions of the new reformers fit with those of the nineteenth century post-Quincy era and categorically not with those of the New Deal or Great Society.

---

[4] Patti Waldmeir, 'Ladder out of Poverty', *Financial Times*, 8 Apr. 1997. This is an admirably crisp and accurate characterization of the new programme.
[5] Noble (1997*b*: 1).

SOCIAL CITIZENSHIP AND US POLITICAL VALUES

The social rights of citizenship celebrated in T. H. Marshall's post-war essay have been less firmly entrenched in the United States than in Europe.[6] Public opinion surveys find an enduring difference in perception toward social programmes based on insurance contributions compared with those relying upon assistance, the former only approximating with social rights. It is the non-insurance programmes which have loomed largest in recent policy debate and reforms. And, in a recent essay, Hugh Heclo argues that even these weakly based social rights have been further eroded in the United States, in part because of significant changes to intellectual discourse in public life: 'social citizenship is an idea that presumes a common narrative in society.' No assumption of commonality can be made, Heclo suggests: 'intellectual trends since the end of World War II have been more or less in the opposite direction . . . It has been in intellectual fashion to argue that "shared vision" is a code word for oppression and that membership in racial, ethnic, and gender groups constitutes the most fundamental truth of each individual's experience.'[7] The centrality of race in American politics is one manifestation of this development.[8]

The weakness of social citizenship also stems from identifiable historical and institutional legacies. Thus, Michael Katz notes that the values of workfare in the USA date from at least the early nineteenth century, when 'legislators tried to balance their obligation to care for the helpless and deserving poor with their fear of promoting dependence'. This aim implied making public assistance the least attractive choice for the indigent: 'the preferred policy became refusing help to people in their homes and forcing them into institutions.'[9] It was the mirror image of the British nineteenth-century reform discussed in Chapter 7.

The dominance of this work ethic assumption in pre-1930s welfare discussions in the United States engendered a suspicion of arguments about social rights of citizenship. James Patterson stresses the historical importance of the assumption that 'hard work led to economic advancement'. Consequently, 'public aid was therefore unnecessary (save in an emergency) . . . The Populists in 1892, though favoring public works in hard times, reaffirmed, "if any will not work, neither will he eat." A few years later, Theodore Roosevelt, himself a hero of the people, celebrated the "strenuous life." "Nothing in this world," he said, "is worth having or worth doing unless it means effort, pain, difficulty." '[10] Katz correctly emphasizes the extent to which excising the undeserving able-bodied waster from the

---

[6] See Esping-Andersen (1990), Schram (1995).   [7] Heclo (1995: 679).
[8] King (1998a), Lieberman (1998).   [9] Katz (1993b: 7).   [10] Patterson (1981: 32).

assistance system has been elevated into a leitmotiv of US welfare policy: 'the core of most welfare reform in America since the early nineteenth century has been a war on the able-bodied poor: an attempt to define, locate, and purge them from the rolls of relief.'[11] This characterization holds for the most recent, 1996, welfare law.

Changing perceptions of gender have further eroded the idea of social citizenship. Being a parent—particularly a single mother—on welfare benefits who justifies it by reference to this parental role has proved to be less and less acceptable to the American electorate; since close to half of the female labour force with children under 3 are working, those who choose not to are stigmatized as the anomalous population.[12] The racial dimension of the debate about welfare further dilutes the universalism required for entrenched social rights: many Americans believe that welfare benefits are absorbed principally by African Americans,[13] although in fact the majority of recipients of welfare, food stamps, and Medicaid are white.[14]

In sum, to be out of work implies, both historically and contemporaneously, laziness and indolence, in a sense which the English Poor Law commissioners of 1832–4 would have keenly appreciated. These cultural attitudes were institutionalized in nineteenth-century policy.

THE CULTURAL AND INSTITUTIONAL CONTEXT

Two sets of factors are examined in this section. First, the influence of the English institutional inheritance for welfare policy; and second, cultural attitudes toward welfare policy as expressed in public opinion surveys, this latter strongly marked by racial cleavages and perceptions of dependency.

The English inheritance

The *deterrent* approach to the unemployed is recognizable as part of the English inheritance structuring the US welfare system. Relief was made a responsibility of local government and reflected English practices: 'the system of local poor relief was transplanted root and branch to the Eastern seaboard from Elizabethan England in the ruthless early seventeenth century, and was later carried by pioneer settlers across the continent.'

---

[11] Katz (1986: 18).

[12] Bane (1988), Bane and Ellwood (1994), and Fraser and Gordon (1997).

[13] Gilens (1996), Hochschild (1995), and Quadagno (1994).

[14] Jencks (1992). In 1994 only 37% of AFDC families were headed by an African American: US House of Representatives, *Background Material and Data on Programs within the Jurisdiction of the Committee on Ways and Means* (Washington DC: GPO, 1994).

Negative views of the poor were also transplanted: 'this English heritage made poverty a disgrace, branded the poor man as unworthy and shiftless, and attached to relief an indelible stigma.'[15] The English Poor Law was established as the framework for relief in almost all the states. In Josephine Brown's assessment, not only did the payments provide a meagre relief but the system cemented hostility to the poor: 'far worse than the laws themselves are the vicious attitudes of scorn and superiority towards poverty and the poor which the system engendered, and which were so deep-seated and persistent.'[16] Anglo-Saxon expectations about individualism and self-reliance, a commitment to local administration and imitation of the English Poor Law, spread throughout the United States with industrialization. These attitudes fed into the view, entrenched between the 1880s and 1920s, that private institutions and means of relief were inherently superior to systems of public relief, if suitably guided by the experts available as part of the Progressive era.[17]

Thus, the United States inherited and adopted its welfare system from Britain,[18] designed to deter the undeserving from seeking state support. Institutions mirroring the poorhouse, the Labour Yard, and outdoor relief abound in nineteenth-century America. However, the main emphasis of American policy was to eliminate outdoor relief (that is, assistance provided to supplicants without any requirement that they become resident in a workhouse institution) through a policy institutionalized in poorhouses. The American version of this policy was not notably more successful than its British counterpart.

The shift to poorhouse relief and the rejection of outdoor relief were motivated by an allegedly unacceptable increase in the number of paupers. For the source of this perception, scholars identify the influential Quincy Report issued in Massachusetts in 1821 which, together with comparable reports in other states, documented a growth of pauperization.[19] It was based on a rudimentary questionnaire sent to towns and parishes in the state about their administration of the poor laws. Pauper payments were rising at an alarming rate, according to the Quincy Report and with pernicious consequences.

The Quincy Report marshalled what became the quotidian distinction

---

[15] Brown (1940: 3).   [16] Ibid. 3–4.   [17] Finegold (1995).

[18] Michael Katz (1986: 13) observes that 'throughout the colonial period and the early nineteenth century, poor relief policy in England profoundly influenced American practice. On both sides of the Atlantic, rising expenses for relief and anxieties about both labor supplied and social order stimulated searching reexaminations of poor laws.'

[19] Massachusetts, General Court, Committee on Pauper Laws, *Report of Committee to Whom Was Referred the Consideration of the Pauper Laws of the Commonwealth*, 1821, chaired by Josiah Quincy, reproduced in Sophonisba P. Breckinridge, *Public Welfare Administration in the United States: Select Documents* (Chicago: University of Chicago Press, 1927), 30–9.

between the worthy and the waster types of needy: 'the poor are of two classes: first, the impotent poor, in which denomination are included all who are wholly incapable of work, through old age, infancy, sickness, or corporeal debility; second, the able poor, in which denomination are included all who are capable of work of some nature or other; but differing in the degree of their capacity and in the kind of work of which they are capable.'[20] A fear of unwittingly aiding the able-bodied poor—'the able poor'—preoccupied policy-makers. Such assistance would diminish the work ethic by 'destroying the economical habits and eradicating the providence of the laboring class of society'.[21] Quincy fully recognized the difficulty of discriminating systematically between the deserving and idle supplicants, and despaired of local overseers resolving this snag: 'in executing the trust they will almost unavoidably be guided by sentiments of pity and compassion, and be very little influenced by the consideration of the effect of the facility or fullness of provision to encourage habits of idleness, dissipation and extravagance among the class which labor.'[22] Poor relief harmed its recipients by eroding the 'just pride of independence'.[23] Quincy recommended poorhouses as suitable institutions for addressing hardship, with work activities attached to such relief: 'the most economical mode is that of almshouses having the character of workhouses or houses of industry, in which work is provided for every degree of ability in the pauper, and thus the able poor made to provide, partially at least, for their own support, and also to the support or, at least, the comfort of the impotent poor.'[24] It urged the formulation of such a policy. While the Quincy Report did not recommend terminating outdoor relief, it plainly favoured an institutionalized solution to need and destitution focused on some work activity in poorhouses. A report prepared for the New York State legislature, a few years after Quincy, reached similar views from its survey of the state's pauper system. The most significant problem was the absence of work for paupers and the consequent failure to foster or support the work ethic: 'there is no adequate provision for the employment of the poor throughout the state.' As a consequence, 'no industrious habit can be effectually inculcated under our present system. This is indeed a very principle defect. Without providing employment for the poor, no system can be productive of much good, either to the public, or the paupers themselves.' Indeed, the poor laws encouraged the 'sturdy beggar' and 'profligate vagrant' to become 'pensioners upon the public funds'.[25] It urged a new policy to address paupers' idleness. This response consisted principally in building new 'houses of employment', in which paupers were to be 'maintained and employed' preferably in agricultural work.[26]

---

[20] Ibid. 32.   [21] Ibid. 33.   [22] Ibid.   [23] Ibid. 34.   [24] Ibid. 37.
[25] New York Legislature, *Report and Other Papers on Subject of Laws for Relief and Settlement of Poor*, reproduced ibid. 47.   [26] Ibid. 50.

Thus, from the 1830s, poorhouses were the preferred solution to poverty and destitution. When the able-bodied poor found themselves confined to a poorhouse, then they had to engage in some sort of labouring work, commonly on farms. Poorhouses were designed as a form of social engineering: the indolence of the poor, of which so many commentators bitterly complained, was to be extinguished.

Whether measured in terms of either preventing pauperism (conditions and health within their confines were generally deplorable) or reforming the character and behaviour of their inmates, poorhouses failed. The behavioural changes which their most ardent supporters believed they would induce amongst the poor did not materialize. Administration and management in poorhouses was commonly inadequate, as Michael Katz describes: 'inmates did a great deal of the routine work around poorhouses. They not only nursed other inmates and gardened but also often cooked, cleaned, sewed, and did other small jobs. Inmates virtually ran the larger poorhouses . . . [O]fficials had little control over life on the wards, and large poorhouses turned into rowdy, noisy places in which discipline was almost impossible.'[27] Admission and departure from poorhouses was monitored indifferently, many inmates leaving before they had worked off the cost of their stay. Categories of unemployed and needy were not distinguished, and members of these different groups found themselves lumped together. Enforcement of the work requirement in the poorhouse was lax, and during winter months when outdoor labouring or farm work was negligible, it was generally non-existent.

The vagaries of poorhouses and their singular failure to deter able-bodied paupers from seeking assistance ensured the survival and diffusion of outdoor relief. As a system of assistance, outdoor relief had a significant place in most states' assistance regimes by the end of the nineteenth century. Josephine Brown reports that outdoor relief was, throughout the nineteenth century, considered costly and assumed to 'encourage idleness and increase pauperism'.[28] Yet, as in Britain, its use proved unavoidable. Outdoor relief was an emergency response, with most of those in need directed into almshouses or workhouses, a trend assisted by the Quincy Report's recommendation. County superintendents of the poor, berated from all sides about both the excessive cost of outdoor relief and its damaging effect on the work diligence of the able-bodied, defended outdoor relief as a necessary evil, without which the scale of poverty and misery would be unmanageable. These officials responded sceptically to the efforts of rationalist reformers—advocates of scientific charity—to end the system and separate the needy from the loafers. In practice, the use of

---

[27] Katz (1986: 28).   [28] Brown (1940: 8). And see Abbott (1940).

outdoor relief gave poorhouses a residual role, housing the sick and infirm or the aged, as the able-bodied poor took advantage of outdoor benefits. This process was aided by reformers determined to exclude the able-bodied from these institutions: 'the poorhouse remained a complex institution. Indeed, to reformers its complexity signaled an indiscriminate and unjustifiable mixing of categories of dependents, and after the early 1870s they directed most of their effort to siphoning off everyone except the elderly.'[29] The difficulty in making poorhouses efficient institutions is conveyed by the warden of a Chicago poorhouse speaking in 1884: 'it has long been my earnest desire to render some department of this institution self sustaining, in part, at least, but after numerous trials of the same I am compelled to acknowledge that owing to the infirm and decrepit condition of the inmates received in this institution I have found it almost impossible to carry my ideas into effect.'[30]

Quincy's report had condemned outdoor relief as expensive and wasteful, and 'most injurious to their [the poor's] morals and destructive to their industrious habits'.[31] In his case study of public assistance in Chicago in the nineteenth century, James Brown finds that newspaper opinion in Chicago echoed this assessment, frequently citing the British (1832–4) Poor Law Commission's condemnation of outdoor relief. Once implemented, the cuts in relief had predictable results: 'a few impostors were actually disposed of, but large numbers of poor persons were reduced to such wretchedness that, one by one, exceptions had to be made and some form of private assistance given.'[32] Outdoor relief was positively assessed in New York in 1857 by a state Senate Select Committee, which recommended its extension from New York City to the remainder of the state.[33] Nonetheless, the dominant trend, in the 1840s and 1850s, was to limit outdoor relief as concern about alleged 'welfare impostors' was encouraged amongst newspaper and elite opinion.

Reducing outdoor relief resulted, at a national level, in increased destitution, according to Josephine Brown: 'each depression left the relief load larger than it had been before and this load each time brought much bitter criticism upon public officals for incompetency and upon the relief system itself on the now familiar ground, confusing cause and effect, that it increased both shiftlessness and poverty. These criticisms culminated in the abolition of outdoor relief in several of the largest cities in the country during the 1880s.'[34] In these latter cities, public relief was established only

---

[29] Katz (1986: 91).　　[30] Cited in Brown (1941: 139).
[31] *The Pauper Laws of the Commonwealth* (Boston, 1821).　　[32] Brown (1941: 40).
[33] *Report of the Select Senate Committee to Visit Charitable and Penal Institutions, 1857*, reproduced in Breckinridge, *Public Welfare Administration in the United States*, 149–69.
[34] Brown (1940: 9).

after the onset of the great depression in 1929. The system was administered, at the county level, by committees whose members were appointed by local politicians (mechanisms even more harmful to the insane than paupers). It remained in place until the 1930s. As in Britain, paupers or recipients of relief mostly forfeited their voting rights, and even as late as 1934, fourteen states' constitutions removed relief recipients' right to vote or to hold public office.[35] Surveying the three decades before the crisis of the 1930s, Josephine Brown finds a common attitude amongst local administrators, throughout the states, toward the destitute. It was an attitude formed in the Poor Law tradition: 'the conviction still prevailed generally that relief should be made so disagreeable to the recipient that he would be persuaded or forced to devise some means of self-support in order to get off the list as swiftly as possible.' This deterrent approach constituted the only early poor relief method of rehabilitation. Furthermore, 'it was conceived as a stern warning to those on the borderline of dependency to practice thrift and keep out of the pauper class and as a stimulus to those who were already "on the town" to struggle doubly hard to better their condition.'[36] To ensure diligence, relief payments were always kept below the lowest wage. This principle equated with that of 'less eligibility' borrowed from the New Poor Law.

The principal target of critics of relief was able-bodied unemployed men, many of whom did indeed use the poorhouse during temporary periods of adversity (particularly in the winter) and many of whom encountered difficulty in finding employment throughout their working lives. Making it more arduous for such unemployed able-bodied men to seek refuge in poorhouses was supposed to push them forcefully and irreversibly into the labour market. But this result did not occur: 'even in the best of times thousands of men were unemployed, and, of course, during the severe depressions that punctuated late nineteenth and early twentieth century America, many men could not locate work of any kind ... Ejecting the ablebodied from almshouses and outdoor relief could not eliminate the problem; it only could displace it.'[37] Temporary lodgings, which developed into the grim flophouse archipalego, eventually became the place in which able-bodied unemployed men sought shelter. Institutions, such as the Chicago Municipal Lodging House or Baltimore's Wayfarer's Lodge, strictly limited the number of consecutive nights that lodgers could stay and extracted payment through some work test (that is, requiring some work from the lodgers).

It was this system, with its minor modifications, which faced unemployed able-bodied men when the Great Depression descended, and which

---

[35] Brown (1940: 10).   [36] Ibid. 17.   [37] Katz (1986: 94).

proved incapable of absorbing the mass unemployment of the 1930s. During economic downturns many cities introduced work relief programmes on a modest scale in which recipients of benefit undertook some work activity, so-called 'made work', such as leaf raking. These initiatives increased after the stock market crash of 1929 and before the New Deal schemes established from 1933. They were in the 'made work' tradition of nineteenth-century local relief, whereby work was required from recipients of assistance but the dispensers of the benefits were little interested in the value of the work undertaken.[38] They underlined the duties accruing to welfare recipients as a condition of help. These were described by one scholar as work projects, 'invented as an excuse for work, obviously made for the purpose of creating means whereby recipients of relief could make some payment for what they received. The projects were usually of questionable value.'[39]

By the early 1930s, when economic crisis reached catastrophic proportions, the world of relief was dominated by private charities and organizations, many organized on a national level. Public departments of social welfare had been established in only a minority of cities and states. Rather, the 'social work world was still dominated by private agency attitudes, philosophy and methods which so influenced public opinion that, when the depression came, community after community logically looked to the private agencies to meet the overwhelmingly increasing demands for relief'.[40] Brown argues that the relentless dissemination of ideas hostile to public relief, particularly those of Malthus and American philanthropists, had 'conditioned public opinion to a far greater extent than was realized even by many of the family welfare leaders themselves'[41] against the publicly funded alleviation of relief. The exhaustion of local volunteers and depletion of community chests in the two years after 1929 set the stage for national action, eventually manifest in the New Deal.

Neither the New Deal nor the Great Society utilized workfare in its deterrent form. The former set of programmes were a quasi-type of workfare in that the public works schemes provided activities for their participation in exchange for benefits. But it lacked a punitive character, thereby temporarily breaking with the nineteenth-century tradition, and never approximated a permanent arrangement (though some of the agencies' administrators aspired to making them permanent). The New Deal schemes were clearly contractual in spirit but the enormity of destitution

---

[38] For discussions of late nineteenth- and early twentieth-century made work, mostly conducted in cities, see Joanna C. Colcord, *Emergency Work Relief as Carried out in Twenty-Six American Communities 1930–31* (New York: Russell Sage Foundation, 1922) and Brown (1940).
[39] Brown (1940: 239–40).   [40] Ibid. 55.   [41] Ibid.

and scale of unemployment made this an academic feature; however, Roosevelt and his advisers strove to avoid simply providing relief without any accompanying work activity. Great Society programmes assumed, by American standards, a remarkably benign view of the victims of unemployment and poverty: prompted powerfully by the civil rights movement these programmes were also embarked upon during a period of prosperity (and in fact, were directed at unacceptable pockets of poverty amongst general affluence) and lacked any punitive or illiberal imposition upon participants.[42] Such generosity in public policy evaporated in the 1970s and it was the expanded non-insurance welfare programmes which attracted greatest controversy. Ending these latter institutions has been the aim of critics of welfare, an ambition realized in the 1996 legislation.

The English inheritance of the poorhouse administrative arrangements not only developed distinctly in the United States but was fundamentally mediated by federal and state welfare programmes. In respect of income-maintenance programmes the most important of these has proved to be Aid to Families with Dependent Children (AFDC, originally ADC), established as a federal-state programme in 1935 (as part of the Social Security Act) and terminated in 1996 by President Clinton in the Personal Responsibility and Work Opportunity Act. Initiated during the New Deal with a concern that widowed mothers would lack the means to support their families, AFDC has since the 1960s become controversial as a consequence of more general social trends. These include the expanded level of female participation in the labour force, taxpayers' frustration with welfare programmes (constantly the subject of criticism amongst political and policy elites), some hostility rooted in racism, and a vocal and salient debate between advocates and opponents of welfare policy.[43] These issues are addressed in the ensuing discussion of the cultural context of welfare policy.

The cultural legacy

Workfare[44] has a long pedigree in the USA, sitting comfortably with the exalted status given to work in this polity. Its economic logic (there should be a punitive cost to the receipt of welfare benefits) coalesces with its political purpose (Americans believe in self-help and achievement through application). The principle that someone capable of working should do so permeates US political culture and accords work a unique position in its moral economy. Disapproval of able-bodied adults who receive benefits

---

[42] Weir (1992) and Davies (1996).
[43] This last is especially well analysed in Teles (1998).
[44] For conceptual definitions see Tsebelis and Stephen (1994).

without working, or who continue to live off benefits over a number of years, is high. This view is captured in Hugh Heclo's 'welfare as self-sufficiency' notion, which he imputes as one of two views held by Americans: it 'is a conception of well-being that is supremely individualistic, for it has to do with the capacity of an individual to get his own way, to enjoy the fruits of his own labor, to be unbeholden, unentangled, able to make it on his own.'[45] From their survey research, Page and Shapiro conclude that 'most Americans don't like the idea of welfare programs that give cash payments to people, some of whom may be truly helpless and may thereby be discouraged from helping themselves'.[46] Steven Teles, reflecting also on opinion poll data, identifies work as 'a central means by which our society provides for itself and to avoid work is to survive on the efforts of others'. This assumption renders work-centred welfare schemes politically attractive: 'work programs, regardless of how they are explained, are popular because they seem to engage all sides of the public's mind: its egalitarian desire to help those in need, its hierarchical desire to enforce a central societal norm, and its individualist desire to foster independence and self-reliance.' In sum, 'work for those on welfare is a popular issue because it is seen, at least at the level of slogan, as the kind of program that connects all sides of the nation's political culture.'[47] And, of course, perceptions of who should and should not work are historically dynamic and sociologically structured. In the 1930s, when relatively few women worked, it was more acceptable to provide a public assistance programme specifically for widowed or single mothers; fifty years later most women work and generosity toward those who do not has weakened massively. Reinforcing this trend is a changing perception of the racial composition of welfare recipients: as we will see below, by the 1980s and 1990s, welfare programmes were commonly seen as consumed in a racially highly uneven way, a perception which did not strengthen public support for such schemes.

Amongst many case workers, responsible on a daily basis for coping with welfare recipients, it is more common to assume that beneficiaries would rather work than not. This opinion is less and less common among national policy-makers and their supporters. For instance, the mayor of Milwaukee, John Norquist, an ardent welfare reformer, declares that 'voters don't want us to take money away from people with work to give it to people who don't.'[48] If welfare is dispensed, it should have some sanctions attached, in this view, as part of the contractual duties arising from membership of a liberal democracy. This reluctance to assist people unconditionally and in an unstructured way is a key theme of critics of welfare programmes, and

---

[45] Heclo (1986: 182).   [46] Page and Shapiro (1992: 126).   [47] Teles (1998: 55).
[48] Quoted in N. Timmins, 'America's great experiment', *Financial Times*, 28 Nov. 1997.

one source of the major reforms enacted in 1988 and 1996. In Charles Murray's judgement, representative of conservative views, welfare pro- grammes are positively harmful: 'social programs in a democratic society tend to produce net harm in dealing with the most difficult problems. They will inherently tend to have enough of an inducement to produce bad behavior and not enough of a solution to stimulate good behavior; and the more difficult the problem, the more likely it is that this relationship will prevail.'[49] Even though President Lyndon Johnson used the notion of a 'hand, not a hand-out' to describe the Great Society welfare programmes, it is the image of able-bodied people receiving benefits in exchange for idleness which fires many welfare critics (and advocates of workfare) his- torically and contemporaneously.

This perception of a hostility to welfare amongst American citizens needs disaggregating in two ways: first, hostility is focused mainly on non- insurance programmes, not non-means-tested insurance ones; and second, the unpopularity of non-insurance programmes is rooted partly in racial cleavages and the historical animosity to dependency, or as Fraser and Gordon remark, 'in current debates, the expression "welfare dependency" evokes the image of "the welfare mother," often figured as a young, unmarried black women (perhaps even a teenager) of uncontrolled sexu- ality'.[50] Both of these conclusions can be illustrated from opinion surveys.

The federal government has, since the 1930s, taken on a range of welfare commitment of both a universalist and means-tested kind. Public opinion toward welfare programmes in the United States reveals support for some of them and hostility toward some components. From a telephone survey of 1,209 interviewees (conducted in 1986) and a study of 58 members of Congress, Cook and Barrett found considerable support for the seven major existing programmes, both insurance and means-tested ones (that is, Medicare, supplementary security income, Social Security, Medicaid, unemployment insurance, AFDC, and food stamps).[51] Few respondents wanted programmes decreased (2.5 per cent for Medicare, 13.0 for unem- ployment insurance, 15.5 for AFDC, and 24.4 per cent for food stamps). Thus despite the public and political debate over AFDC, Cook and Barrett find only one in six respondents want its benefit reduced. Examining atti- tudes in more depth in respect of social security, Medicaid, and AFDC, the authors found, as would be predicted, more support for social security (and for raising its level), and less for the non-insurance programmes, AFDC and Medicaid: 'Social Security seems doubly blessed—it has both sup- porters who are more actively committed and opponents who are less active. AFDC, on the other hand, is doubly cursed with less active sup-

[49] Murray (1984: 218).   [50] Fraser and Gordon (1997: 123).
[51] Cook and Barrett (1992: 62).

porters and more active opponents.'[52] Further evidence from their survey confirmed the political vulnerability of AFDC, though this hostility is less strongly held than might have been inferred from public debate: 'almost two-thirds of the public appear to support AFDC when the question posed has to do with their preferences and does not imply behavioral obligations, but only a third are willing to stand behind their beliefs with actions.'[53]

The picture in respect of welfare recipients is complex. Cook and Barrett find relatively little evidence for the 'undeserving' hypothesis, in contrast to the journalistic stereotype: 'despite common stereotypes, the majority of the respondents disagree that recipients are responsible for their own dependence. Perceptions of blamelessness are greatest for Medicaid (75 per cent) and Social Security (75 per cent), and over half of the respondents disagreed with the statement that AFDC recipients cause their own state of need (61 per cent).' They spell out the contrast with political perceptions: 'even when we examine only those respondents who feel strongly that recipients are not to blame and omit those respondents who only somewhat disagree, the picture is still not as negative toward recipients as might be surmised from media and other portrayals of welfare recipients.' Of this part of the sample, 'a relatively large 41 per cent still completely disagree that AFDC recipients are responsible for their own state of poverty, and nearly 60 per cent feel the same way about Medicaid and Social Security recipients.' Nonetheless, 'respondents are considerably more likely to hold AFDC recipients at fault than other recipients.'[54]

Overall, recipients of social security are viewed as blameless, deserving of their benefits, and prudent in spending them; they are believed to want and to value independence and self-sufficiency, admired values in the American political culture. Sixty-nine per cent of the respondents accepted the neediness of AFDC recipients but 50 per cent believed they wasted their benefits. This division between attitudes toward social security and AFDC is reproduced in questions about the programmes' relative effectiveness: social security is very positively evaluated whereas 'AFDC, and to a lesser degree Medicaid, is seen by some as helping recipients gain their independence but by others as actually making them dependent.' The latter is evidence for the conservative critics of welfare dependency. Furthermore, AFDC is considered more vulnerable to fraud, and it 'is less widely believed to be a benefit to the entire society'.[55] Page and Shapiro report broadly similar views, finding both high support for helping the poor in principle and a suspicion about the laziness of recipients: 'along with general sentiment in favor of helping the needy, there is doubt about some income maintenance programs, especially about "welfare" which for some

[52] Ibid. 67.   [53] Ibid. 70.   [54] Ibid. 99.   [55] Ibid. 121.

people (particularly after the antiwelfare publicity of the 1970s and early 1980s) has conjured up images of laziness and dependency and of black welfare mothers giving birth to illegitimate children.'[56]

The public has no objection to welfare programmes whose contributory source is universal, and is well disposed toward helping the needy. Unquestionably, the principal programme for the poor—the AFDC system, created in 1935—generates some hostility amongst some voters, constituting an issue for political conflict in the 1980s and 1990s (with both Presidents Reagan and Clinton passing reforms) on grounds of its fostering of dependence instead of independence, and its rewarding of idleness.

Steven Teles provides more recent survey evidence about attitudes to AFDC. Correctly emphasizing that 'support for single mothers was originally based upon a moral consensus that, by the early 1960s, was beginning to unravel'[57] as more women worked and the federal budget tightened, Teles finds a growing hostility in the early 1990s: 'between 1991 and 1993, antiwelfare sentiments exploded, from 39.6 per cent in 1991 to 56.6 per cent in 1993, a level near the historic highs of the mid-1970s.'[58] Teles argues that by the 1990s the politics of welfare had changed and that therefore 'the public has come to demand that welfare change as well. The public expects that the values that regulate life for the majority of citizens apply equally to those currently on welfare.'[59] Analytically, Teles underlines the policy and ideational context of the AFDC reform debate. This thesis has two dimensions: first, policy debate about welfare programmes was conducted at one remove from recipients of welfare benefits who lacked participation in the relevant organizations such as think tanks; and second, because of the absence of direct input from the affected individuals (that is, those receiving the benefits), the debate could assume an exaggerated ideological form, as activists with alternative views and agendas exploited welfare policy to advance these more general ends. Thus Teles argues that, 'AFDC politics is dominated by "advocates," those who claim to speak for those without voices, rather than representatives, who have a regular and structured relationship to those they claim to speak for.' As a consequence, 'there is more opportunity for AFDC politics to express the priorities of elites (who are not disciplined by a rank and file that can remove them from their positions), who can use the issue as a way of furthering their position on the larger cultural conflict.'[60] This absence of grass-roots constraints has all sorts of effects, as comprehensive and bold reform initiatives, such as those of Presidents Richard Nixon and Jimmy Carter,[61] were undercut by those activists who judged them too radical or too piecemeal.

---

[56] Page and Shapiro (1992: 124).   [57] Teles (1998: 40).
[58] Ibid. 45.   [59] Ibid. 59.   [60] Ibid. 11.   [61] King (1996).

The increased public hostility toward AFDC in the early 1990s, despite the passage of the relatively tough Family Support Act in 1988, combined with presidential candidate Bill Clinton's promise (in 1992) fundamentally to reform federal welfare programmes by making work more central— giving greater discretion to the states and reducing federal fiscal involvement—appeared to provide an opportunity for legislation. In fact, as several accounts document[62] it was not until the pressure mounted by Republicans in Congress, victorious in the 1994 mid-term elections and embracing their own highly radical reform plan, that President Clinton felt compelled politically to sign the new law in August 1996. The final legislation retained some of his earlier New Democrat proposals but also incorporated significant parts of those advocating a punitive approach to welfare recipients, as discussed below.

Welfare and race

It is crucial to add a racial dimension to this evidence: Americans appear to link poverty peculiarly with African Americans. Martin Gilens spells this implication out forcefully from his survey research:

although there are more whites among welfare recipients than there are blacks, beliefs about blacks in general, and black welfare mothers in particular, are substantially more important in shaping whites' welfare views than are beliefs about the poor or perceptions of white welfare mothers. Thus, the demographics of poverty cannot fully account for whites' tendency to think about welfare in racial terms. Instead, this tendency must be understood as the product of a particular social and cultural context within which blacks' overrepresentation among the poor acquires an exaggerated salience for white Americans.[63]

Given that race is central to US politics,[64] it is unsurprising that the perceived close association between African Americans and welfare has made welfare programmes so salient an issue nationally.

White Americans are sharply divided in many of their opinions, especially about the role of government, from African American members of the electorate, as Kinder and Sanders have recently demonstrated. These two authors comment that, 'the most striking feature of public opinion on race is how emphatically black and white Americans disagree with each other. On the obligation of government to ensure equal opportunity, on federal efforts to help blacks, and on affirmative action, a huge racial divide

---

[62] See, for example, Teles (1998), Weaver (1998).
[63] Gilens (1996: 602).
[64] For recent statements see Carmines and Stimson (1989), Sniderman and Piazza (1993), Dawson (1994), Kinder and Sanders (1996), Massey and Denton (1993), Kelley (1993, 1997) and Goldfield (1997).

opens up.' They also find sharp disagreement by race on 'policy questions that are racial only by implication' and, significantly for the discussion here, 'over how generous the American welfare state should be'.[65] These racial divisions constitute a weak foundation for the establishment of social rights of citizenship.

MODERN WORKFARE: INTEGRATING CONTRACT AND DETERRENCE

Since the 1970s, the pressure to include a contractual workfare component in American welfare assistance, specifically the AFDC programme, has intensified.[66] This pressure, presaged in the Work Incentive Program (1967), resulted, as part of the Omnibus Budget Reconciliation Act of 1981, in a provision permitting states to introduce voluntary workfare schemes if they so chose. This option was taken up in the ensuing years by over half the states, in versions of workfare which ranged from punitive ones, in which the work component was menial and imposed without a serious commitment to training the participants, to training-oriented schemes whose designers ambitiously aimed to remove welfare dependents from the relief system by equipping them for permanent employment. However, the pressure for more substantial change resulted in the passage of the Family Support Act in 1988.[67]

This pressure came from several sources. It was fanned politically by President Reagan (manifest, for instance, in the emphasis upon welfare reform in his 1986 and 1987 State of the Union addresses) and his Republican supporters in Congress, with the full acquiescence of some key Democrats such as Senator Daniel Patrick Moynihan. In addition the governors lobbied for fiscal assistance; and conservative critics of the welfare state, notably Charles Murray whose 1984 book, *Losing Ground*,[68] had a significant influence in advancing a critical analysis of welfare in public discourse, despite challenges of its analysis by academic and other welfare policy experts.[69] The importance of welfare policy advocates and think tanks in the formation of legislation is central to Steven Teles's persuasive analysis of the development of AFDC since the 1960s. Teles

---

[65] Kinder and Sanders (1996: 33).

[66] King (1995), Quadagno (1994), and Mink (1998).

[67] For a detailed account see J. M. Edelman, 'The Passage of the Family Support Act of 1988 and the Politics of Welfare Reform in the United States', D.Phil thesis, University of Oxford, 1995. See also Mead (1992), Berkowitz (1991), and Nathan (1993).

[68] Murray (1984).

[69] See the essays in Jencks and Peterson (1991), Jencks (1992). For a vivid and often harrowing account of the reality of life on welfare see Dash (1996).

remarks that 'the public looks at issues of personal responsibility, generosity, work, and family as matters to be reconciled, but elites see them as either–or choices, to be decided one way or another.'[70] These elites have been relatively insulated from direct electoral or political pressures and thus able to sustain a significant debate about how best to make welfare policy compatible with broader ideological aims.

The Family Support Act (FSA) included a Job Opportunities and Basic Skills (JOBS) programme, mandating in federal policy work requirements for welfare recipients. The FSA required, from October 1990, each state to design and implement a JOBS programme which included five services: (i) educational activities to provide high school graduation literacy equivalent or English as a second language; (ii) job skills training; (iii) job readiness programmes; (iv) job development and placement services; and (v) child-care and transportation support services. Participants received Medicaid (health insurance) during their first year in work, an advantage over the many low-income workers with no health insurance coverage. For the work requirement component, states had to offer two of the following four options: (i) job search assistance; (ii) on the job training; (iii) work supplementation—under which scheme a recipient's benefits are used by the welfare department to subsidize their employment rather than provided directly to the recipients; or (iv) the Community Work Experience Program (CWEP), the scheme first earning the appellation 'workfare', and generally consisting of menial community work (such as tree planting or leaf raking) undertaken by the welfare recipient.

The JOBS requirement was enforced by the states who, in order to retain their federal funding, had annually to increase the number of participants discharging a work or training activity. The justification for the JOBS programme was presented in the language of contractual obligations. It modified the Marshallian social rights of citizenship framework by the specification of matching social obligations (a programmatic theme developed in Lawrence Mead's work[71]). The reform was influenced by arguments advanced by the state governors, whose New Democratic majority wanted a radical change to the welfare system (in some part because of the growing fiscal burden posed by welfare expenditures) and one of whose leading lights was Governor Bill Clinton of Arkansas. In its blueprint for welfare reform, the National Governors' Association underlined creating job opportunities as central to reducing the number of welfare recipients: 'public assistance programs must provide incentives and opportunities for individuals to get the training they need and to seek jobs. It is our aim to create a system where it is always better to work than be

---

[70] Teles (1998: 59).   [71] Mead (1985).

on public assistance.'[72] Speaking in Congress in 1987 to hearings on welfare reform, Governor Clinton explained what the governors envisaged as the core aim of new legislation:'we believe that every welfare recipient should sign a contract with the State, making a personal commitment in return for benefits to pursue an individually-developed path to independence. That includes education, training, and eventually work.'[73]

The language of contract is significant here. By 1988, it had become accepted amongst both conservative critics of the welfare state, concerned to reduce its scope, and liberal supporters, worried about its failure to help recipients break away from dependence, that work was the key component for reform. For both liberal and conservative reformers, welfare policy needed to become work centred whether this was through a punitive or supportive arrangement. The welfare policy expert, David Ellwood, later a member of President Clinton's administration, concluded that 'the notion of mutual responsibility is not controversial any more. It seems that in both the liberal and conservative policy-making communities, there is widespread acceptance of the notion that it is legitimate to ask people to fulfill some obligations and that, in exchange, the government must provide some training, jobs, or other programs.'[74] Ellwood's view may have downplayed the extent to which some left-wing critics viewed welfare as an instrument of control applied unequally across gender and race.[75] This perceived consensus certainly underestimated the subsequent Republican resurgence which prioritized deterrence over contractual obligations (a difference observable in the differences amongst think tanks and advocates of reform): indeed work was an element of reform proposals promulgated by the Nixon and Carter administrations.[76] What changed in the 1980s and 1990s was the new stress upon deterrence.

The pressure for further reform did not abate with passage of the Family Support Act in 1988. Many politicians, particularly Republicans and so-called New Democrats, criticized the new JOBS system as too generous and disconnected from the labour market. Critics maintained that the 1988 reform was too timid, its exemptions too generous, the provisions for childcare and Medicaid excessive, and that only a small number of welfare dependents were likely to be pushed into full-time employment. Contractual workfare supporters recognized the articulation of their aims in the Family Support Act's JOBS component, but regarded the sanctions

---

[72] National Governors' Association, *Job-Oriented Welfare Reform* (Washington, DC: NGA, Feb. 1987), 2.
[73] Hearings before the Committee on Finance, US Senate, *Welfare Reform*, 100th Congress, 1st Session, 9 Apr. 1987, Part 1, p. 17.
[74] Ellwood (1988: 226).
[75] Block and Noakes (1988), Block et al. (1987).
[76] For details of these abortive proposals, see King (1996).

as insufficiently robust. And the contract did not stretch widely enough, in the view of many critics, since mothers with small children were exempted. Overall, to the chagrin of conservative welfare critics, relatively few people were likely to be forced to work under the Family Support Act.[77]

These reservations and criticisms received decisive political support with the election of the Newt Gingrich-led Republican majority in the House of Representatives in 1994. Part of the Gingrich 'Contract with America' programme was a rigorous reform of welfare, which proposed to integrate a robust deterrent element into the contractual workfare framework.[78] It was this priority which was realized in the welfare reform signed into law in 1996: it made AFDC a block grant programme to the states, thereby removing its entitlement status; stringent work requirements were attached; and eligibility for welfare not only tightened but subjected to time limits. We turn now to the details of this measure designed 'to end welfare as we know it'.[79]

Clinton's reform

The most significant reform to welfare and unemployment measures since 1935 was enacted in 1996. In August of that year, Congress passed, and President Clinton signed, the tendentiously entitled Personal Responsibility and Work Opportunities Reconciliation Act.[80] The Act established a new cash welfare block grant, given by the federal government to the states for their allocation, called Temporary Assistance for Needy Families (TANF). This new block grant consolidates and replaces four previous grants: Aid to Families with Dependent Children (originally established as Aid to Dependent Children in 1935), AFDC Administration, the Job Opportunities and Basic Skills Training (JOBS) programme, and the Emergency Assistance Program. TANF allocates $16.4 billion annually until 2002. Each state receives a proportion of this annual sum calculated by the amount it had received from the four terminated programmes. To have its annual block grant renewed under TANF, a state must have spent a sum equal to or higher than 75 per cent of the allocation it used to spend

[77] On the implementation of FSA see US Department of Health and Human Services, Memo on 'JOBS Participation Rate Status Update', June 1992 (Washington DC: USDHHS).

[78] See David S. Broder, 'A Remarkable Right Turn from the 104th Congress', *Washington Post*, 22 Sept. 1995, and 'Speaker wants his platform to rival the Presidency', *Congressional Quarterly Weekly Report*, 4 Feb. 1995, pp. 331–5.

[79] Weaver (1998).

[80] 'Clinton signs bill cutting welfare: states in new role', *New York Times*, 23 Aug. 1996; 'Welfare's New World' *Washington Post*, 23 Aug. 1996; and J. L. Katz, 'After 60 years, most control is passing to states', *Congressional Quarterly Weekly Report*, 3 Aug. 1998, pp. 2190–6. For an early analysis see Noble (1997*b*).

in fiscal year 1994 on the TANF eligible population. It must also satisfy federally specified work participation rates or increase its own state's fiscal contribution to the programme, potentially to 80 per cent of the aggregate sum of the four displaced programmes. TANF funding is to be fixed at an annual rate every six years.

In signing the bill into law, President Clinton supplied plenty of rhetoric about its importance and the new opportunities the legislation heralded for the poor: 'today we are taking a historic chance to make welfare what it was meant to be: a second chance, not a way of life.' This statement meant that the welfare system created dependence. To make this perspective more explicit, Clinton hastened to differentiate the modern welfare client from those he identified as the intended beneficiaries of the Social Security Act in 1935, in language familiar from the Reagan presidency: 'the typical family on welfare today is very different from the one that welfare was designed to deal with 60 years again.' The modern American beneficiaries, 'trapped on welfare for a very long time, exiling them from the entire community of work that gives structure to our lives'. Clinton ended his speech in grandiloquent style: 'today we are ending welfare as we know it. But I hope this day will be remembered not for what it ended, but for what it began: a new day that offers hope, honors responsibility, rewards work and changes the terms of the debate so that no one in America ever feels again the need to criticize people who are poor or on welfare.'[81]

TANF builds on and expands the workfare regime established under the 1988 JOBS programme. After two years on TANF, adults are required to work (a federal requirement permits states to shorten this period). 'Work' is defined by the states within some federal guidelines. Failure to meet the work criterion results in exclusion from the benefits programme. If, after two months on TANF, they fail to find a job, the federal mandate requires that participants undertake some form of 'community service'. Single parents with children under the age of 6 are exempted from this last element. There is a lifetime limit of five years for any adult to receive TANF benefits (a period which states may shorten if they choose). Welfare loses its status as an entitlement for citizens, weakening the notion of social citizenship, and becomes more of a deterrent than contractual workfare system. Eligibility to receive TANF benefits ends after five years regardless of whether the potential recipient still exhibits the criteria which triggered an initial entitlement to assistance. An entitlement to food stamps and Medicaid after the five-year period may be permitted by the states. The position of children in such families is uncertain: they are entitled to

---

[81] 'Clinton signs bill cutting welfare'.

TANF through their parents whose benefit will expire after five years. Possibly, such children will be taken from their parents and placed in foster care programmes. To receive TANF benefits, unmarried teenage mothers are required, under the 1996 law, to live at home with their own parents or in an agreed adult-supervised home and must attend high school. The law empowers states to penalize mothers who have additional children while on TANF benefits, the so-called 'family cap' (a measure already in place in some states before 1996). The penalty is giving no extra benefits to the family despite the additional child.

Although the new law massively increases the role of states in administering welfare benefits, federal regulations remain.[82] The states must satisfy specified work participation rates in their TANF population to retain the block grant. The work rate participation requirement increased by 5 per cent a year to achieve a 50 per cent participation level for TANF beneficiaries by 2002. For two-parent TANF familes, 75 per cent must have one adult in a workfare scheme by 1997, a figure required to reach 90 per cent by 1999. Failure to meet these targets results in a reduction in TANF block grant to the states. Workfare is broadly defined. It includes job-readiness courses, on-the-job training, subsidized public sector employment, unsubsidized employment, and subsidized private sector employment; this last position must not be one arising from the layoff of another worker holding a substantially equivalent job, however. It is possible for waivers and exemptions to be granted within the new law. The Department of Health and Human Services, which administers the federal welfare programme, granted a ten-year waiver to the District of Columbia. It is exempted from meeting some of the requirements of the new law: the District can continue to help recipients after the five-year period has passed, much to the chagrin of Republican architects of the act.[83]

The Personal Responsibility and Work Opportunity Reconciliation Act introduces tough criteria into the US welfare system (and these have been applied[84]). It defines the problem as welfare dependence, mostly sidestepping or disregarding poverty as a reason for receiving benefits; and welfare dependence is identified as a problem (indeed, a moral failing), of the individuals affected, though it is seen as a condition created in part by the values of the welfare system. The arguments of neo-conservative critics of the extant welfare system—that since the 1960s a welfare regime has

[82] Marilyn Werber Serafini, 'Workfare: Wimping Out', *National Journal*, 18 Oct. 1997, pp. 2072–5.

[83] See P. Kilborn, 'Agency is accused of eroding welfare cuts', *New York Times*, 22 Aug. 1996.

[84] See 'Behind the Cheers for Welfare Reform, some Rough Figures', *Washington Post*, 20 Mar. 1998, which reports that several states have cut their caseloads by using sanctions. See also 'US welfare cuts fail to push people into jobs', *The Times*, 25 Mar. 1998.

evolved which fosters dependence, encourages intergenerational or life-time dependence on benefits, and generates its own supporting culture—have been accepted and made the central point of attack in this new programme. The political scientist Steven Teles lays particular stress upon the intellectual and political impact of Charles Murray's arguments for abolition of a federal welfare role, arguments supported by Republicans in Congress.[85] In a development of his *Losing Ground* argument, Murray wrote, in the *Wall Street Journal*, that ending 'all economic support for single mothers' by abolishing AFDC would send a sharp and pellucid message to this part of the population: 'from society's perspective, to have a baby that you cannot care for is profoundly irresponsible, and the government will no longer subsidize it.'[86] This view echoes President Reagan's approach to welfare, when he argued that: 'the welfare tragedy has gone on too long. It is time to reshape our welfare system so that it can be judged by how many Americans it makes independent of welfare . . . In 1964 the famous war on poverty was declared and a funny thing happened. Poverty, as measured by dependency, stopped shrinking and then actually began to grow worse. I guess you could say poverty won the war.'[87] By introducing a workfare system, the work element of the programme perpetuates this focus upon the failings of individual welfare recipients, downplaying structural problems in the labour market. This latter context has been favourable recently but the 1996 law devotes little attention to job creation or enhanced employment opportunities.

In sum, this is a dramatic rewriting of the welfare system, as one former federal official rightly explains: 'the change in the structure is total.' The old system had 'a national definition of eligibility [and] any needy family with children could get help'. Although 'there were rules about participation in work and training' as long as recipients 'played by the rules [they] could continue to get assistance'. Furthermore, 'if people were thrown off the rolls without justification, they could get a hearing to set things right, and could go to court if necessary.' These features no longer hold: 'the system will no longer work that way.'[88]

TANF in operation

Helpfully, the welfare population in most states had declined in the years before the enactment of TANF. The combined effects of the workfare

---

[85] Teles (1998: 152).

[86] C. Murray, 'The Coming White Underclass', *Wall Street Journal*, 29 Oct. 1993, cited in Teles (1998: 151).

[87] From President Reagan's weekly radio talk, quoted in *New York Times*, 16 Feb. 1986.

[88] Edelman (1997: 49).

element (the JOBS programmes) of the 1988 Family Support Act, which set work participation requirements for states to receive federal funding, and a strong, partly labour market driven, economy, resulted in a 20 per cent reduction in state welfare rolls between 1988 and 1994.[89] Nonetheless, hundreds of thousands of welfare dependents are affected by TANF and sanctions have ensured that recipients are losing their benefits. For instance, according to one acount, 'federal statistics show that in one three-month period [in 1997], 38 per cent of the recipients who left welfare did so because of state sanctions, ordered for infractions from missing appointments with caseworkers refusing to search for work'[90]; this trend was evident several months later. Even those getting jobs commonly find themselves in unattractive positions.[91]

Welfare recipients lose their food stamps if, after three months, they are not working at least twenty hours a week or participating in a workfare programme. The initial impact of this stringent law will be, rather as in the case of Britain's Work Project, to drive off those most able to get some sort of job, an obvious aim of the legislation. In particular, the prospect of a place on a workfare programme is a deterrent, in the sense that those who look likely to be forced into a workfare scheme to retain food stamps seem to disappear.[92] New York City has opted to place homeless people in workfare programmes to retain their food stamps entitlement, a decision contested in the State Supreme Court.[93] There have been success stories, much publicized, of former welfare recipients finding jobs. One story concerned Virginian resident, Laura Askew, who got a place in the White House mail room; she is one of 10,000 federal positions opened by President Clinton to help welfare dependents move into work, of which six are in entry-level positions in the White House.[94] Askew, aged 29, was typical of one welfare recipient type, in that she had graduated from high school and worked for eight years in a computer chip plant before being made redundant. Comparable schemes are found in most states.[95] Other welfare recipients lack high school education or work experience, however.

In Detroit's depressed inner city, the Tireman district, welfare workers are attempting to alter the cultural aspirations of their clients (or 'customers'), to convince them that succeeding through work is a realistic option for them. One case worker, herself a former welfare dependent,

[89] 'Ladder out of Poverty', *Financial Times*, 8 Apr. 1997.

[90] B. Vobejda and J. Havemann, 'Sanctions: A Force behind Falling Welfare Rolls', *Washington Post*, 23 Mar. 1998.

[91] R. L. Stanfield, 'Cautious Optimism', *National Journal*, 2 May 1998, pp. 990–3.

[92] Rachel Swarns, 'Survival against the odds', *New York Times*, 7 July 1997.

[93] 'Workfare screening of homeless starts, then stops', *New York Times*, 21 Aug. 1996.

[94] 'From welfare to the White House', *Los Angeles Times*, 4 Aug. 1997.

[95] 'Welfare mothers prep for jobs, and wait', *New York Times*, 31 Aug. 1997.

underlines the scale of the cultural challenge for beneficiaries in the 19–25 age group: 'their grandmother was on assistance, their mother was on assistance, and that's where they think they are supposed to be.'[96] Despite this characterization, welfare case workers believe, according to many reports, that most people would rather be in employment than on benefits. A major problem with achieving this aim is finding jobs which offer genuine prospects of advancement into better paying ones with full benefits. Most welfare dependents go into unskilled, low-wage, and no-benefit positions, often with few obvious advancement prospects.

That large numbers of welfare recipients are leaving, or being expelled from, the rolls is clear.[97] The number of AFDC welfare claimants has fallen by over 25 per cent since 1993, with the fall approaching 50 per cent in some states.[98] In its harshest version, as for example in Wisconsin, the new system permits any benefit from a dependent without participating in some kind of job-search programme. One account describes the changes thus:

what makes Wisconsin different is its treatment of those deemed most capable of work, those considered job ready. These are often welfare mothers who are neither fully self-sufficient nor fully dependent on public assistance. They cycle on and off the system or receive some benefits to supplement their part-time, low-wage jobs. Other states will continue to help these women while they look for jobs or work part time. In Wisconsin, those deemed job ready, even if they have worked sporadically at the minimum wage, are soon to lose their welfare checks, regardless of whether they have a job now or money to pay the bills.[99]

In Wisconsin this requirement may be extended to single mothers with young children.[100]

The Wisconsin system has attracted national interest.[101] It is tougher than other states and more innovative. The former characteristic is manifest in the pressure to get people off the welfare rolls quickly and the attenuation of cash assistance from September 1997. The latter is illustrated by the comparatively lavish child and health care system the state has established for low-income workers; and the contracting of private placement agencies to assist in finding work for those deemed job ready. This

[96] Quoted in Patti Waldmeir, 'Ladder out of Poverty', *Financial Times*, 8 Apr. 1997.

[97] On Milwaukee, a regularly cited instance, see 'US City pioneers a shift off welfare to workfare', *International Herald Tribune*, 8 May 1997.

[98] N. Timmins, 'America's Great Experiment', *Financial Times*, 28 Nov. 1997.

[99] 'Strict rules, hard choices in Wisconsin: welfare changes mean "job ready" recipients will lose benefits', *Washington Post*, 26 Aug. 1997. For a thorough discussion of the Wisconsin programme and the historical context see Mead (1998).

[100] 'Congress set for new battle over welfare', *The Times*, 3 Sept. 1997.

[101] For one good account see Jason DeParle, 'Getting Opal Caples to work', *New York Times Magazine*, 24 Aug. 1997. For a critical evaluation see 'Welfare in the USA: Some British Misunderstandings' *Working Brief* (July 1998).

use of private contactors is now part of a national trend. Increased child-care expenditure satisfies one of the persistent complaints brought by critics of the welfare reform. Bringing in private employment agencies is further indictment of the public employment service's historical inability to assist low-skill workers to find positions. Before President Clinton's 1996 law, Wisconsin had already taken major steps in reforming its welfare system, Republican Governor Thompson aligning himself with New Democrats in the state legislature. As yet, the bold experiment is producing more stories of good fortune and personal transformation than of hardship. A recession or loss of jobs may test this workfare approach, however, and the safety-net protection it provides. One senior state official in Wisconsin claims that this package of policies has succeeded in breaking the 'cycle of dependency' of welfare recipients and advocates the emulation of its 'work first' strategy.[102] The tough strategy has undoubtedly reduced the welfare case load significantly in Wisconsin (and also in California, which has also structured its workfare programme around 'work first' aims) and in a favourable economic era the capacity of the Wisconsin programme to get people into jobs has been impressive.

President Clinton's endorsement of the 1996 welfare reform upset many of his supporters, particularly those committed to a less draconian social policy regime. The decisive shift to workfare (a priority for Republicans) and the imposition of lifetime limits on the receipt of benefits stung such campaigners. (Promises by President Clinton to dilute the system through flexible regulations are unlikely to materialize.) Clinton's tentative efforts to make participants on workfare schemes eligible to the benefits and protections available to conventional waged workers received little congressional support, though the US Department of Labor has interpreted the position of people on workfare as equivalent to regular employees.[103] This approach is bitterly contested by governors who claim it makes workfare unworkable and expensive, and undercuts its very purpose of shifting people into regular work. Both the US Conference of Mayors and the National Coalition for the Homeless have charged that the 1996 law has increased the number of families living in shelters for the homeless, and that others are going homeless.[104] Increasingly, the need to spend more on child care, transportation, and other support services is apparent.

One searing critique of the 1996 law, and of President Clinton's decision to enact it, came from Peter Edelman, an Assistant Secretary at the

---

[102] Quoted in N. Theodore, 'Welfare Reform in the American Heartland', *Working Brief* (Dec. 1997–Jan. 1998), 28.

[103] Marilyn Werber Serafini, 'Workfare: Wimping Out', *National Journal*, 18 Oct. 1997, pp. 2072–5.

[104] 'Poor find welfare pill hard to swallow', *Financial Times*, 17 Dec. 1997.

Department of Health and Human Service (a position from which he resigned in protest at the new law).[105] Edelman argued that the new law will do nothing to address poverty and welfare hardship but will increase misery and destitution. It will cause especial distress, Edelman opines, for the children dependant, through their families, on welfare. In common with other liberal critics, Edelman argues that the test of the system will come when employment contracts: either when the five-year limit is being reached by a significant number of welfare recipients or when a recession inflates unemployment and those with the least marketable skills find themselves in least demand. Edelman stresses the shortage of jobs already: 'the basic issue is jobs. There simply are not enough jobs now. Four million adults are receiving Aid to Families with Dependent Children. Half of them are long-term recipients. In city after city around America the number of people who will have to find jobs will quickly dwarf the number of new jobs created in recent years.'[106] Edelman argues that it is in securing good jobs with proper benefits, which implies training the unemployed, where the real solution to welfare dependency lies. And even though the numbers on welfare dropped by 20 per cent in the year after the Act was enacted, the proportions acquiring secure positions with prospects remains the subject of dispute amongst analysts.[107] To date, however, these sorts of concerns have failed to materialize: there is no direct evidence of mass impoverishment (though many administrators express anxiety about the fate of some former welfare recipients and their families), and the record of some state programmes of getting former welfare recipients into work has been promising. There is no doubt that such trends will be, at the least, challenged during a slowdown in economic growth and job expansion. When this latter occurs, as Teles notes, the programme's structure may prove problematic: 'the block grant structure is biased to work better in good economic times than in bad, giving states more money per recipient when caseloads are dropping and less money per recipient when caseloads are rising.' This characteristic precisely reverses the counter-cyclical logic of Keynesian pump priming: 'the new welfare law is procyclical. That is, it emphasizes, rather than counteracts, the swings of the economic cycle.'[108] The economics Nobel laureate, Robert Solow, also doubts the capacity of state workfare schemes effectively to address the needs of those targeted, commenting from a statistical study of California's programme that 'the burden of proof is on anyone who thinks that welfare recipients forced into the labor market will be very successful in the search for jobs'.[109]

---

[105] Edelman (1997).   [106] Ibid. 52.

[107] See the views of experts reported in R. L. Stanfield, 'Cautious Optimism', *National Journal*, 2 May 1998, pp. 990–3.

[108] Teles (1998: 183).   [109] Solow (1998*a*: 36).

Edelman's lament is that of the old philosophy, the allegedly tarnished New Deal and Great Society approach,[110] dismissed by critics of the system in place after the 1960s, whose modern critique maintains that welfare dependency reflects the welfare system, not need. It is this latter view which has become the orthodoxy amongst the welfare policy expertise consulted by policy-makers in the White House and Congress. And while Teles is correct to characterize this as a debate about ideas which has been conducted through think tanks and advocacy groups—and as such express basic ideological divisions in the United States polity—it is important to appreciate that policy for those receiving benefits has followed a twenty-year trend of increasing severity whether this is presented as an escape from dependency, an induction into liberal citizenship, or a fresh start. There may be conflict between welfare policy experts but only the punitive side of this debate—influential equally with Republican and Democrat presidencies—has shaped legislation since the 1980s.

CONCLUSION

Although workfare has strong historical and cultural roots in the United States and its advocates consistently underline the failings of recipients of welfare, its form has varied over time. Both the nineteenth-century 'made-work' system and the reform enacted in 1996 are examples of deterrent workfare: that is, policy is designed to deter citizens from seeking assistance (whether outdoor relief in the nineteenth century or TANF benefits in the 1990s), and to set limits on the receipt of benefit. This policy of limitation is pronounced in the 1996 reform: each individual now faces a lifetime limit of five years' receipt of welfare benefits. It is this characteristic which differentiates deterrent workfare from contractual workfare of the sort initiated in the 1960s, which culminated in the JOBS programme of the Family Support Act enacted in 1988. The various measures implemented over these two decades, and given federal force in the mandatory work participation programme of the 1988 legislation, underlined the contractual status of receiving welfare benefits: in exchange for those benefits recipients had, as part of the contractual responsibilities and rights arising from citizenship, an obligation to do something in exchange. What is particularly novel about the 1996 welfare reform, with its lifetime limit, is the blunt abrogation of this contract: after five years, you are on your own, the contractual obligation of government exhausted. While on welfare the contractual obligation to undertake work or training is pivotal. Furthermore,

---

[110] For one elegant formulation see Beer (1978).

in common with other illiberal policies this new stringency has received support from both the political right, the Republicans, and the left, Clinton's New Democrats.

This modern workfare programme is not driven solely by pragmatic needs or electoral pressures. Rather, two other factors are crucially important. First, conservative welfare policy experts have successfully advanced the view amongst federal policy-makers that existing institutional and policy arrangements are not only inadequate but consequentially harmful. Existing welfare programmes have permitted the development of a culture of welfare dependency, critics have charged, and to eradicate these flaws has required the revival of effective deterrents amongst potential welfare claimants. The thesis of institutional durability, popular with scholars of comparative politics, looks rather inadequate in this context: the 1996 reform marks a significant break with existing arrangements. Second, reformers and critics of welfare alike have been exercised by a moral concern: being on welfare and not working is considered an unacceptable status, from which those affected should be shifted. This priority is not simply economic, but reflects moralistic motives too, of the sort we can read about in the Poor Law Commission of 1834 and are intrinsic to liberal democratic values. It is testimony to the remarkable staying power of such arrangements and values in market democracies that they have stimulated new legislation in both Britain and the United States in the 1990s.

PART V

Conclusions

9

The Future of Social Citizenship

RECALLING his time in a reconditioning camp in Glenbranter, 80-year-old Willie Eccles told a national newspaper that he was treated inhumanely and degradingly, reflecting that 'when I look back I realise that the way we were treated was not much different from the way the Nazis treated people'.[1] Another ex-trainee, Charles Ward, said the centres 'were like chain gangs without the chains. It was slave labour, They used to stand over us and bawl and shout at us to work harder ... *None of us wanted to go there but we were forced to*.'[2] Carrie Buck, the subject of the US Supreme Court's *Buck* v. *Bell* judgement in which Justice Holmes issued his celebrated warning that 'three generations of imbeciles' was enough, was unable to have children as a consequence of her sterilization. Stephen Jay Gould wrote about Buck when she was aged 72 and lived near Charlottesville: 'neither she nor her sister Doris would be considered mentally deficient by today's standards. Doris Buck was sterilized under the same law in 1928. She later married ... a plumber. But Doris Buck was never informed [about her sterilization]: 'I broke down and cried. My husband and me wanted children desperately. We were crazy about them. *I never knew what they'd done to me*.'[3] Throughout Britain, under the New Deal for Lone Parents scheme, single mothers are called to Benefit Agency offices whose officers attempt to help them get jobs and off benefits. For some it is a welcome expression of concern by the state's caring officials; for others it is a bullying and demeaning intervention.[4] These US or British citizens were affected directly and significantly by the social policies examined in this study. To use the aphorism 'the magic spear that heals as well as wounds' (taken from Wagner's *Parsifal*[5]), liberal democratic states both

---

[1] Quoted in Mark Austin, 'Revealed: "Slave Camps" of Labour's First New Deal', *Sunday Times*, 9 Aug. 1998.

[2] Quoted ibid., emphasis added. His compulsion to attend is not explained in the article.

[3] Gould (1981: 336), emphasis added.

[4] It is a role which the Department of Social Security intends to expand, with an increasingly mandatory component. See 'Lone parents face benefit cuts', *Independent*, 27 Oct. 1998 and R. Taylor, 'Minister extends New Deal for lone parents', *Financial Times*, 27 Oct. 1998.

[5] In *Parsifal*, the spear that pierced Christ's side was preserved in the Grail Castle but stolen by the magician Klingsor, who wounds Amfortas with it and carries it off to his own castle. Amfortas lives in constant pain, controlled only by the daily sight of the Grail. Parsifal

provide resources with which to ameliorate the social and economic circumstances of their citizens and the means for restricting their freedoms through illiberal measures. In fact, the way in which these two tendencies are reconciled in public policy gives meaning, in part, to liberal democracy.

Policies of the sort examined in this book assume importance because of their influence on the definition of citizenship and its development in liberal democratic polities: they contribute to how the boundaries of the public and private are distinguished, and determine how the balance of rights and obligations changes historically. It should already be plain why such policies matter: they create differential experiences of citizenship, foster distinctions between different groups within the same political system, and bolster or erode public spiritedness amongst some citizens. As many scholars have recognized public policy influences, in significant ways, both the content of citizenship and attitudes (including trust in government) within civil society.[6] The communitarian Amitai Eztioni asserts that 'public policies can nourish communities by ensuring that the state does not take over activities that provide opportunities for communities to act,'[7] and welcomes moral dialogues in society, an agenda also embraced by proponents of deliberative democracy:[8] some illiberal policies plainly compromise these aims. The most blatant form of such special or differential treatment are politically unsustainable in the long run (for example, the USA's Chinese Exclusion Act of 1882) but subtle and incipient differentials are observable. The historian Robin Kelley's discussion of how young African Americans' speech is studied—as a 'ritual'—points to a more general problem likely to be associated with illiberal measures: 'the very use of the term *ritual* to describe everyday speech reinforces the exoticization of black urban populations, constructing them as Others whose investment in this cultural tradition is much deeper than trying to get a laugh.'[9] The establishment of a Social Exclusion Unit or the delineation of an 'underclass' each runs the danger of reifying some notion of 'Otherness' of those defined as falling within these categories: instead of working directly for an advancement of inclusive, socially mixed communities, these strategies appear to underline the excluded status of the targeted groups in the population (and quite often fail to distinguish which groups very precisely).[10] It is a difficult balance but one to which we should be alert.

recaptures the spear from Klingsor, returns it to the Grail Castle and heals Amfortas. See Beckett (1981: 56).

  [6] For a good discussion see Tichenor (1995).   [7] Etzioni (1997: 149).
  [8] Elster (1998).   [9] Kelley (1997: 32–3).
  [10] I concur with Robert Goodin's observation that 'built into the very logic' of the notions of inclusion and exclusion 'is a focus on precisely that marginality which those who politically invoke values of "inclusion" hope to transcend' (1996b: 346). In contrast to the language of citizenship, policies such as workfare which treat selected citizens differently from others serve to underline those differences as Goodin argues: 'talking in terms of citizenship fixes

Mathew Thomson's historical account of eugenists' efforts to extend the boundary of citizenship to assessments of mental preparedness is illustrative here ('the very category of the mental defective was intentionally related to the contemporary desire to construct democratic subjects'[11]), as is many experts' discussion of the poor as a group apart and distinguished by separate behavioural traits.

For convenience, these concerns can be thought of as raising two broad questions about citizenship. First, who should be a member of the polity? And, second, once accorded citizenship what obligations are incurred (if only as a corollary of the rights acquired)? The latter is an issue which results in two sorts of public policy: first, social engineering schemes to alter the economic and social circumstances facing citizens (usually through collectivist experiments), and second, attempts directly to modify the behaviour of individuals by altering the balance of rights and obligations defining their relationship to the state, principally by restating or reinforcing obligations.

Since citizenship is fundamental to liberal democracy, how these answers—to questions which recur historically—are formulated in public policy is crucial to American and British political development. Hitherto, scholars have given too little attention to the interweaving of liberal and illiberal policies in these two political systems and hence are poorly prepared to evaluate the implications of new policies. 'End of history' triumphalism about liberal democracy also ill prepares us for the recurrence of illiberal policies. It is both too teleological and too ahistorical in its failure to recognize how such policies recur.

What governments do 'in the name of liberalism'—even within the illiberal policy categories analysed in this book—are diverse. The comparative case studies have regularly thrown up distinct aspects of each country, not least in the way liberal and illiberal elements have interacted. And although the analysis has addressed commonalities in US and British liberal democracy, there are differences sufficiently important to underline distinct national traditions. Some of the similarities arise from the cross-fertilization of ideas and elites. The British poor law relief tradition was imported to US local and state governments in the nineteenth century, and the approaches of 'scientific' charitable reformers were also shared in this period. In both countries social reformers and politicians articulated

attention on what is common and central. It fixes attention on what all citizens share. Talk of "inclusion" and "exclusion", in contrast, fixes attention—and necessarily so—on boundaries and margins, on what differentiates one class of persons from another' (1996b: 356). Of course, these concerns do not imply any doubts about the sincerity of those policy-makers responsible for administering policies for the socially excluded.

[11] Thomson (1998: 304).

philosophies justifying a significantly expanded government role in addressing unemployment and hardship in this century. Elites have shared views and arguments about eugenic proposals and, most recently, punitive approaches to recipients of public income-maintenance programmes.

Despite such similarities and shared information, the implementation of these programmes has differed in some ways too. One crucial source of difference between the two countries is the way in which liberal democratic values combine with distinctive national and cultural identities, resulting in effect in *sui generis* liberal traditions. The most obvious source of this contrast is US racial politics, as the empirical cases make clear. Historically and at present there is a fundamental racial dimension to the formulation and implementation of workfare schemes: white Americans both attribute a disproportionate number of African Americans compared with whites as recipients of welfare and express greater concern about welfare because of the racial composition of its population.[12] One way in which the inter-war experiment with work camps, the New Deal CCC, was made compatible with liberal democracy was its treatment of African Americans, who were offered places in segregated camps and rarely placed in positions of authority (a function no doubt, in part, of the small pool of African Americans eligible for such positions). Such patterns meant that the Corps mirrored rather than disturbed prevailing US racial politics.

Both the question of who is judged suitable to admit to liberal democracy and what balance of rights and obligations membership attracts are much influenced by the views of experts when such views are exploited politically. The doggedness of the eugenic campaigns in Britain and the United States resulted in the political articulation of eugenic grounds for selective exclusion; the remorseless ascription of the poor as an underclass differentiated behaviourally from the mainstream of society played no small role in justifying workfare. The empirical cases have found ideas to be of importance to the policy process. Diluted, distorted, or modified as they are, intellectual debate and dialogues underpin and provide a context to political debate. What this claim implies is that winning the argument about political ideas matters, as implied by Thatcherism or New Labour, since it enables those successful to dominate the content of political discourse. Ideas are not sufficient to generate policy, however, as we have seen, since they require political sponsors and legitimators. Experts can rarely effect policy without political support at the highest levels. In respect of the British eugenics example, civil servants and policy experts did attempt to implement policies independently of any public demand for them, and the existence of the Brock Committee itself resulted in large

---

[12] Gilens (1996).

part from interest group pressure. After the Eugenics Society, which led the campaign for sterilization, failed in its efforts to lobby parliament directly, it sought with success to secure its own representation on the Brock Committee and to use it as a means to advance eugenic aims. Thus, by the early 1930s, a specific interest had colonized a potentially influential corner of the civil service and used it to pursue aims which did not accord with those of the British public. The archival evidence demonstrates both that the committee felt the need to justify the case with reference to scientific evidence,[13] *and* that it was prepared to read into the evidence conclusions which, by the chairman's own admission, the committee had reached in advance of receiving submissions from the British scientific community. These conclusions arose from the prominent intellectual and ideological position attained by eugenics, which enjoyed extensive support in British elite circles.

WHO SHOULD BE ADMITTED TO MEMBERSHIP IN LIBERAL DEMOCRACY?

It is unremarkable that societies take decisions about whom they admit to full membership and citizenship. Nonetheless, the grounds for such decisions should not be immune from scrutiny. This task can be undertaken in two ways: historically and in terms of the intellectual criteria employed in policy choices.

Historically, both Britain and the United States live with the outcome of decisions about membership on a range of dimensions: geographical, nationality, generational, eugenic, and so forth. Two have been examined in this book. The contrast between the eventual failure of the Brock Committee's recommendation for eugenic sterilization compared with the success of US eugenists in influencing the national framework of immigration policy has been drawn intentionally to illustrate the way in which illiberal choices create consequential legacies. Thus, US immigration policy had fundamentally to be revised to excise the discriminatory restrictions embodied in the 1924 Johnson–Reed law. In contrast, British advocates of a voluntary sterilization campaign, advanced on grounds of scientific evidence about who should be encouraged to reproduce, implying a redrawing of the boundary of citizenship in terms of mental competence, ultimately failed to determine policy because of politicians' apprehension about the illiberality of such measures and potential violation of democratic norms. An assessment of either country's policy in these areas—

---

[13] Much American work, and the forced voluntary sterilization which it recommended, was rejected by the Committee ostensibly on the grounds of its inadequate scientific quality.

immigration policy in the USA and health policy for those with severe learning disability in Britain—needs to take account of how these particular initiatives, even if unenacted, structured the process of defining eligibility for membership in these two liberal democracies.

Intellectually, the presence of a concern with mental competence has not diminished in liberal democracy as a criterion specified for membership, though it is manifest in new spheres. For example, the development of genetic engineering techniques to a sophisticated and replicable standard unquestionably raises the potential for choices about membership in a powerful form. The question of admission to membership is drawn sharply as for instance in China where the 1995 law, the Maternal Infant Health Care Law (suspended in 1998) permitted doctors to sterilize people with serious genetic conditions.[14] Frank Dikotter's observation that 'open democracies with a vibrant civil society, such as Britain and the Netherlands, were generally less inclined to adopt extreme eugenic proposals than authoritarian regimes in Germany and the People's Republic of China,' somewhat overlooks US history.[15] The 1997 film *Gattaca* conveyed the dilemma of membership in its imaginary society divided into the 'higher race' and others, with entry to the former strictly monitored. The point of these examples is to emphasize the continuing influence of approaches to rationality, mental competence, or degree of intellectual ability as decisions about apposite qualities for membership in liberal democracy. Such pressures point again to the indirect presence of illiberal traditions; their recurrence in public policy might usefully be anticipated.

The comparison between eugenists' positive or negative schemes and genetic screening should not, of course, be overdrawn, as the science writer Matt Ridley fairly cautions: 'there is a big difference between genetic screening and what the eugenists wanted in their heyday. Genetic screening is about giving private individuals private choices on private criteria. Eugenics was about nationalizing that decision; to make people breed not for themselves but for the state.'[16] Ridley perceives a distinction between private choices about genetic screening compared with the state's use of genetic information, and argues that past eugenic excesses reflect uncontrolled state activity rather than scientists' inflated powers (though his own view that scientists enjoy the flattery of 'being treated as experts in a new

---

[14] 'China suspends sterilization of people with genetic ills', *International Herald Tribune*, 18 Aug. 1998.

[15] Dikotter (1998: 476).

[16] Ridley (1998: 47). And see British Medical Association (1998: 8) whose authors write: 'while people have always been faced with difficult decisions about how to evaluate and balance the risks and benefits medicine offers to them as individuals, genetic choices are far more likely to touch the lives of others.' It is this characteristic which disinguishes the new genetics: 'this is the main ethical area where genetic technology differs from other areas of medicine, in which the individual's values and priorities may be the sole determinant.'

technocracy'[17] sits uneasily with this judgement). To support this thesis, he cites the contrast between the Chinese state sterilization laws noted above and the US Committee for the Prevention of Jewish Genetic Disease, whose efforts have 'virtually eliminated' cystic fibrosis among American Jews. Ridley's distinction is an attractive one but perhaps runs the danger of underestimating the importance of state policy when evidence and expertise indicates it is appropriate to act and political contingencies provide a motive. It is not always easy to draw a line between private choices and state decisions, as recent debates about certain forms of universal vaccination make pellucid. In fact, significantly to denigrate the importance of political choices may be an error. Liberal democracy depends upon political choices exercised on the basis of reason, evidence, and calculations about the future—exercises unquestionably structured by politicians' self-interest too—and it is the freedom of expression and ability to influence debates through reasoned argument which fosters a strong civil society of the sort which in Britain permitted forceful individualist libertarian arguments against eugenics in the inter-war decades.

GOVERNMENT POLICY AND CITIZENSHIP

Governments engage in two sorts of policies which impinge upon and modify citizenship in liberal democracies, as the preceding chapters have indicated. First, through social amelioration projects, including collectivist experiments, they attempt to modify the attitudes and behaviour of citizens in a way which often results in special treatment for some members of the polity. Second, although membership of a liberal democracy is supposed to accord equality of rights and treatment (as we saw in Chapter 1), it has also been associated, both historically and at present, with specified obligations.

Making citizenship

Policies driven by strong expertise arguments are particularly likely to effect illiberal consequences because a robust evidential basis cannot easily be ignored. This feature has strengths and drawbacks. It is desirable in that it reflects values in our society which respect rationality and scientific results. It is problematic however, because it can produce policies without consideration of their political and social effects, a vulnerability James Scott amply demonstrates in his pungent analysis of selected social

[17] Ibid. 45.

engineering schemes.[18] Even apparently straightforward policies such as vaccination may have these results, as recent debate about Crohn's disease illustrate. One useful response is a rigorous process of scrutiny[19] followed by political choices.

James Scott's study of large-scale government initiatives also suggests some reasons why such undertakings have been controlled in the USA and Britain compared with the excesses of social engineering observable else-where. In an analysis of the growth and scope of the modern state, Scott argues that what he calls 'the most tragic episodes of state development'[20] rest upon three factors. The first is the presence of a well-developed 'high modernism' ideology, a conviction that with scientific analysis and rational planning society can be restructured in a desired way. Such ambitions descend directly from the Enlightenment conception of progress and ratio-nality. Second, Scott identifies the 'unrestrained use of power of the modern state as an instrument for achieving these designs'.[21] And third, a weak civil society removes potential constraints upon state intervention. He applies this framework to the examples of Soviet collectivization, the Tanzanian compulsory villagization programme and scientific agricultural schemes. Scott finds a general propensity amongst officials of the twentieth-century state toward social restructuring and standardization:

the modern state, through its officials, attempts with varying success to create a terrain and a population with precisely those standardized characteristics that will be easiest to monitor, count, assess, and manage. The utopian, immanent, and con-tinually frustrated goal of the modern state is to reduce the chaotic, disorderly, constantly changing social reality beneath it to something more closely resembling the administrative grid of its observations.[22]

The twentieth century certainly provides no shortage of examples of such general tendencies. In liberal democracies, however, civil society is strong, policy and political legacies about the appropriate sphere of gov-ernment consequential, and electoral dynamics require politicians to defend their policy choices and political decisions. This does not, as we have seen, remove the potential for illiberal policy—and indeed I have argued that it is in part intrinsic to the composition of a liberal democracy that such policies are adopted from time to time for well-argued reasons which are, in fact, compatible with liberalism—but it does translate into significant strictures upon such ambitions. All the recent literature on trust in government and the importance of civil society suggests that the pres-ence of such strictures are healthy and desirable aspects of an enduring

[18] Scott (1998).
[19] Advocated for instance by Collingridge and Reeve (1986).
[20] Scott (1998: 88).   [21] Ibid. 88–9.   [22] Ibid. 81–2.

and democratic polity. Civil society matters in part because it encodes informal practices, Scott argues, which can never be fully documented: 'formal order is always and to some considerable degree parasitic on informal processes, which the formal schemes does not recognize, without which it could not exist, and which it alone cannot create or maintain.'[23] Civil society also matters because it constitutes a basis for critical evaluation of policy and political choices. Furthermore, a market economy, with which a liberal democracy coexists, is testimony to the limits of statecraft and intervention, a point stated most forcefully by Hayek in the middle of the twentieth century as he reflected upon the disastrous statism of numerous European countries, an observation which can be contrasted with the non-disastrous statism of the New Deal.

It is striking that policies which, in other countries, became the basis for odious and oppressive regimes were restrained in Britain and the USA. This comparative pattern has long attracted scholarly attention (see, for example, de Tocqueville's reflections in *Democracy in America*) but most recently the notion of 'social capital' as a prerequisite to civil communities has gained prominence. This attractive theory is presented in Robert Putnam's influential book, *Making Democracy Work*, which, in providing an explanation of the differences in civic cultures between north and south Italy, develops an argument about the presence of historically rooted 'social capital' conducive of democracy in the northern region.[24]

These arguments about the importance of social capital and a strong civil society imply the following propositions. First, a strong civil society—valued as a source of stability—presumes that all citizens consent to the government's policies. This precept has limited application for illiberal measures under which marginal groups in the population are often targeted and whose consent may not be sought. Such a limitation can be counteracted by making programmes voluntary rather than coercive. The inter-war work camps were voluntary but in the British case the degree of voluntariness was plainly qualified and they were disliked. Workfare programmes clearly are not voluntary but coercive. Second, viewing trust as a source of social order—in Misztal's words as a 'social lubricant'[25]—implies that government policy ought ideally to contribute to fostering trust in the institutions of the state. Since social capital of this sort is, according to Robert Putnam, 'produced as a byproduct of other social activities',[26] government policy that undermines trust in public institutions will be harmful. Illiberal measures—such as employing eugenic criteria to single out some citizens for special treatment because of their alleged

---

[23] Ibid. 310.
[24] Putnam (1993). For a useful commentary see Rothstein (1996).
[25] Misztal (1996: 96), and see Seligman (1992, 1997).   [26] Putnam (1993: 170).

mental incompetence—may increase trust amongst some groups (those not affected directly by the policy) while concurrently eroding confidence in public policy amongst others. As Putnam puts it, making a broader point: 'the trust that is required to sustain cooperation is not blind. Trust entails a prediction about the behavior of an independent actor,'[27] in this case the state. Citizens look to governments to mediate and where appropriate dilute or modify expert advice, and not to privilege some schemes at the expense of their own needs. Third, social capital arguments resonate particularly powerfully in the United States, where de Tocqueville's nineteenth-century analysis of the polity highlighted the incidence and vibrancy of its civic society. The interactions necessitated by a strong civil society—manifest in participation in a range of associations—permits the forging of high interpersonal trust, an underpinning of social capital. It is of its nature voluntary and dependent on informal rather than formal arrangements. Involuntary or coercive measures by governments are unlikely to have a comparable effect. Furthermore, high levels of inter-personal trust can be achieved simultaneously with the marginalization of significant minorities, such as welfare recipients or African Americans.

A similar point emerges from Margaret Levi's research on conscription. She finds that how potential conscripts view government policy funda-mentally affects their attitudes toward the state.[28] If they think the mech-anisms for conscription are fair and that the burden is likely to fall equally upon other citizens then the conscripts will be more positive about the state. Thus Levi argues that the 'study of the history of military service in democracies reveals critical elements of the relationship between citizens and the state'. She argues that, while 'military service is one of the oblig-ations constitutive of citizenship' its implementation is important: 'in democracies, however, this citizen obligation carries with it a correspond-ing obligation of government toward its citizens.' To be politically accept-able, it is, therefore, 'incumbent upon democratic governments to use a system of conscription which is fair, or at least perceived as fair. Inequities in the system may be understood as a failure on the part of government officials to keep their side of the conscription bargain and, thus, license for citizens to withdraw their cooperation.'[29] Illiberal policies present a com-parable set of dynamics, except that it is often a marginalized section of the population that is affected. This is a reason for transparency and clarity of purpose in public policy.

The way in which the USA and Britain developed illiberal policies illus-trates the limits to such institutions and how their formulation is an intrin-sic part of liberal democratic political development. The reluctance to

---

[27] Putnam (1993: 171).   [28] Levi (1997).   [29] Ibid. 207–8.

implement the recommendation of the Brock Committee to introduce voluntary eugenic sterilization is an instance of such a characteristic as is the
way in which the Civilian Conservation Corps's collectivism was made
compatible with the USA's democratic individualist ideology in the 1930s.
John Field argues that the Corps's basis for success was ideological: 'the
CCC offered young men the opportunity to participate in a vital national
crusade, the enrollees waving goodbye at the railway stations in the belief
that they were on their way to rebuild the nation, as in more than one
respect they were.'[30]

Unsurprisingly, the significance of a federal polity looms large in the
comparative analysis. This is manifest in several ways. First, a federal
system in which some genuine policy discretion is left to state governments
permits greater experimentation and variation in public policy. Thus, we
have seen how many of the US states adopted eugenic-inspired sterilization before the Supreme Court sanctioned it in 1927. Most recently, workfare programmes have been pursued rigorously by many states since
regulations in 1981 were relaxed according them the opportunity to diver-
sify and experiment. States are thus the laboratories of democracy. In a
federal system, furthermore, there are significant constraints on state government excesses: both judicial review and federal oversight provide
avenues through which state initiatives can be evaluated, protested, and
on occasions abrogated (though the former failed to halt eugenic
programmes).

This state role as 'policy experimenters' does not provide a model only
for the US federal government. As we have seen, British policy-makers
were also aware of state variation in welfare programmes and their own
proposals were informed by this variety. The fact that British policy specialists paid close attention to sterilization policies and welfare reform in
American states is a reminder of the mobility of new policy ideas, findings,
and experiences during the past century.

Second, although federal structures provide a greater number of points
through which innovative ideas or proposals can be presented, the diffusion of political authority makes national policy-making complex. Experts
may gain direct access to policy-makers (a process enhanced by the comparative weakness of political parties in the United States) but whether
they are acted upon remains a function of political mobilization and coalition building within Congress and between it and the presidency, a frag-
mentation which also advantages opponents of a new policy. As Margaret
Weir notes in her study, *Politics and Jobs*, federal institutions constitute
additional barriers to the administration of a policy: 'the need to negoti-

[30] Field (1992: 153).

ate the different levels of the federal system affects the way political actors decide how policy goals should be achieved or, indeed, whether they are possible at all.'[31] Weir argues that these constraints create a policy-making environment best characterized as 'organizationally bounded'.

The Corps is an instructive example in other ways too. The comparative context of the 1930s was certainly one conducive to extremist youth movements directed uncritically toward national goals. As Field observes, 'almost every nation has, at some time, established work camps.' Overwhelmingly, they have been targeted on the marginal sectors of the labour force: 'names differ, but it is possible to identify some kind of remote labour system for a group or subgroup of citizens who are defined in some way as marginal to or even outside the wider socio-economic community.'[32] In explaining the demise of the British experiment with work camps, Field underscores their weak democratic legitimacy: 'the British experiment suggests that the system was fatally weakened by its internal fragility, which in turn arose from its lack of legitimacy in a society which placed such high value in its dominant ideology upon the consent of the governed and on the freedom of labour.'[33] Field's quasi-Marxist framework may encourage him to exaggerate the importance of the mechanisms he identifies as crucial to the constraints imposed upon the work camp experiment. There is, in fact, remarkably little direct evidence—in civil service memoranda or Cabinet committee papers for instance—that concern about the 'consent of the governed' exercised these policy-makers (which is not the case in the British flirtation with eugenic proposals where the political reluctance of the Conservative minister, Sir Edward Hilton Young, to act was decisive). There were robust defences of the camps in parliament but not in these terms. Field seems to be echoing the political scientist Bo Rothstein's view, encountered in Chapter 1,[34] in assuming that all citizens must consent equally for policy to be enacted. At a general level, such constraints as 'consent of the governed' operate but not all groups of citizens have the same influence upon politicians, especially if an interest-driven view of the latter is adopted.

Examined comparatively, it is clear that the British experience of work camps had some similarities with those in Canada, New Zealand, and Australia but none with those of totalitarian systems (and such analogies seem groundless); and that the CCC achieved a remarkable singularity in its legitimacy, popularity, and embodiment of its society's dominant values. As Field correctly notes: 'it was the only work camp system that was both large-scale and innovatory, yet at the same time rested on widespread popular acceptance, amounting at times to enthusiasm.'[35]

---

[31] Weir (1992: 23).   [32] Field (1992: 141).   [33] Ibid. 141.
[34] Rothstein (1998).   [35] Field (1992: 155).

These comparative observations highlight the significance of the political values and culture of the polity within which work camps were established. They also indicate the importance of how the institution operated. Interestingly, the work activity undertaken in work camps in the inter-war decades varied little cross-nationally—mostly heavy manual labour with some rudimentary training in conservation—but the way this was discharged and the conditions of the camps did vary. Despite being voluntary, however, the mere requirement of having to travel to spend time in a residential work camp was a drawback for the participants and desertion was steady if modest, even from the CCC. The recently aired memories of the British camps suggests, however, that they were quite unpopular and often strongly disliked by many of the participants, even if attendance was nominally voluntary. Dissent, however, was relatively mute.[36]

As we saw, there were significant pressures to militarize the Civilian Conservation Corps and to make it a permanent institution as a quasi-form of conscription (with the Peace Corps perhaps its descendant). Yet these initiatives were resisted: the Corps's structure as a collectivist experiment consistent with US political culture ensured its constrained development. Alan Brinkley's more general comment on New Deal agencies is apt in respect of the CCC too: 'the New Deal has often seemed as significant for its failures and omissions as for the things it achieved.' He adds: 'many of the New Deal's most prominent and innovative efforts—its work relief programs, its community and national planning initiatives, its community-building efforts, its public works agencies—did not survive the war.'[37] This assessment applied to the CCC too, whose development was constrained by several factors. First, the weak evidential basis for collectivist solutions to unemployment meant a lack of authority compared with other cases such as eugenic schemes or the often repeated arguments about certain types of welfare state programmes; second, the fundamental incompatibility between collectivism and individualism in a liberal democracy, despite President Franklin Roosevelt's efforts to justify the former strategy; and, third, contingencies not least the increasing publicity of the European fascist regimes, the USA's participation in the Second World War, and President Roosevelt's astute judgements about the limits of such experiments in liberal democracy. Historically and culturally, however, the decision to terminate the Corps and the way in which it functioned ensured the institution's contribution to the consolidation of US democracy (as practised then[38]) rather than threatening its embeddedness—a small example, no doubt, but still relevant. In racial terms, the Corps reinforced

---

[36] For details see Field (1992) and Colledge (1989).
[37] Brinkley (1998: 33–4).
[38] On its inadequacies see Smith (1993, 1997).

the prevailing prejudices of segregationist America, illustrating how central illiberal measures can be to a polity's history.

The obligations of membership

Members of liberal democracies acquire a basket of rights and obligations. One right is the fundamental entitlement to equality of treatment. As explained in Chapter 1, in social policy, the discourse of the last fifty years amongst politicians and advocates has been dominated by a Marshallian conception of social rights. And although it is fashionable now to observe that this focus on the social rights of citizenship implied no diminution or neglect of the obligations, in practice the discussion of obligations or duties associated with social citizenship has unfolded amongst academics only in the wake of the political success of the neoliberal politics of the Reagan and Thatcher administrations. This reorientation has proved to be one of profound importance, since it not only coincided with the collapse of communism (and the serious weakening of its socialist relatives), but set the political context for and defined the political language within which left–right politics is now debated (overwhelmingly to the benefit of neoliberal principles and at the expense of conventional socialist aims). Although these political developments often appear—or are interpreted—as recent, the idea of social obligations of citizenship is one which, as we have seen, has deep historical roots.

The way in which obligations have been formulated in respect of citizenship includes the following.

1. *Loss of rights*.[39] Historically, liberal democracies have made political rights a condition of wealth. Thus, in Britain paupers forfeited the right to vote if they received relief under the Poor Law Act of 1834 (a disfranchisement which ended in 1918).[40] A modern version of this principle is those state welfare programmes in the United States which penalize single mothers who have additional children while in receipt of assistance by providing no upkeep for the new child and, in some cases, reducing the benefits already provided. New Jersey practised a form of this policy before the 1996 federal reform, and in its programme included bonuses, such as subsidized childcare, if the single mother found a job. Abrogating rights is probably the most difficult approach for a government to adopt since such

---

[39] The obverse of a loss of rights—some form of positive discrimination—is also illiberal in the sense it treats some citizens differently; however, the reason for its adoption is fundamentally different from the cases examined here. Positive discrimination arises from historical inequalities, which its measures are designed to rectify or mitigate.

[40] Vincent (1991: 14). Of course, no paupers would have had the right to vote at the founding the New Poor Law but the clause was relevant for some later in the century.

measures rarely withstand judicial challenge (as recent restrictions on legal immigrants in the USA testify).

2. *Citizenship duties.* Partly to instil a sense of civic pride and allegiance to the state, conscription has commonly been required of citizens.[41] In the USA and Britain, however, conscription has been historically linked with wartime needs and compared with many continental European countries, it is a policy of limited importance. The idea of fostering liberal democratic citizenship through education is an enduring one, however, surveyed in Eamonn Callan's recent book.[42] Aside from classes in civics education, there is a general assumption that school education is designed to inculcate a sense of civic obligation.

Most recently, the communitarian agenda has invoked a major emphasis upon how citizens' behaviour contributes to the creation of a 'good society' situated between individualism and a strict social order.[43] Amitai Etzioni argues that 'integral to the social order of all societies are at least some processes that mobilize some of their members' time, assets, energies, and loyalties to the *service of one or more common purposes.*' Furthermore, a good society requires '*an order that is aligned with the moral commitments of the members*'.[44] He formulates this as a 'golden rule' with which to organize society: 'the challenge for those who aspire to a good society is to form and sustain a social order that is considered legitimate by its members, not merely when it is established (as contract libertarians would have it) but continuously.' To realize this golden rule, citizens must address the 'tension between one's preferences and one's social commitments . . . by increasing the realm of duties one affirms as moral responsibility—not the realm of duties that are forcibly imposed but the realm of responsibilities one believes one should discharge and that one believes one is fairly called upon to assume'.[45] He makes voluntary contribution to the construction and maintenance of such a social order pivotal to its enduring strength. And yet such a contribution cannot be 'voluntary' in its entirety: a state is required to impose some values, or at least to facilitate their development.

Etzioni argues that the USA requires a regeneration to restore these values. The development and consolidation of moral values rests upon a moral voice since 'the sociological fact is that values do not fly on their own wings'.[46] Community-based and reinforced morality is central to Etzioni's communitarian vision of an attractive social order, and he concludes that 'the weaker the community the thinner the social web and the slacker the moral voice'.[47] A key aspect of this framework is imposing

---

[41] See Levi (1997).   [42] Callan (1997).   [43] Tam (1998) and White (1998).
[44] Etzioni (1997: 10,12). The author's emphasis.
[45] Ibid. 12.   [46] Ibid. 119.   [47] Ibid. 187.

limits upon the role of the state but arguments about active citizenship or forms of civic conscription provide some ways for the fostering of duties amongst citizens. It is difficult to see how such values can be fostered without an active state role.

3. *Coercive obligations.* Some measures purposefully discriminate between groups by requiring obligations as a condition of receiving assistance. Test work and made work, discussed in Chapters 7 and 8, are historical examples of this practice. In the USA and Britain at present it is workfare which best epitomizes this approach. Its effect upon recipients of welfare is mixed. Some do not object to the requirement while others consider it stigmatizing and a compromise of the equality of treatment fundamental to citizenship and their efficacy as programmes is unsettled.[48] As formulated in New Labour's New Deal's four options there is arguably some choice left to the affected citizens but no choice about whether to participate or not. Coercive obligations appeal to politicians as a way of assuaging taxpayers.

As we saw in Chapter 8, the British Prime Minister, Tony Blair, has placed obligations at the centre of New Labour's restructuring of welfare policy (and Labour Party membership cards include the phrase 'the rights we enjoy reflect the duties we owe'). Indeed, an emphasis upon obligations has become a defining feature of the so-called 'Third Way' political strategy promoted by intellectuals associated with the Clinton Democrats and Blair's New Labour.[49] Anthony Giddens, in his book of this title, puts obligations at the core of Third Way politics: 'one might suggest as a prime motto for the new politics, *no rights without responsibilities*. Government has a whole cluster of responsibilities for its citizens and others, including the protection of the vulnerable. Old-style social democracy, however, was inclined to treat rights as unconditional claims.'[50] Giddens challenges the

---

[48] Solow (1998).

[49] Giddens (1998), and Novak (1998). A seminar on this topic with Prime Minister Blair and President Clinton present was organized at New York University on 21 Sept. 1998. Although the occasion coincided with the US Congress's decision to release the video of Clinton's appearance before the Grand Jury convened by Special Prosecutor Kenneth Starr, nonetheless the joint discussion of the Third Way continued. On the intellectual links between the two administrations, Sydney Blumenthal was quoted in the *Sunday Times* (27 Sept. 1998), as saying '"I communicate regularly with prime minister Tony Blair directly, his chief-of-staff Jonathan Powell, director of policy David Miliband, official spokesman Alastair Campbell, Peter Mandelson and various other aides, ministers and members of the British government."'

[50] Giddens (1998: 65). For an intellectually persuasive and coherent discussion of the Third Way see White (1998). For the influence of these arguments in government thinking about welfare reform see both Department for Education and Employment, *A New Contract for Welfare: The Gateway to Work* (London: HMSO, 1998, Cm. 4102) and Department of Social Security, *New Ambitions for our Country: A New Contract for Welfare* (London: HMSO, 1998 Cm. 3805).

importance of the development of Marshallian social rights of citizenship, arguing that they were more contingent upon the modern state's preparation or participation in war than commonly appreciated: 'citizenship rights and welfare programmes were mainly established as states sought to engage their populations and hold their support.' Scholars have exaggerated the degree to which the development of the welfare state was 'self-contained', rather than a consequence of short-term pressures.[51]

In response to changing political circumstances, Giddens advocates decentralizing power and reinvigorating rights and obligations by, for instance, stipulating a contractual arrangement for child rearing: 'contractual commitment to a child could be separated from marriage, and made by each parent as a binding matter of law, with unmarried and married fathers having the same rights and the same obligations.'[52] In addition, 'children should have responsibilities to their parents, not just the other way round.'[53] Presumably children will be able to sue their grandparents for having the children who, as their parents, failed them.

The major danger of a coercive obligations framework in social policy— or what Janoski terms the need for 'a renewed emphasis on notched and low-level sanctions'[54]—is its potential authoritarianism, resulting from the imposition of excessive burdens upon those targeted by the relevant policies. Even when such measures are dressed up in the language of rights and responsibilities or mutual obligations, policy administrators are likely to find themselves—historical experience suggests—much more exercised about the discharge of duties than dispensing entitlements. This weakness is intrinsic to a rights/duties balance which is underpinned by 'coercive obligation' precepts and, to those affected, can appear more oppressing than emancipatory. Most startlingly, the language of rights and responsibilities—as articulated by those developing Third Way politics—fails to acknowledge the basic inequalities of power common between partners entering into such contractual formality.

4. *Paternalist policy.* Paternalist policy consists of measures designed to improve the circumstances and behaviour of targeted individuals. Its proponents presume that they know what is best for the targeted subjects, and often make no pretensions to involve them in those decisions. Paternalist policy, however, tends also to have a sharp edge: it is directive and highly interventionist. Historically, this sort of approach was manifest amongst nineteenth-century charitable organizations such as the Charity

---

[51] Ibid. 71. See Dryzek and Goodin (1986).
[52] Giddens (1998: 95).   [53] Ibid. 97.
[54] Janoski (1998: 234). White (1998) writes that, as past of the ethic of civic responsibility, and 'as a matter of justice, the state should clearly define, and, where necessary, enforce the obligations which derive from . . . basic responsibilities'.

Organization Society.[55] The Society was focused exclusively upon individuals, bolstered by an individualist philosophy,[56] aiming through detailed and systematic casework to uplift the poor, through integration into the work habits of modern industrial society. Employing the Victorian principle of self-help, the COS's officers believed that 'the aim of all charitable work and action ... must be the strengthening or at least not the weakening, of the individual's will to help himself. The individual should be persuaded, but if necessary goaded, into achievement through his own efforts.'[57] Gareth Stedman Jones underlines the class context of these endeavours: 'the elaborate methods of investigation and classification devised by the C.O.S. were an attempt to reintroduce the element of obligation into the gift in districts where a small number of mainly non-resident rich were confronted with a vast and anonymous mass of poor applicants.'[58]

There are two modern versions of this paternalist approach. First, there is that form of attention recently characterized as the 'therapeutic state', that is, the panoply of experts, civil servants, and advisers collectively constitutive of 'the state' who form a set of received opinion and expertise about addressing the problems which face the democratic polity. Writing of social policy, Andrew Polsky defines the 'therapeutic state' as the personnel and agencies responsible for those citizens identified as socially and politically marginal. The latter are those members of society who need 'to acquire the value structure that makes for self-sufficiency, healthy relationships, and positive self-esteem,' and who, to learn these traits, 'become the clients of behavioral specialists, clinicians and social workers'.[59] The sociologist James Nolan has taken this metaphor further, imputing a 'therapeutic culture' throughout the institutions of US government, and identifies a 'new priestly class' fostering this cultural approach. This class is composed of representatives of the modern expert, he contends: 'these psychologists, psychiatrists, counselors, therapists and social workers have been granted a high level of prestige and social recognition in American society for their ability to help individuals make sense of life in the modern world.'[60] Nolan alights upon the significant convergence between Democrats and Republicans in respect of the language, principles, and aims in which welfare reform is discussed. Both parties' members appeal to what Nolan terms 'therapeutic themes', such as self-esteem.[61]

---

[55] See Lewis (1991: 302–11). Gerstle (1994: 1044) distinguishes the New Deal reformers from their Progressive predecessors in terms of the latter's concern with individual amelioration: 'missing from the New Deal was the Progressive preoccupations with individual virtue and vice. Progressives had been intent on reforming individuals and improving character.'

[56] Mowat (1961).   [57] McBriar (1987: 55).   [58] Jones (1971: 257).
[59] Polsky (1991: 1).   [60] Nolan (1998: 8).   [61] Ibid., ch. 6.

A second form of paternalism is that which some scholars, such as Lawrence Mead, have detected as a revival of a nineteenth-century style focus upon individuals. In contrast to the therapeutic form of paternalism, this new type sets out energetically to direct and reform the behaviour of welfare state recipients rather than reinforcing existing patterns. Mead defines paternalism as consisting of those 'social policies aimed at the poor that attempt to reduce poverty and other social problems by directive and supervisory means. Programs based on these policies help the needy but also require that they meet certain behavioral requirements, which the programs enforce through close supervision.'[62] Such modern paternalist policies are mandatory, that is, they require specified actions by those targeted; it is this legal authority which decisively differentiates modern paternalism from nineteenth-century precursors. James Q. Wilson takes this approach and celebrates it, concluding from a survey of some paternalist programmes that 'we do better in changing people when we tell them how they are supposed to behave ... [there is a] case for the government enforcing *outcomes* instead of merely providing resources or offering opportunities.'[63] In its emphasis upon individual amelioration and combination of rewards with sanctions, paternalism plainly revives aspects of nineteenth-century charitable programmes, and links them with quasi-communitarian principles. Using instruction, government is acting on behalf of the community systematically to integrate those individuals estranged from mainstream values or the practices of the social order. It is likely to be a costly strategy because, to succeed, the schemes are very labour intensive (although the sincerity and concern of its practitioners is usually not in doubt). The principal problem is whether there can be agreement on the content of the values apposite to such regimes in societies whose basis is individualism and the concomitant diversity it encourages.

In sum, while these four types of social policy are differentiated by the way in which they balance rights and responsibilities, they share a role for government which can result in illiberal measures. Importantly, such policies can coexist and are identifiable at different points in the history of the USA and Britain. For instance, directive paternalism of the sort Mead now proposes may seem anachronistic because it did not feature in the post-1945 so-called mature welfare state era but is unquestionably a feature of social policy in the 1990s. Similarly, the return of social obligations of citizenship—most saliently in Third Way politics—releases characteristics of government policy long dormant.[64] It also contains unanticipated consequences. For example, as the political theorist John Gray notes, 'forcing the unemployed to take work presupposes that there is work to be had'. He adds: 'fairness and common sense demand that, if the unemployed are obliged to work, society is obliged to provide them with it. And that obligation can be discharged only if the state is ready to step in as employer of last resort.'[65] Gray's statement can be expanded to note that the work discharged under workfare requirements should have long-term value to the person obliged to do it. There is always 'work' to do, but it is almost everywhere tree planting or conservation: useful tasks undoubtedly but not to the people whose only taught skill is to plant trees.[66]

The policies discussed in this book have tested each country's liberal democracy. They have both broadened it (the embrace of an obligations-based workfare regime is the best example here) and clarified its unassailable barriers (for example, the unacceptability of a eugenic-based criterion in determining citizenship). While these tests to liberal democratic values and institutions point to their political durability in the USA and Britain they also demonstrate the recurrence of illiberal pressures upon policy-makers rather than the 'end of history'. These implications should warn us that liberal democracy is a dynamic not a static set of institutions and values, the content of which should never be assumed but instead periodically scrutinized.

[65] Gray (1998: 29). It is notable that the duties attributed to government in the 'new welfare contract' (which are to provide people with help in finding work, to make employment pay, to support those who can't work, to help parents in raising children, to regulate pensions, to relieve old age hardship and to make the welfare system transparent) does not include that of creating work. See Department of Social Security, *New Ambitions for our Country: A New Contract for Welfare* (London: HMSO, 1998, Cm. 3805), 80.

[66] No workfare scheme succeeds in providing the kind of education an apprenticeship would do. The life chances of those who do it are not enhanced, except in the short term. As the economist Robert Solow concludes about the recent US reform, 'we have been kidding ourselves. A reasonable end to welfare as we know it—something more than just benign or malign neglect—will be much more costly, in budgetary resources and also in the strain on institutions, than any of the sponsors of welfare reform have been willing to admit' (1998a: 27). See also Solow (1998b).

BIBLIOGRAPHY

PRIMARY

Britain

Public Record Office

Ministry of Health records (MH51, MH58, MH79).
Home Office records (HO144).
Treasury records.
Cabinet papers and minutes.
Ministry of Labour.

Modern Records Centre, Warwick

TUC records.

Parliamentary and Governmental Departmental Sources

Report from His Majesty's Commissioners for Inquiring into the Administration and Practical Operation of the Poor Laws, Published by Authority (London, 1834).

Report on Free and Pauper Colonies in Holland by Sir John McNeill, Appendix A to 8th Annual Report of the Board of Supervision for Relief of the Poor (Scotland), in *Parliamentary Papers*, vol. xxix.

Report on Agencies and Methods for Dealing with the Unemployed (London: HMSO C-7182), in *Parliamentary Papers*, vol. lxxxii.

Report of the Interdepartmental Committee on Physical Deterioration (London: HMSO, 1904, Cd. 2175).

Royal Commission on the Care and Control of the Feeble-Minded. Minutes of Evidence and Reports (London: HMSO, 1908, Cd. 4215–21, 4202).

Report of the Royal Commission on the Poor Laws and Relief of Distress, Poor Law Commissioners (London: HMSO, 1909, Cd. 4499).

Report of the Interdepartmental Committee on Mental Deficiency 1925–1929 (Wood Report), 3 vols., 4 parts (London: HMSO, 1929).

Report of a Special Inquiry into Various Forms of Test Work, Ministry of Health (London: HMSO, May 1930, Cmd. 3585).

Royal Commission on Unemployment Insurance (London: HMSO, 1931), Minutes of Evidence.

Report of the Departmental Committee on Sterilisation, chaired by Sir Laurence Brock (London: HMSO 1934, Cmd. 4485). In *Parliamentary Papers*, vol. xv (1934).

A Clinical and Genetic Study of 1280 Cases of Mental Defect (The Colchester

Survey) by L. S. Penrose (London: HMSO 1938/Medical Research Council Special Report Series 229).

Report on Social Insurance and Allied Services, by William Beveridge (London: HMSO, 1942, Cmd. 6404).

Report of the Committee on the Provision for Social and Economic Research, chaired by Sir John Clapham (London: HMSO, 1946, Cmd. 6868).

House of Commons Sessions 1995–6, Employment Committee, Second Report, *The Right to Work/Workfare* (London: HMSO, 13 Feb. 1996).

Department of Social Security, *New Ambitions for our Country: A New Contract for Welfare* (London: HMSO, 1998, Cm. 3805).

Department for Education and Employment, *A New Contract for Work: The Gateway to Work* (London: HMSO, 1998, Cm. 4102).

Parliamentary Debates

Local Government Board, *Sixteenth Annual Report 1886–87*.
Ministry of Health, annual reports 1925–35.
Ministry of Labour, annual reports 1929–39.

The United States

National Archives and Record Administration

Record Group 35, Records of the Civilian Conservation Corps:
  Advisory Council minutes
  Division of Selection
  Personal Correspondence of the Director
  Reference Files
  Report of Conference.
Record Group 85, Records of the Immigration and Naturalization Service.
Record Group 119, Records of the National Youth Administration.
Record Group 233, Records of the US House of Representatives:
  Committee on Immigration and Naturalization
Record Group 307: Records of the National Science Foundation, Office of the Director, General records 1949–63.

Library of Congress, Manuscript Division

Papers of Calvin Coolidge.
Papers of Franklin MacVeagh.
Papers of the National Association for the Advancement of Colored People.

Truman State University, Special Collections Department, Pickler Memorial Library
Papers of Dr Harry Laughlin

Congressional Sources

Civilian Conservation Corps, *The Civilian Conservation Corps and Colored Youth* (Washington, DC: CCC Office of the Director, 1939).

Report of the Immigration Commission (Washington, DC: GPO, 1910–11),
US House of Representatives, 66th Congress, 2nd Session, 'Biological Aspects of Immigration', hearings before the Committee on Immigration and Naturalization (17 Apr. 1920).
——68th Congress, 1st Session, 'Europe as an Emigrant-Exporting Continent: the United States as an Immigrant-Receiving Nation', hearings before the Committee on Immigration and Naturalization (8 Mar. 1924).
——69th Congress, 2nd Session, 'Americanization of Adult Aliens', hearings before a Subcommittee of the Committee on Immigration and Naturalization (17 Feb. 1927).
——70th Congress, 1st Session, 'The Eugenical Aspects of Deportation', hearings before the Committee on Immigration and Naturalization (21 Feb. 1928).
——75th Congress, 1st Session, 'To Make the Civilian Conservation Corps a Permanent Agency', hearings before the Committee on Labor 14 and 15 Apr. 1937 (Washington, DC: GPO).
——76th Congress, 1st Session, 'To Make the Civilian Conservation Corps a Permanent Agency', Hearings before the Committee on Labor, 9, 23, and 24 Feb. 1939 (Washington, DC: GPO).
——*Background Material and Data on Programs within the Jurisdiction of the Committee on Ways and Means* (Washington, DC: GPO, 1994).
US Senate, 69th Congress, 2nd Session, Document No. 190, 'National Origins Provision of the Immigration Act of 1924', message from the President of the United States (7 Jan. 1927).
——US Senate, 100th Congress, 1st Session, hearings on Welfare Reform, Committee on Finance, 9 Apr. 1987 (Washington, DC: GPO).

Theses

EDELMAN, J. M., *The Passage of the Family Support Act of 1988 and the Politics of Welfare Reform in the United States*, D. Phil thesis, University of Oxford, 1995.
THOMSON, M. P., '*The Problem of Mental Deficiency in England and Wales*, D. Phil thesis, University of Oxford, 1992.

Books and Articles

ABBOTT, E., *Public Assistance* (Chicago: University of Chicago Press, 1940).
BLACKER, C. P., 'The Sterilization Proposals: A History of their Development', *Eugenics Review*, 22 (1930), 239–47.
BLYTHE, S. G., 'Camps for Jobless Men', *Saturday Evening Post*, 27 May 1933.
BRACKENBURY, H. B., 'The Mental Deficiency Acts and Their Administration', *Eugenics Review*, 15/2 (July 1923), 393–401.
BRECKINRIDGE, S. P. (ed.), *Public Welfare Administration in the United States: Selected Documents* (Chicago: University of Chicago Press, 1927).
COLCORD, J. C., *Emergency Work Relief as Carried out in Twenty-Six American Communities 1930–31* (New York: Russell Sage Foundation, 1922).
COOK, W. G. H., 'English and Foreign Marriage Laws in Relation to Mental Disorder', *Eugenics Review*, 13/1 (Apr. 1921), 352–60.

CROLY, H., *The Promise of American Life* (New York: Macmillan, 1909).

—— *Progressive Democracy* (New York: Macmillan, 1915).

DARWIN, L., 'First Steps toward Eugenic Reform', *Eugenics Review*, 4/1 (Apr. 1912), 26–38.

—— 'How should our Society now strive to advance?' *Eugenics Review*, 13/3 (Oct. 1921), 439–55.

—— 'Sterilization in America', *Eugenics Review*, 15/1 (Apr. 1923), 335–44.

—— 'Programme of Eugenic Reform', *Eugenics Review*, 15/3 (Oct. 1923), 595–6.

—— 'Analysis of the Brock Report', *Eugenics Review*, 26 (Apr. 1934), 9–13.

DAVENPORT, C. B., 'The Work of the Eugenics Record Office', *Eugenics Review*, 15/1 (Apr. 1923), 20–5.

DUGDALE, R. L., *The Jukes: A Study in Crime, Pauperism, Disease and Heredity* (New York: G. P. Putnam & Sons, 1877).

ELLIS, H., 'The Sterilization of the Unfit', *Eugenics Review*, 1/3 (Oct. 1909), 203–6.

FAIRCHILD, H. P., *The Melting-Pot Mistake* (Boston: Little Brown & Co., 1926).

FISHER, R. A., 'Positive Eugenics', *Eugenics Review*, 9/3 (Oct. 1917), 206–12.

FOX, E., 'The Mental Deficiency Act and its Administration', *Eugenics Review*, 10/1 (Apr. 1918), 1–17.

GILBOY, E. W., *Applicants for Work Relief: A Study of Massachusetts Families under the FERA and WPA* (Cambridge, Mass.: Harvard University Press, 1940).

GODDARD, H. H., 'Heredity of Feeble-Mindedness', *Eugenics Review*, 3/1 (Apr. 1911), 6–60.

—— *The Kallikak Family* (New York: Macmillan, 1912).

—— *Feeblemindedness: Its Causes and Consequences* (New York: Macmillan, 1914).

GRANT, M., *The Passing of a Great Race* (London: G. Bell, 4th edn., 1921).

HALDANE, J. B. S., *Heredity and Politics* (London: George Allen & Unwin, 1938).

HANNINGTON, W., *The Problem of the Distressed Areas* (London: Victor Gollanz, 1937).

KIRBY, A. H. P., 'Notes on the Present Working of the Mental Deficiency Act, 1913', *Eugenics Review*, 7/2 (July 1915), 133–5.

KOPP, M. E., 'Legal and Medical Aspects of Eugenic Sterilization in Germany', *American Sociological Review*, 1 (1936).

LAUGHLIN, H. H., 'Eugenics in America', *Eugenics Review*, 17 (Apr. 1925), 28–35.

LIDBETTER, E. J., *Heredity and the Social Problem Group* (London: Arnold, 1933).

McCLESKEY, J. B., 'Economic Conservation Made Practical', *Plant Flower and Fruit Guild Magazine* (May 1932).

MALLET, Sir BERNARD, 'The Social Problem Group: The President's Account of the Society's next Task', *Eugenics Review*, 23 (Oct. 1931), 203–6.

MUDGE, G. P., 'The Menace to the English Race and to its Traditions of Present-Day Immigration and Emigration', *Eugenics Review*, 11/4 (Jan. 1920), 202–12.

MYERSON, A., 'Some Objections to Sterilization', *Birth Control Review*, 12 (1928), 81–4.

—— *Eugenic Sterilization* (New York: Macmillan, 1936).

NEWTON CRANE, R., 'Recent Eugenic and Social Legislation in America', *Eugenics Review*, 10/1 (Apr. 1918), 24–9.

PEARL, R., 'Sterilization of Degenerates and Criminals Considered from the Standpoint of Genetics', *Eugenics Review*, 9/1 (Apr. 1919), 1–6.

PEASE, E., *The History of the Fabian Society* (New York: E. P. Dutton, 1916).

PHILLPOTT, H. R. S., 'Concentration Camps', *Daily Herald*, 15, 16, 17, 19, 22 Mar. 1934.

——'Those "Concentration Camps"', *Labour: A Magazine for all Workers*, 1 (Apr. 1934).

SCHUSTER, E., 'Methods and Results of the Galton Laboratory for National Eugenics', *Eugenics Review*, 3/1 (Apr. 1911), 10–24.

TAIT, D. C., 'Unemployment of Young People in Great Britain', *International Labour Review*, 31 (Feb. 1935), 177–89.

TREDGOLD, A. F., 'Eugenics and the Future Progress of Man', *Eugenics Review*, 3/2 (July 1911), 94–117.

WEBB, S., 'Eugenics and the Poor Law', *Eugenics Review*, 2/2 (Nov. 1910), 233–41.

SECONDARY

ABBOTT, E. (1940), *Public Assistance* (Chicago: University of Chicago Press).

ADAMS, M. (ed.) (1990), *The Wellborn Science: Eugenics in Germany, France, Brazil and Russia* (New York: Oxford University Press).

ADDISON, P. (1975), *The Road to 1945* (London: Jonathan Cape).

——(1992), *Churchill on the Home Front 1900–1955* (London: Jonathan Cape).

AINLEY, P., and VICKERSTAFF, S. (1933), 'Transitions from Corporatism: The Privatisation of Policy Failure', *Contemporary Record*, 7: 541–56.

ALLEN, G. E. (1986), 'The Eugenics Record Office at Cold Spring Harbor, 1910–1940: An Essay in Institutional History', *Osiris*, 2nd series, 2: 225–64.

——(1987), 'The Role of Experts in Scientific Controversy', in H. Tristram Englehardt Jr. and A. L. Caplan (eds.), *Scientific Controversies* (Cambridge: Cambridge University Press).

AMENTA, E. (1998), *Bold Relief: Institutional Politics and the Origins of Modern American Social Policy* (Princeton: Princeton University Press).

ANDREWS, G. (1991), *Citizenship* (London: Lawrence & Wishart).

ARCHDEACON, T. J. (1983), *Becoming American: An Ethnic History* (New York: Free Press).

ARNESON, R. J. (1990a), 'Liberalism, Distributive Subjectivism and Equal Opportunity for Welfare', *Philosophy and Public Affairs*, 19: 158–94.

——(1990b), 'Is Work Special? Justice and the Distribution of Employment', *American Political Science Review* 84: 1127–48.

ASHBY, P. (1989), 'Training and Enterprise Councils: Assessing the Gamble', *Policy Studies*, 10: 31–9.

BADGER, A. J. (1989), *The New Deal* (Basingstoke: Macmillan).

BAILYN, B. (1971), *The Ideological Origins of the American Revolution* (Cambridge, Mass.: Harvard University Press).

BALDWIN, P. (1990), *The Politics of Social Solidarity* (Cambridge: Cambridge University Press).

BANE, M. J. (1988), 'Politics and Policy of the Feminization of Poverty', in Weir, & Orloff, and Skocpol 1988.

——and ELLWOOD, D. T. (1994), *Welfare Realities* (Cambridge, Mass.: Harvard University Press, 1994).

BARKAN, E. (1992), *The Retreat of Scientific Racism: Changing Concepts of Race in Britain and the United States between the World Wars* (Cambridge: Cambridge University Press).

BARKER, D. (1983), 'How to Curb the Fertility of the Unfit: The Feeble-Minded in Edwardian Britain', *Oxford Review of Education*, 9: 197–211.

——(1989), 'The Biology of Stupidity: Genetics, Eugenics and Mental Deficiency in the Inter-War Years', *British Journal of the History of Science*, 22: 347–75.

BARRY, B. (1995), *Justice as Impartiality* (Oxford: Clarendon Press).

——(1996), 'Political Theory, Old and New', in Goodin and Klingemann 1996.

BARRY, N. (1990), *Welfare* (Milton Keynes: Open University Press).

BATES, R. H., GREIF, A., LEVI, M., ROSENTHAL, J. L., and WEINGAST B. R. (1998), *Analytic Narratives* (Princeton: Princeton University Press).

BAUMGARTNER, F., and JONES, B. (1993), *Agendas and Instability in American Politics* (Chicago: University of Chicago Press).

BECKETT, L. (1981) *Parsifal* (Cambridge: Cambridge University Press).

BEER, S. H. (1978), 'In Search of a New Public Philosophy', in A. King (ed.), *The New American Political System* (Washington, DC: American Enterprise Institute).

BELLAMY, R. (1992), *Liberalism and Modern Society* (Oxford: Polity).

BENNETT, C. J. (1991), 'How States Utilize Foreign Evidence', *Journal of Public Policy*, 11: 31–54.

BENTLEY, M. (1987), *The Climax of Liberal Politics* (London: Edward Arnold).

BERKOWITZ, E. D. (1991), *America's Welfare State* (Baltimore: Johns Hopkins University Press).

——and McQUAID, K. (1992) *Creating the Welfare State* (Lawrence, Kan.: University Press of Kansas).

BERLIN, I. (1969), *Four Essays on Liberty* (Oxford: Oxford University Press).

BERMAN, S. (1998), 'Path Dependency and Political Action: Reexamining Responses to the Depression', *Comparative Politics*, 30: 379–400.

BIRD, R. D., and ALLEN, G. (1981), 'The Papers of Harry Hamilton Laughlin, Eugenicist', *Journal of the History of Biology*, 14: 339–53.

BLEDSTEIN, B. J. (1976), *The Culture of Professionalism* (New York: Norton).

BLOCK, F., and NOAKES, J. (1988), 'The Politics of New-Style Workfare', *Socialist Review*, 18: 31–58.

——CLOWARD, R. A., EHRENREICH B., and PIVEN, F. F. (1987), *The Mean Season* (New York: Pantheon Books).

BOWLER, P. J. (1993), *Biology and Social Thought 1850–1914* (Berkeley, Calif.: Office for History of Science and Technology).

BOWLES, N. (1987), *The White House and Capitol Hill* (Oxford: Clarendon Press).

BRESLAU, D. (1997), 'The Political Power of Research Methods: Knowledge Regimes in U. S. Labor-Market Policy', *Theory and Society*, 26: 869–902.

BRIGGS, E., and DEACON, A. (1974) 'The Creation of the Unemployment Assistance Board', *Policy and Politics*, 2: 43–62.

BRINKLEY, A. (1982), *Voices of Protest* (New York: Knopf).

—— (1998), *Liberalism and its Discontents* (Cambridge, Mass.: Harvard University Press).

British Medical Association (1998), *Human Genetics: Choice and Responsibility* (Oxford: Oxford University Press).

BRITTAN, S. (1975), 'The Economic Contradictions of Democracy', *British Journal of Political Science*, 5: 129–59.

—— (1996), 'Making common cause? How liberals differ, and what they ought to agree on', *Times Literary Supplement*, 20 Sept.

BROBERG, G., and ROLL-HANSEN, N. (eds.) (1996), *Eugenics and the Welfare State: Sterilization Policy in Denmark, Sweden, Norway and Finland* (East Lansing, Mich.: Michigan State University Press).

BROCK, W. R. (1988), *Welfare, Democracy and the New Deal* (Cambridge: Cambridge University Press).

BROGAN, H. (1985), *The Pelican History of the United States* (Harmondsworth: Penguin Books).

BROWN, J. (1941), *The History of Public Assistance in Chicago 1833 to 1893* (Chicago: University of Chicago Press).

BROWN, J. C. (1940), *Public Relief 1929–1939* (New York: Henry Holt & Co.)

BROWN, M. B. (1998), *Defending the Welfare State* (Nottingham: Spokesman).

BRYNER, G. (1998), *Politics and Public Morality: The Great American Welfare Reform Debate* (New York: W. W. Norton).

BULMER, M. (ed.) (1987), *Social Science Research and Government* (New York: Cambridge University Press).

——BALES, K., and SKLAR, K. K. (eds.) (1991), *The Social Survey in Historical Perspective 1880–1940* (Cambridge: Cambridge University Press).

BURLEIGH, M. (1994), *Death and Deliverance* (Cambridge: Cambridge University Press).

BURTT, S. (1993), 'The Politics of Virtue Today: A Critique and a Proposal', *American Political Science Review*, 87: 360–8.

CALLAN, E. (1997), *Creating Citizens: Political Education and Liberal Democracy* (Oxford: Clarendon Press).

CAREY, A. C. (1998), 'Gender and Compulsory Sterilization Programs in America: 1907–1950', *Journal of Historical Sociology* 11: 74–105.

CARMINES, E. G., and STIMSON, J. A. (1989), *Issue Evolution* (Princeton: Princeton University Press).

CHECKLAND, S. G., and CHECKLAND, E. O. A. (eds.) (1974), *The Poor Law Report of 1834* (Harmondsworth: Penguin).

CHRISTIE, I. (1999), 'Return of Sociology', *Prospect* (Jan.), 34–7.

CLARKE, P. (1988), *The Keynesian Revolution in the Making 1924–1936* (Oxford: Clarendon Press).

COBB, R. W., and ELDER, C. D. (1972), *Participation in American Politics: The Dynamics of Agenda Building* (Boston: Allyn & Bacon).

COCKETT, R. (1994), *Thinking the Unthinkable* (London: Harper Collins).

COLLEDGE, D. (1989), *Labour Camps: The British Experience* (Sheffield: Sheffield Popular Publishing).

——and FIELD, J. (1983) '"To Recondition Human Material . . .": An Account of a British Labour Camp in the 1930s', *History Workshop Journal*, 15: 152–66.

COLLINGRIDGE, D., and REEVE, C. (1986), *Science Speaks to Power* (London: Frances Pinter).

COOK, F. L., and BARRETT, E. J. (1992), *Support for the American Welfare State: The Views of Congress and the Public* (New York: Columbia University Press).

COPP, D. J., HAMPTON, J., and ROEMER, J. (eds.) (1993), *The Idea of Democracy* (Cambridge: Cambridge University Press).

CRANE, D. (1972), *Invisible Colleges: Diffusion of Knowledge in Scientific Communities* (Chicago: University of Chicago Press).

CROUCHER, R. (1987), *We Refuse to Starve in Silence: A History of the National Unemployed Workers' Movement, 1920–46* (London: Lawrence & Wishart).

CROWTHER, M. A. (1981), *The Workhouse System 1834–1929* (London: Batsford, 1981).

DAHRENDORF, R. (1995), *LSE* (Oxford: Oxford University Press).

DANIEL, W. W. (1990), *The Unemployed Flow* (London: Policy Studies Institute).

DASH, L. (1996), *Rosa Lee* (New York: Basic Books).

DAVID, P. (1985), 'Clio and the Economics of QWERT', *American Economic Review: Papers and Proceedings*, 75: 332–7.

DAVIES, G. (1996), *From Opportunity to Entitlement* (Lawrence, Kan.: University Press of Kansas).

DAWSON, M. C. (1994), *Behind the Mule* (Princeton: Princeton University Press).

DEACON, A. (1976), *In Search of the Scrounger* (London: Macmillan).

——(1993), 'Richard Titmuss Twenty Years on', *Journal of Social Policy*, 22.

——(1996), 'The Dilemmas of Welfare: Titmuss, Murray and Mead', in S. J. D. Green and R. C. Whiting (eds.), *The Boundaries of the State in Modern Britain* (Cambridge: Cambridge University Press).

——(1997), *Benefit Sanctions for the Jobless: 'Tough Love' or Rough Treatment?* (London: Employment Policy Institute).

——(1998), 'The Case for Compulsion,' *Poverty*, 98: 8–10.

——and BRIGGS, E. (1974), 'Local Democracy and Central Policy: The Issue of Pauper Votes', *Policy and Politics*, 2: 347–64.

——and MANN, K. (1997), 'Moralism and Modernity: The Paradox of New Labour Thinking on Welfare', *Benefits* (Sept.–Oct.), 2–6.

DEAN, H. (1991), *Social Security and Social Control* (London: Routledge).

——(1996), *Welfare, Law and Citizenship* (Brighton: Harvester Wheatsheaf).

——and TAYLOR-GOOBY, P. (1992), *Dependency Culture: The Explosion of a Myth* (Hemel Hempstead: Harvester Wheatsheaf).

DEAN, M. (1991), *The Constitution of Poverty: Towards a Genealogy of Liberal Goverance* (London: Routledge).

DEEG, R. (1995), 'Institutional Transfer, Social Learning and Economic Policy in Eastern Germany', *West European Politics*, 18: 38–63.

DESAI, R. (1994), 'Second-Hand Dealers in Ideas: Think-Tanks and Thatcherite Hegemony', *New Left Review*, 203: 27–64.

DE SCHWEINITZ, K. (1943), *England's Road to Social Security* (New York: Barnes).

DEWEY, J. (1935), *Liberalism and Social Action* (New York: Capricorn Books).

——(1946), *The Public and Its Problems* (Chicago: Gateway Press).

DIKOTTER, F. (1998), 'Review Essay: Race Culture: Recent Perspectives on the History of Eugenics', *American Historical Review*, 103: 467–78.

DIVINE, R. A. (1957), *American Immigration Policy 1924–1952* (New Haven: Yale University Press).

DOLOWITZ, D. (1996), 'Reflections on the UK Workfare System', unpublished mimeo, Birmingham.

——(1997), *Learning from America* (Falmouth: Sussex Academic Press).

——, and MARSH, D. (1996), 'Who Learns What from Whom: A Review of the Policy Transfer Literature', *Political Studies*, 44: 343–57.

DOWBIGGIN, I. R. (1997), *Keeping America Sane: Psychiatry and Eugenics in the United States and Canada, 1880–1940* (Ithaca, NY: Cornell University Press).

DOWDING, K. (1995), 'Model or Metaphor? A Critical Review of the Policy Network Approach', *Political Studies*, 43: 136–58.

DOWNS, A. (1957), *An Economic Theory of Democracy* (New York: Harper).

DRIVER, S., and MARTELL, L. (1998), *New Labour: Politics after Thatcherism* (Oxford: Polity).

DRYZEK, J., and GOODIN, R. E. (1986), 'Risk-Sharing and Social Justice: The Motivational Foundation of the Post-War Welfare State', *British Journal of Political Science*, 16: 1–34.

DUDZIAK, M. L. (1986), 'Oliver Wendell Holmes as an Eugenic Reformer: Rhetoric in the Writing of Constitutional Law', *Iowa Law Review*, 71: 833–67.

DUNLEAVY, P. (1991), *Democracy, Bureaucracy and Public Choice* (Hemel Hempstead: Harvester Wheatsheaf).

EDELMAN, P. (1997), 'The worst thing Bill Clinton has done', *Atlantic Monthly* (Mar.), 43–58.

ELLISON, N., and PIERSON, C. (eds.) (1998), *Developments in British Social Policy* (London: Macmillan).

ELLWOOD, D. T. (1988), *Poor Support: Poverty in the American Family* (New York: Basic Books).

ELMORE, R. F. (1983), 'Social Policymaking as Strategic Intervention', in E. Seidman (ed.), *Handbook of Social Intervention* (Beverly Hills, Calif.: Sage).

ELSTER, J. (ed.) (1998), *Deliberative Democracy* (Cambridge: Cambridge University Press).

——and SLAGSTAD, R. (eds.) (1988), *Constitutionalism and Democracy* (Cambridge: Cambridge University Press).

ESPING-ANDERSEN, G. (1990), *The Three Worlds of Welfare Capitalism* (Oxford: Polity).

ETZIONI, A. (1995*a*), *The Spirit of Community: Rights, Responsibilities and the Communitarian Agenda* (London: Fontana).

——(ed.) (1995*b*), *New Communitarian Thinking* (Charlottesville, Va.: University Press of Virginia).

——(1997), *The New Golden Rule: Community and Morality in a Democratic Society* (London: Profile Books).

FAULKS, K. (1998), *Citizenship in Modern Britain* (Edinburgh: Edinburgh University Press).

FIELD, F. (1997), 'Re-inventing Welfare: A Response to Lawrence Mead', in Mead 1997*b*.

——and OWEN, M. (1994) *Beyond Punishment: Pathways from Workfare* (London: Institute of Community Studies).

FIELD, J. (1992), *Learning through Labour* (Leeds: Leeds Studies in Continuing Education).

FINEGOLD, K. (1995), *Experts and Politicians: Reform Challenges to Machine Politics in New York, Cleveland and Chicago* (Princeton: Princeton University Press).

FINN, D., BLACKMORE, M., and NIMMO, M. (1998), *Welfare-to-work and the Long Term Unemployed* (London: Unemployment Unit).

FITZGERALD, K. (1996), *The Face of the Nation: Immigration, the State and National Identity* (Stanford, Calif.: Stanford University Press).

FRASER, D. (ed.) (1976), 'Introduction', *The New Poor Law in the Nineteenth Century* (London: Macmillan).

FRASER, N. (1997), *Justice Interruptus* (New York: Routledge).

——and GORDON, L. (1997), 'A Genealogy of "Dependency"', in Fraser 1997.

FRAZER, E., and LACEY, N. (1993), *The Politics of Community* (Hemel Hempstead: Harvester Wheatsheaf).

FREDRICKSON, G. M. (1987), *The Black Image in the White Mind* (Hanover, NH: Wesleyan University Press).

FREEDEN, M. (1978), *The New Liberalism* (Oxford: Clarendon Press).

——(1979), 'History and Progressive Thought: A Study in Ideological Affinity', *Historical Journal*, 22: 645–71.

——(1996), *Ideologies and Political Theory* (Oxford: Oxford University Press).

FRYER, P. (1984), *Staying Power: The History of Black People in Britain* (London: Pluto).

FUKUYAMA, F. (1992), *The End of History and the Last Man* (New York: Free Press).

——(1995), *Trust* (London: Hamish Hamilton).

FULBROOK, J. (1978), *Administrative Justice and the Unemployed* (London: Mansell).

GAMBETTA, D. (ed.) (1988), *Trust* (Oxford: Blackwell).

GIDDENS, A. (1998), *The Third Way* (Oxford: Polity).

GILBERT, B. (1970), *British Social Policy 1914–1936* (London: Batsford).

GILENS, M. (1996), '"Race Coding" and White Opposition to Welfare', *American Political Science Review*, 90: 593–604.

GERSTLE, G. (1994), 'The Protean Character of American Liberalism', *American Historical Review*, 99: 1043–73.

GLAZER, N. (1997), *We are all Multiculturalists now* (Cambridge, Mass.: Harvard University Press).

GLENNERSTER, H., and Midgley, J. (eds.) (1991), *The Radical Right and the Welfare State: An International Assessment* (Hemel Hempstead: Harvester Wheatsheaf).

GOLDFIELD, M. (1997), *The Color of Politics* (New York: The New Press).

GOLDMAN, L. (1987), 'A Peculiarity of the English? The Social Science Association and the Absence of Sociology in Nineteenth-Century Britain', *Past and Present*, 114: 113–71.

——(1998), 'Exceptionalism and Internationalism: The Origins of American Social Science Reconsidered', *Journal of Historical Sociology*, 11: 1–36.

GOLDSTEIN, J. (1988), 'Ideas, Institutions and American Trade Policy', *International Organization*, 42: 179–217.

——(1989) 'The Impact of Ideas on Trade Policy: The Origins of U.S. Agricultural and Manufacturing Policies', *International Organization* 43: 31–71.

GOODIN, R. E. (1985), *Protecting the Vulnerable* (Chicago: University of Chicago Press).

——(1988), *Reasons for Welfare* (Princeton: Princeton University Press).

——(1996a), 'Institutions and Their Design', in R. E. Goodin (ed.), *The Theory of Institutional Design* (Cambridge: Cambridge University Press).

——(1996b), 'Inclusion and Exclusion', *Archives européennes de sociologie* 37: 343–71.

——and KLINGEMANN, H.-D. (eds.) (1996), *A New Handbook of Political Science* (Oxford: Oxford University Press).

GOODWIN, J. L. (1997), *Gender and the Politics of Welfare Reform* (Chicago: University of Chicago Press).

GOULD, S. J. (1981), *The Mismeasure of Man* (Harmondsworth: Penguin).

GRAHAM, L. (1977), 'Science and Values: The Eugenics Movement in Germany and Russia in the 1920s', *American Historical Review*, 82: 1133–64.

GRAY, J. (1989), *Liberalisms: Essays in Political Philosophy* (London: Routledge).

——(1993), *Post-Liberalism* (London: Routledge).

——(1995), *Liberalism* (Milton Keynes: Open University Press, 2nd edn.).

——(1998) 'A Strained Rebirth of Liberal Britain', *New Statesman* (21 Aug.).

GUTMANN, A., and Thompson, D. F. (1996), *Democracy and Disagreement* (Cambridge, Mass.: Harvard University Press).

HALL, P. A. (1986), *Governing the Economy* (New York: Oxford University Press).

——(ed.) (1989), *The Political Power of Economic Ideas* (Princeton: Princeton University Press).

——(1993), 'Policy Paradigms, Social Learning and the State: The Case of Economic Policymaking in Britain', *Comparative Politics*, 25: 275–96.

HALLER, M. (1963), *Eugenics: Hereditarian Attitudes in American Thought* (Brunswick, NJ: Rutgers University Press).

HALPERN, R., and MORRIS, J. (eds.) (1997), *American Exceptionalism?* (London: Macmillan).

HALSEY, A. H. (1996), *No Discouragement: An Autobiography* (London: Macmillan).

HAMBY, A. L. (1985), *Liberalism and Its Challengers: FDR to Reagan* (New York: Oxford University Press).

HANDLER, J. F., and HASENFELD, Y. (1991), *The Moral Construction of Poverty: Welfare Reform in America* (Newbury Park, Calif.: Sage).

——————(1997), *We the Poor People: Work, Poverty and Welfare* (New Haven: Yale University Press).

HARDIN, R. (1982), *Collective Action* (Baltimore: Johns Hopkins University Press).

HARRIS, J. (1972), *Unemployment and Politics* (Oxford: Clarendon Press).

——(1977), *William Beveridge: A Biography* (Oxford: Clarendon Press).

——(1996), 'Political Thought and the State', in S. J. D. Green and R. C. Whiting (eds.), *The Boundaries of the State in Modern Britain* (Cambridge: Cambridge University Press).

HART, V. (1994), *Bound by Our Constitution: Women, Workers and the Minimum Wage* (Princeton: Princeton University Press).

HARTZ, L. (1955), *The Liberal Tradition in America* (New York: Harcourt, Brace).

HATTAM, V. C. (1993), *Labor Visions and State Power* (Princeton: Princeton University Press).

HAYEK, F. A. (1944), *The Road to Serfdom* (London: Routledge & Kegan Paul).

HECLO, H. (1974), *Modern Social Politics in Britain and Sweden* (New Haven: Yale University Press).

——(1978), 'Issue Networks and the Executive Establishment', in A. King (ed.), *The New American Political System* (Washington, DC: American Enterprise Institute).

——(1986), 'General Welfare and Two American Political Traditions', *Political Science Quarterly*, 101: 179–96.

——(1995), 'The Social Question', in K. McFate, R. Lawson, and W. J. Wilson (eds.), *Poverty, Inequality and the Future of Social Policy* (New York: Russell Sage Foundation).

HIGHAM, J. (1988), *Strangers in the Land: Patterns of American Nativism 1860–1925* (New Brunswick, NJ: Rutgers University Press, 2nd edn., 1st pub. 1955).

HIRSCHMAN, A. O. (1977), *The Passions and the Interests* (Princeton: Princeton University Press).

——(1982), 'Rival Interpretations of Market Society: Civilizing, Destructive or Feeble?', *Journal of Economic Literature*, 20: 1463–84.

HOCHSCHILD, J. (1995), *Facing up to the American Dream* (Princeton: Princeton University Press).

HOFSTADTER, R. (1955*a*), *The Age of Reform* (New York: Vintage).

——(1955*b*), *Social Darwinism in American Thought* (Boston: Beacon).

HOLMES, S. (1993), *The Anatomy of Antiliberalism* (Cambridge, Mass.: Harvard University Press).

——(1995), *Passions and Constraints: On the Theory of Liberal Democracy* (Chicago: University of Chicago Press).

HOOD, C. (1983), *The Tools of Government* (London: Macmillan).

——(1998), *The Art of the State* (Oxford: Clarendon Press).

HOOVER, H. (1938), *Addresses upon the American Road 1933–1938* (New York: Charles Scribner's Sons).

HOWE, D. W. (1997), *Making the American Self* (Cambridge, Mass.: Harvard University Press, 1997).

HUMPHRIES, S., and GORDON, P. (1994), *Forbidden Britain* (London: BBC Books).

HUTCHINSON, E. P. (1981), *Legislative History of American Immigration Policy 1798–1965* (Philadelphia: University of Pennsylvania Press).

IGNATIEV, N. (1995), *How the Irish Became White* (New York: Routledge).

IMMERGUT, E. M. (1998), 'The Theoretical Core of the New Institutionalism', *Politics and Society*, 26: 5–34.

JACOBSEN, J. K. (1995), 'Much Ado about Ideas: The Cognitive Factor in Economic Policy', *World Politics*, 47: 283–310.

JANOSKI, T. (1998), *Citizenship and Civil Society* (New York: Cambridge University Press).

JENCKS, C. (1992), *Rethinking Social Policy* (Cambridge, Mass.: Harvard University Press).

——and PETERSON, P. (eds.) (1991), *The Urban Underclass* (Washington, DC: Brookings).

JONES, G. (1980), *Social Darwinism and English Thought* (Brighton: Harvester Press).

——(1982), 'Eugenics and Social Policy between the Wars', *Historical Journal*, 25: 717–28.

——(1986), *Social Hygiene in Twentieth Century Britain* (London: Croom Helm).

JONES, G. S. (1971), *Outcast London* (Oxford: Oxford University Press).

JONES, H., and MACGREGOR, S. (eds.) (1998), *Social Issues and Party Politics* (London: Routledge).

JONES, J. (1992), *The Dispossessed: America's Underclasses from the Civil War to the Present* (New York: Basic Books).

KATZ, M. (1986), *In the Shadow of the Poorhouse* (New York: Basic Books).

——(ed.) (1993a), *The Underclass Debate* (Princeton: Princeton University Press).

——(1993b), 'The Urban "Underclass" as a Metaphor of Social Transformation', in Katz 1993a.

KATZNELSON, I. (1981), *City Trenches* (New York: Pantheon).

——(1996a), *Liberalism's Crooked Circle* (Princeton: Princeton University Press).

——(1996b), 'Knowledge about What? Policy Intellectuals and the New Liberalism', in Rueschemeyer and Skocpol 1996.

——(1997), 'Structure and Configuration in Comparative Politics', in M. I. Lichbach and A. S. Zuckerman (eds.), *Comparative Politics: Rationality, Culture and Structure* (New York: Cambridge University Press).

——(1998), 'The Doleful Dance of Politics and Policy: Can historical institutionalism make a difference?', *American Political Science Review*, 92: 191–7.

KELLEY, R. D. G. (1990), *Hammer and Hoe* (Chapel Hill, NC: University of North Carolina Press).

——(1993), '"We are not what we seem": Rethinking Black Working-Class Opposition in the Jim Crow South', *Journal of American History*, 80: 75–112.

——(1997), *Yo's Mama's Disfunktional: Fighting Cultural Wars in Urban America* (Boston: Beacon Press).

KESSELMAN, J. R. (1978), 'Work Relief Programs in the Great Depression', in J. L. Palmer (ed.), *Creating Jobs: Public Employment Programs and Wage Subsidies* (Washington, DC: Brookings).

KEVLES, D. J. (1986), *In the Name of Eugenics* (Harmondsworth: Penguin Books).

KEVLES, D. J. (1988), 'American Science', in N. O. Hatch (ed.), *The Professions in American History* (Notre Dame, Ind.: University of Notre Dame Press).

——(1998), 'Grounds for Breeding', *Times Literary Supplement*, 2 Jan.

KINDER, D. R., and SANDERS, L. M. (1996), *Divided by Color* (Chicago: University of Chicago Press).

KING, D. (1995), *Actively Seeking Work? The Politics of Unemployment and Welfare Policy in the United States and Great Britain* (Chicago: University of Chicago Press).

——(1996), 'Sectionalism and Policy Formation in the United States: President Carter's Welfare Initiatives', *British Journal of Political Science*, 26: 337–67.

——(1997), 'Creating a Funding Regime for Social Research in Britain', *Minerva*, 35: 1–26.

——(1998*a*), 'A Strong or Weak State? Race and the US Federal Government in the 1920s', *Ethnic and Racial Studies*, 21: 21–47.

——(1998*b*), 'The Politics of Social Research: Institutionalising Public Funding Regimes in the United States and Britain', *British Journal of Political Science*, 28: 415–44.

——and WALDRON, J. (1988), 'Citizenship, Social Citizenship and the Defence of Welfare Provision', *British Journal of Political Science*, 18: 415–43.

KINGDON, J. W. (1995), *Agendas, Alternatives and Public Policies* (New York: Harper Collins, 2nd edn.).

KLEINMAN, D. L. (1995), *Politics at the Endless Frontier* (Durham, NC: Duke University Press).

KLOPPENBERG, J. T. (1986), *Uncertain Victory: Social Democracy and Progressivism in European and American Thought 1870–1920* (New York: Oxford University Press).

KLOSKO, G. (1993), 'Rawls's "Political" Philosophy and American Democracy', *American Political Science Review*, 87: 348–59.

KUHL, S. (1994), *The Nazi Connection* (New York: Oxford University Press).

KUSHNER, T. (1994), *The Holocaust and the Liberal Imagination* (Oxford: Blackwell).

KYMLICKA, W. (1990), *Contemporary Political Philosophy* (Oxford: Clarendon Press).

LARSEN, O. (1992), *Milestones and Millstones* (New Brunswick, NJ: Transaction Books).

LARSON, E. J. (1991), 'The Rhetoric of Eugenics: Expert Authority and the Mental Deficiency Bill', *British Journal of the History of Science*, 24: 45–60.

——(1995), *Sex, Race, and Science: Eugenics in the Deep South* (Baltimore: Johns Hopkins University Press).

LEES, L. H. (1997), *The Solidarities of Strangers* (Cambridge: Cambridge University Press).

LEMANN, N. (1991), *The Promised Land* (New York: Knopf).

LEUCHTENBURG, W. E. (1963), *Franklin D. Roosevelt and the New Deal 1932–1940* (New York: Harper & Row).

LEVI, M. (1997), *Consent, Dissent and Patriotism* (New York: Cambridge University Press).

LEWIS, J. (1991), *Women and Social Action in Victorian and Edwardian England* (Stanford, Calif.: Stanford University Press).

——(1992), 'Gender and the Development of Welfare Regimes', *Journal of European Social Policy*, 2: 159–73.

LIEBERMAN, R. C. (1995), 'Race and the Organization of Welfare Policy', in P. E. Peterson (ed.), *Classifying by Race* (Princeton, NJ: Princeton University Press).

——(1998), *Shifting the Color Line: Race and the American Welfare State* (Cambridge, Mass.: Harvard University Press).

LINDBLOM, C. E. (1980), *The Policy-Making Process* (Englewood Cliffs, NJ: Prentice Hall, 2nd edn.).

LISTER, R. (1990), 'Women, Economic Dependency and Citizenship', *Journal of Social Policy*, 19: 445–67.

——(1993), 'Tracing the Contours of Women's Citizenship', *Policy and Politics*, 21: 3–16.

——(1997), *Citizenship: A Feminist Perspective* (London: Macmillan).

LOMBARDO, P. A. (1985), 'Three Generations, No Imbeciles: New Light on *Buck v. Bell*', *New York University Law Review*, 60: 30–62.

LOWE, R. (1986), *Adjusting to Democracy: The Role of the Ministry of Labour in British Politics, 1916–1939* (Oxford: Clarendon Press).

——(1993), *The Welfare State in Britain since 1945* (London: Macmillan).

LUDMERER, K. (1972), *Genetics and American Society* (Baltimore: Johns Hopkins University Press).

McBRIAR, A. M. (1987), *An Edwardian Mixed Doubles: The Bosanquets versus the Webbs* (Oxford: Clarendon Press).

MACEDO, S. (1990), *Liberal Values* (Oxford: Clarendon Press).

MACGREGOR, S. (1998), 'A New Deal for Britain?', in Jones and MacGregor 1998.

MACKENZIE, D. A. (1976), 'Eugenics in Britain', *Social Studies in Science*, 6: 499–532.

——(1979), 'Karl Pearson and the Professional Middle Class', *Annals of Science*, 36: 125–43.

——(1981), *Statistics in Britain 1865–1930: The Social Construction of Scientific Knowledge* (Edinburgh: Edinburgh University Press).

McKIBBIN, R. (1990), 'The Social Psychology of Unemployment in Inter-war Britain', in R. McKibbin, *The Ideologies of Class* (Oxford: Clarendon Press).

——(1998), *Classes and Cultures* (Oxford: Oxford University Press).

McNAMARA, K. R. (1998), *The Currency of Ideas* (Ithaca, NY: Cornell University Press).

MACNICOL, J. (1987), 'In Pursuit of the Underclass', *Journal of Social Policy*, 16: 293–318.

——(1989), 'Eugenics and the Campaign for Voluntary Sterilization in Britain between the Wars', *Social History of Medicine*, 2: 147–69.

——(1992), 'The Voluntary Sterilization Campaign in Britain 1918–39', *Journal of the History of Sexuality*, 2: 422–38.

MANDELL, B. R. (ed.) (1975), *Welfare in America: Controlling the 'Dangerous Classes'* (Englewood Cliffs, NJ: Prentice-Hall).

MANDLER, P. (1987), 'The Making of the New Poor Law *Redivivus*', *Past and Present*, 117: 131–57.

MARCH, J., and OLSEN, J. (1989), *Rediscovering Institutions: The Organizational Basis of Politics* (New York: Free Press).

MARSH, D., and RHODES, R. A. W. (1992*a*), *Policy Networks in British Government* (Oxford: Oxford University Press).

——(1992*b*), *Implementing Thatcherite Policies* (Buckingham: Open University Press).

MARSHALL, T. H. (1964), *Class, Citizenship and Social Development* (New York: Doubleday).

MASSEY, D. S., and DENTON, N. (1993), *American Apartheid* (Cambridge, Mass.: Harvard University Press).

MAYHEW, D. R. (1991), *Divided We Govern* (New Haven: Yale University Press).

MAZUMDAR, P. M. H. (1992), *Eugenics, Human Genetics and Human Failings* (London: Routledge).

MEACHAM, S. (1987), *Toynbee Hall and Social Reform 1880–1914* (New Haven: Yale University Press).

MEAD, L. M. (1985), *Beyond Entitlement* (New York: Basic Books).

——(1992), *The New Politics of Poverty* (New York: Basic Books).

——(ed.) (1997*a*), *The New Paternalism* (Washington, DC: Brookings).

——(1997*b*), *From Welfare to Work*, ed. A. Deacon (London: Institute of Economic Affairs).

——(1997*c*), 'Citizenship and Social Policy: T. H. Marshall and Poverty', *Social Philosophy and Policy*, 14: 197–230.

——(1998), 'Statecraft: The Politics of Welfare Reform in Wisconsin', Paper presented to the annual meeting of the American Political Science Association.

MILKIS, S. M. (1993), *The President and the Parties* (New York: Oxford University Press).

MILL, J. S. (1972), *On Liberty* (London: J. M. Dent, 1st pub. 1859).

MILLER, D. (1989), *Market, State and Community* (Oxford: Clarendon Press).

MINK, G. (1998), *Welfare's End* (Ithaca, NY: Cornell University Press).

MISZTAL, B. A. (1996), *Trust in Modern Societies* (Oxford: Polity Press).

MORONE, J. A. (1990), *The Democratic Wish: Popular Participation and the Limits of American Government* (New York: Basic Books).

MOWAT, C. L. (1961), *The Charity Organisation Society 1869–1913: Its Ideas and Work* (London: Methuen).

MUCCIARONI, G. (1990), *The Political Failure of Employment Policy, 1945–1982* (Pittsburgh: University of Pittsburgh Press).

MULHALL, S., and SWIFT, A. (1992), *Liberals and Communitarians* (Oxford: Blackwell).

MURRAY, C. (1984), *Losing Ground* (New York: Basic Books).

——(1990), *The Emerging British Underclass* (London: Institute of Economic Studies).

NAGEL, T. (1991), *Equality and Partiality* (New York: Oxford University Press).

NATHAN, R. P. (1993), *Turning Promises into Performance* (New York: Twentieth Century Fund).

NELSON, B. (1996), 'Class, Race and Democracy in the CIO: The "New" Labor history meets the "wages of whiteness" ', *International Review of Social History*, 41: 351–74.

NOBLE, C. (1997*a*), *Welfare as we knew it* (New York: Oxford University Press).

——(1997*b*), 'The End of the Welfare State? Devolution and the Future of American Social Policy', Paper presented to the annual meeting of the American Political Science Association.

NOLAN, J. L. Jr. (1998), *The Therapeutic State: Justifying Government at Century's End* (New York: New York University Press).

NORRIS, D. F., and THOMPSON, L. (eds.) (1995), *The Politics of Welfare Reform* (Newbury Park, Calif.: Sage).

NOVAK, M. (1998), *Is There a Third Way?* (London: Institute of Economic Affairs).

NYE, J. S. Jr., ZELIKOW, P. D., and KING, D. C. (eds.) (1997), *Why people don't trust government* (Cambridge, Mass.: Harvard University Press).

NYE, R. A. (1993), 'The Rise and Fall of the Eugenics Empire: Recent Perspectives on the Impact of Biomedical Thought in Modern Society', *Historical Journal*, 36: 687–700.

O'CONNOR, J. S. (1996), 'From Women in the Welfare State to Gendering Welfare State Regimes', Special Issue *Current Sociology*, 44.

OLIVER, D., and HEATER, D. (1994), *The Foundations of Citizenship* (Hemel Hempstead: Harvester Wheatsheaf).

OLIVER, M. J. (1996), 'Social Learning and Macroeconomic Policymaking in the United Kingdom', *Essays in Economic and Business History*, 14: 117–31.

OPPENHEIM, C. (1998), 'Welfare to Work: Taxes and Benefits', in J. McCormick and C. Oppenheim (eds.), *Welfare in Working Order* (London: Institute for Public Policy Research).

ORLOFF, A. S. (1993*a*), 'Gender and the Social Rights of Citizenship: The Comparative Analysis of Gender Relations and Welfare States', *American Sociological Review*, 58: 303–28.

——(1993*b*), *The Politics of Pensions* (Madison: University of Wisconsin Press).

OWEN, D. E. (1964), *English Philanthropy 1660–1960* (Cambridge, Mass.: Harvard University Press).

PAGE, B. I., and SHAPIRO, R. Y. (1992), *The Rational Public* (Chicago: University of Chicago Press).

PATTERSON, J. T. (1981), *America's Struggle against Poverty 1900–1980* (Cambridge, Mass.: Harvard University Press).

PAUL, D. (1984), 'Eugenics and the Left', *Journal of the History of Ideas*, 44: 567–90.

——(1992), 'Eugenic Anxieties, Social Realities and Political Choices', *Social Research*, 59: 663–83.

PECK, J. A. (1991*a*), 'Letting the Market Decide (with Public Money): Training and Enterprise Councils and the Future of Labour Market Programmes', *Critical Social Policy*, 31: 4–17.

——(1991*b*), 'The Politics of Training in Britain: Contradictions of the TEC Initiative', *Capital and Class*, 44: 23–34.

——(1996), *Workplace: The Social Regulation of Labour Markets* (London: Guildford Press).

PEDERSEN, S. (1993), *Family, Dependence and the Origins of the Welfare State* (New York: Cambridge University Press).

PICK, D. (1989), *Faces of Degeneration* (Cambridge: Cambridge University Press).

PIERSON, C. (1991), *Beyond the Welfare State?* (Oxford: Polity).

PIERSON, P. (1994), *Dismantling the Welfare State?* (New York: Cambridge University Press).

——(1996), 'The Path to European Integration', *Comparative Political Studies*, 29: 123–63.

PLANT, R., and BARRY, N. (1990), *Citizenship and Rights in Thatcher's Britain: Two Views* (London: IEA Health and Welfare Unit).

——LESSER, H., and TAYLOR-GOOBY, P. (1980), *Political Philosophy and Social Welfare* (London: Routledge & Kegan Paul).

POLANYI, K. (1944), *The Great Transformation* (Boston: Beacon).

POLANYI, M. (1967), 'The Growth of Science in Society', *Minerva*, 5: 533–45.

POLSKY, A. J. (1991), *The Rise of the Therapeutic State* (Princeton: Princeton University Press).

POWELL, G. B. (1992), 'Liberal Democracies', in M. Hawkesworth and M. Kogan (eds.), *Encyclopaedia of Government and Politics* (London: Routledge).

PRICE, D. K. (1988), 'The Profession of Government Service', in N. O. Hatch (ed.), *The Professions in American History* (Notre Dame, Ind.: University of Notre Dame Press).

PROCTOR, R. N. (1988), *Racial Hygiene: Medicine under the Nazis* (Cambridge, Mass.: Harvard University Press).

PUTNAM, R. (1993), *Making Democracy Work* (Princeton: Princeton University Press).

QUADAGNO, J. (1994), *The Color of Welfare* (New York: Oxford University Press).

RAFTER, N. H. (ed.) (1988), *White Trash: The Eugenic Family Studies 1877–1919* (Boston: Northeastern University Press).

RAWLS, J. (1971), *A Theory of Justice* (Oxford: Oxford University Press)

——(1993), *Political Liberalism* (New York: Columbia University Press).

RAY, L. J. (1983), 'Eugenics, Mental Deficiency and Fabian Socialism between the Wars', *Oxford Review of Education*, 9: 213–22.

RAZ, J. (1986), *The Morality of Freedom* (Oxford: Clarendon Press).

REILLY, P. R. (1983), 'The Surgical Solution: The Writings of Activist Physicians in the Early Days of Eugenical Sterilization', *Perspectives in Biology and Medicine*, 26: 637–56.

——'Involuntary Sterilization in the United States: A Surgical Solution', *Quarterly Review of Biology*, 62: 153–70.

——(1991), *The Surgical Solution: A History of Involuntary Sterilization in the U.S.* (Baltimore: Johns Hopkins University Press).

RHODES, R. A. W. (1997), *Understanding Governance* (Buckingham: Open University Press).

RICHARDS, H. (1997), *The Bloody Circus: The Daily Herald and the Left* (London: Pluto).

RIDLEY, M. (1997), *The Origins of Virtue* (Harmondsworth: Penguin).

——(1998), 'Eugenics and Liberty', *Prospect* (Aug.–Sept.), 44–7.

RINGEN, S. (1988), *The Possibility of Politics* (Oxford: Oxford University Press).

ROCHE, M. (1992), *Rethinking Citizenship* (Oxford: Polity Press).

RODGERS, D. T. (1998), *Atlantic Crossings: Social Politics in a Progressive Age* (Cambridge, Mass.: Harvard University Press).

ROEDIGER, D. (1991), *The Wages of Whiteness* (London: Verso).

ROSE, R. (1993), *Lesson-Drawing in Public Policy* (Chatham, NJ: Chatham House).

ROTHSTEIN, B. (1996), 'Political Institutions: An Overview', in Goodin and Klingemann 1996.

——(1998), *Just Institutions Matter* (Cambridge: Cambridge University Press).

RUESCHEMEYER, D., and SKOCPOL, T. (eds.) (1996), *States, Social Knowledge, and the Origins of Modern Social Policies* (Princeton: Princeton University Press).

RUNCIMAN, W. G. (1966), *Relative Deprivation and Social Justice* (London: Routledge & Kegan Paul).

SALMOND, J. A. (1965), 'The Civilian Conservation Corps and the Negro', *Journal of American History*, 52: 75–88.

——(1967), *The Civilian Conservation Corps, 1933–1942: A New Deal Case Study* (Durham, NC: Duke University Press).

SANDEL, M. J. (1982), *Liberalism and the Limits of Justice* (Cambridge: Cambridge University Press).

——(1996), *Democracy's Discontent: America in Search of a Public Philosophy* (Cambridge, Mass.: Harvard University Press).

SAUTTER, U. (1991), *Three Cheers for the Unemployed: Government and Unemployment before the New Deal* (New York: Cambridge University Press).

SCHNEIDER, A., and INGRAM, H. (1993), 'Social Construction of Target Populations: Implications for Politics and Policy', *American Political Science Review*, 87: 334–47.

SCHNEIDER, W. H. (1990), *Quality and Quantity: The Quest for Biological Regeneration in Twentieth-Century France* (Cambridge: Cambridge University Press).

SCHORR, A. L. (1986), *Common Decency* (New Haven: Yale University Press).

SCHRAM, S. F. (1995), *Words of Welfare* (Minneapolis: University of Minnesota Press).

SCHWARZMANTEL, J. (1998), *The Age of Ideology* (London: Macmillan).

SCOTT, J. C. (1998), *Seeing Like a State* (New Haven: Yale University Press).

SEARLE, G. R. (1971), *The Quest for National Efficiency* (Oxford: Blackwell).

——(1976), *Eugenics and Politics in Britain 1900–1914* (Leiden: Noordoff Publishing International).

——(1979), 'Eugenics and Politics in Britain in the 1930s', *Annals of Science*, 36: 159–69.

——(1981), 'Eugenics and Class', in Webster 1981.

——(1998), *Morality and the Market in Victorian Britain*.

SELIGMAN, A. (1992), *The Idea of Civil Society* (New York: Free Press).

——(1997), *The Problem of Trust* (Princeton: Princeton University Press).

SHAFER, B. E. (1996), 'The United States', in B. E. Shafer (ed.), *Postwar Politics in the G-7* (Madison: University of Wisconsin Press).

SHKLAR, J. N. (1998), *Redeeming American Political Thought* (Chicago: University of Chicago Press).

SHONFIELD, A. (1965), *Modern Capitalism* (Oxford: Oxford University Press).

SIMMONS, H. (1978), 'Explaining Social Policy: The English Mental Deficiency Act of 1913', *Journal of Social Policy*, 11: 387–403.

SKOCPOL, T. (1992), *Protecting Soldiers and Mothers* (Cambridge, Mass.: Harvard University Press).

——and RUESCHEMEYER, D. (1996), 'Introduction', in Rueschemeyer and Skocpol 1996.

SMITH, R. M. (1989), ' "One United People": Second-Class Female Citizenship and the American Quest for Community', *Yale Journal of Law and the Humanities*, 1: 229–93.

——(1993), 'Beyond Tocqueville, Myrdal and Hartz: The Multiple Traditions in America', *American Political Science Review*, 87: 549–66.

——(1995), 'American Conceptions of Citizenship and National Service', in Etzioni 1995*b*.

——(1997), *Civic Ideals* (New Haven: Yale University Press).

SNIDERMAN, P. M., and PIAZZA, T. (1993), *The Scar of Race* (Cambridge, Mass.: Harvard University Press).

SOLOMON, B. (1998), 'Hatching Good Ideas', *National Journal* (2 May), 980–5.

SOLOMON, B. M. (1956), *Ancestors and Immigrants* (Chicago: University of Chicago Press).

SOLOW, R. M. (1998*a*), 'Guess who pays for workfare?' *New York Review of Books* (5 Nov.), 27–37.

——(1998*b*), *Work and Welfare* (Princeton: Princeton University Press).

SOLOWAY, R. A. (1995), *Demography and Degeneration: Eugenics and the Declining Birthrate in Twentieth Century Britain* (Chapel Hill, NC: University of North Carolina Press).

SPENCE, C. (1985), *The Salvation Army Farm Colonies* (Tucson, Ariz.: University of Arizona Press).

STANFIELD, R. L. (1998), 'Cautious Optimism', *National Journal* (2 May).

STEINMO, S., THELEN, K., and LONGSTRETH, F. (eds.) (1992), *Structuring Politics: Historical Institutionalism in Comparative Analysis* (New York: Cambridge University Press).

STEPAN, N. (1982), *The Idea of Race in Science: Great Britain 1800–1960* (London: Archon Books).

——(1991), *The Hour of Eugenics* (Ithaca, NY: Cornell University Press).

STEWART, A. (1995), 'Two Conceptions of Citizenship', *British Journal of Sociology*, 46: 63–78.

STONE, D. (1996), *Capturing the Political Imagination* (London: Cass).

STONE, D. A. (1997), *Policy Paradox: The Art of Political Decision Making* (New York: W. W. Norton).

SUGRUE, T. J. (1996), *The Origins of the Urban Crisis* (Princeton: Princeton University Press).

TAM, H. (1998), *Communitarianism: A New Agenda for Politics and Citizenship* (London: Macmillan).

TANNER, M. (1996), *The End of Welfare: Fighting Poverty in the Civil Society* (Washington: Cato Institute).

TAYLOR, C. (1989), *Sources of the Self: The Making of the Modern Identity* (Cambridge, Mass.: Harvard University Press).

TAYLOR, P. (ed.) (1998), *Choice and Public Policy: The Limits to Welfare Markets* (London: Macmillan).

TELES, S. M. (1998), *Whose Welfare? AFDC and Elite Politics* (Lawrence, Kan.: University Press of Kansas).

THANE, P. (1982), *Foundations of the British Welfare State* (London: Longman).

——(1984), 'The Working Class and State "Welfare" in Britain 1880–1914', *Historical Journal*, 27: 877–900.

THOMSON, M. (1998), *The Problem of Mental Deficiency* (Oxford: Clarendon Press).

TICHENOR, D. J. (1995), 'Immigration and Political Community in the United States', in Etzioni 1995*b*.

TIMMINS, N. (1996), *The Five Giants: A Biography of the Welfare State* (London: Fontana).

TITMUSS, R. M. (1967), *Choice and 'the Welfare State'* (London: Fabian Tract 370).

——(1968), *Commitment to Welfare* (London: Allen & Unwin).

——(1974), *Social Policy: An Introduction* (London: Allen & Unwin).

——(1976), *Essays on 'the Welfare State'* (London: Allen & Unwin).

TONGE, J. (1998), 'Workfare, "trainingfare" or neither? New Labour and Employment Policy Innovation', Paper presented to the annual Political Studies Association meeting.

TRENT, J. W. Jr. (1994), *Inventing the Feeble Mind: A History of Mental Retardation in the United States* (Berkeley and Los Angeles: University of California Press).

TSEBELIS, G., and STEPHEN, R. (1994), 'Monitoring Unemployment Benefits in Comparative Perspective', *Political Research Quarterly*, 47: 793–820.

TWINE, F. (1994), *Citizenship and Social Rights* (London: Sage).

VAN PARIJS, P. (1995), *Real Freedom for All: What (if anything) can justify capitalism?* (Oxford: Oxford University Press).

VAN STEENBERGEN, H. (ed.) (1994), *The Condition of Citizenship* (London: Sage).

VEYSEY, L. (1988), 'Higher Education as a Profession: Changes and Continuities', in N. O. Hatch (ed.), *The Professions in American History* (Notre Dame, Ind.: University of Notre Dame Press).

VINCENT, D. (1991), *Poor Citizens* (London: Longman).

WALDRON, J. (1993), *Liberal Rights* (New York: Cambridge University Press).

WALKER, J. (1969), 'The Diffusion of Innovations among the American States', *American Political Science Review*, 68: 880–99.

WARE, A. (1996), *Political Parties and Party Systems* (Oxford: Oxford University Press).

WEALE, A. (1983), *Political Theory and Social Policy* (London: Macmillan).

WEAVER, R. K. (1998), 'Ending welfare as we know it', in Weir 1998.

WEBSTER, C. (ed.) (1981), *Biology, Medicine and Society 1840–1940* (Cambridge: Cambridge University Press).

WEINSTEIN, J. (1968), *The Corporate Ideal in the Liberal State 1900–1918* (Boston: Beacon Press).

WEIR, M. (1992), *Politics and Jobs* (Princeton: Princeton University Press).

——(ed.) (1998), *The Social Divide* (Washington, DC: Brookings Institution).

——ORLOFF, A. S., and SKOCPOL, T. (eds.) (1988), *The Politics of Social Policy in the United States* (Princeton: Princeton University Press).

——and SKOCPOL, T. (1985), 'State Structures and the Possibilities for "Keynesian" Responses to the Great Depression in Sweden, Britain and the United States', in P. Evans et al. (eds.), *Bringing the State back in* (New York: Cambridge University Press).

WEISS, S. F. (1987), 'The Race Hygiene Movement in Germany', *Osiris*, 2nd Series, 3: 193–236.

WENNERBERG, T. (1997), 'Sterilization and Propaganda', *New Left Review*, 226, 146–53.

WHITE, M. (1991), *Against Unemployment* (London: Policy Studies Institute).

——and LAKEY, J. (1992), *The Restart Effect: Evaluation of a Labour Market Programme for Unemployed People* (London: Policy Studies Institute).

WHITE, S. (1997), 'Liberal Equality, Exploitation, and the Case for an Unconditional Basic Income', *Political Studies*, 45: 312–26.

——(1998), 'Interpreting the "Third Way": Not One Road, but Many', *Renewal*, 6: 17–30.

WHITESIDE, N. (1991), *Bad Times* (London: Faber).

——(1998), 'Employment Policy', in Ellison and Pierson 1998.

WICKHAM-JONES, M. (1992), 'Monetarism and its Critics', *Political Quarterly*, 63: 171–85.

WILENSKY, H. L. (1975), *The Welfare State and Equality* (Berkeley and Los Angeles: University of California Press).

WILSON, J. Q. (1997), 'Paternalism, Democracy and Bureaucracy', in Mead 1997*a*.

WINCH, D. (1993), 'The Science of the Legislator', in M. J. Lacey and M. O. Furner (eds.), *The State and Social Investigation in Britain and the United States* (Cambridge: Cambridge University Press).

YEE, A. S. (1996), 'The Causal Effects of Ideas on Policies', *International Organization*, 50: 69–108.

WILLETTS, D. (1998), *Welfare to Work* (London: Social Market Foundation).

INDEX

DATE DUE